THE PRACTICAL ILLUSTRATED GUIDE TO

JAPANESE GARDENING
AND GROWING BONSAI

THE PRACTICAL ILLUSTRATED GUIDE TO

JAPANESE GARDENING AND GROWING BONSAI

Essential advice, step-by-step techniques and projects, plans, plant listings and over 1500 photographs and illustrations

CHARLES CHESSHIRE AND KEN NORMAN

Special photography by Alex Ramsay
and Neil Sutherland

HERMES
HOUSE

This edition is published by Hermes House, an imprint of Anness Publishing Ltd, Blaby Road, Wigston, Leicestershire LE18 4SE

info@anness.com;www.hermeshouse.com; www.annesspublishing.com

If you like the images in this book and would like to investigate using them for publishing, promotions or advertising, please visit our website www.practicalpictures.com for more information.

Publisher: Joanna Lorenz
Editorial Director: Helen Sudell
Project Editors: Emma Clegg and Caroline Davison
Designers: Simon Daley, Mike Morey and Lisa Tai
Jacket design: Balley Design
Additional materials and equipment text: Jenny Hendy
Illustrators: Anna Laflin and Anna Koska
Special photography:
  Alex Ramsay and Neil Sutherland
Additional photography (materials and equipment):
  Peter Anderson
Production Controller: Mai-Ling Collyer

ETHICAL TRADING POLICY
At Anness Publishing we believe that business should be conducted in an ethical and ecologically sustainable way, with respect for the environment and a proper regard to the replacement of the natural resources we employ.
  As a publisher, we use a lot of wood pulp to make high-quality paper for printing, and that wood commonly comes from spruce trees. We are therefore currently growing more than 750,000 trees in three Scottish forest plantations: Berrymoss (130 hectares/320 acres), West Touxhill (125 hectares/305 acres) and Deveron Forest (75 hectares/185 acres). The forests we manage contain more than 3.5 times the number of trees employed each year in making paper for the books we manufacture.
  Because of this ongoing ecological investment programme, you, as our customer, can have the pleasure and reassurance of knowing that a tree is being cultivated on your behalf to naturally replace the materials used to make the book you are holding.
  Our forestry programme is run in accordance with the UK Woodland Assurance Scheme (UKWAS) and will be certified by the internationally recognized Forest Stewardship Council (FSC). The FSC is a non-government organization dedicated to promoting responsible management of the world's forests. Certification ensures forests are managed in an environmentally sustainable and socially responsible way. For further information about this scheme, go to www.annesspublishing.com/trees

© Anness Publishing Ltd 2011

Previously published in two separate volumes,
A Practical Guide to Japanese Gardening
and *Growing Bonsai: A Practical Encyclopedia*

PUBLISHER'S NOTE
Although the advice and information in this book are believed to be accurate and true at the time of going to press, neither the authors nor the publisher can accept any legal responsibility or liability for any errors or omissions that may be made nor for any inaccuracies nor for any loss, harm or injury that comes about from following instructions or advice in this book.

Contents

▶

Introduction

The horticultural arts of Japanese gardening and bonsai have their roots firmly implanted in the East, in both China and Japan. First used by the Chinese and then developed by the Japanese, bonsai is the older art, believed to have been first practised in the Han Dynasty (206BC–AD220). Japanese gardening emerged in the 7th century AD when Chinese Buddhist and Taoist ideas were absorbed by Japan – and what resulted was a gardening style that was an amalgamation of these ideas with the Japanese culture and its ancient religion, Shinto. With such backgrounds, both art forms have spirituality and symbolism in abundance. This makes studying them immensely rewarding – as practical arts that can be appreciated on many different levels.

Above: Acer palmatum *'Ukon', styled into a beautiful twin-trunk bonsai and typical of a mature Japanese maple, but in miniature.*

THE APPEAL OF TWO ART FORMS

The Zen monks and painters of Japan were isolated from the rest of the world from the 1630s to over 200 years later and spent this time nurturing extraordinary and unique styles of architecture, poetry, painting, flower arranging and gardening. When artists, architects and designers in the West were finally exposed to these Japanese arts in the late 19th century, they were astonished by what they found.

The technique of Japanese gardening continues to capture the imagination of Western gardeners. Architecture, water, rocks, gravel, bridges, stepping stones, paths and walkways and low-key planting and greenery – from moss and bamboo to maples and topiary – are all elements that are creatively combined to form a garden vocabulary that is calming and relaxing.

The Japanese word 'bonsai' means a plant, tree, or group of trees or plants growing in a container (from bon 'basin' and sai 'to plant'). Bonsai is all about growing miniature trees in the form of full-size mature trees, mostly using the same species and varieties from which the full-size trees are grown. It is a living art form that can provide hours, weeks, months or even a lifetime of working with and understanding trees.

Acquiring a ready-grown specimen is how most people enter the world of bonsai. What might start as a hobby will invariably develop into a lasting obsession. The detailed study of trees through the art of bonsai, whether they

Left: *A patchwork of different species of moss in the dappled sunshine at Sanzen-in, Ohara, near Kyoto. The soft velvet carpets of moss under Japanese cedars (*Cryptomeria*) produce a magical effect.*

are full-size or miniature, certainly has a therapeutic quality and gives the practitioner a rewarding familiarity with the growth patterns of the trees.

JAPANESE GARDENS: AN OVERVIEW

The original Japanese gardens of the medieval period, especially those constructed of stone and sand (some of which survive from the 15th century), have become the benchmark of abstract garden art throughout the world. Even a modest knowledge of Japanese history, especially the country's relationship with China and Buddhism, will go a long way towards helping to understand the art of the Japanese garden, and thereby enabling us to reproduce it.

Japanese landscape gardens can be broken down into five main styles – pond gardens, dry gardens, tea gardens, stroll gardens and courtyard gardens – and each of these has a long and intimate relationship with the history of Japan.

Plants are fundamental to all but a few Japanese gardens. Most of the plants used possess symbolic significance, including the twisted pine, scattered cherry blossom, pendulous wisteria, the lotus and fiery Japanese maple. Plants are placed with restraint and care, and gardeners celebrate the seasons through their fleeting beauty. Everything in the garden – plants, rocks, lanterns and water – serves a role in the creation of a unified, harmonious and poetic picture. This is an art in which the whole is far greater than the sum of its parts.

Water is one of the most important elements in the Japanese garden. It can often be found in the form of a pond, a stream or a simple small water basin. Even when water is absent, its presence is often suggested through areas of sand and gravel, or dry streams. Rocks are equally important

and are regarded as possessing a kind of spiritual and living essence that needs to be respected if they are to be placed successfully.

An understanding of the elements of rock and water, through careful observation in nature, forms a good basis for creating Japanese-style gardens. The more the natural law is understood, the easier it becomes to treat them in abstract ways.

It is this abstraction of nature that is most difficult to reproduce successfully. But don't be put off: it is perfectly possible to assimilate some of the simple beauty of Japanese gardens without delving into the often esoteric meaning behind them.

Right: *Moss is used to great effect in Japanese gardens, here covering a bridge in the gardens of Saiho-ji in Kyoto.*

BONSAI: AN OVERVIEW

The technique of bonsai involves dwarfing trees by the strategic pruning of the roots and stems of the selected tree, shrub or plant, alongside the restriction of its roots. Junipers and other needle-bearing evergreens are always popular for this purpose, but there are many other options such as *Buxus* (box), *Cotoneaster* or *Ficus* (fig). Bonsai growers need to select their plant or tree and grow it on, using various horticultural techniques, common sense and a touch of artistic expression. The final specimen needs to blend with its pot or container to give a convincing impression of a mature tree in miniature.

The actual tree is only one part of the complete picture, the others being the pot, the appearance of the soil surface and – most importantly of all – the shape and style of the tree. The tree, container and soil surface must all complement each other in terms of size, shape, colour and texture.

So there is more to bonsai than growing a small plant in a pot. Bonsai can, in fact, be almost any size, ranging from 2.5cm (1in) high to probably so large that it would need to be carried by two or more very strong people.

As a beginner it is probably advisable to start with small-to medium-sized trees, but if you become an enthusiastic grower, you might then want to move on to growing larger and larger trees. There is a much greater scope to develop ideas when growing large trees, but it is very important not to become too ambitious too soon in the process.

Instead, move forward slowly using logical steps, proceeding with caution, so that you absorb all of the very varied techniques employed in bonsai culture. Taking time to become familiar with these techniques will mean that they will remain with you as an invaluable reference for all future projects.

HOW TO USE THIS BOOK

This book is divided into two sections. The first shows you how to create a beautiful and individual Japanese garden. Chapters take you through the history of the gardening style and the environmental and cultural elements that have inspired and influenced it, in particular Zen, and attitudes and beliefs concerning the natural world. This section also describes ways in

TYPICAL BONSAI FEATURES

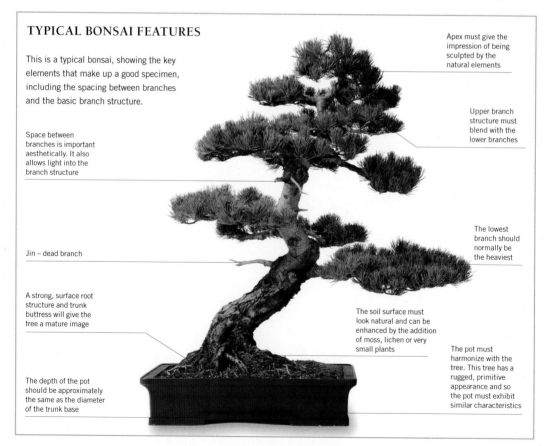

This is a typical bonsai, showing the key elements that make up a good specimen, including the spacing between branches and the basic branch structure.

Apex must give the impression of being sculpted by the natural elements

Upper branch structure must blend with the lower branches

Space between branches is important aesthetically. It also allows light into the branch structure

The lowest branch should normally be the heaviest

Jin – dead branch

A strong, surface root structure and trunk buttress will give the tree a mature image

The soil surface must look natural and can be enhanced by the addition of moss, lichen or very small plants

The pot must harmonize with the tree. This tree has a rugged, primitive appearance and so the pot must exhibit similar characteristics

The depth of the pot should be approximately the same as the diameter of the trunk base

Above: *This forest bonsai grouping uses a number of Japanese larch (*Larix laptolepis*) trees to create a woodland scene.*

Above: *This formal upright style using a Chinese juniper (*Juniperus chinensis*) needs a straight trunk and an even taper from base to apex.*

pinching, as well as more advanced skills such as creating sharimiki. A section on Bonsai Styles introduces 15 of the most popular shapes, with advice on how to achieve them, followed by a chapter on Indoor Bonsai, showing the requirements of tropical and subtropical plants. Advice on pots and containers, accessories, stands and accent planting is then given in a chapter on Displaying Bonsai. The Bonsai Directory provides information on a variety of popular species for both indoors and outdoors.

The concluding section on care and maintenance gives advice on weeding, pruning, trimming, shaping, raking and tidying the Japanese garden and watering, feeding and general maintenance of bonsai, as well as how to cope with common pests and disease.

The techniques of Japanese garden design and bonsai have ancient and traditional roots as well as popular appeal. The former continues to exert a powerful and mystical grip on the gardening world and the style also suits the creation of modern, minimal gardens and courtyards. Bonsai needs meticulous cultivation, with pruning, drainage, feeding and watering, and the specimens you create have the potential to dramatically enhance your interior and exterior spaces.

which the principles have been interpreted over the years, and suggests how you might continue this tradition by adapting them.

The five main Japanese garden styles (pond, dry, tea, stroll and courtyard) are outlined in their traditional forms so you can think about which ones most appeal. Chapters on Natural Materials and Creative Constructs introduce essential elements, with practical explanations of how to achieve them, and a section on Water Features shows how to plan all the water-based items. Creating a Garden looks at each style more closely, each one presenting a detailed garden plan and showing how to combine three key practical elements to create part of a garden. The Plant Directory gives a selection of plants for use in the Japanese garden.

The second section of the book looks at bonsai. Bonsai Essentials gives a background to the craft, advises on the best trees and shrubs and explains the importance of bonsai size, proportion and aesthetics. A Bonsai Gallery then provides an inspiring selection of mature bonsai specimens.

In the core chapter on Bonsai Techniques, practical guidance is given on basic approaches such as shoot

Right: *The autumn tree colours, the gravel landscape and the geometric form of the path at this garden at Tenju-an in Kyoto are all classic elements of the Japanese garden.*

Far right: *Flowering cherries, such as these Yoshino cherry flower heads (*Prunus x yedoensis*) are a favourite sight in Japanese gardens in the springtime.*

Japanese Gardening

The Japanese garden is a place of beauty created by a masterful and artistic composition of elements. A harmonious balance of individual features is achieved through the interrelation of plants, sand or gravel, water and rocks. These gardens are not frenetic, busy and colourful; they are calming, restrained, co-ordinated and meaningful.

A typical Japanese garden landscape will show re-creations of the myths of the Ancient Isles in the use of rocks and forms on the land and in the water. A Japanese garden also aims to create an interesting journey for the garden visitor, with pathways, attractive viewpoints and unexpected elements.

This section takes you through everything you could possibly need to create your own garden in the style of Japan – the journey starts with the history and interpretation of the garden style, then an analysis of the classic elements, and finishes with the five garden styles and practical advice on how to put them together.

Opposite: *The Japanese maple (Acer japonica vitifolium) is a deciduous tree valued for its autumn colours.*

Above: *Boxwood, clipped into rounded shapes ,and a stepping stone path are two distinctive features of the Japanese garden.*

A HISTORY OF JAPANESE GARDENING

The story of this gardening tradition is both long and fascinating. Understanding its history and learning about the people who were involved in its development gives an insight into the philosophy that inspires the Japanese garden. With such knowledge, we can plan and create gardens in this style with confidence and conviction. Although the essential style of Japanese gardens can be imitated simply by copying their outward form and appearance, reproducing their spirit requires a much deeper understanding.

The following chapter leads us through the main Japanese historical periods, made distinct by wave after wave of Chinese and Buddhist influences. These have combined with the Japanese people's strong sense of self, and their glorious landscape and native religion, to produce the uniquely curious and beautiful art form that is the Japanese garden. It is remarkable that garden styles from over 1,000 years ago still inform today's gardens. Even in the most avant-garde modern gardens you can often find motifs from Heian romanticism, the dry gardens of the Muromachi period or the tea gardens of the Momoyama period.

Above: *A chequerboard of stone squares sunk into a sea of moss.*
Left: *A tea house at Saiho-ji Moss Temple in Kyoto.*

The evolution of the garden

There are six important periods in the history of the Japanese garden, most of them coinciding with dramatic changes in Japan's history. The division into six is an oversimplification, but it helps to explain the evolution of some of the distinct styles of these gardens. Each period is defined not only by the practicalities and customs of contemporary Japanese life, but also by the conflicts and changes brought by religion, culture, politics and warfare. Chinese artistic influence was strong, and Buddhism brought a sense of spirituality to Japanese garden design.

Above: *A garden of clipped shrubs, which are known as o-karikomi, at Sanzen-in, a garden from the Edo period.*

THE DIFFERENT PERIODS

As recently as the 1970s, a garden from the 9th century was excavated in Nara. The history of the Japanese garden really starts at that time, now known as the Nara period. It continues through the five subsequent periods – the 11th-century Heian period, the 13th-century Kamakura period, the 15th-century Muromachi period, the 16th-century Momoyama period (which all centred around the old capital of Kyoto), and lastly the 18th- and 19th-century Edo period (after the capital moved to Tokyo). The gardens of the 20th century are more complex in their style and are dealt with later under "Modern and Western influences".

NARA PERIOD (710–94)

A period of pond and stream gardens, and gardens for ceremonies (Chinese Tang dynasty, 618–906)
Built in 710, Nara, which lies some 48km (30 miles) south of Kyoto, was the last of the ancient capitals of Japan. Excavations in 1974 found vestiges of an ornamental garden on the site of an old palace. They revealed a winding stream, edged in gravel and pebbles in a naturalistic style, with unique, sophisticated rock arrangements. These gardens were almost certainly used for ceremonial purposes, and were quite similar to those that were constructed in China during the same period.

HEIAN PERIOD (794–1185)

The first wave of Chinese influence and Pure Land Paradise gardens (Chinese Tang dynasty, 618–906; Five Dynasties, 906–60; Chinese Song dynasty, 960–1279)
This, the most romantic period in Japanese cultural history, saw a great many refinements, and also showed a new sensitivity to detail and a focus on the seasons and rituals, all of which evolved under imperial rule in Kyoto. One of the key features was the creation of pond and island gardens that reproduced the Mystic Isles of the immortals and the Pure Land Paradise garden of Buddha Amida, into which the souls of the pure could be reborn after death.

Another new feature was the garden design that enabled court ceremonies, music and poetry readings to be performed in courtyards, on boats and by the side of streams. The *Sakuteiki*, possibly the world's first great garden treatise, was written during this period in the 11th century.

Left: *This woodblock print by Katsushika Hokusai (1760–1849) shows a group of ladies visiting the wisteria gardens at Edo-period Kameido. Traditional Japanese garden design was closely linked to formal social etiquette.*

KAMAKURA PERIOD (1185–1392)

The second wave of Chinese influence with the arrival of Zen (Chinese Song dynasty, 960–1279; Yuan or Mongol dynasty, 1279–1368; Chinese Ming dynasty, 1368–1644)

Minamoto was the first *shogun* (military dictator) in Japan, and his government, based in Kamakura, took little interest in the arts until Buddhist monks began returning from China bringing tea, paintings of the Song dynasty and early artefacts of the Ming dynasty. They were also influenced by the Zen Buddhism of China. The imperial family in Kyoto continued with the same traditions as in the Heian period. Around 1339, the Saiho-ji and Tenryu-ji gardens were created in Kyoto, inspired by scenes from Song-dynasty paintings. Zen monks started to make gardens, and rocks became an important element.

MUROMACHI PERIOD (1393–1568)

The era of the devastating Onin wars and the refining influence of Zen on garden-making (Chinese Ming dynasty, 1368–1644)

The mingling of the warrior classes with the imperial classes in Kyoto led to an extraordinary flowering of the arts. This period saw the building of the Golden Pavilion in the 1390s and the Silver Pavilion in the 1470s by Ashikaga shoguns, whose pond-filled stroll gardens were a departure from the earlier preference for boating lakes. The most important innovation of this period was the creation of "dry water" gardens (*kare-sansui*) that used rocks set in gravel or sand to symbolize water. The designs of these gardens were influenced by Zen Buddhism and the black and white ink landscape paintings. The most famous of these gardens are the Daisen-in (made in about 1513) and the Ryoan-ji (1499).

Right: The Golden Pavilion in Kyoto, which is covered in gold leaf, was built in the 1390s by the first of the Ashikaga shoguns, marking the beginning of the Muromachi period.

MOMOYAMA PERIOD (1568–1603)

The era of the unifiers who would build Japan as a single nation and the rise of the tea masters and the merchant class (Chinese Ming dynasty, 1368–1644)

Three successive military unifiers built gardens using far larger rocks than before, designed as an expression of power, but this excess was also tempered by the modesty of an important new feature: the tea house and garden. The famous tea-ceremony ritual was initially popularized by a merchant called Rikyu, who was one of the most influential figures in Japan.

Above: The gardens around Nijo Castle, in Kyoto, were constructed at the beginning of the Edo period. These gardens used larger rocks than ever before and in greater numbers.

EDO PERIOD (1603–1867)

The era of National Isolation and the private stroll gardens (Chinese Qing dynasty, 1644–1911)

In 1603, the Tokugawa shogunate moved to the eastern capital, Edo (now Tokyo), where strict social structures were enforced. The gardens of this period are characterized by stroll gardens, the most famous being the Katsura Detached Palace, in Kyoto. With its many pond-side tea houses and buildings, and exquisite framed views, it might represent the last great peak in large-scale Japanese garden art.

Meanwhile, wealthy city merchants and samurai developed the small courtyard garden, incorporating motifs from the dry gardens and the tea gardens of earlier ages. In time, gardens became more ostentatious, losing the creative edge and philosophical depth of their predecessors. Since 1867, however, when Japan reopened its borders to the West, gardens have explored the minimalism of Zen and more avant-garde and naturalistic styles, although still incorporating traditional motifs such as the Mystic Isles.

Waves of Chinese influence

Before AD607, Japan was a primitive culture that had received only a trickle of Chinese cultural influence through Korea. After 607, a whole host of influences were suddenly accessible to the Japanese people through their contact with China. When the first Japanese ambassador to China arrived in Ji, the Chinese capital, in 607, he would have seen vast lake-and-island gardens, encircled by pavilions, surrounding the imperial palaces. China must have been a revelation to the Japanese, and this was the beginning of many centuries of cultural exchange.

Above: *The gardens of Tenryu-ji are situated in Kyoto. Created in the 1300s, some parts were later adapted to fit with changing tastes.*

THE CHINESE STYLE

In Chinese gardens, islands were often used to represent the Mystic Isles, the mythical abode of the immortals. The Chinese Emperor Han Wu had built his own lake and a fantastical island garden in the hope of enticing the immortals down to part with the secret elixir for eternal youth. The Mystic Isles were believed to float on the backs of turtles, while the immortals were carried around on the backs of cranes. These myths had a huge impact on the Japanese imagination and, to

this day, the Mystic Isles, cranes and turtles still feature prominently, usually in the form of carefully composed rock groupings. Rocks not only represented islands, however, but also came to symbolize Mount Shumisen, the central mountain in Buddhist mythology and an important mountain-water image that arrived in Japan from China.

BUDDHIST INFLUENCE

A major force in Japan, Buddhism gained particular importance from the mid-6th century onwards,

incorporating additional Chinese influences. Even though the emperor of Japan placed the country under the protection of the Buddha, the indigenous Shinto gods, or kami, retained a strong influence, closely associated with the emperor and with the general well-being of society.

Ponds were central to the Buddhist concept of paradise and became as essential to Japanese gardens as they had been in China. The Amida Buddha's Land of Paradise garden was described as being planted with gem-laden trees, while golden sands edged lily-filled lakes. On these lakes, heavenly hosts waited for devout souls to give them new birth on a lotus blossom in the realm of bliss. The great Amida garden of lakes and islands became the image for Nara- and Heian-style gardens.

THE ONSET OF THE JAPANESE STYLE

In 794, when the capital was moved to what is now Kyoto (Heian Kyo), the pond-and-winding-stream garden was the pre-eminent garden design.

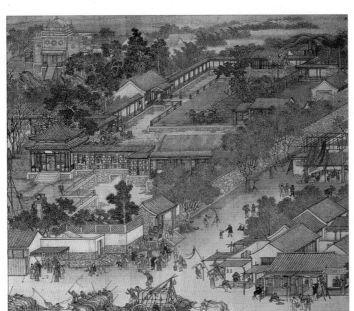

Left: *Ancient Chinese gardens displayed trees and fantastic rocks in their courtyards. The Japanese, although heavily influenced by the Chinese, had a preference for a more naturalistic approach to garden design.*

Above: *The Chinese myths of the Mystic Isles still inspire designers today. In the dry garden of Ryogen-in, created in the 1980s, stands the central mountainous island of Horai.*

Left: *A landscape of mountains and a river by Japanese painter and Zen priest Toya Sesshu (1420–1506). His Zen-inspired landscapes were influential within both the painting and garden design styles of Japan.*

Gradually, during the Heian period, fuelled by the cultured society of Kyoto, a true Japanese garden style began to emerge. This style slowly and indiscernibly blended Buddhism, the Mystic Isles and Shinto's sacred groves into the distinctive art form that is so recognizable today.

GEOMANCY

Meaning the Chinese science of divination, geomancy affected the design of palaces, towns and gardens by its insistence that buildings, plants and rocks must be placed in a very precise manner according to certain forces or lines of energy, to ensure that they were in balance and in tune with the natural order. If a placement was wrong, trouble and ill health could descend on an individual, a whole household or even the nation. In fact, the choice of the site of the new city of

Kyoto, modelled on the Chinese city of Chang'an and its palaces and gardens, followed Chinese geomantic principles.

Each of the elements is linked to a direction: earth at the centre, water in the north, fire to the south, wood in the east and metal in the west. Other Chinese approaches to the elements maintained that each direction could also represent colours, planets, seasons and guardian gods.

The principles of yin and yang also form part of the science of geomancy, but they are not always regarded as precise opposites and may be seen as complementary forces. Most phenomena contain an element of both yin and yang, because bringing them together produces harmonious conditions. For example, combining water (yin) with the sun or fire (yang) creates the right conditions to enable seeds to germinate.

Above: *A turtle island at Konchi-in where the head and flippers can be picked out from among rocks and clipped shrubs.*

PAINTINGS

The next wave of influences on the Japanese garden also came from China, in part through its painters. The Chinese artists of the Tang and Song dynasties painted mountains, pine trees beside waterfalls, streams falling into lakes, and paths weaving through rocks. These artists, more than all of the great Chinese imperial parks, influenced the Japanese garden. Meanwhile, Japanese monks and artists who visited China saw temples of great beauty, as well as hermit monks and artists living a simple life in huts and caves, and they returned home with a desire to emulate the Chinese lifestyle and the arts that they had encountered there.

ZEN BUDDHISM

Japanese monks were eager to practise a purer version of Buddhism without esoteric practices such as the worship of Buddha Amida. They found in China practitioners of Chan (or Zen, as it is known in Japan), a word derived from the Sanskrit *dyana*, which means meditation. Zen Buddhism places much more focus on the individual and on his or her efforts to control the mind, especially through meditation, and the experience of "no-ness".

By the late 1500s, Japanese Zen masters had become the next great garden-makers, once again inspired by Chinese and Japanese paintings featuring dry gardens of sand and rocks. Their gardens became increasingly abstract, often carrying hidden messages of Zen symbolism.

TEA GARDENS AND CEREMONIES

The paintings, poetry and spiritual writings of the Chinese literati were not the only sources of inspiration for Japanese painters and Zen monks. The design of the Japanese tea house was also inspired by the rustic hermitages of the Chinese literati and artists residing in their mountain retreats. As a result, the merchants and monks would develop a completely new style of garden, which included a path (known as a *roji*) that led to a tea house.

By the early 16th century, this new style had evolved into the influential form of the tea garden, and Japanese garden design took a brand new imaginative direction. The Japanese tea garden is one that is very familiar to Western eyes, with its key features such as a tea house, lanterns, water basins and wells.

Top right: *This two-fold screen by Kano Eitoku (1543–90) shows a romantic depiction of birds and a waterfall.*

Right: *In the garden at Konchi-in, various symbolic forms are depicted with rocks and pines, with fine white gravel spread around them to represent the sea.*

Modern & Western influences

From 1633, when shogun Iemitsu declared the Japanese borders closed, until the Americans arrived to reopen them by force in 1852, Japan was a hidden, secret country. Very few links with the West survived during this period, and even the Chinese had little contact with their neighbours. While the country developed in isolation during the major part of the Edo period (1603–1867), Japanese artists continued to express themselves in painting, literature and design, making use of a strong internal cultural tradition in which artistic endeavour could flourish.

THE AMERICAN ATTACK

Until 1852, when the Black Ships of the American Navy fired their first few warning salvos at the Tokugawa shogunate to force the Japanese to open their ports and begin trading with foreigners, the influence of the modern Western world had been limited. Once these trading and communication channels opened, the West's influence

made a mark in technical and artistic terms. This was a two-way interaction, as the impact of Japanese culture in the West was also significant.

The Japanese regime in 1852 was in a sad state of decline. However, after the American attack, the impoverished imperial family replaced the shogunate that had held power for 250 years, and enjoyed a new ascendancy.

Above: *The roof garden of the Canadian Embassy in Tokyo, designed by the Buddhist monk Shunmyo Masuno in the 1990s, and inspired by the Rocky Mountains.*

Below: *Mirei Shigemori, an artist and garden maker, redesigned the garden of Tofuku-ji in Kyoto, in the 1930s. He was the first to see the potential of the Japanese garden to become a vehicle for contemporary expression. He was also influenced by the Western art forms of the time.*

JAPANESE ARTS REACH THE WEST

From the mid-19th century onwards Japan's influence on the West made itself felt, with Japanese prints and artefacts flooding Western markets, invigorating the art world and inspiring the Impressionists, among others. Great architects, such as Frank Lloyd Wright (1867–1959) and Charles Rennie Mackintosh (1868–1928), found a raw simplicity in Japanese gardens and architecture. They also admired the beauty of natural materials, which they used in conjunction with their own modern materials: glass, concrete and steel.

In gardening terms, what particularly appealed to Western eyes was the style of extraordinary gardens such as the Ryoan-ji, in Kyoto, whose brooding mystery affects people as much now as it did when it was built in the 1490s. This Zen-style garden influenced many Western designers who, although perhaps unfamiliar with the concepts of Zen Buddhism, found in the garden an art form that gave expression to their own minimalist, atonal and avant-garde creations.

WESTERN ARTS REACH JAPAN

While the West was absorbing Eastern influences, the Japanese showed an extraordinary capacity to assimilate other traditions, both digesting and also reinventing them. There was (and still is), for example, a hunger for English-style gardens, which were initially copied, as Chinese gardens had been, before being integrated into the Japanese mainstream and given an Eastern slant.

MODERN JAPANESE DESIGN

By the 1930s, however, the design of more traditional Japanese gardens had become rather stale and clichéd, and this situation prompted one or two designers to re-evaluate the use of established materials and motifs. The greatest of these was Mirei Shigemori (1896–1975), who made private and temple gardens from the 1930s to the

Above: *A Japanese tea garden, designed by Maureen Busby for the 2004 RHS Chelsea Flower Show in London. The main feature of a tea garden is a stepping-stone path that passes through a "wilderness".*

1950s. He gave his gardens a modern twist but, interestingly, continued to employ traditional motifs and natural materials alongside the contemporary use of concrete.

Since the 1950s, many newly created gardens have replaced natural rocks and boulders with raw, blasted, quarried materials, plastics and metals, in much the same way as 17th-century gardens blended the artificial with the natural. This incorporation of new materials, while retaining the pure simplicity of Zen gardens, is still the hallmark of contemporary Japanese garden design.

One of the latest movements in the evolution of the Japanese garden is towards a more natural style of garden

design, featuring a combination of both native plantings and naturalistic streams. However, what also stands out with these contemporary Japanese gardens is that Japan cannot entirely shed its cultural and historical past and that, even now, the most up-to-date garden designs still hark back through the ages to the 11th-century Heian gardens in their use of natural materials, as was laid down in the oldest surviving work on Japanese gardening – the *Sakuteiki*.

INSPIRATIONS

The Japanese garden possesses a style quite unlike
any other. This unique character can be attributed to
three factors: the outstanding natural landscape and
the spirit of Zen, which both inspired it, and the
importance of architectural features within the garden.

Japan is an archipelago of rugged coastlines and
has a volcanic mountainous landscape, with steep
rocky streams that tumble through forests. This
wonderful natural topography and native flora inspired
gardeners to recreate in their own gardens what they
saw around them. The ancient Japanese also believed
that the trees, rocks, mountains and water had power
over the gods of their Shinto religion.

The pared-down, minimalist way of interpreting and
recreating the natural landscape around them within
the garden originated in the spirit of Zen, with the
careful use of space and understatement.

A final factor to consider is the spiritual significance
of architectural features in the Japanese garden,
including the tea houses, and the technique of
shakkei, whereby views both within and beyond the
garden are framed by manmade or natural elements.

This chapter looks at the features that make the
character of the Japanese garden distinct, and
explains how this style can be understood and
interpreted in the West.

Above: *Plum blossom is associated with the start of spring.*
Left: *In the garden of Hosen-in in the mountains north of Kyoto,
a clipped hedge frames the natural landscape and draws it in
through the stems of bamboo.*

The natural landscape

Looking out over an expanse of sand raked into perfect lines, set in a perfect rectangular courtyard with one or two rocks, and an azalea or two clipped so much that they barely flower, you might be forgiven for thinking that Japanese gardeners are more inclined to fly in the face of nature than sympathize with it. Yet Japan's own natural landscape of mountains, windswept pines, waterfalls and islands directly inspires and informs their garden designs, resulting in a spiritual style that gives inspiration to gardeners all over the world.

Above: *Under certain conditions, snow will stick to pine needles. In Japan these attractive white baubles are commonly known as "snow flowers".*

AN INSPIRING STYLE

Japanese garden design was initially influenced by the Chinese. However, the natural mountainous and coastal landscapes of Japan, coupled with the people's spiritual reverence for rocks and trees, derived from their native Shinto religion, together created a second powerful influence. By incorporating a careful selection of indigenous plants and imitating the natural features of the countryside, albeit in a restrained, stylized form, Japanese garden designers have developed a unique style.

THE TOPOGRAPHY OF JAPAN

A mountainous archipelago of four main islands, Japan also has hundreds of small rocky islets. The mountains – over 50 of which are volcanic – are steep and wooded and scored with rocky streams, hot springs and rivers. In fact, most are still wooded up to their peaks because, until recently, Buddhism was the official religion and the eating of meat and fish was prohibited. This meant that, unlike in other parts of the world, their hills and mountains have not been stripped of vegetation by sheep, goats and cattle. To this day, natural features such as mountains, rocks and streams continue to inspire Japanese garden designers and are recurring features of the Japanese garden.

THE MOUNTAIN MOTIF

Mountains are a uniquely powerful influence over the imagination and gardens of the Chinese and the Japanese. Through myth and religion, mountains stand as the central feature of many of their garden designs. The Mystic Isles myth (which developed off the Chinese coast) is a typical example. There were five islands, one of which was called P'eng-lai, which later became Horai in Japan. These Mystic Isles, like the real islands of Japan, were large and mountainous, towering thousands of feet high, their sides steep and precipitous, reaching up to high plateaux rich in greenery. Here were misty blue valleys where all the beasts and birds were white, trees bore pearls, the flowers were fragrant and the fruits brought immortality to those who ate them. Along the shores of the islands lived blissfully happy immortal beings in golden, silver and jade pleasure pavilions. The immortals were not gods, but men who suffered no sickness or death, and developed supernatural powers, being able to float through the air. Sometimes they were carried on the backs of giant cranes, another key feature of Japanese design.

Originally, the myth says, the Mystic Isles floated about and were not fixed to the ocean floor. Then, the Supreme Ruler of the Universe commanded the islands to be secured by 15 enormous turtles, but one day a giant cast a net and caught six of the turtles.

Right: *Vermilion Torii gates originate in Shinto religion and symbolize sacred ground. They make a bold feature in the Karlsruhe Japanese garden in Germany.*

SYMBOL OF SHINTO: THE *TORII* GATE

The typical vermilion-painted gateway to Shinto shrines may be found at the entrance to many Buddhist temples as well. The gateway marks the progress of the worshipper from the day-to-day world outside to the sacred world inside, and passing under it is part of the cleansing ritual common to Shinto and Buddhist worship. *Torii* gates are usually made of wood, metal or stone, with two upright supports and two crossbars over the top. The word *torii* is thought to derive from a resting perch for birds; the birds will bring good luck to the temple, as they are considered to be messengers from the gods in the Shinto religion. These days, wealthy visitors to a Shinto shrine may donate a new *Torii* gate to thank the gods for their success in business.

Some others drifted away and were lost, leaving just three. The early Japanese might well have believed that they already lived on these Mystic Isles. Whatever the case, the island of Horai, the crane and the turtle became themes embedded in their gardens, even being reproduced in Mirei Shigemori's garden at the Tofuku-ji, as recently as 1938.

When you add to this ancient myth the divinities of Shinto (see below), the natural landscape of Japan, the influence of the distantly revered and idealized landscapes of China, and the Lands of Paradise promised by some Buddhist sects, the whole concoction becomes an inspirational mix for the development of a very special and beautiful style of gardening.

THE INFLUENCE OF SHINTO

Shinto – the religion of Japanese settlers who arrived by sea, possibly from Korea, in the 3rd or 4th centuries – means "way of the gods". It involved animistic and pagan-style rituals, and centred around rocks,

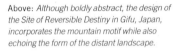

Above: *Although boldly abstract, the design of the Site of Reversible Destiny in Gifu, Japan, incorporates the mountain motif while also echoing the form of the distant landscape.*

trees and plants. It was believed that these objects possessed spiritual aspects that could draw the gods down to earth. There were two kinds of gods, or *kami*: those that descended from above, and those that lived across the sea and gave birth to the main islands of Japan. These two sets of gods were symbolized by sacred rocks and sacred ponds. These rock and pond motifs occur again and again in Japanese gardens, both past and present.

The Shintoists believed that certain places in the wild were inhabited by

the gods. To this day, you will still find trees wrapped in ropes near shrines, as well as old trees and rocks that have become shrines in their own right. *Shime*, the binding of objects or even people with rice straw ropes, may originally have been used to designate territory, while the bound artefacts symbolize land or islands. It is interesting to note that the word *shima*, meaning "garden", comes from shime.

Go-shintai ("the home of the gods") and *iwa-kura* ("seats of the gods") can also still be found throughout Japan. They have been purified and covered with layers of sand and gravel to become *shiki-no-himorogi*, or "sacred precincts". Some special rocks may even have been added.

Such rituals and sacred spaces had an important influence on the use of rocks in gardens and dry landscape gardens. The interplay between the flat expanse of the sea (symbolized by sand or gravel) and the rugged immensity of rocks and old trees provided a kind of aesthetic that inspired the leap from the purely spiritual space of Shinto to the secular space of the garden. This aesthetic

Left: *Detail from a screen (c.1600–1640) illustrating episodes from* The Tale of Genji. *This classic of ancient Japanese literature is interwoven with symbolic references to nature.*

may also explain why the Chinese style of garden was not copied "religiously". Shinto and the natural landscape of Japan provided a fertile influence that adapted the Chinese style into something new.

INTERPRETATIONS OF NATURE

The natural world has been a constant feature of Japanese gardens from the early days of the Heian period (794–1185), when inspiration came straight from the landscape and natural surroundings, right up to the present, when abstract and contemporary gardens still demonstrate a profound understanding of nature. The Italian garden aims to express an intellectual and philosophical vision of nature; the English garden is mainly based on the idealized world of the pastoral idyll; but the Japanese garden uses nature in a highly symbolic way.

More specifically, in the 15th and 16th centuries, Japanese designers turned increasingly to their great landscape painters for artistic inspiration, just as the late 18th-century English picturesque garden was inspired by the paintings of Claude Lorrain and Nicolas Poussin. Along with nature, painting has been a common starting point for many gardening movements.

THE *SAKUTEIKI*

The earliest known treatise on gardening, the *Sakuteiki* – the subtitle of which was "Setting of Stones" – was written in the mid-11th century. It was more of a technical journal for the select few, but many of its rules are still adhered to today as elemental precepts. Stones are said to have "desires", and the book recommends ways of listening to them, vital if they are to be placed correctly in the Japanese garden, as if they were in the wild.

The chapter headed "Nature" describes the remarkable and vivid use of the imagery of coastlines, streams, rocks, islands and waterfalls in garden design, and details a range of features with specific instructions. For example, stones can be used in different ways – perhaps placed in streams in order to modulate the flow of water, used as bottom or solitary stones, or as diffused stones to interrupt and divert the flow. Furthermore, garden streams (*yarimizu*) can be created in various styles, for example as if they are flowing through a valley, or as if they are broad rivers, or mountain torrents. There are also descriptions of, and instructions for creating, different kinds of waterfall, all of which are relevant to the Japanese gardener today.

Garden streams often pour down a waterfall into a lake or pond. These ponds represent lakes or the sea, and are dotted with islands, their shorelines punctuated by promontories made of white sand to evoke the beaches of distant landscapes. Miniature windswept ocean beaches, coves and undulating shorelines are planted with soft grasses. Islands also come in different guises, with rocky shores, for example, or in forest, meadow and wetland styles.

The earliest Japanese gardens, from the Heian period when the *Sakuteiki* was written, still have an important influence on modern garden designers who look to nature for inspiration. These gardens emphasize that we should observe but not slavishly copy nature, consulting the "genius of the place" before transforming it into art. As the *Sakuteiki* suggests, "Visualize the famous landscapes of our country and come to understand their most interesting points. Recreate the essence of these scenes in the garden, but do so interpretatively, not strictly."

HEIAN CULTURE AND DESIGN

In the culture of the Heian period, as distinct from the later austere Zen and Muromachi periods, the aristocracy that had settled around the Emperor in Kyoto enjoyed years of peaceful luxury. They spent much of their time writing poetry, and became more and more detached from the business of running the country. A kind of melancholy pervaded their lives. They believed that they were living in the *Mappo*, the Buddha's period of Ending Law, with declining social and religious mores. They hoped to be transported to his Western Paradise, depicted in their gardens as lakes and islands, for an afterlife of eternal bliss. This life was seen as a fleeting interlude, a dream between two realities.

The Heian aristocracy closely observed nature, noting every whim and expression as a sign and symbol to compare with love, death, honour and the great range of human emotions. These emotions were often symbolized by plants, and the early Heian gardens used many flowering shrubs, such as kerria, deutzia, lespedeza, azalea and osmanthus, as well as cherries, maples, wild roses and irises. In the two great novels of the time, *The Pillow Book* (995) by Sei Shonagon and *The Tale of Genji* (early 11th century) by Murasaki Shikibu, trees and flowers, as well as the weather, were used to symbolize human thoughts and desires.

THE SEASONS AND THEIR PLANTS

Around Kyoto, the seasons are fairly predictable, right down to the first rumblings of thunder over the mountains that herald the beginning of the rainy season in midsummer. By then, the cherry blossom, wisteria and azalea will have long dropped their last blooms and the hydrangeas started to colour. At the same time, it will be sweltering in the sub-tropical south in Kyushu, while in northern Honshu and Hokkaido, trees growing below the melting snows on the mountainsides have not yet come into

Top: *The cherry blossom heralds the height of spring which is the most popular season for viewing gardens in Japan.*

Above: *The mop-headed* Hydrangea macrophylla, *growing profusely in a shaded woodland, is a classic summer flower.*

leaf. Apart from the northern reaches, most of Japan endures uncomfortably hot and rainy summers. This is why the Heian elite in Kyoto placed such a strong emphasis on the two main garden seasons – spring (the most important) and autumn – an emphasis that still exists today. The seasons

were also considered to be part of the geomantic system, with flowers used to depict the cardinal lines of energy; good planting and design helped to protect the household from misfortune.

In modern Japan, the plum and peach blossoms are the fanfare for spring, followed shortly by the cherry blossom.

THE FOUR SEASONS IN JAPANESE GARDENS

Spring

Weather: mild and pleasant – the best growing season and the best time to visit Japan.

Plants: plum, peach and cherry blossom, azalea, wisteria, camellia.

Festivals: many festivals linked with spring flowers, including Golden Week (April/May) to celebrate the abundant cherry blossom.

Summer

Weather: hot, humid and rainy with thunderstorms, oppressive heat day and night.

Plants: iris, hydrangea, lotus blossom.

Festivals: iris festival in late May. Bon, a Buddhist festival honouring the ancestors. Many Japanese people leave the cities and visit the cooler mountain areas of the north.

Autumn

Weather: mild, less humid with sunshine and cold nights. Season of typhoons.

Plants: *Acer palmatum* and *Enkianthus*.

Festivals: local festivals (*matsuri*) linked with rice harvest.

Winter

Weather: very cold, often snowy, but some clear days with winter sun.

Plants: bamboo, pine, cedar and other evergreen trees and bushes.

Festivals: New Year festivals (*Omisoka*) when the whole country takes time off and all businesses are shut.

Top: *Trees are planted extensively in Japanese gardens for their autumn colour, such as this katsura tree in the Tully garden in Ireland.*

Above: *The vivid colour of a traditional Japanese Torii gate stands out dramatically in a snow-covered garden.*

Then come the native camellias, azaleas and floribunda wisterias, while, in early summer, iris festivals are celebrated up and down the country. The lotus, the enduring symbol of Buddhism, also flowers in summer. The autumn is marked by the Japanese maples (*Acer palmatum*) which grow in Japan's forests, as does *Enkianthus*, which sets ablaze the hillsides and hillside temples at this time. Chrysanthemums, symbols of the imperial family, long life and good fortune, are grown especially for festivals in late autumn. In winter, the pine, cedar and bamboo are celebrated.

The Japanese use some native plants, such as cherries, azaleas, pines and bamboos, within their gardens, but tend to ignore a vast range of their native flora. This indicates restraint rather than a limited palette. So a hedge may be made up of a number of evergreen shrubs but will not blend masses of bright-coloured foliage. In this way, the final effect is restrained even when a large number of plants have been used.

The influence of Zen

Zen Buddhism was introduced to Japan from China by monks in the 13th century. Once established, it provided a consistent influence for all aspects of Japanese culture and arts. The "no-ness" of Zen philosophy, in particular, prompted some important developments in garden design – the dry gardens surrounding many Buddhist temples were a rich source of inspiration for Japanese garden designers and the influence of this simple, restrained style, with its symbolic use of raked effects in gravel and the subtle placing of rocks, has been felt from East to West.

Above: *Natural rocks have been replaced by slabs of blasted quarry stone and assembled with fragments of the rock. The mountain image and empty space are typical features of the Zen garden.*

THE ARRIVAL OF ZEN BUDDHISM

The pioneer monks who introduced Zen to Japan initially met with a bleak response from the rather philistine military government based in Kamakura, south of present-day Kyoto. Two or three generations later, however, Zen found new patrons among the rival warlords and the imperial family so that, by the early 1300s, there were some 300 Zen monasteries in Kamakura and Kyoto. These temples, part of what was called the Five Mountain Network, promoted studies in a range of Chinese arts and philosophies. Apart from studying neo-Confucian metaphysics, the monks were also highly skilled in poetry, painting, calligraphy, ceramics, architecture and garden design.

A less erudite group of rural monks, who were known as Rinka (meaning "forest"), practised in another network of Zen temples and devoted themselves strictly to Zazen, or sitting Zen (meditation), as well as *koan* (the writing of riddles). Their self-discipline and loyalty to their masters appealed to the rising warrior class, the samurai, to whom the Rinka monks preached stern moralizing sermons. This philosophy was shared by other followers of Zen, whose teachers or masters also transmitted their values to their disciples. There were no written scriptures, though, and none of the trappings of esoteric Buddhism, such as mandalas, chanting and the reciting of scriptures, which had dominated Japanese life for the previous 500 years.

ZEN AND THE DRY GARDEN

Dogan (1200–53), a monk who lived during the Kamakura period, was well known for emphasizing the "no-ness" of all things (emptiness, void or non-substantiality). This aspect of Zen meant finding what might be called the "perfect expression of pure mind". Garden designers expressed this "no-ness" in the empty space of sand in dry gardens. Sand had already been used within Shinto sacred precincts, then in front of palaces for court

Left: *The stump of an enormous Japanese cedar bound and housed as a shrine in its own right. The Shinto belief that trees, rocks and other natural objects possessed spirits was incorporated into Zen garden design.*

Above: *Rocks in a "sea" of gravel represent the Mystic Isles, from the ancient myth adopted by the Zen tradition.*

Right: *Zen monks were drawn to the world of the Chinese scholar-hermit. They created tea houses, such as this one at Toji-in Temple, and tea paths imbued with the spirit of Zen.*

ceremonies, before evolving into a representation of the sea or a white canvas for painter-gardeners. Under the auspices of Zen practitioners, the empty stretch of sand came to represent a meditative spiritual space. Sometimes these gardens look like familiar landscapes, or brush paintings, and if contemplated for long enough, they induce a sense of calm.

It was mostly the Zen monks who designed the extraordinary spaces known as *kare-sansui* (dry landscapes), which have become synonymous with Japanese gardening, most notably at the famous dry gardens of Ryoan-ji and Daisen-in. Zen exercised a strong influence over Japanese gardening (and still does), and it also gave greater precision and discipline to the art of garden design. Even if you are not steeped in the mysteries of Zen, you can appreciate the extraordinary beauty and sense of style and the pared-down, abstract visions of nature to be found in these gardens.

Right: *At the Canadian embassy in Tokyo, a dry garden with natural rocks and sand pays homage to the past while also displaying the brave cutting edge of modernity.*

ZEN AND THE TEA GARDEN

The evolution of the tea garden had strong links to the Zen monks. Used originally by them as an aid to wakefulness during long periods of meditation, tea soon became an essential part of Buddhist rituals. It was only a short step for Zen monks, as garden makers and tea drinkers, to bring these two arts together. So the tea garden, at first just a simple rustic path to the tea house, became associated with important traditions.

ZEN AND MODERN GARDEN STYLE

When creating a Zen-style dry garden, consider the influences that created them. Many contemporary gardens are made up of a few rocks, a layer of sand or gravel and a bamboo plant or pine tree, and are glibly described as being very Japanese or, worse, very Zen. That is only true, however, if there is no hint of the superfluous. Nor should any one feature dominate. Zen-style dry gardens, or tea gardens, should be imbued with purity and restraint.

THE ESSENCE OF THE ZEN GARDEN

While the first Japanese gardens of the 11th century were poetic readings of nature and 15th-century gardens were inspired readings of the master landscape painters, the gardens of both periods were disciplined attempts to understand the self and the universe. What this meant in practical terms was that there was an avoidance of the trite, the obvious and the emphatic. Unnecessary distractions and the use of excessive colour or form were also avoided. The prime ingredients were those that in the 13th century became defined as the seven aspects of Zen:

- asymmetry
- simplicity
- austere sublimity
- naturalness
- tranquillity
- subtle profundity
- freedom from attachment

These qualities were also applied to other art forms in a Zen style, such as calligraphy and poetry.

Even people with no experience of meditation or of Zen Buddhism can appreciate the calming beauty of a Zen garden. If you want to imbue your garden with the spirit of Zen, you should try to make your garden reflect a quiet, contemplative world and avoid the kind of deliberate gestures that come from a busy, overactive mind. The art is to avoid over-stimulating the senses in the way that you might experience in a Western garden.

A Zen garden will avoid carefully contrived colour schemes, rocks with strange shapes, gushing fountains or brightly painted buildings. For example, the red-painted Chinese bridges that you see in some Japanese gardens would not be seen in a Zen garden because such features were

Above: *The Zen garden of Tenju-an, in Kyoto, dating from the late 14th century, is a superb example of the interplay between geometric, manmade and irregular natural forms.*

seen to divert the eye and stimulate the mind instead of calming it.

It is the approach to the Zen arts that is important, whether it be in garden design, painting or the martial arts. The spirit of Zen, the "emptiness" conveyed by an area of raked gravel in a dry garden, should be as much in the mind of the man with the rake as in the clean sweep of the gravel. Although Zen is a state of mind that takes years to perfect, the garden designer can still plan a garden with the spirit of Zen in mind, making calmness and tranquillity a central feature, avoiding bright colours and ensuring that the landscaping and planting are kept to an absolute minimum.

Zen garden with raked waves

This dry garden in Ryogen-in, Kyoto, was redesigned and constructed in 1980 on the site of an old garden. The "canvas" of this painterly garden is a rectangle of a sea with parallel raked waves. Maintained in a more exaggerated form than older gardens of this style, the essential elements are the same as those of the 15th century. The parallel lines of raked gravel change to deep concentric waves as they lap around the main features in the dry sea. Towards the back is the tallest group of rocks, which represent Mount Horai (*Horai-san*), the foremost of the Mystic Isles. These isles were said to be carried on the backs of turtles, so the main mossy island is designed as a turtle island (*kame-shima*). The immortals lived on these isles, holding the secret elixir for eternal youth and immortality. They travelled around on the backs of cranes, and the third rock arrangement is a crane island (*tsuru-shima*).

The rectangular frame is made from a combination of edging stones and roof tiles. On two sides a border of moss is contained between the edging and the wall, while in the foreground the temple veranda and garden are divided by a border of pebbles. Pine trees have also been planted into the border.

The garden can be read as an artistic impression, with the bolder shapes and the deeper waves creating a dramatic effect on the viewer. Nevertheless, the simplicity of the design and the significance of the main features give a sense of permanence.

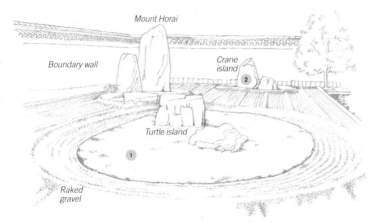

Mount Horai

Boundary wall

Crane island

Turtle island

Raked gravel

Right: *In the dry garden at Ryogen-in, the three main symbols of the Mystic Isles are laid out in a sea of sand. In the foreground is a turtle island; back left is Mount Horai, the tallest of the Mystic Isles; with a crane island at the rear.*

Architectural elements

Up to the Edo period (1603–1867), all major garden styles evolved in towns and were defined by the layout of the main buildings, courtyards, entrances and boundaries. Later, large gardens were laid out in more rural locations, where small buildings such as arbours, pavilions and tea houses were often placed to keep the human focus, so maintaining the relationship between architecture and garden. Another role for architecture was in the technique of *shakkei*, where buildings, trees or shrubs would frame a view of the landscape beyond the garden.

ARCHITECTURAL INTERACTION

The relationship between a Japanese garden and the architecture of the main house, temple or garden buildings is quite unlike that of the formal Western garden. In the West, the details and forms of the architecture tend to influence the design of formal gardens, but by contrast the formal Japanese garden enjoys the interplay between the angularity of the architecture and the curve of natural forms. Although dry and courtyard gardens are often contained within the rectilinear confines of garden walls, the forms of the gardens themselves are more like paintings held within a picture frame.

Above: *In the dry garden at the Tofuku-ji, the architectural line of the* hojo *abbot's quarters, the surrounding walls and the lines of raked sand make it hard to define exactly where the building ends and the garden begins.*

Below: *The view from the temple veranda overlooking the garden at Shoden-ji reveals not only the garden but also the distant sacred Mount Hiei. This capturing of a view was part of the garden design device known as* shakkei.

In other styles of Japanese garden, the natural forms of stepping stones, rocks, pine boughs and bamboos are brought very close to the buildings. Sometimes camellias or azaleas may be clipped into geometric forms to accentuate or even imitate the architecture, but asymmetry and dynamic natural forms within the design are usually preferred.

CHINESE INFLUENCES

The Japanese buildings of the Nara (710–94) and Heian (794–1185) periods, like their gardens, were more or less copies of the Chinese. But differences began to develop during the Heian period: the Japanese already showed a preference for the natural finish of timber, rather than the more flamboyant painted buildings common in China at the time, and roofs were also less sweeping and curved than their Chinese counterparts.

GARDEN BUILDINGS

Japanese garden buildings and structures have particular characteristics that mark them as different from most Western styles:

• the preferred materials are natural, such as bamboo, reed, and sawn or raw timber (sometimes with the bark on);

• materials are not painted, but left to look as natural as possible;

• at times when the Chinese influence was strong, especially the very early Nara period (early 8th century) and the later Edo period (early- to mid-19th century), buildings and structures, such as bridges, were sometimes painted bright red-orange, in dramatic contrast to the typically muted look apparent in the rest of the garden.

The principal style of Heian aristocratic homes was known as *shinden* (literally, "sleeping hall"). This main hall, or *shinden*, was set at the centre of a square building, with two adjacent wings to the sides for concubines and wives. From these two wings, two corridors (the east and the west) led south to the main garden. In the space between these two corridors was an open, sand-covered courtyard, which was reserved for ceremonies and entertainment. Through part of this courtyard, a stream might meander and feed into the main pond beyond.

At the end of the east and west corridors were pavilions, usually named after their primary function – for instance, the fishing pavilion was often built on stilts over the main pond, but was just as likely to have been used by musicians. Another pavilion may have covered the well or the spring that fed the pond.

Over the next 200 years, Japanese architecture evolved into smaller and more refined urban residences. By the Muromachi period, monks and samurai showed a marked preference for the *shoin* style. *Shoin* was a term that referred to the alcove that was set within one of the outer walls of the main building. This alcove had papered walls in order to allow natural light to illuminate a specially designed shelf or a desk for reading and writing. The *shoin* was a kind of library or study that, for the warriors and abbots, symbolized their arrival as members of the intelligentsia or literati. This new architectural style was found in many temples and houses, which also had verandas and sliding panels that opened up to reveal their gardens.

The tea house also employed some aspects of the *shoin* style, especially the alcove, but the general style of tea-house architecture was more rustic. The Japanese tea house, which was originally known as the "mountain place in the city", combined the rustic charm of the thatched hut (*soan*) with the sophistication of a more literary and urban style of architecture (*shoin*). This hybrid style was, and still is, most popular for building tea houses and garden buildings.

The alcove of the tea house, known as the *tokonoma*, was a place in which to display works of art, especially calligraphy scrolls and poems, alongside simple country-style flower arrangements.

SHAKKEI

Many old houses and temples have verandas with pillars that support the roofs. These pillars also frame a view of the garden. The view of the garden from indoors can be regarded as if you are looking at a painting. The art of framing is even more important when a spectacular distant view can be captured – for example, the sight of Mount Fuji, near Tokyo, or Mount Hiei, near Kyoto. This technique is called *shakkei*, or "borrowed scenery", but was once known by the more evocative term *ikedori*, meaning "captured alive". It was an important device that involved more than simply having a "nice view" from your house. *Shakkei* meant that prominent distant features could, in effect, be drawn into the garden itself and so become an intrinsic part of its overall composition.

Although most Westerners wishing to reproduce a Japanese garden will not own a Japanese-style home, they may have verandas, picture windows or other forms of framing that can be used to capture their garden, and perhaps also a more distant view. In this way, architecture can be used to make the garden part of the house.

Above: *The pillars that support the verandas of temples and tea houses can frame the garden beyond them in the same way as the frame of a landscape painting. This design accentuates the contrast between the architecture and the natural form.*

Below: *Sliding rice paper panel doors (*shoji*) open up a view from a tatami-matted tea room at Isui-en, Nara. The square opening interacts with the weaving stems of Japanese maples.*

FRAMING THE VIEW

If you are creating a Japanese garden around a Western-style house, think of how a Japanese house would interface with the garden. You should aim to:

• create key viewing points, where the garden and the distant view are framed as a complete composition;

• use large picture windows to frame the view of the garden and beyond;

• use the supporting pillars of a veranda or an arbour to frame a focal point;

• take extra care to frame the view of a dry garden.

Toji-in tea houses

Yoshimasa, the shogun of the late 15th century who inspired a great flowering of the arts of Japan, is said to have designed this thatched tea house in the garden of Toji-in. The garden is unusual in that it has two tea houses set side by side, and this helps to illustrate the design principles of the tea house. The style is derived from a combination of an older style of *shoin* architecture, including sliding panels, rice paper windows and a place to study, with the *soan* style of rustic huts of mountain farmers. The thatched roof is constructed in the same way as a farmer's house or barn, often including ventilation for silk worms, which were kept in the attic space. The rustic charm alludes to the Taoist hermit monks who lived in such buildings.

Traditional tea houses such as this often combine raw materials. Pillars made from tree trunks with the bark still on might feature, alongside strips of split bamboo and screens of natural plaster. There might also be finely carved shelves and surrounds to the *tokonoma*, the alcove inside the tea house where decorative objects were placed as a focus for the tea ceremony. The floor is laid out with tatami reed mats around a hearth set in the floor to heat the hot water for tea. While simple and appearing to be rustic, tea houses can be quite complicated and elaborate. The Toji-in tea house commands a view over the garden, but tea houses can also be placed in more secluded spots within a garden.

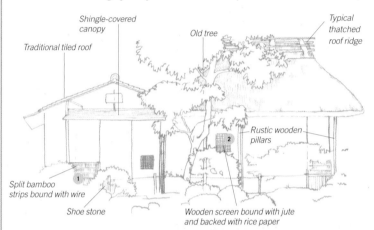

Shingle-covered canopy

Traditional tiled roof

Old tree

Typical thatched roof ridge

Rustic wooden pillars

Split bamboo strips bound with wire

Shoe stone

Wooden screen bound with jute and backed with rice paper

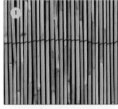

Right: *Two hermitage-style tea houses, built using contrasting materials, are set side by side in the gardens of Toji-in, Kyoto. The simple architecture and thatched roof are modelled on those of rustic farm buildings.*

Understanding the Japanese garden

Despite the complexity of different kinds of Japanese garden, the common Western impression is of a small, carefully cultivated, stylized space, filled with clipped shrubs, rocks and stone artefacts such as lanterns, pagodas and Buddhas. In reality, the finest Japanese gardens are larger than many Western city gardens, and the artefacts are quite superfluous to their design. What counts is the spirit of the garden, and how the different elements are balanced. A sensitively styled Japanese garden should include the following principles.

NATURE AND RELIGIOUS SPIRIT

The beauty of many of the great Japanese gardens lies in their sublime vision of nature. The pleasure people took in the poetic beauty of flowers and cherry blossom that was so evident in the 11th century still lingers on in the celebratory cherry blossom festivals of today. The Japanese also held great reverence for their landscape gods and recognized the power of *yugen* ("hidden depth"), describing the feeling of awe that nature can evoke. This reverence has always been an important influence in the garden designs of Japan, inspiring the recreation of, for example, an open ocean, the way a river flows, and how a mountain range is encircled by mist.

ROCKS AND WATER

The standard elements of rocks and water are designed and placed to imitate as far as possible the way they occur in the natural landscape. So ponds should be created with naturalistic outlines, with inlets and gravel beaches just as if nature had shaped them. Rocks should not be positioned as individual, monolithic pieces, as they are in Chinese gardens, or admired in isolation as one would a piece of sculpture on a pedestal. They are also presented as part of the natural landscape.

NATURAL AND MANMADE ELEMENTS

Although water and rocks are the foundation of the garden, the design of any artefacts and buildings follows a carefully observed and orchestrated relationship between the natural and the manmade. The finely polished wooden panels of the tea house might be in-filled with rough plaster, while the wooden support posts might still have their bark on. The concept of *wabi-sabi* is equally important. This was a poetic term adopted by the tea masters to describe a quality of raw simple beauty, touched with the patina of age.

Above: *Monochromatic ink paintings with their simple brushwork were frequently imitated by the creators of Zen dry gardens.*

ASYMMETRY AND BALANCE

Symmetry is rarely found in Japanese gardens, where the elements are characteristically arranged in odd numbers to bring to mind the asymmetry that characterizes nature.

Below: *The flat expanse of gravel, the horizontal lines of the hedge and some of the rocks in the Karlsruhe Japanese garden are balanced by several vertical rocks and the distant* torii *gate.*

Occasionally, an entranceway will have straight paths bordered by a pair of hedges or a view might be framed by rugged pine trees, but symmetry is generally seen by Japanese gardeners as something that restricts the imagination.

Instead of a symmetrical format, you need to create a design that feels natural, yet has a balanced composition, as well as a good sense of proportion between open and enclosed areas, enough empty space to allow the imagination to roam, and an easy transition from one section of the garden to another. The need for free-flowing movement applies not only to the observer's passage from area to area but also to specific elements. So paths and streams must meander and wander as they do in the wild, and ponds must appear to have naturally formed outlines.

ADDITIONAL NATURAL FEATURES

It can be useful to adopt the approach of the master painters when planning a Japanese garden, starting by dividing the site up into different layers:

• the foreground can be sand, gravel, moss or grass, featuring a water basin, rock or plant;

• the middle section can include a pond, island groups of rocks, and a weathered pine tree or clipped shrub;

• in the background, leave more open space with just the occasional rock, and use any distant view;

• frame the garden with an informal band of evergreens, walls or bamboo fencing.

CREATING LAYERS OF INTEREST

In the past, Japanese garden designers were inspired by old Japanese paintings. Composed with layers of interest and the artful play of light and shade, they helped them create a landscape's essence, framing it and dividing it into foreground, middle and distance.

Every element of a Japanese garden is there as part of the whole, whether a beautiful cherry tree or a millstone placed on a stepping-stone path.

Below: *The warm effect of the azaleas in this garden in Ito Shizuoka, Japan, shows how to integrate colour sensitively within the landscape.*

THE IMPORTANCE OF COLOUR

Although all the elements in a Japanese garden are subservient to the whole, this does not mean that the bright beauty of plum or cherry blossom or the autumn leaves of a maple are harmful to the design; they should be carefully considered for the part they play in celebrating the seasons. At the same time, plant colours should never be allowed to overwhelm a design, so showy, variegated, gold or purple foliage plants should in general be excluded. A good guide is that Japanese maples provide colour in the autumn and azaleas in the spring.

Interpreting a garden

The garden around the temple of Raikyu-ji, in Takahashi, was created by the 17th-century master gardener and tea-master Kobori Enshu. The central island set in a sea of gravel symbolizes Mount Horai and the Mystic Isles, and is wrapped in artistically clipped azaleas. The rounded shapes of the clipped shrubs that hug the main island emphasize the forms around them, either the rocks or the hilly landscapes that lie outside the garden. The effect is highly abstract, quite playful but also very sophisticated.

Each layer of the garden builds on the one before it. The foreground of raked sand, the rocks, the rolling "hills" of azaleas, the background evergreens, the spreading canopies of maples, all build up to the outline of Mount Atago in the distance.

Although essentially asymmetrical, this garden could be considered as very formal, and requires careful maintenance. The topiary, especially, needs a trained eye and a skilled hand to keep the shapes uniform. Each aspect of the design needs to be considered as part of the whole.

Also included are elements of the tea garden. A stepping-stone path starts at the temple and curls across the sea of gravel, behind the Mystic Isles and on around the garden into the shady depths of the trees. Here, a lantern has been carefully placed to light the path and to form another part of the overall composition.

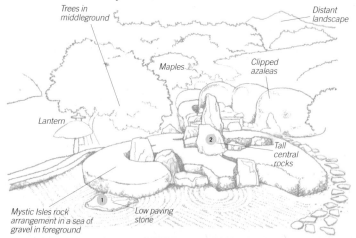

Trees in middleground

Distant landscape

Maples

Clipped azaleas

Lantern

Tall central rocks

Mystic Isles rock arrangement in a sea of gravel in foreground

Low paving stone

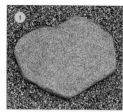

Right: *The garden of Raikyu-ji, one of the masterpieces of Kobori Enshu (1579–1647). The gardens of this designer incorporate many of the essential elements of Japanese gardens in an elegant and balanced manner.*

Translating the style

Garden design in Japan is an ancient art form, and therefore one that is in tune with the country's culture and history. Indeed, Japanese gardens have often inspired other historic Japanese artworks, such as paintings on silk or parchment, porcelain decoration and poetry. The classic heritage of this gardening style is still preserved and valued within Japan and beyond, but it is also open to modern adaptation. There follows an evaluation of 19th- and 20th-century interpretations, and the challenges of using this established style and its traditional elements within modern gardens.

Above: *Although cobbles are often carefully set to imitate the flow of water, in this garden they have been placed with an emphasis that produces a more artistic effect.*

EARLY INTERPRETATIONS

When European and American gardeners became exposed to Japanese gardens in the late 1800s, most of them were only able to "read" them in the context of their own culture or of contemporary Japanese fashions. Japan had by then lost touch with its garden history. Zen was not properly understood at this stage, and it was only in the late 20th century that the true heart of the Japanese garden began to be more accurately interpreted.

Those early imitations of Japanese gardens created by Western gardeners in the late 19th and early 20th centuries included many of the artefacts found in authentic Japanese gardens, such as lanterns and pagodas, but these tended to be placed around ponds that were surrounded by the lush plantings so popular in Europe at the time. Many English "Japanese-style" gardens of this time were quite beautiful, with their blossoming rhododendrons and magnolias, but they were far from authentically Japanese.

These gardens are important for the way in which they illustrate the style of the times in which they were made, with the Japanese Garden at Tatton Park in Cheshire perhaps the best example. While English Victorian and Edwardian gardens in the Japanese style can be appreciated for their own beauty, their creators had little understanding of the principles behind Japanese garden design, and they should not be used as models by those wishing to follow in the Japanese tradition.

MINIMALISM AND ARTISTRY

As an abstract concept, the Japanese garden has become a springboard for modern designers. Minimalist gardens claim to owe much of their inspiration to Zen and its philosophy of "nothingness". While this may be partly true, these gardens often fail to capture the essence of a Japanese Zen garden. They tend to rely on manmade rather than natural materials, and lack the fine sense of proportion and balance so essential to the spirit of the Japanese garden.

Left: *In the precincts of the Shinto shrine of Kamigano, Kyoto, sits this pair of sand cones. Pairs of cones in a sea of sand are also found in some Zen gardens, as symbols of purification.*

GARDEN MATERIALS

One of the problems facing those keen to make Japanese gardens can be finding the right materials. It can be quite tricky and sometimes very expensive to buy some of the exact materials that you might find in a genuine Japanese garden. Rocks of the best kind may not be available in your area, and transport costs may be prohibitive. So you might ask yourself whether rocks are an essential element to your design, and consider the possibility that clipped plants such as azaleas would achieve an acceptable alternative, albeit creating an altogether different result.

The same is true for gravel. The search for the perfect gravel for a dry garden, of the right colour, size and texture, may not always be successful, and if you do use very fine gravel or sand it will require regular and careful maintenance.

To solve this problem you need to ask yourself some basic questions. If you want to avoid the trouble of raking and re-raking the gravel on a regular basis, a more ordinary gravel would be satisfactory and you could then use a simpler design that is easier to maintain.

Below: *Mirei Shigemori was the first Japanese garden designer to break with traditional design. This dry garden dates from the mid-1900s.*

Above: *This contemporary garden in Tofuku-ji interprets traditional brushwood fencing and rock representations with great inventiveness.*

Certainly, the Japanese have used gravel and rocks to such a peak of artistry that any garden design with a spread of gravel and artfully placed rocks will have a clear Japanese influence.

Any style of garden created away from its natural context will require an interpretation that suits your local conditions, your local resources, your budget and the space available. These constraints may in fact help to focus your creativity and inspire you to design a Japanese garden that is truly individual.

MODERN INTERPRETATIONS

There are examples of Japanese-style gardens being built on rooftops, using lightweight but realistic fibreglass rocks, and where the classic profile of the Japanese pine tree has been carved in metal. Similarly, concrete, stainless steel and fibreglass have all been used in contemporary Japanese gardens and are quite acceptable as part of a modern garden scheme. This approach is a different interpretation of the traditional style, but the essence of the Japanese garden is still clearly evident.

In the André Citroën gardens in Paris, the French garden designer Gilles Clément created a riverbed garden using gravel and dwarf willows bordered by silver-leafed shrubs. As in a Japanese Zen design, the garden is framed in a rectangle. He also placed stepping stones in the gravel, but instead of random stone he used raised square wooden blocks to cross over the "dry water" of the riverbed. The design is inspired by Japan in the use of gravel, stepping stones and the rectangular frame, but the whole is no longer identifiable as Japanese. It has transformed into something entirely original and unique.

The dry garden, a model that the Gilles Clément garden in Paris translates with such imagination, is an accessible one to emulate. It can be small, requires a minimum of planting and the basic materials of gravel or sand and rocks. The tea garden, with its reflections of journeys taken along paths through mountain wildernesses, finally arriving at a hermitage, is a concept that is wide open to contemporary interpretation.

Traditionally, pond and stroll gardens contain many artefacts, such as lanterns and pagodas, and these can appear excessive to Western tastes. A modern interpretation could, however, use the principle of a garden based around a pond but achieve this in a minimalist way without artefacts. The courtyard garden has perhaps the greatest potential in a modern garden as it is so intrinsically part of city culture and needs only a small space. This style of garden corresponds as closely with city gardens today as when they evolved in the Edo period in Japan.

Below: *The Jardin Argenté at Parc André Citroën in Paris is a modern and original design vision that has the clear spirit of the Japanese garden at its heart.*

Above: *Japanese black pines in the Huntington Botanical Gardens have been pruned to give a windswept look and combined with a rugged scree and bold rocks.*

CLASSIC GARDEN STYLES

When you start to think about choosing one of the five main styles of Japanese garden design – pond gardens, dry gardens, tea gardens, stroll gardens or courtyard gardens – you should understand that these are an over-simplification of a much more complex art form. But these categories do provide a good initial approach, and having made your choice, you can then add elements from other styles.

The first consideration will be what style will suit your garden or site best. A pond garden will need a fairly large area of at least a quarter of a hectare (roughly half an acre). A dry garden can be laid out in a very small space but ideally a flat one. A tea garden is more of a lifestyle decision than one dependent on the size or quality of the site. Tea gardens while traditionally complex and led by rituals, can in practice be small or extensive; paths can be long or short, undulating or flat; while the tea house can be secluded or prominent. Stroll gardens generally need a fair amount of space and a reliable source of water; they are best on uneven sites, where small hills can be raised and paths can wander around them. Finally, a courtyard garden can be as small as a few square metres (yards). This overview of the traditional styles will help you make your choice before you start to design your garden.

Above: *This rock evokes a Chinese junk floating in a bay.*
Left: *Symmetrical layout contrasts with the natural forms of Japanese maples in the dry garden at Tenju-an, Kyoto.*

Pond gardens

Ponds, lakes and streams have always been central to the Japanese garden, instilling a sense of tranquillity, joy and calm. Water features, such as ponds and streams, always appear totally natural within the surrounding landscape, even if they are constructed artificially, and obvious manmade features, such as fountains, are avoided. You do not need a particularly large garden to include an expanse of water, although the results will obviously be much more dramatic if you are able to construct a feature of some size and presence.

Above: *A turtle island carrying Mount Horai, from the myth of the Isles of the Immortals, in the Heian period garden of Motsu-ji.*

THE HISTORY OF POND GARDENS

There is a general nostalgia in Japan for a romantic period in Japan's history, exemplified by the stories in *The Tale of Genji* by Murasaki Shikibu. Although written in the 11th century, this is still a very popular novel. In it you will find references to many kinds of plants and to boating parties. Both in the 17th century, at the Katsura Palace, and in the 19th century, after the restoration of the emperor as the head of state, gardens were created to reawaken the spirit of those times. So although this style of garden is very old, it still has a place in the hearts of the Japanese today. The naturalistic aesthetic makes it all the more relevant in times when nature is so much under threat, especially in Japan.

THE POND GARDEN OF MOTSU-JI

We can gain some inspiration for the design of present-day pond gardens by looking briefly at a famous example from Japan's past, Motsu-ji, in Hiraizumi, Iwate, which is one of the very few surviving pond and island gardens from the 12th century. Today, you can still see Motsu-ji's great lake, which is bordered by formal iris beds and dramatic rock arrangements. Nothing remains of the palace and temple complexes, but remarkably there are sufficient vestiges of this garden to conjure up images of how it might have been used. These glimpses into the past are intriguing. Guests at great "winding-water" banquets would sit by streams that wove through meadows before entering the lake. Resplendent garden parties were held in which painted dragon barges, filled with musicians dressed in elaborate costumes, were rowed and punted around the lake. At special ceremonies, people might pray for rain to fall in

Above: *The garden of the Moss Temple at Saiho-ji was a 12th-century pond garden, with islands linked by wooden bridges. It has now become famous for its velvet carpets of moss.*

Left: *An ambitious waterfall scheme in the Rheinaue Garden, Germany, creates drama through well-observed rock arrangements and in the ways that the water spills over the rocks.*

order to water the rice fields, or they might evoke Amida Buddha in his Paradise garden.

The lakes of early pond gardens such as Motsu-ji were broad and well-lit, glimmering under the sun, moon and stars, while weeping willows swayed and shaded their banks. Birds and fish would have added movement and colour to this intoxicating scene. The lakes had a pebbled bottom or were edged with beaches of silver sand and backed by low hills planted with trees and shrubs. This style of pond garden differs from the later stroll gardens in having none of the more familiar tea houses, lanterns or water basins. Instead, the pond contained islands, often linked by bridges.

LATER POND GARDENS
Pond gardens remained popular in Japan, but as they became smaller, their outline became increasingly complex and indented and the rock arrangements more artistic and painterly. The sumptuous gowns of the ladies of the Heian period would have made it impossible for them to stroll around large lakeside gardens, and so in the Kamakura and Muromachi periods, ponds became smaller, and formed part of the first

Above left: Recycled materials, such as these millstones, make beautiful stepping stones. Old temple pillar bases and sections are also popular in Japan.

Above: The gardens of the Heian shrine, in Kyoto, were created in the late 19th century to recreate the spirit of the 10th- and 11th-century gardens of the Heian period.

KEY CONSIDERATIONS

Location	Choose the lowest part of the garden to make your pond, as this will look most natural and you will have a good view of the water.
Lining the pond	If you have room for a large pond, you can line it with clay and make it deep enough for boating. If your pond is small, line it with a butyl liner.
Surroundings	You will be able to use the soil dug out for the pond to make natural-looking small hills and undulating ground around the edges.
Edges	Use the natural contours of your pond to make beaches of cobbles or sand, caves or grottoes. A small sandy beach may be just the place to moor a small boat and launch it into the water.
Water flow	Ponds are usually filled by a natural or manmade stream. The water can be re-circulated using an electric pump. Different types of feeder stream will work well, from a flat meandering type to a steep waterfall.
Rocks	The placing of rocks in a feeder stream or waterfall and around the edges of a pond must be handled carefully. Try out the position of each rock until it looks perfectly natural in its setting, following the "request" or "desire" of the stone and bearing in mind which way the water will flow. Rocks can also be used as part of an island, particularly if you are making a crane or turtle shape, or as a bridge between the island and the mainland.
Extra features	Irises are the most common plants in Japanese ponds. You can also construct an island in your pond in an asymmetrical position, perhaps with a bridge linking it to the mainland.

TURTLE AND CRANE ISLANDS

Another common feature of the pond garden was the group of islands that represented the Isles of the Immortals. Some of these took the form of turtles and cranes. They can be included in today's gardens, although it is important to point out that Japanese representations of the crane or turtle are rarely naturalistic. The crane island is made up of a group of rocks, with one taller rock usually sitting up like a wing. In the groups of rocks representing turtles, the head and flippers are sometimes discernible, but more often the image is utterly abstract and only a trained eye can appreciate what is being depicted.

Turtle and crane motifs are not essential to a pond garden, but they can be included if they are treated with some sensitivity. To recreate a crane or turtle island, look at some famous examples. You will find that some are made entirely of groups of

real stroll gardens, a style of Japanese garden that we will look at later on. Most of these later pond and stream gardens were confined within walls, which meant that their size was fairly limited – a factor that makes it easier for us to envisage the practicalities of trying to create one in a smaller Western garden.

In trying to reproduce such a style, one has to imagine a far more poetic time, as well as one in which there was a far greater reverence for nature. While later gardens were influenced by painters and Zen philosophy, the Heian pond garden takes nature in its well-observed form as a principle feature in the design.

FOLLOWING NATURAL FORMS

The *Sakuteiki*, which was written in Heian times, names many forms of pond styles, islands, streams and waterfalls, and even notes the best techniques for planting trees. Even now, we can draw on this ancient work for inspiration when designing contemporary pond gardens. For example, when placing rocks or choosing the course of a stream, you need to follow the "desire" or "request" of the stone or water. Inanimate rocks were, and still are in Japan, thought to possess

personalities that must be treated with respect. By doing this, you will achieve a balanced and harmonious design for your garden.

It is also important to remember that the design of a water garden should be asymmetrical, even though the adjoining architecture may be symmetrical. This interplay between the formality of the architecture and the informality of the garden is part of the genius of Japanese gardens. The design of the pond is key, and achieving a pleasing shape is vital to the success of the finished pond.

rocks, while others are islands of earth with rocks protruding into the lake, which can be seen as flippers, a tail or a head. You are not aiming to create literal reproductions of these animals.

PINE ISLANDS

A favourite for Japanese gardens is a pine island, which is evocative of the windswept pine-clad islands of Matsushima, a scenic site in northern Japan, famous throughout Japanese garden history. Large pond gardens may include several pine islands of varying sizes, but if there is just one island, this could be reached by a traditional Chinese red-painted bridge, the most popular style of bridge when the Matsushima garden was made.

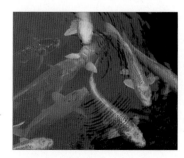

Above: *Japanese koi carp , considered to be a symbol of prosperity and good luck, were developed from the basic black carp, or* Magoi.

PLANNING A POND GARDEN

The pond or lake is the central feature of this style of garden and should be large enough and deep enough for a small boat, which can be kept moored to a stone or on view in an open-sided, ornate Chinese-style boathouse. There should be at least one island in the pond, often two, linked by bridges. By the 14th century, when ponds became smaller, the curved Chinese bridges were replaced by bridges made from less ornate materials such as rocks or unpainted timber. Small islands can be planted with pine trees or grasses.

The outline of the pond can be indented with coves, beaches and grottoes. The land around the pond might be hilly, with the hills planted naturalistically with groups of trees. You can easily create a pond garden planted with iris beds and dotted with well-placed rock arrangements, possibly with a gently sloping sandy beach area. Imagine recreating those splendid outdoor celebrations with an *al fresco* pond-side supper for friends, perhaps lit with some paper lanterns.

READING AROUND THE SUBJECT

There is a range of useful background reading material to help the gardener to understand the roots of the pond garden style. Despite their age, the

Above: *Placing a lantern at the end of a gravel spit is still a popular recreation of the famous natural scenic site of the Amanoshidate Peninsula on the north coast of Honshu.*

following books still have a place in the hearts of the Japanese.
• The *Sakuteiki* contains a wealth of practical ideas to inspire gardeners, with descriptions of streams, waterfalls and the symbolism of rock forms.
• *The Tale of Genji* by Murasaki Shikibu, written around the same time as the *Sakuteiki*, provides another important source of garden styles.
• *The Pillow Book* by Shonagon, also a contemporary of the *Sakuteiki*, makes amusing observations on the culture and gardens of the period.

Above: *A pine island in the tranquil lake setting of the Heian shrine, in Kyoto.*

Dry gardens

Dry gardens are often referred to as *kare-sansui*, which literally means "dry mountain water". This is a style of garden in which water has been replaced by sand, gravel or pebbles. These gardens have also become synonymous with what we now often call a Zen garden. Dry gardens were conceived by the Japanese with abstract designs, often just consisting of gravel, and as deeply spiritual and symbolic landscapes. They can also be enjoyed by visitors as peaceful and restorative environments where they can be appreciated for their calm beauty.

Above: *An unusual treatment for a dry garden at Shisendo, Kyoto. The fine sand has been brushed with a besom around a tree stump.*

THE HISTORY OF DRY GARDENS

Dry gardens have inspired garden designers throughout the world. An understanding or, better still, an experience of Zen will help you to find their spiritual essence, but another way to look at dry gardens is to see them as minimalist landscape art.

Before looking at the main features of the dry garden and how it can be successfully created in the West, it will be helpful to consider some of the historical, artistic and religious principles behind this unique garden style. The precise origins of such dry gardens remain a little obscure. References to dry landscapes occur as early as the 11th century, but they refer to the natural placement of rocks in grass or moss, and not to dry representations of water.

It is possible that the early Shinto shrines were a starting point. The great shrines at Ise stand in vast rectangles of gravel. This gravel was replaced every 20 years as part of the rituals of renewal and cleansing, while rocks were (and still are) used to represent the Buddha and the Buddhist Trinity. The earliest dry rock arrangements that preceded the *kare-sansui* may have been at Joeji-in, near Yamaguchi, where a collection of rocks was laid in an area of moss between the temple and the pond. This garden, which was created in the mid-1400s, is attributed to Sesshu, the great Japanese painter who reproduced his angular brush strokes in the garden using flat-topped and angular rocks. Sesshu was a monk, and also a painter and gardener, therefore possessing a rare

Below: *The rocks in this area of the garden at Nanzen-ji in Kyoto are arranged to display the innate quality of the stones.*

combination of talents. Looking at his paintings can be a source of inspiration even today.

These dry gardens were not created because of a natural absence of water. (Indeed, there is an abundance of water in many of the temple gardens around Kyoto. At the Ryoan-ji, for example, there is a large pond on the other side of the wall from the dry garden.) Instead, they were created for a mixture of artistic and philosophical reasons. The first reason was based on the example of Japanese painters, whose artistic work inspired gardeners to use a monochromatic treatment of the landscape, and the second was linked to the philosophy of Zen.

THE INFLUENCE OF ZEN
Most dry gardens appear in Zen temples and are therefore strongly associated with Zen Buddhism and meditation.

The dry gardens in Zen temples tend to be framed within rectangular courtyards close to the abbot's quarters (*hojo*). They can be viewed as paintings, illustrating distant and idealized landscapes "hung" within

Above: The Mystic Isles rock arrangement at Tofuku-ji has immense power. The designer, Mirei Shigemori, used much larger and darker rocks than in more traditional arrangements.

their rectangular frame. As garden style evolved throughout the 15th century, its influences shifted away from art as an inspiration for natural landscapes towards art as a means of teaching Zen tenets.

In Zen, one reaches one's true self by diverting one's gaze from the material to the spiritual world. Through

Above: This garden near Kyoto was created in a small, rectangular framework. Raked sand and a single maple in a mossy mound prove how little you need to create a perfect scene.

meditation, one can experience what is known as the "void", a formless state of no-self, which Zen defines as the original human state. Time spent in this state is a form of spiritual renewal. This "meditative void" can be equated to those areas of unpainted whiteness in a picture and to the empty space of raked sand in a dry garden.

Right: The garden of Tenju-an, in Kyoto, is a superb example of the interplay between geometric manmade and irregular natural forms.

Above: *At Nanzen-ji, in Kyoto, over two-thirds of the dry garden is composed of sand. The rest is dedicated to this group of rocks and shrubs.*

Below: *The raked circles of sand in the Ryoan-ji garden represent the rough seas and the rocks the sacred mountains of the Mystic Isles.*

Whereas lay people might look at a Zen garden and see islands in an ocean or mountain tops circled in mist, Zen practitioners will simply see space, a reflection of the infinite space that lies deep within us. Many of the arts of Zen employ the use of space to encourage this kind of self-awareness. The act of raking gravel is a meditative practice for Zen monks, while some Zen gardens include arrangements of rocks that signify aspects of Buddhism, for monks to contemplate.

RYOAN-JI

The Ryoan-ji garden, in Kyoto, is a timeless example of the exceptional degree of artistry and the deep understanding of the painters, monks and garden-makers of the late 15th century, when it is thought that this garden was constructed. The Ryoan-ji is a rectangular courtyard bordered on three sides by a clay and oil wall and on the fourth side by the abbot's quarters, where a long veranda overlooks the garden from about 75cm (30in) above the level of the garden. The area is about the size of a tennis court, and is neatly edged in a frame of blue-grey tiles. The whole of the inner space is spread with a fine, silvery grey quartzite grit that is raked daily along its length in parallel lines. This "sea" of sand is the background canvas to 15 rocks in five groups of 5-2-3-2-3 (see page 72), fringed by moss. This pattern recurs throughout the Far East, even in the rhythm of music and the chanting of Buddhist texts. The parallel lines of raked gravel break their pattern and form circles around the groups of rocks like waves lapping against island shores.

The magical way that the rocks are grouped and spaced has gripped generations of visitors, and not just monks, artists, poets and gardeners. No one knows the exact meaning of these groupings. Some have described them as a tiger taking her cubs across a river, while others see them as mountains in the mist or as islands

surrounded by sea. One reason for this puzzle is that Zen practitioners probably started with an idea, but ended up focusing on universal truths and abstract, natural shapes. When creating your own arrangements, bear in mind that the setting of the stones should follow their own "desire". The stones or rocks need not be particularly exceptional in themselves and should not be set as individual pieces of sculpture.

DESIGNING A DRY GARDEN

In the intial stages of planning a dry garden, first imagine a distant misty mountain landscape, a stream with waterfalls or a rocky shoreline. Look at how streams and rivers flow, how waves lap against rocks, and you will learn how to use the inspiration of nature to make raked gravel patterns around rocks.

Once you have composed a picture in your mind, then let go of the superfluous and simply allow the

Above: *Dry rock arrangements are often centred around a main stone, which may have symbolized the Buddha, the sacred mountain of Shimusen or Mount Horai of the Mystic Isles.*

essence of the composition to take over, and minimize it. Remember that an unfilled space is just as important as a space containing objects or plants. This "minimalism" has inspired many contemporary garden designers to reproduce the dry garden in modern urban environments. After all, dry gardens were often created in domestic courtyards, not just in Zen temples. A simple composition could be created with a rock or two, a stone lantern, a water basin and a section of bamboo fence set simply in a stretch of sand.

USING PLANTS IN THE DRY GARDEN

Dry gardens are not restricted to just sand, gravel and rocks – they also involve plants. At the garden of the Shoden-ji, in north-west Kyoto, rocks have been replaced by mounds of clipped azaleas in more or less the same kind of pattern as the rocks at the Ryoan-ji. The azaleas are clipped so much that they do not flower very well, but form is considered far more important than colour in this style of Japanese garden. If you liken these gardens to the monochrome paintings that inspired them, it is clear that colour is of little or no importance, while composition and space are paramount.

CONTEMPORARY INTERPRETATION

Dry gardens may appear to be quintessentially Japanese, but the appeal of their pared-down, minimalist style is both universal and contemporary. Once you have understood how and why the original 15th-century dry gardens were created, you may want to employ new, exciting methods of expressing the same principles, but in ways and with materials that are more relevant to your own culture and landscape.

Above: *The dry "silver" garden created by Gilles Clément at the Parc André Citröen in Paris is Japanese-inspired and represents a dry river bed planted with silver shrubs.*

Tea gardens

Tea gardens were designed as places in which to appreciate *sado*, the tea-drinking ceremony. These spaces were seen to represent a break in a journey from a busy urban centre to a secluded country retreat. The design and philosophy of the tea garden can easily be adapted for the modern garden, and suits city life now as much as it did in the 16th century. Each element of a tea garden – for example, the stepping stones, lanterns, water basins and even the tea house itself – can easily be created using modern materials.

Above: *Every tea garden has a* tsukubai *arrangement – a low water basin filled with fresh water and accompanied by a lantern.*

THE HISTORY OF TEA GARDENS

Tea, imported from China, had been drunk at the imperial court since the 9th century, but its cultivation did not start in Japan until the 13th century. The Buddhist monk Eisai, returning from pilgrimages to China, is credited with introducing both Zen Buddhism and tea plants to Japan.

Tea was drunk by Buddhist monks as an aid to wakefulness during their long hours of meditation. It also became popular among the poets, intellectuals, samurai and merchants at the end of the 15th century. The monks and intellectuals brought the worlds of Zen Buddhism, poetry, fine porcelain and art appreciation together into the theatre of tea drinking, and created what is known as the "tea ceremony", drawing the simple act of drinking tea into the realm of high art. By the mid-16th century, tea ceremonies, tea houses and tea gardens were part of the culture of Japan.

The first great tea masters of the 16th century built their tea houses to imitate the mountainside hermitages of the Chinese sages. These sages were learned in the arts, philosophies and religions of their time. The Japanese also built their own style of hermitage that evolved into the tea house, not in the mountains, but right in their back gardens in cities such as Kyoto, Nara and the port of Sakai, near present-day Osaka. The gardens

Below: *Tea houses are most often constructed from natural materials that are allowed to weather. This tea house has a tiled roof, whereas many others are thatched.*

Below: *A bamboo panel tied with jute is framed between two branches. At the step, guests remove their shoes before entering the tea house.*

Right: *Not all tea ceremonies take place inside a tea house. A special lacquered table is prepared for an outdoor tea ceremony (no-da-te), often conducted in an informal style.*

around these "mountain places in the city", as they became known, were originally based on paths, symbolizing the routes taken by pilgrims on their way to meet sages in their hermitages. The tea garden, or *roji*, which means "dewy path" or "dewy ground", evokes those mountain paths and gradually evolved to include an elaborate set of sophisticated symbols.

The greatest tea master was the 16th-century Sen no Rikyu, who had a preference for the rustic and the rough. His successors, such as Furuta Oribe and Kobori Enshu, who created gardens in the early 17th century, were from the samurai class and had more of a taste for sophisticated manmade materials. By the 17th century, tea paths were often made of formal square paving and millstones. The tea houses also changed, becoming more refined, more open and less humble.

Later still, tea houses evolved into tea arbours, where tea might be drunk while looking out over the garden. The changing aesthetic from the Muromachi period through to the Edo period shows a slow evolution from *wabi-sabi* ("withered loneliness"), indicating a taste for the impoverished, to *asobi*, which is a more playful and artistic style.

THE TEA GARDEN RITUAL

After generally passing through a main gate, guests would enter the first half of the tea garden, known as the outer *roji*. They might then be asked to wait, often in a small shelter or booth, before being led deeper into the garden, then to the tea house. On the way, they might pass through a middle "stooping gate", perhaps with a lantern nearby, designed to force the guests to bow slightly – a moment of enforced humility to stimulate an awareness of the material world the

guests were leaving behind and of the higher, purer realms of consciousness they would encounter in the tea house.

After passing under the stooping gate, the guests would enter the inner *roji* that surrounded the tea house. This part of the garden was the "wilderness", which represented the wild mountain landscape that might surround a Chinese hermitage. The guests would

then wash their hands and mouths at a low basin called a *tsukubai* (or "stooping basin"). This a lower style of basin than the taller *chozubachi*, which is a water basin more frequently found near the veranda of the main house.

Below: *Planting in tea gardens is generally less tightly controlled and more suggestive of a wilderness.*

A lantern often accompanies the *tsukubai*, as many tea ceremonies took place in the evening.

After cleansing themselves, the guests would proceed to the tea house, remove their shoes and enter through a small hatch-like entrance, the *nigiriguchi*. This entrance was made too small for a samurai still wearing his sword to enter, so some tea houses had special racks built outside to hold swords. Once inside, the guests would admire a seasonal flower arrangement and a scroll hanging in an alcove, known as the *tokonoma*. The most important guest would sit with their back to the *tokonoma*. The tea ceremony would then begin.

Above: *The style of the* roji, *or tea path, evolved over the centuries, from one that was natural and simple to a more artful and complex style, like this one at Nanzen-ji.*

CONSTRUCTION OF THE TEA HOUSE

The tea house was often built to look like a rustic thatched hut, but it was always constructed with the finest planed timber. Elegant rush matting, called *tatami*, lined the floor. The rustic appearance of the tea house, combined with the refinement of domestic and temple architecture, created a whole new language in garden architecture – a discipline that is still studied today.

THE FEATURES OF A TEA GARDEN

A tea garden can include a range of decorative features, such as gates, water basins and lanterns, as well as following certain aesthetic rules,

Left: *Inside the tea house or tea room is a specially designed alcove (*tokonoma*), decorated with a simple "country-style" flower arrangement and a calligraphy scroll.*

such as an attention to detail and cleanliness, which are apparent in all Japanese gardens.

The tea house itself could be quite traditional in appearance, built with a thatched roof and sliding panels. One shogun even had a portable tea house built that was gilded throughout, as a symbol of his power. Thus, the basic principles of the tea garden could be adapted to suit the aspirations and taste of the owner.

TEA GARDENS IN MINIATURE

In small town gardens where space may not allow for a tea house, the Japanese will convert one room in the house into a tea room with a *tatami*-matted floor. For the tea garden they would still devise a path, or *roji* that wanders through a "wilderness" of just a few paces from one door, then returning via a side door, perhaps with a *nigiriguchi*, into the tea room. The whole point is to be able to create an illusion of wandering through a wild mountainside. The onus is placed on the guests to comprehend that the journey they are taking is "real", but to help them, the garden designer will include pointers and hints as to the symbolic nature of each element.

If a whole *roji* is reduced to a few metres (yards) in length, it would still include a few stepping stones, a water basin, a lantern and one or two plants, such as a camellia or a bamboo, to suggest the wilderness. A rock might indicate a mountain, while a post might be enough to suggest a middle crawl-through gate (see page 178). That is the essence of the tea garden: creating a spiritual, rather than a literal, journey.

THE FLEXIBILITY OF THE TEA GARDEN

Once the significance of the tea garden has been grasped, you can be as creative as you want, just like the

designers of the 16th century. While one tea master might have enjoyed a natural look, another might have preferred a creative mix of the manmade and the natural. Such adaptability is the main reason why tea houses and tea gardens never really died out, reappearing in stroll gardens and courtyard gardens to the present.

A tea garden does not have to be imbued with the tenets of Zen to be intriguing or even beautiful. Indeed, when Zen Buddhism went out of favour in Japan and Confucianism was in the ascendancy, the tea ceremony continued to thrive, but it evolved to express a more outward and cultured refinement than the deeper inner transformative power of Zen. This illustrates just how flexible the concept of the tea ceremony and garden can be, and that it can easily be reinterpreted to accommodate virtually any culture.

When you are creating a tea garden of your own, you could make a simple layout with just a few scattered rocks, bamboos, natural paving and bamboo

gates, or a much more elaborate affair. You could build your own tea house, to whatever level of complexity and authenticity you want, or you could simply convert any garden building into a tea house, even with chairs and tables, although the space should be kept clean and treated with a certain degree of reverence, so that you can entertain guests in a quiet and respectful atmosphere. All you really need for a tea garden is a path.

Right: *A waiting booth* (koshikake) *in the inner tea garden, or* roji, *at Chishaku-in, Kyoto. This simple square construction has a thatched reed and bamboo roof and a pair of benches.*

Stroll gardens

A stroll garden is one in which the visitor is encouraged to amble slowly along paths that circle around a small pond or lake. Although there had been stroll gardens in Japan since the 14th century, they came to the fore in the Edo period of the 17th century and beyond. Unlike the earlier pond and stream gardens, where the emphasis was on the water, and boating was the main activity, the emphasis in a stroll garden was on the paths that wound among a new set of garden motifs. Classic examples are all large gardens, but, as long as there is room to wander, smaller ones are possible.

Above: *Most stroll gardens have a path that circles around a central pond, with specially contrived views at strategic points.*

THE HISTORY OF STROLL GARDENS

The stroll garden is one of the most familiar Japanese garden styles, partly because it incorporates so many aspects of other styles. You will find stepping-stone paths, lanterns, water basins and tea houses from the tea garden; expanses of sand with a rock or two, usually near the main building, from the dry garden; and the use of water in streams, waterfalls and ponds from the pond garden. Other elements might include bamboo fences and bridges of all kinds. The tea houses, tea arbours, lanterns, bridges and contrived views of scenes reproduced from historic or famous places around Japan or even China that could be found here were all carefully placed to entertain the stroller.

When the stroll garden was developed in the 17th century, the pervasive aesthetic of the times was not as "spiritual" as that of the earlier dry and tea gardens. There was more of a sense of playfulness (*asobi*) as well as a desire for the sumptuous and magnificent, and Japanese garden owners prided themselves on their connoisseurship of the arts.

Nevertheless, stroll gardens managed not to be overly ostentatious because they still employed the restraint and cultivated poverty of many of the aspects of the tea garden. This restraint in garden design was known as *shibumi* (meaning "astringent"), which underlined their markedly minimalist, unpretentious and subdued beauty. *Shibumi* is a term that can also be used to describe many contemporary Japanese gardens.

Although some of the gardens of the *daimyos* (land-owning lords) were somewhat grandiose, there were other, smaller gardens that were delightfully playful in their use of plants, water and architecture. A stroll garden could be as large as 20 hectares (50 acres) or be created in as little as 25sq m (about a sixteenth of an acre). Through the careful use of space and meandering paths, smaller areas can be made to look much larger than they actually are. One device that was commonly practised in stroll gardens was the "borrowing" of scenery, such as distant buildings and hills outside the bounds of the garden, as part of the garden plan – a technique known as *shakkei* (see page 36).

In the years following the fall of the Tokugawa shogunate at the end

Left: *Azaleas in flower in the small stroll garden at Shisendo, Kyoto. A simple garden, it has fine sand paths, rounded azaleas and a small pool with irises.*

of the Edo period and the emperor's restoration as the head of state (Meiji period), there was a return to more romantic ideals, as seen in the Heian period 1,000 years earlier. Some of these late-19th-century stroll gardens adopted a more naturalistic form, in which streams were designed to look like those found in wooded mountains. This style was more appealing to Western gardeners than the earlier very prim and trimmed stroll gardens.

ROCKS AND TOPIARY

In most stroll gardens, rocks played a far less prominent role than they had in the earlier Kamakura and Muromachi periods, partly because the Edo period was based on the new capital, Edo (Tokyo), where rocks were far scarcer than they had been around the previous capital, Kyoto. This scarcity led garden designers to rely more on clipped shrubs for dramatic form. This distinctive form of topiary, known as *o-karikomi*, is a fine

Above: The 19th-century garden of Murin-an is full of illusions. A pair of wild-looking mountain streams appear almost like great rivers flowing through the "hills" of azalea.

art that is still practised extensively today. All kinds of plants were clipped: shrubs were trimmed into hedges or rounded forms like small hills, and sometimes huge evergreens were carved into abstract shapes. These mounds of clipped shrubs were mostly azaleas and

Left: A mass of clipped azaleas is typical of the planting style in Edo-period stroll gardens. A few rocks are interspersed among them, but rocks feature less prominently than in earlier styles. This was because rocks were scarce around the then new capital of Edo, present-day Tokyo.

Right: An early Edo-period stroll garden in Kyoto. Here the rocks are dramatic and symbolic of the power of the shogun, Tokugawa Ieyasu, who built this garden at Nijo Castle, with the exaggerated masses as a statement of his own prestige.

camellias, but any number of different evergreens might be employed and, occasionally, even deciduous shrubs such as enkianthus, whose leaves glow fiery red in the autumn.

When rocks were used in a stroll garden, they might be smaller stones strung like beads along the edge of ponds or used as stepping stones along paths or across inlets. Some of these stones were recycled architectural fragments such as temple pillar bases, old bridge supports or millstones. This practice of recycling materials was known as *mitate* ("to see anew").

VIEWING POINTS

Although stroll gardens are designed to be walked around, they are also meant to be viewed from the main house or from arbours in the garden. Traditional Japanese houses had verandas, raised above ground level, from which you look over an expanse of brushed or raked sand stretching as far as the pond. At the near edge of the pond you will find clipped azaleas and an occasional rock. Distant shores might be overhung by pines, their branches supported by posts.

STREAMS

At one end of the pond, a stream might enter, with a wide estuary traversed with stepping stones. These may be made from natural stone or formal slabs. Bridges that cross over streams or inlets can be a single slab of curved, carved granite, or a curved wooden bridge, sometimes painted red like a Chinese bridge. In more naturalistic settings, log bridges or natural stone can be used. The stream babbles over pebbles as it enters the pond. Further upstream, it is narrower, tumbling between rocks and over waterfalls, and hugged by ferns and sedges.

If you are blessed with a natural fall of land, you can create a stream that follows the slope of the ground.

If your garden is flat, you can still create the illusion of a mountain or hillside from which a stream might naturally flow. In most cases, you will need a pump to recycle and oxygenate the water, especially if your pond is stocked with fish such as koi and carp, but the water should be kept fairly shallow, only about 60cm (2ft) deep, so the fish can be easily seen. Deeper bays and shelters can be built to give the fish some shade and protection in the extreme heat or cold.

THE ROUTE TO THE TEA HOUSE

If you plan to make a tea house or arbour, your visitors will be drawn along paths of stepping stones, guided by bamboo fences and through gates, past lanterns and water basins, to the tea house itself. Tea arbours are more open than tea houses, as they were used for less formal occasions where the emphasis was on a commanding view of the garden. Other buildings might include a thatched umbrella shelter or a Chinese-style hexagonal summerhouse. Paths may pass through groves of cherries or maples, sometimes in an open grassy glade, or under-carpeted with moss where the shade is deeper.

DESIGNING A STROLL GARDEN

Although stroll gardens can include many elements, the individual components should not distract from the whole. The plan can simply include a path, a pond, a few clipped shrubs, a lantern and some trees, such as maples, pines or cherries. Decorative elements such as flowering plants or statues should be used with care and restraint.

Even though stroll gardens may lack the spirituality of other styles, they obey certain rules of balance, and look to nature or famous scenes for their inspiration. When planning a garden in this style, focus on a simple design that includes a well-shaped pond and an interesting path, rather than an assorted handful of Japanese artefacts.

Above: *Although generally they are more elaborate and impressive, stroll gardens often include features found in earlier pond gardens, such as the stone bridge here.*

Right: *The azaleas in the stroll garden of Murin-an are clipped into abstract shapes and dispersed quite randomly.*

Courtyard gardens

The history of the courtyard garden starts in the early 17th century, but for contemporary designers the small, enclosed space adjoining a building still offers fantastic design possibilities. The design is generally simple, sometimes planned as a light extension to the house with large windows and doors, sometimes as a usable outdoor space. Small courtyard gardens, designed to be viewed through glass panels or set within atriums open to the sky, are now being created everywhere from large museums and corporate headquarters to private homes.

Above: *Courtyard gardens in contemporary settings can give a designer the chance to experiment with new materials.*

THE FIRST COURTYARD GARDENS

In the Heian period, courtyard gardens, or *tsubos*, were simple, small, enclosed spaces, perhaps inhabited by a single plant. The rooms that overlooked them, and the courtyards themselves, were named after these plants: the

Below: *Courtyard gardens borrow motifs from other styles, such as the rocks and sand of the dry garden and the stepping-stone path of the tea garden.*

Imperial Palace of Sento, in Kyoto, still has a Wisteria Court. Although the medieval residences of the samurai would have had *tsubos*, it was the rise of the merchant class in the late 16th century and throughout the Edo period that led to the refinement of the art of the courtyard garden (*tsubo-niwa*) in the early 17th century.

The small Edo courtyard gardens, like the much larger stroll gardens of the same period, were amalgams of

preceding garden styles, but they often lacked the coherent principles and philosophies that lay behind their parent styles. For instance, when the inspiration was a tea garden, tea paths were rarely used, nor did religion play a role. Instead courtyard gardens appropriated the motifs and artefacts

of previous styles. Where it was not possible to build a tea house, a room in the house might be used. The journey to this room could be via a "path" (*roji*) that would lead guests on a detour through the "wilderness" in the garden to maintain the illusion that they were heading somewhere special.

As the Edo period progressed, the insularity of the shogun's policies made the landed nobility (*daimyo*) poorer, while the merchants accumulated great wealth. The merchants were afraid to show off their money, as they could have had it confiscated, despite their importance within the national economy. In those days, the merchants were considered to be the lowest class; this was to prevent them from using their money to exert too much influence. Consequently, they constructed modest shop fronts to conceal a complex world of deep rooms and small enclosures, passages and courtyard gardens (*machiya*) hidden from the public in a style that made incredibly economic use of space. Some of these original gardens can still be seen in cities throughout Japan, but more such small gardens are being built today, often owing to lack of space

Above: *An entrance garden to the Silver Pavilion (Ginkaku-ji) in Kyoto illustrates the exceptional artistry of combining natural forms with the geometric.*

Below: *This Zen-style hotel courtyard has two shapes set in the sand: a grass circle and a grass gourd shape. These shapes are recognized symbols of hospitality.*

Below: *This tiny garden at Sanzen-in is a welcome island of green in the centre of the building, where there is only just enough light for plants such as ferns, mosses and bamboos to grow.*

explored Japan in the mid-19th century were astonished by the stroll gardens, but were equally amazed by these beautiful small town gardens.

Temple complexes also had *tsubo-niwa* gardens, usually simple dry gardens with one or two rocks and a "pool" of raked gravel. So, too, did restaurants, where narrow passageways were made into elaborate gardens with stone paving bordered by lanterns and clipped evergreens such as azaleas, mahonias, nandinas and bamboos. These gardens were, and still are, invariably too shady and too small for most flowering shrubs or cherries, limiting the range of plants to glossy evergreen shrubs such as aucubas, fatsias and camellias, as well as shade-loving ferns, bamboos and farfugiums. There is also often a carpeting of moss, just as would have been found in a traditional tea garden with its shady walks and scattered rocks.

rather than out of any need to hide them – making this style of garden particularly relevant today.

In addition to the entranceway garden, if there was one, most of the original merchants' houses featured a small central garden, which served to separate the trading area from the living quarters, and an even smaller courtyard garden termed a *tsubo-niwa*.

TSUBO-NIWA

The term *tsubo-niwa* derives from a measurement that is equivalent to 2 *tatami* mats. Many Japanese today still measure their houses and rooms in *tatamis*, approximately 1.85 x 0.9m (6 x 3ft), a measurement close to that of the average human being when lying down. So a *tsubo* is roughly 3.3sq m (18sq ft) – an indication of just how small these gardens can be.

THE ELEMENTS OF A COURTYARD GARDEN

In addition to their aesthetic appeal, minuscule courtyard gardens perform the important role of bringing light and air into the home, while the verandas running around their edges join together the *machiya*'s various areas. Though tiny in scale, the quality of the garden's lanterns, rocks and other components were and still are clear indicators of the taste and affluence of the *machiya*'s occupants.

Through the use of sliding screens, fence panels and bamboo blinds, it is possible to view these internal gardens from different angles, with each aspect framed within the rectilinear bounds of doors and window frames. The distinction between indoors and outdoors disappears. Westerners who

Above: Dry gardens can give surprising life to inner courtyards where few plants would grow. The great waves of sand add a sense of movement in this garden at Ryogen-in.

Right: *A serene courtyard garden at Kodaiji Temple, a 16th-century Buddhist temple in Kyoto's Higashiyama district. It is spacious enough to include several small trees.*

Another form that a courtyard garden might take is to create a scenic picture with miniature landscapes (*shakkei*) created to be viewed from one of the surrounding rooms.

A MODERN INTERPRETATION

In many ways, the courtyard style – a hybrid between the dry garden and the tea garden – suits the modern world well, and is often highly refined. Some of these gardens have everything from lanterns, water basins, small bridges, gravel and rocks to shady plants and sections of fencing used as a partition or to create privacy. Intricate journeys are hinted at, but it's never more than a hint. Courtyard gardens are often interpreted in a minimalist style today, maybe consisting simply of a single clump of bamboo planted off-centre or a group of rocks with ferns and moss. In fact the courtyard garden is an ideal medium for the contemporary garden designer, as the minimalist style is now so popular.

Roof gardens can also be classified as courtyard gardens, even though they may include views over the outside world. The raw, open, soil-less space on top of a building is perfect for the dry-landscape treatment, particularly where there are worries that excess weight from plants, pots, soil and water might damage the building's structure. The use of sand, lightweight plants and even fibreglass rocks in the Japanese style is often the ideal solution to this.

THE VERSATILITY OF THE COURTYARD GARDEN STYLE

In a sense, the courtyard garden can provide anything you want it to. It can be a dry garden, a tiny tea garden, a miniature landscape, or simply an area that encapsulates nature as a motif, or even a tranquil contemplative space. The courtyard garden can be both a retreat from the busy streets outside and an opportunity for escapist fantasy. It may also function in a mundane pragmatic way, simply by allowing more light to be drawn into the surrounding rooms.

In its design, the courtyard garden absorbs the best of Japanese culture, where one often sees one art form impacting on another. Just as a

flower arrangement may influence a tea room, so too does the tea ceremony influence the nature of the garden, and so on. Once we appreciate one art form, we will gain a better understanding of another. This cross-pollination is also at the heart of the courtyard garden style – an art form that is itself in a constant process of evolution.

Above: *The corner of this courtyard garden combines the rocks and gravel from a dry garden style with an* oribe *lantern, a popular feature of the tea garden.*

Above: *Most Japanese gardens use a grey-white quartzite grit, but this modern garden uses red gravel. Mirei Shigemori designed this garden in the Tofuku-ji temple complex in the 1950s.*

NATURAL MATERIALS

In the Japanese garden, the shapes of nature are celebrated, with great prominence typically given to one beautifully shaped rock or boulder set in subtly coloured gravel. This chapter looks at the natural materials that commonly feature in Japanese gardens. It explains how to source them, how to use them and also offers useful step-by-step features and practical illustrations to demonstrate specific techniques and designs. Paving and stepping stones are used, both decoratively and to create pathways. Gravel, grit and sand are also essential, traditionally designed to imitate the whiteness of a painter's canvas and the flow of water. In combination with rocks, gravel and sand form the vocabulary for the familiar dry-water features of the Japanese garden, such as waterfalls and streams, that are also illustrated here.

Ground cover, in particular moss, and the use of plants both make an important contribution. Moss grows profusely in Japan and is a natural ground cover that allows more freedom with planting than grass. While some gardens eschew the use of plants altogether, especially with dry garden designs, certain garden plants, such as azaleas, are used as substitutes for rocks or are clipped to imitate distant hills using the art of topiary.

Above: *Cobbles feature strongly in dry gardens.*
Left: *The intrigue of a Japanese garden is largely to do with natural forms, used in artful imitation of nature.*

Rocks & boulders

Rocks have formed the foundation of the Japanese garden from the earliest days. No other culture has made rocks so central to its garden art. It is possible to trace the history of the placement of rocks, from their first use in shrines and later as motifs for sacred mountains to their grouping in and around water. Later, in the dry gardens of the Muromachi period (1393–1568), water was replaced by sand, while in the gardens of the Edo period (1603–1867) rocks were replaced by clipped shrubs, which were used to imitate hills and mountains.

SPIRITUAL QUALITIES AND SYMBOLISM
Rocks were originally thought to possess spirits and the ability to draw the gods down to earth. They were later used to represent the mountain homes of the immortals, as well as the Buddha and his attendants. However, Zen monks, who had little time for superstition, rejected much of the esoteric symbolism of rocks and gave them more philosophical and decorative roles.

Above: *The central rock in this arrangement represents the Buddha, with two subservient attendant stones.*

Below: *The scale and quantity of these rocks at Nijo Castle were intended to express the power of Ieyasu Tokugawa (1543–1616) in the early 1600s.*

Although rocks were, and still are, placed in symbolic groups, they now tend to be arranged according to certain aesthetic rules. It takes a well-trained and experienced eye to read the symbolism in a group of stones. Groups of rocks that appear entirely natural may actually possess a number of possible symbolic meanings. Therein lies the genius of the Japanese rock-setters. Do not let this put you off creating symbolic arrangements in your own garden. Historians and Zen practitioners may like to read complex messages in classic rock arrangements, but it is not necessary to have such a deep understanding to compose successful groupings. It was, after all, the study of Chinese and Japanese minimalist ink-and-brush paintings that inspired them. Take a look at some of those paintings. The important thing to remember is that less is more, and not to be too decorative in your approach. What you leave out is almost more important than what you put in, and neither the stones nor the plants need be fancy or remarkable in themselves.

CREATING A ROCK GARDEN

We are fortunate that the Japanese have always rated rocks so highly because excavations of ancient gardens can still give a good idea of what they looked like, and this may help with the placement and grouping of the rocks. One garden in the city of Nara, 48km (30 miles) south of Kyoto, which was excavated in the 1970s, was found to be over 1,000 years old. There, the rocks are arranged in a surprisingly naturalistic way around a pond and stream, providing us with a useful example to follow.

Above right: *Gleaming rocks form a dramatic centrepiece in this* ryu-ten *("teashop in the garden") in Koraku-en, in Okayama.*

Right: *The setting of rocks, usually within gravel, the latter often representing the sea, is the central creative dynamic in the making of most Japanese gardens.*

Avoid using rocks with fantastic shapes. These have never been popular in Japan, except during a brief Edo/Confucian period. Chinese gardeners, in general, were much keener on using fantastic sculptural rocks, many of which were raised from lake beds, standing them on pedestals as symbols of immortality. The Japanese, on the other hand, are more interested in discovering a rock's natural inner essence.

From a design point of view, there is endless scope when working with larger rocks, but don't get carried away with design ideas and remember the inner essence of the rocks if you wish to achieve a natural effect that does not jar with the rest of the setting you have created in your garden.

MAKING ROCK GROUPINGS

Rocks are generally placed in groups. Seven was an auspicious number to the Chinese, as it is in many cultures, and was the original number of the Mystic Isles. Music was composed in units of 7-5-3 beats, while the prayers recited to Buddha Amida were chanted 7, 5 and 3 times in succession. By the 15th century, all kinds of objects were arranged in groups of 15, including rocks. The Ryoan-ji, for instance, is a 5-2-3-2-3 arrangement.

Most groups will consist of one main stone and up to five accessory stones, with one or more unifying stones to stabilize the group. Others might be used as linking stones to join together the members of one group, as well as different groups. The accessory stones can be placed to the front, rear or side of the main stone, huddled up against it or

Below: The garden of the Ryoan-ji was first laid out in 1499. The composition of 15 rocks is set in a rectangle of sand, against a backdrop of an oil and clay wall overhung with trees.

Above: At the Konchi-in, in Kyoto, the eye is drawn to the rocks as they sit in the centre of a layered composition, with its foreground of raked sand and backdrop of evergreens.

some distance away, but should never obscure it. Try making the attendant stones respond to or echo the angle or position of the main stone. These stones should respond to the energy of the main stone in one of the following seven ways:
Receptive A rock that is placed to receive the energy from the main stone that is leaning towards it.

Transmitting An attendant rock that transmits energy from the main stone towards others in the group.

Pulling A rock that is angled to counteract a main stone that leans away from it.

Pursuing Set behind a main stone that leans away from it, this rock is angled in the same direction, as if following it.

Stopping An upright main stone is stabilized by an accompanying one.

Attacking The accompanying rock leans towards a neutral, upright main stone.

Flowing This rock is a passive conductor rather than a more active transmitter; often flat, it acts as a kind of conduit to others.

These terms are not meant to be rigid, but they help to describe the relationship of the stones to each other and to clarify what might work in a particular grouping. They also highlight the subtle approach that is required to make such a grouping work. If your grouping does not look right, then work through these terms to help give the stones an authentic Japanese touch.

By far the best way of learning how to arrange rocks, however, is by studying good, authentic examples. Because of the static nature of rocks, it is possible to do this from looking at photographs, but note that arrangements must look good from any angle (which a photograph might not show), although they will tend to have one front side that gets the most attention. Also bear in mind that it is better not just to copy an arrangement but to be creative, seeking out and following the "desires" of your own particular rock.

Left: *Mirei Shigemori's use of rocks at the Matsuo Shrine in Kyoto defies the traditional naturalistic use of rocks, but still uses natural form to create a remarkable sense of drama and mystery.*

Choosing rocks & boulders

Whether you're planning a naturalistic stream garden, a Zen-influenced dry garden (*kare-sansui*) or a small Japanese-style courtyard, the care and attention you spend when selecting the rock elements will have a profound influence on the finished look and feel of the space. Rocks supply the strong yang (positive, bright and masculine) element in Japanese gardens, and larger, more sculptural pieces can be full of character. In dry gardens, they often form the main focus, so the size, shape and texture of individual rocks in a grouping is critical.

Above: *This classic trio of rocks has symbolic meanings in Japanese gardens but also works as a sculptural and harmonious arrangement.*

When selecting rocks for a Japanese garden, choose ones that you find interesting, but are not too eccentric in shape, and which can be partially buried. It is interesting to note that the rocks of the famous Ryoan-ji garden are not individually that remarkable: their hypnotic power lies in their arrangement, inspired by the way rocks and boulders can be seen poking out of the sea or a lake.

The most favoured rocks are often angular, with either pointed or flattish tops. These shapes echo the angular strokes of a paintbrush, but such distinctive shapes also stand out well when viewed from a distance. When you are using rocks as symbols – perhaps to represent Mount Horai, Shumisen or Sanzon, or crane and turtle islands, for example – make sure they are subtly arranged so that they have a quiet, still presence.

WEATHERED STONE

Stone that shows signs of weathering is particularly valued in Japanese gardens of all kinds. In these kinds of stones, a surface colonization of plants – mosses, liverworts and lichens or larger plants rooted into crevices – is of great benefit in the overall effect. This kind of natural weathering is more marked in softer, porous rock types, such as limestone and sandstone, that absorb moisture. However, you can encourage lichen growth on all types of rock by coating them with yogurt or diluted manure, and keeping them moist to get the aged effect.

It is sometimes possible to buy reclaimed stone, for example pieces from a demolished dry stone wall, either from stone merchants or architectural salvage yards. Do not, however, take a beautiful stone from the wild landscape: this is potentially damaging to the environment and individual ecosystems.

ROCKS FOR WATER FEATURES

Harder rocks like granite (a Japanese garden favourite), schist and slate tend to weather slowly, but this can be advantageous in and around water features. Sandstone and limestone are not so successful in water gardens, as porous sandstone quickly darkens with algae when wet, leaving the dry stone surround much paler, while limestone can dissolve into water, raising the pH level and adversely affecting fish.

Large, rounded boulders work very well for natural stream features since they have a water-worn quality and always combine pleasingly with cobbles and pebbles. When building cliffs and banks for a waterfall or other

Left: *Here large rounded boulders with a beautiful patina of age are set well into the ground and are surrounded by plants.*

features, ensure that the rock colours and the direction of strata of sedimentary rocks match up and look as natural as possible.

ROCKS FOR DRY GARDENS

Slate and schist shear in thin layers, producing pieces with dramatic, jagged outlines – ideal for mountainous "islands" in dry gardens. Slate may be very dark when wet with rain and is a particularly good choice for more abstract, contemplative arrangements, including black-and-white schemes. You can purchase plum- and green-toned slates, as well as more colourful kinds with reddish-brown iron deposits. Granite comes in a wide range of shades from almost white through pink and brown to almost black, and is subtly mottled and flecked. Though salts and minerals permeate many different rock types, adding colour and textural interest, it may be safer to go for more restful tones such as greys and browns, especially in a small space.

SOURCES OF NATURAL ROCK

Local garden centres are unlikely to have pieces that are the right size and shape to act as focal points, although they may have smaller rocks to choose from. Stone merchants (listed in your local telephone directory) can usually help, but for very large projects it may be advisable to visit a quarry. There you could discover pieces that have been standing for some time, distinct from the freshly quarried material, and with that all-important aged quality.

When buying by the tonne from a stone merchant or quarry, make sure you specify the rock size and quality to avoid the weight being made up with unusable rock waste. It's very important that you are at home when the stone arrives so that you can supervise the delivery process. Rough handling of rocks may damage the surface patina or cause pieces to shear off, revealing the brighter, unweathered interior, and the stone could take years to recover.

Above: Decorative stones like these rainbow cobbles can be used sparingly as features.

Above: The markings on these gneiss boulders are more subtle, making them easier to place.

Above: Rockery stones may be too small for Japanese gardens. Always hand select them.

Above: Smooth, sea-worn boulders have a pleasing texture and work well with cobbles.

Above: Boulders of Welsh green granite offer the perfect way of adding a rugged feel to any garden landscape.

Above: You would be advised to use thicker pieces of slate for stepping stones, as thin pieces tend to crack under any pressure.

Do as much preparation as possible before the delivery of your rocks in the way of digging out holes or dry stream courses. You may also need to hire a bulldozer or digger to lift heavy stones into their sockets; alternatively you can use a block-and-tackle pulley system. Ensure that the new rocks are well protected and cushioned to prevent any possible damage caused by cables during lifting.

MANMADE ALTERNATIVES

Where access to a garden is restricted or weight is an issue, for example on load-bearing surfaces such as roofs and balconies, use resin or fibreglass rocks and boulders instead. These are hollow and easy to lift but can look very realistic when bedded in and surrounded by plants and perhaps a few cobbles. You can buy them on-line or from landscaping exhibitions.

Moving rocks & boulders

Stones and rocks can vary enormously in weight, size and shape. Your choice of rocks may be determined by your budget, and also by how they can be manoeuvred into place. In a small garden, or behind a house with only a narrow gated entrance, you may have problems in getting the rocks into position. In more open spaces there will be no such limitation, but you should still consider the weight and potential unwieldiness of large pieces and be prepared to hire professionals to move them. If moving smaller rocks, take great care with your back.

MOVING SMALL ROCKS WITH A BAR

You will need
- two people to carry the rock
- strong straps (from a hire shop)
- a scaffolding pole and shackle

1 If a rock is the right size for strapping, wrap the two loose ends of the strap around a scaffolding pole, securing them with a shackle.

2 Ensure the length of strap is equal to a little less than the height to the carriers' shoulders. This will mean that the rock only need be lifted off the ground a short way, just enough to move it. It will also be safer if the rock is hung as close to the ground as possible, in case it should fall out of the straps.

3 One person at either end of the pole can lift the pole on to their shoulders, and then the two people can lift and move the rock.

MOVING SMALL TO MEDIUM ROCKS WITH A SACK TRUCK

You will need
- a sack truck, preferably with pneumatic tyres as this will make it easier to pull over soft ground – hard wheels will easily get bogged down, even in gravel

1 Lift up one end of the rock until it stands on end and slide the sack truck as close up to the rock as you can.

2 Roll the rock over on to the plate of the sack truck. You may be able to slide the plate under the rock without having to roll the rock by lifting one end a little bit off the ground.

Above: Mount Horai is the tallest of the mythical Mystic Isles, often portrayed by the tallest rock. Moving such large rocks into position requires careful thought and planning, and the right equipment.

3 Place one foot against the axle of the truck as you pull the handle back. Small rocks are easy to move around like this with the handle at around 45 degrees. It is easier to pull than to push.

NARROW ENTRANCES

If the garden has a narrow entrance, a sack truck is useful to move smaller stones. For larger stones, you may need to hire a crane to lift the rocks over the house. Although expensive, cranes will carry a lot more weight.

MOVING ROCKS WITH A SKID LOADER

You will need
- a hired skid loader
- medium-size rocks

1 You may be able to drive the bucket under the rock without having to move the rock.

2 Otherwise, either prop up one end of the rock using a post or a crow-bar while the bucket slides underneath, or, with help if the rock is too large, roll the rock into the bucket.

SELECTING THE BEST METHOD

The size of rocks you need to move will dictate the method you use:

- to move rocks by hand, they must be small but you can control positioning;

- a sack truck will carry small–medium rocks, and will fit through narrow gaps;

- a skid loader can be used to transport medium rocks, and the weight is taken by the equipment;

- a mini-digger or foreloader can move rocks up to its weight limit.

MOVING MEDIUM TO LARGE ROCKS WITH A MINI-DIGGER OR FORELOADER

You will need
- a mini-digger or foreloader on a tractor, or back-hoe, plus a skilled licensed driver
- hard hats, steel toe-capped boots and gloves
- a block of wood or fencing post
- lifting straps with looped ends – these can be hired, and are classified according to the weight they are designed to carry. Go for heavier straps than you think you will need.
- U-shaped shackles to bind the ends of the straps

1 If the rock is lying flat, prop up the top end in order to slide the straps underneath. Use the digger to lift up one end and slide a block of wood underneath to prop it up.

2 Wind the straps two or three times around the rock at approximately a third of the way from the top. This position should keep the rock secure when the straps tighten around it. Tighten the two ends by pushing one end through the loop at the other end. Make the two ends with equal length to spare and ensure they end up at either side of the rock. This will allow it to hang more vertically when you lift it up.

3 Wind the two loose ends around a secure point on the lifting bucket, and bring the two loops close enough to each other to be secured together. Using a suitable shackle, clamp the two loops together.

4 Lift the machine loader bucket up until the straps are tense and lift the bucket gently and slowly until you can see how the rock will hang from the bucket.

5 It may take two or three attempts until the straps are secure and the rock is hanging so that it can be manipulated into place.

SAFETY NOTE

Before moving the rock, ensure that it is hanging securely and that everyone is at a safe distance.

Paving & stepping stones

Paving is another important element of a Japanese garden. Pathways through the Japanese garden can be made of different kinds of stone, from new or manmade paving stones to reclaimed stone from various sources. Stepping stones are often used in water features or gravel areas. Straight lines and right angles are usually best avoided, as curves and natural forms complement the concept and style of a Japanese garden better. If care is taken at the planning stage, the final result can look completely natural and spontaneous.

Above: Granite setts are rough hewn and therefore more suitable for Japanese gardens where natural-looking materials are preferred.

RANDOM PAVING

This kind of paving, using irregularly cut stone pieces, is popular in Japanese gardens. The stone is generally bought by the tonne and needs careful laying to accommodate pieces of varying thickness and to minimize the width of mortar joints. Random stone can be laid as a pathway "filler" in conjunction with straight-edged, rectangular pieces and adjacent to sections of geometric patterning, for example next to pavers set as a line of diamonds. Kerbstones and stone setts are also used to define pathways and to separate areas of differing colour, pattern or function.

Left: Weathered stone slabs covered with mosses and lichens are used here as stepping stones in a sea of pebbles. Note how they are set proud of their surroundings. Rectangular pieces are often mixed with irregular ones.

RECLAIMED STONES

Paving that is reclaimed, with a rough-hewn look or with worn or weathered surfaces is much sought after. Japanese gardeners will often incorporate pieces once used for other purposes, including original millstones, old gateposts and worn stone door lintels or steps. A good source of reclaimed stones is architectural salvage yards.

STEPPING STONES

A very common feature of Japanese gardens, stepping stones are used in both wet and dry locations. A zigzagging pathway might artfully combine rounded stepping stones with rectangular elements, often also mingled with cobbles or pebbles. Handcrafted granite stepping stones, broadly circular and with softly bevelled edges, are laid following age-old patterns.

Whatever the location – crossing a pool, a mossy woodland floor or in a gravel area – the stones are always set slightly proud of the surrounding surface. Stepping stones should be well bedded into the substrate to give the path stability and also to create a

"rooted" quality. This means that individual stones are likely to need a depth of at least 15cm (6in).

TYPES OF NATURAL STONE FOR PAVING

Certain types of sedimentary rock can be split very easily along the overlying layers, making them ideal contenders for paving. These include pale grey or creamy coloured limestone, which often has visible remnants of fossilized organisms and shells. Sandstones, such as buff-coloured York stone paving and millstone grit in Britain, and flagstone and bluestone in the US, are also used for paving. Good-quality reclaimed York stone commands a high price, but nowadays imported Indian sandstone can be more economical and just as effective. It ranges in colour from almost black to buff with pink or yellow tinting. If possible, look at samples of the different colour types laid as paving, both dry and wetted, before making your selection, as the colour may change dramatically when the stone is wet, perhaps making it not the perfect choice after all.

Indian sandstone is widely available in a wide range of sizes, and is hand cut to leave a bevelled, rough-cut edge

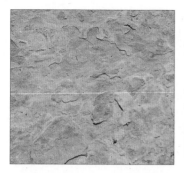

Above: *Indian sandstone comes in a wide range of colours.*

Above: *York stone paving slabs covered with lichen and moss.*

Above: *Limestone is a sedimentary rock that gives an aged patina to paving.*

Above: *Traditional granite stepping stones are usually rounded or irregular in shape.*

Above: *Slate stepping stones look wonderfully glossy and dark after rain.*

Above: *Used sparingly, stepping stones with imprinted symbols or patterns can add interest.*

with a more rustic appearance than diamond- or machine-cut stone. There are, however, some practices to do with the labour and sourcing of Indian sandstone that mean that this material is not guaranteed to be ethically sourced, so you might want to look for alternatives until better standards are established.

When buying any regular-cut stone, buy by the square metre/yard rather than by the tonne, and specify a minimum and maximum thickness.

Granite is traditional in Japanese gardens. As it is one of the most resistant stones to wear and tear, it is much sought after, especially when the surface shows signs of erosion, as this signifies great age. In shady or damp paved areas, granite and other non-porous rock types have an advantage over limestone and sandstone because, with the more porous stone, moisture absorption leads

to the growth of slippery algae, which must be removed periodically for safety. This does not apply to granite, which is less absorbent. Choose hand-finished granite paving or tumbled granite setts for a natural effect.

Slate is another excellent paving option, although pieces tend to be cut relatively thinly, so they must be laid on a full mortar bed to give adequate support. Check before buying imported slate to ensure that the pieces are thick enough for external use and that they are of outdoor quality, meaning that they won't shatter or flake on exposure to the elements.

MANMADE ALTERNATIVES

Manufacturers of concrete paving now produce very convincing stone reproductions using old stone pavers as moulds to give a natural-looking effect. But these products can wear

and chip, then exposing the concrete interior, and the slabs tend not to be as thick as natural stone. However, driveway setts (small blocks) are a good option for paving close to buildings and in more formal areas.

If used with care, poured concrete can be an effective and inexpensive material for making large stepping stones or areas resembling exposed bedrock. The mix is poured into a mould of sufficient depth to prevent cracking, using curved shuttering. Before it completely hardens, it is textured with a wetted nylon hand brush and various tools. Alternatively, you can add pebbles and shingle to the concrete to create an interestingly textured surface, then use a soft brush and watering can to expose some areas, thus mirroring the processes of natural erosion.

Cobbles, pebbles & paddlestones

Often used for pathways, in open areas or by water features, the smooth, rounded surfaces of cobbles, pebbles and paddlestones make a pleasing contrast to rough-surfaced regular paving slabs or flat stepping stones. They can be a wonderful foil for plants, especially those with linear or strap-like foliage. Different schemes call for different sizes and types of pebbles or cobbles, in keeping with the scale and nature of the garden. Remember that the beauty of the stone may be revealed only when wet, so when you are buying stones ask to see samples in and out of water.

Above: *Graded pebbles camouflage the edge of a butyl-lined pond or stream, creating a beach or natural stream bank effect.*

COBBLES

Acting as a helpful transition from large rounded boulders to smaller pebbles, cobbles tend to be required in relatively small quantities for ordinary domestic garden schemes.

In fact, in a compact urban space such as an enclosed courtyard or roof garden, you may need only a handful, which is just as well because they tend to be sold individually and can be quite expensive.

Some cobbles are relatively unmarked but range in colour from white, through brown, red and grey to almost black, reflecting different rock types. Paler greys and browns may also show attractive banding, for which you will pay a premium. When hand-selecting small numbers of stones, look carefully to ensure that they are the colour, shape and texture you want, as cobbles are sometimes split or damaged in transit.

Large cobbles of the sort originally used to surface the roads and stable yards of old are sometimes available from reclamation yards. Bigger garden centres often have a few large cobbles for sale, stored in crates or on palettes. Cobbles may be commercially dredged from the sea bottom or taken from gravel pits. For larger quantities, visit your local stone merchant or a gravel pit if there's one in your area. You can't just go to the beach and help yourself, though – laws normally prohibit the removal of cobbles or pebbles from a beach or the bank of a stream.

Left: *It is important to place larger stones and cobbles by hand to create a naturalistic effect. Here there is the impression of a stream trickling down into a larger, deeper pool. The cobbles are graded by size and infilled with gravel.*

PEBBLES

In nature, pebbles often represent a wide mixture of rock types, fragments of which have been worn smooth and rounded by the action of water or ice. When wet, they glisten and may show an extraordinary range of colours, flecks and stripes. Suppliers normally have samples in buckets for you to examine. Pebbles may also be colour selected so that, as well as the natural mixed shades, you can buy pure white or jet black for special projects.

In small quantities, pebbles are sold in bags or sacks, but they are extremely heavy – the average car could safely transport only three or four bags at a time. You can also buy them bagged or loose by the tonne delivered from stone merchants. Pebbles are graded and sold by size – you'll normally find at least two or three sizes at larger garden centres.

MIXING COBBLES AND PEBBLES

Sometimes cobbles and pebbles are used together in Japanese gardens to create a pleasingly natural look. When you are using these stones as ground cover, mix cobbles and pebbles of different sizes. If you want to create a beach effect at the margin of a butyl-lined pond, or in a dry stream bed, lay cobbles, pebbles and shingle in graded bands and curving sections, reflecting the strata formed by water in nature. Check that the various types you have in mind are compatible in terms of colour and texture. If you intend to use cobbles and pebbles in and around your pond or by a stream, check that they are fish friendly and wash them thoroughly before use to avoid contaminating the water.

PADDLESTONES

These flat or paddle-shaped pieces of stone with gently rounded edges come in sizes from 15cm (6in) across to as much as 60cm (24in). Although they are sometimes used for ground cover and for creating interesting surface textures, these stones are ideal for representing a stream because the pieces can be laid to overlap and "flow" in the direction of the imaginary water. They can also be used to suggest the rippled surface of a pool or, on a much larger and more ambitious scale, a lake or even a sea. Paddlestones have a markedly different look to cobbles and pebbles and are therefore best laid with some visual barrier to separate them from these more rounded, glossy aggregates.

Above: *You can buy pebbles graded by size bagged or loose from builders' merchants.*

Above: *Slate pebbles eroded by the action of water are softer looking than chippings.*

Above: *These red marble pebbles have been set into cement to create a textured surface.*

PREPARING THE GROUND

Do not lay cobbles, pebbles and paddlestones directly on to soil, because this is likely to contain perennial weed roots and annual weed seeds. Instead use a black horticultural or landscape membrane, which will allow water to pass through but which prevents soil and weeds from coming to the surface.

Above: *Ask to see pebbles wet before you buy as they can look quite different.*

Above: *Paddlestones are characterized by their large, flat, broadly oval shapes.*

Above: *White marble pebbles are sometimes used for more stylized designs.*

Sand, grit, gravel & slate

A feeling of space is very important in Japanese gardens, and open sand or gravel areas help to keep the structure of the garden simple and are easy to maintain if laid carefully. Sand or grit can be raked into patterns, as in a traditional Zen garden, and although gravel cannot be raked into quite such well-defined designs, it makes an interesting and subtly coloured backdrop to a large rock or boulder. Whichever kind of ground cover you choose, make sure that the preparation is meticulous and you will be rewarded with a natural-looking, easy-to-keep area.

Above: *Pieces of natural stone here form an informal pathway. Clay tiles have been used to separate the two types of gravel.*

SAND AND FINE GRIT
A well-known feature of many Japanese gardens is an area of sand or fine grit, raked into swirling patterns to represent forms in nature. (See overleaf for some examples.) This can be a practical option for a newly created Japanese garden if thought is given to the materials, the size of the area and its location within the garden. In dry gardens, the patterns represent the movement of water. More abstractly, in the Zen tradition, these raked sand or gravel patterns can also represent the tranquil mind.

The best location for this effect is in a sheltered garden or courtyard. The fine material traditionally used is not suitable for very open, windy locations as the patterns will be disturbed too quickly. After periods of heavy rainfall or strong winds, you may well find that designs need to be re-raked or brushed quite frequently.

A number of grades and colours of sand and grit can be used to create your design. In bright, sunny locations, and especially for larger areas, avoid pure white sand, as this can create an uncomfortable glare – darker shades are more tranquil. However, paler coloured sands can bring light into a shaded passageway or courtyard area, or an enclosed space that is viewed through a window.

Prepare the area by separating the sand and base material from the underlying soil using landscape membrane. Make sure that you keep the sand or grit well away from areas of lawn as it can damage mower blades.

COARSE GRIT AND GRAVEL
Gravel is a relatively inexpensive ground cover when compared to paving. When laid over landscape membrane, it can also be surprisingly low maintenance. Finer gravels may be used as an alternative surface around rock formations in a dry Zen garden, though they won't allow for intricately raked patterns.

You can buy gravel in a range of grades. The coarser types (up to 2cm/¾in across) are best for walking on, especially if the area is close to the house, because they don't get caught in the treads of shoes and tend to bed down well and stay put. You should try to avoid using fine grit and gravel under trees, as it will be difficult to clear fallen leaves in the autumn. However, you can use a leaf blower on larger diameter gravels and pebbles without disturbing them.

Finer gravel can be kicked about by foot traffic and all too easily makes a seed bed for weeds, so it will need more maintenance than the coarser varieties.

For water gardens, you will find that river gravels and beach shingles give a natural look, being composed of rounded, water-worn pieces that glisten when wet. They normally come in a combination of browns and greys – soft, neutral colours that work well in restful Japanese gardens and also

Above: *Where fine sand is used, be prepared for regular maintenance, even in sheltered areas.*

Above: *Gravel is often used as a representation of water in the Japanese garden.*

combine nicely with pebbles and cobbles (see pages 80–81). Avoid golden-coloured gravels or coloured chippings, which tend not to look very natural.

DIFFERENT SOURCES

To purchase sand or grit for raking, you may need to contact a specialist Japanese garden supplier as it is not easy to find the right grade or colour in ordinary garden centres, stone merchants or builders' merchants. The type of grit used in Japan is made from degraded rock fragments that measure about 3mm (⅛in) in diameter. However, certain types of horticultural grit may make an acceptable alternative if you cannot find it.

Though bagged gravel is readily available from garden centres, you can buy it more economically from builders' merchants. Having bags or truckloads delivered will also avoid unwanted wear and tear to your car. In this case, tell the supplier what area you plan to cover and to what depth and they will calculate exactly how much to deliver.

OTHER GROUND COVER

Stone chippings of hard rocks such as granite are also suitable for ground cover, and they come in a wider range of colours than gravel, including black, shades of grey, plum, green, brownish-red and white. You can purchase a range of grades. Whatever colour you choose, make sure that it blends with or makes a suitable contrast to the type of rock you are using as a central feature. In general, chippings, with their jagged, sharp edges, tend to work better in a dry garden setting than in a water garden. In a water garden you would expect the natural substrate to be smooth and water-worn rather than spiky and frost-shattered.

Slate waste is now widely available in garden centres as an alternative surfacing material to gravel for paths and open areas. The flat shards bed down well and don't tend to get kicked about like fine gravel. This material is also resistant to weed growth, although like the other ground cover materials it benefits from being laid on a horticultural or landscape membrane. Slate is usually sold in bags, and comes in dark grey, or with plum or green tones.

Larger pieces of slate can be laid like paddlestones to create the effect of flowing water in a dry stream feature, and finer grades can be applied as a mulch around plants or to create the illusion of a body of still water in a dry garden. Fine slate works well to make a dry "pool" crossed by an arched bridge or stepping stones, or at the base of a stone waterfall.

Above: *These 5mm (¼in) diameter granite chippings are ideal for traditional-style gardens.*

Above: *Pearly quartz chippings can be used to lighten shady courtyards.*

Above: *Blue slate "waste" is readily available and useful for creating dry pools and streams.*

Above: *Dark-coloured Welsh granite chippings could be used to contrast with pale cobbles.*

Above: *Always lay chippings over permeable landscape membrane to limit weed problems.*

Above: *Use coloured or pale granite chippings sparingly in more naturalistic settings.*

CHOOSING SAND OR GRAVEL

The sand or gravel can be 3–10mm (⅛–⅜in) in diameter. If it is too fine, it will get blown about and will not rake well into patterns, although in the famous garden of Shisendo, in Kyoto, the sand is very fine and is brushed with a twig broom into delicate patterns rather than raked. The ideal size is 4–6mm (³⁄₁₆in) in diameter. A mixture of sizes and a degree of roughness will help the stones in the ridges to bind with one another. If they are too round and smooth, the stones tend to roll and the ridges flatten out too readily.

The sand can be laid over a concrete base, but it is important to ensure that the whole site is well drained. An alternative would be a firm but open base of hardcore overlaid with rough stone and sand mix (known as hoggin or scalpings) in order to allow the surface to drain.

The most sought-after gravel in Kyoto is made of a silvery-grey granite and quartz grit. It is very precious, very expensive and becoming quite difficult to obtain, even in Japan. In other countries it may be difficult to find the ideal kind of gravel or sand, though situations will vary. Avoid white marble chips, as these will be

Above: *With the right type of fine gravel, you can create a range of clearly defined patterns.*

Below: *In the temple garden of Tofuku-ji, "waves" of gravel have been raked into abstractions. The main set of lines runs parallel throughout the garden while those closest to the edge curve to meet it.*

USING GRAVEL: KEY ELEMENTS

Finding the right site Gravel "pools" of water should always be laid on a level site. Don't try to make them on even a gentle slope.

Colour of gravel Don't use gravel that is bright white as this will glare in bright sunshine; try to find a colour that is light enough to feel like water and to show up in moonlight.

Size of gravel Gravel size can be as small as 3mm (⅛in) and up to 10mm (¾in) in diameter, depending on the kind of pattern you want to make and the area to be covered. The ideal size for raked gravel is 4–6mm (³⁄₁₆in). If the gravel is too small and smooth it will collapse too readily.

Depth of gravel Gravel should be laid to a depth of about 5cm (2in) to give enough material to rake.

Raking without leaving footprints
Simply start in the middle of the "canvas" and work outwards.

Making a satisfying and authentic pattern The bulk of your space should be empty and raked in parallel lines. In the most famous dry garden in the world, the Ryoan-ji, the lines are all parallel except the concentric waves that lap around each of the 15 rocks.

Keeping it simple Avoid making too much of the space busy with too many different and elaborate patterns as this will defeat the calming influence of the water effect. Simple is best.

Imitating the flow of water Around rocks and plants, you can rake as if the waves were lapping against their shores. In other places you can "draw" whirlpools, waving patterns, or patterns that imitate the variable flow in rivers (always remembering that your overall pattern should be simple). Dry streams made of gravel can also be raked to imitate the flow of small brooks.

Stream current

Stylized wave

Ocean wave

Surf pattern

Brook

Stylized ocean wave

Concentric ocean wave

Combination: whirlpool and stream current

Concentric ripples

Whirlpool

Elliptical concentric ripple

far too bright and look a bit funereal. Darker colours can be used but they will tend to look more like muddy water than the reflective purity that is so ideal in these gardens.

If you would prefer not to commit yourself to frequent raking, then any kind of gravel that is not too chunky would do; however, even in this case you will need to rake it from time to time to keep it looking clean and tidy. If you like the raking process, you could make it a regular practice. How frequently you need to rake a dry garden will depend on the degree to which the patterns get disturbed by heavy rains, wind, birds and small animals, or in autumn by how many leaves fall on them. Before you re-do the raking, level out the whole site

with a broom, a board or the flat side of a hay rake, so that you are working on a blank canvas.

SAND AND GRAVEL PATTERNS

In Zen temples, dry gardens often have areas of sand or gravel raked into elaborate patterns. These are simple abstract imitations of the movement of waves on water. The simplicity and rhythm are also symbolic of the spiritual life. They create a sense of space and wonder, helping the mind to enter a state of contemplation and quiet – one of the goals of Zen Buddhism. The raking of the sand is part of the spiritual practice of Zen monks, who enter a state of "no-mind"

as they walk backwards, drawing their rake and pulling the sand into ridges and troughs.

The traditional patterns made by the monks are a closely guarded secret. If you enjoy the effect of these dry gardens but are less interested in the high goals of Zen meditation, simply imagine that you are "painting" a sea in sand. The sand can be the wide open sea or a river; it also represents the white "canvas" background of a landscape painting. Knowing this can open up numerous possibilities for abstract patterns, but keep the overall pattern simple or you will distract the mind of the viewer, rather than soothing it into a state of calm.

Dry water

The original dry landscape gardens focused on the placement of rocks in moss or grass. In later dry gardens, rocks were set in sand, gravel and among pebbles, with these elements arranged and spread to imitate the qualities of water: either as a stream, when on a flat surface, or as a waterfall, when carefully constructed on a slope (see pages 88–89). The important concept with a dry waterfall is to have high stones at the back of the design to represent the waterfall height. It can then end in a dry stream or pond when it reaches the foot of the slope.

Above: *At Tofuku-ji, in Kyoto, the 20th-century artist-designer Mirei Shigemori used sand to imitate water, recalling ocean waves lapping at island shores.*

DRY STREAMS: KEY ELEMENTS

Assessing the slope A dry stream can be built down a gentle slope. On a steeper slope you will need to create a series of dry falls, or alternatively make the stream take a wandering course.

Making a meandering dry stream You can use the same principles as for a meandering water stream (see pages 104–107), on a flattish site with a wider expanse of stones.

Paths and bridges Design paths that can cross over the stream or that look as though they can, so that you can build a slab stone bridge across the stream. Bridges will add to the illusion of a real stream.

Adding waterfalls Small "falls" can be built into the stream to make it look more realistic.

Exaggerating the effect Remember that you are suggesting a stream rather than making an exact copy, so the effect should ideally look as artistic as it is naturalistic. If it is too naturalistic, the stream will simply look as though the water has run dry.

Planting Place clumps of plants that have a "wet" look on the sides of the stream, for example sedges, hostas or tricyrtis.

ROCKS AND PEBBLES

The first two great gardens with rocks set in moss or grass were the 14th-century Saiho-ji, or Moss Temple, and Tenryu-ji. At the latter there is a superb dry waterfall, known as the Dragon Gate Waterfall, created with all the power of a real waterfall. At the Saiho-ji, there is a large turtle representation and a hillside with dramatic arrangements of rocks. The

Below: *This dry garden at St Mawgan in Cornwall shows the same kind of enterprising spirit seen in many of Shigemori's designs. The effect is like that of a flooded inland river basin.*

Zen monks who created such dry gardens realized that the imagination is more captivated by a suggestion than by reality. Or, as they might have put it, the power of the imagined shape yields a far greater truth than one locked up in the real. This is what is meant by the poetic term *yugen*, or "the spirit of hidden depth".

Streams, as opposed to still water, are portrayed in their "dry" form by

the use of river-washed pebbles laid out carefully in overlapping patterns to indicate a sense of flow. The image is completed by the use of a few larger boulders or rocks, as well as bridges made of large stone slabs.

MODERN INTERPRETATIONS

There is great design potential for contemporary designers to use a dry rock-and-sand garden to create even more abstract patterns, using quarry-blasted rocks rather than naturally occurring weathered stones. This takes the "suggestive" nature of the dry landscape into the realm of contemporary design. If you are careful with the composition, space and balance of the layout, these gardens can be very successful, as well as fairly easy to manage. Not all modern Japanese garden designers follow Zen precepts; they have become more Western in outlook. However, the overall design of these modern gardens remains essentially Japanese.

Above: *This dry garden at the Brunei Gallery roof garden in London can be interpreted as a river with large natural boulders being crossed by a staggered carved stone bridge that stretches from bank to bank.*

Below: *A dry waterfall in Kew Gardens shows a carp stone placed at the base of the waterfall. This symbolizes the striving of the individual to rise above himself. A carp who reaches the top of the waterfall is transformed into a dragon.*

DRY WATERFALLS: KEY ELEMENTS

Using a flat site In a flat, rectangular courtyard setting, a dry waterfall can be set into one corner.

Using a hilly site In a natural setting, a dry waterfall should be built into the side of a hill or a steep slope to look effective.

Exaggerating the effect Good dry waterfalls should have a "monumental" feel to look impressive, as if a lot of water fell down them at one time. Don't be afraid to exaggerate this effect. Some versions use very large rocks.

Choosing the top stones Find some flat-topped stones for the points at which the water would have flowed over the waterfall. The top stone should always have two larger stones on either side of it. For a simple arrangement, these three stones might be enough.

Imagining the water Always imagine the flow of the waterfall as if it had real water in it. This will help you decide how to lay the stones.

Making pools Some waterfalls have small pools halfway down them. In a dry waterfall these are filled with gravel to imitate the standing water.

Making a dry waterfall & stream

Waterfalls in Japanese gardens can be real sources of water, or they can alternatively be dry cascades (*kare taki*) in which stones simply suggest the movement of a waterfall. *Kare taki* exist in various forms, ranging from a single cascade to a more complex one of multiple stages. Each one is documented in Japan's earliest known manual of gardening, the *Sakuteiki*, which describes ten different forms of waterfall construction, stipulates the proper height and width of a cascade, and advises the reader on the appropriate types of stones to use for such a feature.

This dry cascade is suitable for a garden with a natural slope, and uses a plastic liner and a stepped selection of rocks from the top to the base. Such a dry waterfall is seen as highly symbolic by Japanese garden masters, and the aesthetic positioning of rocks, often in groups of three, is key. The dry waterfall forms part of a dry landscape, which might also include evergreen trees and shrubs, moss and raked sand, which symbolizes streaming water. Here the dry stream at the bottom is represented by gravel and more well-positioned rocks.

Above: *Dry waterfalls are often built on a series of levels, so that the gravel that imitates the water can be held in the "pools" as the dry cascade descends down the slope.*

Opposite: *Sedges and ferns tucked around the rocks recall the plants that you might find alongside a mountain stream.*

You will need
- 2 people to move the stones
- a large backing stone
- 2 side stones
- various other large stones and boulders
- concrete
- plastic sheeting
- gravel
- a long base stone to represent a bridge
- a shovel

1 Prepare the location by digging over the land following the shape of the proposed waterfall and stream. Then dig a hole to fit the backing stone and manoeuvre the stone into position.

2 Set the backing stone and pack the soil around it tightly so that it remains steady. Larger stones and boulders should be set in the hole with concrete to ensure they remain solidly in place.

3 Having achieved the basic stepping-stone shape from backing stone to lower level stone, prepare the ground to accommodate two side stones.

4 Place stones to form a pool structure, as shown here, that is positioned directly below the four key waterfall stones.

5 For the dry stream, prepare the land beneath the pool. The stream should appear on a lower level again to maintain the illusion of falling water.

6 Position further stones to frame the shape of the stream, judging their positions as you go.

7 Having completed your stone structure, cut plastic sheeting to line each of the enclosed areas. This ensures that plants will not grow into the gravel.

8 Shovel gravel on top of the plastic sheeting to cover it fully. Ensure that the gravel layer representing the stream is at least 2.5cm (1in) thick.

9 As a finishing touch, position another long, flat stone across the two base stones around the stream to represent a bridge.

Plants & planting

The "hard" elements of a garden – gravel, rocks and architectural features – are important in Japanese garden design. However, "soft" elements – plants, trees and shrubs – are also vital. Many people regard Japanese gardens as making little use of plants, and while it is true that they are often less central than in, for example, a traditional English cottage garden, many Japanese gardens use a great range of plants. The crucial point is that the plants are always subservient to the overall design, and will be carefully placed and managed to this end.

Above: *On the west coast of Europe, near the sea, there is enough moisture in the air for moss to grow on the ground and over the trees.*

GROUND COVER

An important ingredient in most Japanese gardens for ground cover, moss requires the right balance of sun and shade to grow well. In Kyoto, for example, it will grow virtually anywhere because of the high rainfall during the summer. The variety of different species of moss gives the surface of the garden a beautiful velvety texture in all shades of green, often highlighted by the dappled sun if the moss is growing beneath trees. By contrast, the popular Western ground cover of grass is not widely used in Japanese gardens. The advantage of growing moss rather than grass is that it gives the Japanese designer much more freedom in terms of positioning plants, as it does not need to be mown in the same way as grass. It does, however, need to be cared for and weeded to keep it in shape. Rocks can also be positioned without the constraints placed on gardens in which grass is the main foundation. If you are not blessed with a climate in which moss grows freely, you can easily improvise by using a ground cover of mondo grass (*Ophiopogon*) or perhaps instead some shorn bamboos.

Below: *It is important to have the right amount of light and shade to maintain the moss cover. Too much sun and it burns out; too little and it dies out. Many species of moss have combined to knit this carpet at Sanzen-in.*

Below: *This uneven chequerboard of stone squares sunk into a sea of moss and edged with roof tiles is at the garden of Tofuku-ji; this garden harmonizes the natural, the architectural and the contemporary.*

Right: *Although most Japanese gardens exhibit restraint in their colours, some late Edo-period gardens grew a number of brightly coloured azaleas, such as these at the Karlsruhe Japanese garden in Germany.*

Grass is rarely used as ground cover in the Japanese garden except in very large gardens, where drought-resistant zoyza grass can be planted. This deep-rooting grass is not mown tight to the ground, and should be left at a height of approximately 8cm (3in), which gives a dense, cushiony turf. However, this grass does turn brown in the winter. Grass on banks and between rocks in Japanese gardens should be trimmed and clipped as neatly as in a Western garden.

SYMBOLIC PLANTS

While plants are not used as much as in Western gardens, when they are used they are not simply a design element but often hold symbolic significance too. So most Japanese gardens will contain one or more of the most symbolic plants, such as plum, cherry, bamboo, pine or maple. The Japanese plum (*Prunus mume*) is a symbol of purity and hope; the cherry (*Prunus serrulata*) with its short-lived blossom reminds us of our mortality, while the Japanese maple (*Acer palmatum*) is a symbol of longevity.

JAPAN'S NATURAL FLORA

Although Japan's mountains, streams and coastlines are brimming with superb flora, the disciplined restraint of Japanese gardens focuses on certain types of plants. The native plant area in Kyoto's botanical garden is full of plants that Western gardeners would relish, but most of them would not find a home in a Japanese garden.

The problem with many Western imitations of Japanese gardens is that designers cannot resist using attractive Japanese plants that would not normally be chosen by a Japanese designer – for example, those that are considered too colourful or are the wrong shape. However, this restraint does not mean that the Japanese do not appreciate plants. On the contrary, the Japanese celebrate flowers perhaps more than any other nation, especially flowers that signify seasonal change or are associated with certain festivals.

SEASONAL VARIETY

As the last snows melt in spring, the plum trees (or Japanese apricots) start wafting out their scent and are appreciated with a quiet reverence. The cherry blossom season then attracts thousands to gardens with the best displays, with parties gathering under their boughs. Although there are a number of native shrubs that flower in late spring – some deutzias, spiraeas and kerrias – they are considered as secondary to the cherries, wisterias, peonies, azaleas and camellias.

The summer begins with a show of irises that grow in swampy ground at the heads of ponds, and in pots as prized and cosseted specimens. Hollyhocks (*Alcea rosea*), hydrangeas, the lotus (*Nelumbo*) and the morning glory (*Ipomoea*) are all cultivated to keep the season going as long as possible. Many plants originating in different climates do not grow well in the hot, wet Japanese summers, but will revive in the spring and autumn.

Right: *Garden with azaleas in bloom in the Rikugien Garden in Tokyo, Japan.*

In Autumn Japanese maples are just as important as the spring cherries in the Japanese calendar. Their fiery reds contrast with the deep greens of the evergreen pines and the fleeting blossom of the autumn-flowering camellia (*Camellia sasanqua*). Bush clover, balloon flower, toad lilies and *Farfugium* all add extra interest.

The most favoured plants for winter interest are bamboos and pines, and these can withstand the cold impressively. Snow-covered pines make a beautiful sight. Japan is also blessed with an exceptional number of evergreen shrubs that thrive in its acidic soil and temperate climate.

PLANTING STYLES

Most shrubs in the Japanese garden are set out in random, natural-looking groups or as individual specimens. Formal, symmetrical styles are rarely used, and shrubs and flowers are not planted for their textures or colours.

Below: *A pathway through the bamboo garden at the Hakone Gardens in Saratoga, California. This part of the garden contains many highly prized types of bamboo, including a black-stemmed variety.*

In tea gardens, you will find plants such as ferns that lend a wild quality to the design. In stark contrast, other gardens are planted with clipped evergreens, a look at its most artistic in the 17th-century art of *o-karikomi*, in which groups of shrubs, usually azaleas and camellias, are clipped into abstract topiary shapes (see pages 94–97). Hedges are another important feature for which a great miscellany of shrubs can be used. While some hedges look fairly uniform from a distance, they may actually contain as many as 20 or more genera from a list including *Elaeagnus, Pieris, Camellia, Rhododendron, Ficus, Aucuba, Osmanthus* and *Nandina*.

The Japanese garden is by no means devoid of colour and scent. Town gardens might include hydrangeas, hollyhocks, sweet peas (*Lathyrus odoratus*), morning glories and clematis or azaleas growing in pots outside the door. This planting effect is something that would be simple to recreate in any small city garden. The pots themselves can be in all shapes and sizes but in Japan are often quite small. The compost (soil mix) would be annually renewed to ensure a good supply of nutrients.

Above: *A dwarf Japanese red pine creates a much softer look than the harsher and more rugged black pine.*

PLANTS THROUGH THE SEASONS

Spring
Plum blossom (*Prunus mume*)
Cherry blossom (*Sakura*)
Deutzia
Spiraea
Japanese rose (*Kerria*)
Wisteria
Peony (*Paeonia*)
Azalea
Camellia

Summer
Iris
Hollyhock (*Alcea rosea*)
Hydrangea
Lotus blossom (*Nelumbo*)
Morning glory (*Ipomoea*)

Autumn
Japanese maple (*Acer*)
Evergreen pines
Autumn-flowering camellia (*Camellia sasanqua*)
Bush clover (*Lespedeza*)
Balloon flower (*Platycodon*)
Toad lily (*Tricyrtis*)
Farfugium

Winter
Bamboos
Evergreen pines and other shrubs

PLANTING TECHNIQUE

Although you can plant pot-grown plants at almost any time of year, you may need to water them more frequently if you plant in late spring or summer. The ideal time of year for planting is autumn but if your chosen plant is tender, especially when young and small, it would be better to wait until the late winter or early spring. It is not a good idea to attempt to plant anything when the ground is very hard and dry, very wet and boggy, or when it is frozen solid.

The standard planting technique shown below should be adapted around the different types and sizes of plant available as well as around the type of roots the plant has. Before you start the process of planting, you will need to be prepared with a garden spade and fork, some well-rotted manure, a rake and a watering can.

Right: Take care when planting some species of bamboo as they can be invasive. Root barriers can be placed in a circle around the plant to prevent it from invading the garden.

1 Place the plant, still in its pot, where you want to plant it and mark around the spot with your spade or place a cane. Then put the plant to one side, digging a hole 50% wider than the pot and 5–7.5cm (2–3in) deeper. Break up the soil in the bottom of the hole and replace it.

2 While holding the pot, turn it over. Squeeze the sides gently with the hand holding the base of the pot and ease it off with the same hand. If it doesn't come off readily, give the rim a firm tap on something hard and check that no roots have emerged through the holes in the pot and are holding the plant in.

3 Before planting, check that the hole is the correct depth – normally, the same as it was in the pot. In very heavy soil, planting slightly higher would help to avoid waterlogging, and in light soil you could plant deeper to increase the water supply. Add one or two forkfuls of well-rotted manure to the soil that you removed from the hole and mix the two.

4 If the plant has been well grown then you will not need to tease the roots out, but if the plant is at all pot-bound, spread some of them out. Now, still holding the plant with one hand on the top and one underneath, turn the plant over and carefully lower it into the hole.

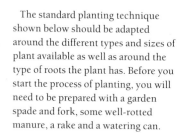

5 Backfill around the plant with the manure/soil mixture. There is no need to put any of this mix under the plant as most "feeder" roots grow out laterally.

6 Firm the soil with your foot. If it is very wet, wait before you do this, as the firming may cause compaction and bad drainage. Water the plant generously to help the soil settle in around the plant and remove air pockets. Water at least once a week until established.

Topiary

The Japanese love clipping plants. Often this is simply to manage the growth of a tree or a shrub so that it doesn't become too overgrown, or it may be to allow more light into a garden or on to the mossy woodland floor. In many gardens in Japan, almost every shrub is clipped into rounded mounds, in layers or in squares. This clipping, known as *o-karikomi*, is something very familiar to Westerners when they think of Japanese gardens. But don't make the mistake of attributing very elaborate topiary to the Japanese, when that particular style is, in fact, more Chinese.

AUTHENTIC STYLES

Topiary has been part of the way the Japanese have represented the abstraction of nature in their gardens since the earliest gardens of the Nara and Heian periods. It is worth taking a closer look at how the Japanese approach topiary. In the most famous traditional Japanese gardens, you will find very few examples of the kind of "cloud pruning" that you often find in copies of Japanese gardens, especially in the USA, where all kinds of plants from juniper to boxwood are clipped

into a series of rounded "cloud" forms. These sculptured plants can be spectacular but can also, in the wrong setting, look rather comical. Topiary needs a skilled eye; without it, these plants can look more like clipped poodles than part of an elegant design. This brings us back to the recurring theme of the Japanese garden: that the overall composition should not be overwhelmed by excessive forms or colours that may be too distracting.

Although "cloud" pruning is an oriental practice, it was originally

Above: *These massive blocks of clipped azaleas in Raikyu-ji resemble huge waves, cloud formations or even mountain ranges.*

(and still is) highly developed in China and Korea. The practice of these countries influenced the art in Japan, but the Japanese way is different. The art of clipping shrubs, like so much of their art, is modest and meaningful when carried out by good designers. In the same way that the Japanese enjoy the simple and natural form of rocks while the Chinese enjoy eccentric and convoluted forms, Japanese garden designers also use their form of topiary with sensitivity and restraint. In the 16th and 17th centuries this practice of *o-karikomi* reached its peak of artistry. With consideration, it can be utilized in a Japanese garden in any of the main styles, using all kinds of plants.

Pines are often trained rather than clipped into remarkable shapes, but this is not strictly *o-karikomi*. These trees are restructured to imitate the weathered, windswept look of wild seaside and mountain-top pines – a favoured feature of many gardens.

Left: O-karikomi *reached its peak during the 17th century. Although the clipping in this garden imitates natural forms, the artistic hand is very apparent. The plants are made up of a mixture of azalea, camellia, pieris and photinia.*

Above: *This natural hill form of clipping has become popular in Western-style gardens. Sometimes all you have to do is follow the "desire" of the plant. Here, the result is a gentle flowing outline of a range of small hills.*

Below: *Planting azaleas or boxwood so that they can be clipped into rounded shapes of differing sizes will create a dynamic design, especially when placed to contrast with the natural outline of rocks.*

Above: *Cloud pruning is used to give plants an eccentric individual character. Although intriguing, these forms are not always easy to fit into an overall design, and are generally best placed as individual specimens.*

KOBORI ENSHU

The man acknowledged as the master of *o-karikomi* was Kobori Enshu (1579–1647). A soldier, town planner, tea-master and garden designer, Enshu introduced the clipping of great masses of evergreens, most often blocks of azaleas but using mixed plantings too, into abstract forms that suggested the movement of waves, the folding of hill ranges, and even, in the garden of Daichi-ji near Kyoto, a treasure-ship on an ocean. In the temple garden of Raikyu-ji, in Takahashi, Enshu combined the art of *o-karikomi* with the art of *shakkei*, clipping blocks of azaleas into forms that, in one part of the garden, imitate ocean waves around the Mystic Isles of the immortals, while in another the forms echo and draw in the outline of the surrounding hills. The overall effect makes for a brilliant composition.

AZALEAS IN TOPIARY

Clipping into such ambitious schemes is not the commonest form of topiary. It can also be the simple trimming of evergreen azaleas into rounded shapes on the banks of a small hill, by the side of a path or pond, or virtually anywhere in the garden. These shapes should complement each other. In the dry garden of Shoden-ji, the clipped azaleas are used in place of rocks and are arranged in artistic groups in a 3-5-7 arrangement, as in the Ryoan-ji. Rounded mounds of azaleas are often seen with square clipped hedges or camellias trimmed with a stem and a round head. This can be seen at Sanzen-in, in Ohara.

There are two varieties of azalea that are clipped differently. 'Hi-ra-do' is a large-leafed evergreen azalea, usually with pink or white flowers, that is clipped into large mounds, while 'Satsuki', with its tighter growth and deeper pink flowers, can be shorn very low, sometimes only 15cm (6in) from the ground. This technique can be used to make the azalea flow down hills, or hug the bases of rocks. Clipping, often carried out in spring and autumn, can result in many plump flower buds being removed.

Above: *This white-flowered form of* Camellia sasanqua *has been clipped into three layers. The autumn flowering should not be affected.*

Enough flower buds remain to give a display, but the number is moderate compared to the profuse flowering that azaleas might otherwise produce, often smothering the plant with so much colour that no leaf can be seen.

WHEN TO CLIP

To maintain a neatly trimmed look, follow these guidelines:

• azaleas, box, hollies and most other evergreens can be clipped from autumn to spring, preferably straight after flowering, followed later in the year by a gentle autumn tidy-up;

• hard prune in spring, to give the plant time to recover its vigour by the end of the growing season;

• avoid serious pruning from mid- to late summer, as this might stimulate a late flush of growth that is likely to be damaged by early autumn frosts.

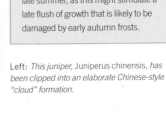

Left: *This juniper,* Juniperus chinensis, *has been clipped into an elaborate Chinese-style "cloud" formation.*

SQUARE FORMS

Some gardens use linear hedge clipping to draw the eye into the garden or as a device across the line of vision to separate the foreground and background – a feature that actually unifies the composition more than it divides it. Rectangular topiary or clipping into square forms is more familiar in Western gardens. In Japan this kind of topiary and square shaping is used as an interplay between the architecture of the buildings and the informal landscapes beyond them. This may have been influenced by the culture of Western design, since this art developed in the 17th century when the Japanese were first exposed to Western culture after centuries of isolation.

By the 19th century (the late Edo period), much of the clipping of shrubs lost the genius of Enshu's art and became rather over-elaborate. This clichéd style has often been imitated by Western gardeners.

MIREI SHIGEMORI

In the 20th century, Mirei Shigemori (1896–1975), who was a landscape architect and scholar, transformed the design of the Japanese garden, incorporating old motifs and new together in a dramatically abstract manner. His work was also known for using the Western formality of squares, particularly in the gardens around the Hojo of Tofuku-ji. Here he used the device of repeated low squares of azaleas positioned in a chequerboard pattern.

PLANTS SUITABLE FOR *O-KARIKOMI*

Although deciduous shrubs could be used, the following plants are exclusively evergreen and are the most common ones used for *o-karikomi*:

Genus	Species	Common name
Rhododendron	vaious hybrid azaleas	azalea
Camellia	sasanqua	camellia
Camellia	japonica and others	camellia
Ilex	crenata	holly (Japanese holly)
Taxus	baccata	yew
Taxus	cuspidata and others	yew
Buxus	sempervirens	box
Buxus	microphylla	box

For large blocks and hedges of mixed evergreens, you could include:

Pieris	japonica and others	pieris
Photinia	glabra and others	photinia
Aucuba	japonica and others	spotted laurel
Prunus	lusitanica	Portugal laurel
Prunus	laurocerasus	cherry laurel
Nandina	domestica	heavenly bamboo
Osmanthus	heterophyllus	osmanthus
Osmanthus	delavayi	osmanthus
Osmanthus	burkwoodii	osmanthus
Taxus	cuspidata	yew
Taxus	baccata	yew
Thuja	plicata	western red cedar
Chamaecyparis	obtusa	hinoki cypress
Cryptomeria	japonica	Japanese cedar
Juniperus	chinensis	juniper

For clipping as individuals into cloud formations and other dramatic forms, choose:

Camellia	sasanqua	camellia
Osmanthus	burkwoodii	osmanthus
Prunus	lusitanica	Portugal laurel
Taxus	baccata	yew
Chamaecyparis	obtusa	hinoki cypress
Cryptomeria	japonica	Japanese cedar
Juniperus	chinensis	juniper

Far left: O-karikomi *can be used to enhance, or play with, existing architectural forms; this idea is similar in many ways to Western-style topiary.*

Left: *At Tofuku-ji, a Buddhist temple in Kyoto, Mirei Shigemori took some of the Western influence of topiary to create a chequerboard of clipped azaleas to evoke an old system of land use in China. The bold squares contrast with the white wall and its blackened vertical wooden posts.*

WATER FEATURES

The original Japanese word for landscape was *shan-shui*, meaning "mountain-water". Most Japanese gardeners find their inspiration in the mountain landscapes of their country, with their pools, tumbling streams and waterfalls. For this reason water and rocks have become central to Japanese garden design.

While sometimes it is the spirit of water that is encapsulated in dry water features such as waterfalls made with rocks, and streams and still areas of water constructed with sand or gravel, actual water features give lifeblood to any garden they are used in. This is true whether they are pond or stroll gardens with large ponds, meandering streams and natural waterfalls, or tea and courtyard gardens with smaller-scale examples of ponds and streams and self-contained features, such as *tsukubai* (water basins), *shishi-odoshi* (deer scarers) and *sui-kinkutsu* (echo chambers). At whatever level they are used, the Japanese are always meticulous about integrating water features sensitively within the garden landscape.

Above: *A waterfall in the gardens next to Himeji Castle, Japan.*
Left: *This pond view illustrates the technique of* shakkei, *a way of incorporating a distant view into a garden.*

Streams, waterfalls & ponds

Water has a naturally mesmerizing quality and it is easy to understand the spiritual significance of its various incarnations in the Japanese garden. The choice of Kyoto as the new capital in the 10th century was partly due to the way the hills frame the area, but also to the southward and westward flow of its rivers. In geomantic terms, the southward course towards the sun (fire) was said to bring life, growth and good fortune. While mountains were said to have a meditative quality, and were seen as symbols of the gods and the Buddha, water was a source of joy and detachment.

Above: *A naturalized stream in the Japanese garden at Newstead Abbey, England.*

WATER IN THE JAPANESE GARDEN

In the past, streams would have been used on ceremonial occasions in Japan as settings for poetry readings and for drinking tea and saki. They would typically lead in and out of shallow ponds, often home to koi and the common carp. Ponds were also combined with small islands, and a pine on an island is one of the classic images of Japan. The bridges that cross from the mainland to the island give a good viewing point for the fish and flowers in the shallow water.

Waterfalls are the third water element, believed by Japanese gardeners to be best placed where they can reflect the moon. This stunning effect can be recreated in your garden so long as you take care to place the waterfall so that it looks as natural as possible.

STREAMS

The first Japanese gardens of the Nara and early Heian periods had winding streams that bordered the courtyard before feeding the main pond. These were often edged with rocks, the two forming an important relationship. An august stone might be used to mark the headwater of the stream as it entered the garden. Other rocks would "follow the desire" of this stone, responding to its position and shape, forcing the water this way and that, changing its mood as it approached the pond. Mountainside, torrent-style streams required the scattering of many more random stones, which caused the stream to divide and flow rapidly through narrowing channels.

A *yarimizu* is a meandering stream of the type that might be found flowing through a meadow, and it can be used in gardens to create a wetland area including an estuary planted with reeds and irises – popular in the Japanese garden. The stream's point of entry into this wetland should be indiscernible, and the water level should be kept fairly high, like a flooded estuary. These estuaries are often crossed by zigzag, eight-plank bridges (*yatsuhashi*) that weave over iris beds or baskets of irises secured to the stream or pond bed. (See pages 140–141, *Making a yatsuhashi bridge.*)

Left: *This is a quintessential and perfectly enchanting Japanese garden at Hosen-in, Ohara. The pond reaches almost up to the veranda.*

STREAMS: KEY ELEMENTS

Assessing the flow A meandering stream will need a large pump to keep a good flow of water. The smaller the flow, the narrower the channel should be. Narrow channels will produce a more rapid flow.

Using intermittent flow If the flow is intermittent, make your stream into a series of small pools that have the look of a stream. This way, when there is no flow from a pump or a natural source, the stream bed will not empty out.

The sound of water Streams make a pleasant sound if allowed to trickle over stones and pebbles.

Planting Be careful not to let plants draw too much water from the sides of a stream. Thirsty plants can lower water levels considerably, so make sure the supply is always topped up.

Above: *With its naturally crushed quartzite beaches and well-formed boulders, the stream that tumbles down the mountains above Nagoya is shaded by groves of wild Japanese maples.*

Below: *Shigemori's double winding stream is highly abstract. The rocks, set in a naturalistic manner, contrast with the smooth-set cobbling and gravel beaches. The idea owes some of its inspiration to the streams of the Heian period.*

WATERFALLS

These are another essential feature of pond and stream gardens and stroll gardens. They are often built to represent the Buddhist Trinity, with one large stone at the centre, over which the water tumbles, supported on either side by two attendant stones that stand slightly further forward. Large and important waterfalls were often known as dragon-gate waterfalls after the Chinese symbol for waterfall, which included a dragon and water.

A stone might be placed at the waterfall's base to represent a carp, as if it were about to leap. This "carp stone" symbolized spiritual and mental effort in Buddhist and Confucian terms. The carp, symbolically, would change into a dragon on reaching the top of the waterfall. The carp stone points to the strivings of an individual to better themselves. It is also, on a more practical level, the part of the waterfall that receives the full force of the flow as it hits the bottom.

Above: *A thin stream of water falls on to a flat stone, creating a louder sound and making a more decorative pattern than if it had simply fallen into a pool of water.*

Left: *The eccentric rock forms in the Huntington Botanical Gardens are more Chinese in spirit, but the overall design follows the natural ethos of the Japanese.*

WATERFALLS: KEY ELEMENTS

Position Waterfalls will look too artificial if mounded up in the middle of a garden. Try to use a natural hill or slope near the edge of the garden.

Siting the inlet Try to disguise the inlet of the water as much as possible. To do this, choose a dark, mysterious corner of the garden for the emergence of your stream.

Installing a pump It will usually be necessary to use a circulating pump for artificial waterfalls.

Losing water It is easy to lose water down the sides of a waterfall through splashing, so be thorough and generous in laying out a liner beneath any nearby rocks and make sure the water is channelled back into the system.

PONDS

Whether it moves through a stream or waterfall, the water needs eventually to flow into a pond. In Japanese gardens, ponds tend to be no deeper than 45cm (18in), so that they are easily kept clean and clear, and the fish can be seen. Try to include a stream flowing out of the pond for authenticity, they are believed to carry away evil spirits. When planting the pond with lotuses (*Nelumbo*) or water lilies (*Nymphaea*), make sure that they do not become too choked or the pond may silt up after a few years.

The proposed design of the pond edges will determine what happens to the water. For example, the water might appear to lap against a rocky shoreline, with a few solitary stones jutting out into the water, or it could become a wide inlet bordered by a sand bar. One sand-bar scene – the Aminoshidate peninsula in western Honshu – is so famous that it is cited as one of the three most important landscapes in Japan. It is often symbolically reproduced in Japanese gardens, often shown with a lantern on a promontory to represent a lighthouse. The shapes of ponds should, wherever possible, recall a natural scene, perhaps even the seaside.

The edges of ponds can be supported by rocks or timber posts. If you are using a pond liner, ensure that the liner is hidden by edging stones, timbers or plants. Japanese ponds are often designed using the shape of an ideogram, maybe symbolizing the word for "heart", "water" or "gourd", or they can be loosely outlined in the shape of a turtle or crane, however, it is more usual to find islands in these shapes representing the Mystic Isles.

ISLANDS

The islands in Japanese gardens might reproduce special scenes, such as the hundreds of extraordinary rocky islets in Matsushima Bay, near Sendai, in northern Honshu. Some of these islands are very small, but most have some kind of plant life, particularly pines, growing in their rocky crevices. The pine is a resilient tree that can take on fantastic forms as it is buffeted by salty winds. The Japanese take great care in pruning the pines in their gardens to give this characteristically wizened and windswept look.

Apart from the pine-covered island, there are other island styles, including the Rocky Islet and Cove Beach Island, all described in the *Sakuteiki*. The Meadow Isle is made up of low rocks, moss and autumn grasses. Forest Isles have random trees and grass, while Cloud and Mist Islands have sandy beaches planted in a spare, wispy way. These styles can all be recreated in your Japanese garden by growing suitable plants to set an atmospheric scene.

Islands were originally placed towards the middle of the pond, but slightly off-centre, to create a sense of mystery so that, whether you were boating or walking, you might find an inlet, waterfall, grotto, or even another island behind them. Use this element of surprise if you are designing a pond with islands.

Below: In the gardens of Nijo Castle, the shogun used unusually large rocks as a means of exhibiting his own power.

PONDS: KEY ELEMENTS

Shape Mimic the outline of natural ponds or choose a Japanese ideogram.

Using streams Most ponds have a wider inlet for the stream. This could be a good place to plant water irises.

Stepping stones When placing stepping stones across ponds with a butyl liner, make sure the liner is well protected from their weight.

Edging the pond Beware of how much the edges of a liner might show if there is a big drop in water level. Exposed liners are unattractive and can be damaged by animals and too much sunlight.

Position Choose a site where water might naturally lie in your garden.

Drainage Beware of any potential problems with drainage, and make provisions for overflow water.

Pumps Before buying a circulation pump for your pond, be aware of the running costs – it may have to run throughout the day to keep a pond healthy and clean.

Stocking a pond A pond with a good balance of plants and fish will stay naturally healthy.

Preparing the watercourse

Running water in the Japanese garden gives pleasure in terms of both sight and sound, but careful thought and planning is needed to make a water feature such as a stream or a series of cascades look natural. It may be easy to decide on the kind of feature you like, but its setting and the way it blends with other parts of the garden should be considered. As always, the preparation of the ground is vital, and you will need to use a variety of ground cover materials in the surrounding areas to hide tanks and pumps.

Above: *A carp stone at the base of a waterfall in the gardens of the Golden Pavilion. This tall upright stone is traditionally used in waterfalls.*

PREPARATION

Whether you are designing a broad, shallow stream to meander gently through the landscape (ideal for a flat site), or a rocky cascade feature (for a sloping garden), the watercourse first needs to be dug out as accurately as possible. Next you should remove any sharp stones. You will need a rubber liner, but before you lay this on the bed of the watercourse you should cover the channel with soft sand and/or a cushioning underlay to prevent the rubber liner being punctured. Specialist mail order companies and larger aquatic garden outlets will make a stream course liner for you, saving you the difficult task of manhandling, cutting and sealing a large, heavy piece of butyl rubber.

If you wish to make a waterfall on flat ground, the garden would have to be artificially contoured with the addition of several tonnes of soil, hardcore or subsoil covered with topsoil to achieve a suitable height. At the same time the rear of the waterfall feature should be camouflaged so that the water appears to be coming in from beyond the garden boundary. If this all sounds like a major upheaval, why not make a stream with a broader course on a gentle manmade slope instead? These can look and sound just as delightful in a Japanese garden.

ARRANGING THE ELEMENTS

Whether you are making your water feature on a natural or manmade gradient, carefully arrange the wall of rocks to create your cascade or waterfall, especially in the steeper sections. The strata and rock seams should line up to look as natural as possible. Use spare pieces of liner folded over several times to cushion the impact of large rocks sitting on the pool or stream liner and be careful not to tear the liner when arranging the stone.

Whatever liner you use, ensure that the overlapping pieces make a good seal and do not allow water to seep back through into the ground. For the same reason bring the edges of the liner well up on either side of the stream course, tucking them under the soil to hold them firmly in place to preserve the water.

Left: *This broad, meandering stream with gravel banks and large rocks in the Augsburg Japanese garden in Germany creates a restful scene. Artificial stream beds such as this are lined with butyl rubber.*

Right: *In the Augsburg Japanese garden, the water curtain provides movement within a static composition of clipped evergreens. To create the impression of a stream-fed pool, position a rock barrier with a hidden reservoir behind and pump water over the edge.*

Camouflaging the water inlet and outlet of your stream requires a certain amount of ingenuity. For a re-circulating system where the stream appears to run through the garden, the water flows into an underground reservoir made by burying a plastic dustbin (trashcan), hidden by plants and perhaps a large slab of stone or a galvanized metal grill covered with pebbles and cobbles. Alternatively, the water can flow into a base pool or pond. A submersible pump sends water back from there to the top of the stream via a length of corrugated plastic delivery pipe buried underground and protected with a row of tiles.

Ask an aquatic or pond specialist to calculate the size of pump needed for your scheme and the diameter of delivery pipe required. You can do a rough estimation of the required flow rate by pouring measured buckets of water down the watercourse over a set time to achieve the look you want. Multiply up to calculate a litres-per-hour or gallons-per-hour figure.

A header pool, which could be made using a small, preformed fibreglass pond, at the top of a rock cascade ensures a steady flow of water with no sudden surges when the pump is switched on. The stream could also appear to rise directly from a spring, if you camouflage the end of the delivery pipe with rocks and plants.

Take time to select the piece of rock needed at the top of a large waterfall as it will be quite a feature even when the water is switched off. A flat spillstone on top ensures that the water curtain cascades evenly over the stone. Different shapes, sizes and arrangements of stones will affect the fall of water over cascades and, with careful positioning, a relatively small water output can be made to look like a much bigger flow. After cementing in the main rocks, experiment with loose stones, seeing how they can further deflect and direct the cascading water in a pleasing manner.

READY-MADE ALTERNATIVES

Stream courses and cascade features can be purchased ready made as rigid fibreglass sections, and are obtainable from aquatic specialist outlets as well as mail order or internet companies. These are fashioned to resemble rocky watercourses, but will need to be carefully camouflaged. This will be achieved by bedding them well into the earth and rock surroundings, giving them a more natural appearance. Adding gravel, pebbles and cobbles along the length of a fibreglass-lined or butyl rubber-lined stream softens the look, especially with the addition of overhanging plants and the occasional large rock or boulder.

Above: *Choose a preformed stream unit to blend in with the surrounding rocks and gravel.*

Above: *A preformed stream unit and water basin with a sandstone rock finish.*

Above: *Simple, dark stream liners may blend more easily. Use gravel to camouflage them.*

Building a meandering stream

Japanese gardens often have a meandering stream on a site where there is little natural gradient, and this is made using a flexible liner. The stream does not have to be dominated by rocks but can have softer, more rounded stones and boulders along its course, looking as if they have been deposited naturally along an old river bed. If you don't want to have a pump running continuously, the stream can be built as a very long narrow pool or series of pools with small falls along its length that are designed to overflow as soon as the pump introduces more water.

The header pool for a meandering stream does not have to be conspicuous – it simply provides the illusion of natural water entering the garden. The essential factor in creating a natural-looking scheme is to devise a wandering route that widens in parts and follows as closely as possible the direction that water would take naturally when flowing over a flat site.

The first thing to do is to check the garden levels. This is because even a relatively flat site will have a slope, no matter how slight. If you can identify the highest point, plan a scheme that has this as the source of the stream. This will not only avoid the difficulty of building the stream against a slope but also do away with the need to make slight changes in the levels.

Above: *This stream wanders through a moss-covered landscape. The shadowy enclosed garden and the shafts of sunlight breaking through give a feeling of solitude.*

Below: *The winding stream that runs into the large ponds at Motsu-ji has been restored to show how they were used during the 11th and 12th centuries. The placing of rocks and plants is understated, in the style of a slow stream weaving through a meadow.*

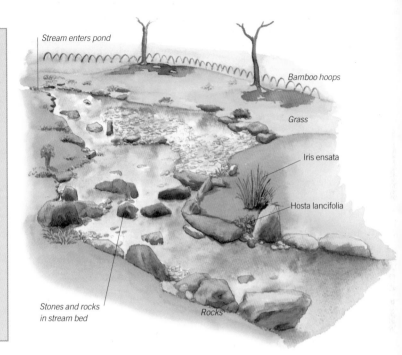

Stream enters pond

Bamboo hoops

Grass

Iris ensata

Hosta lancifolia

Stones and rocks
in stream bed

Rocks

You will need

- string, canes or garden hose
- wooden pegs, about 2.5cm (1in) in diameter and 15cm (6in) long
- a hammer
- a straight-edged piece of wood
- a spirit level
- a spade
- a plastic sheet
- a rake
- underlay and flexible liner
- a thin, flat stone
- ready-mixed mortar
- a mortaring trowel
- cobbles or river gravel
- corrugated plastic pipe, measuring 1–2.5cm (½–1in) in diameter
- roof tiles
- rounded boulders
- a submersible pump
- a flow-adjusting valve

1 Having chosen the source, mark out the route of the stream with string, canes or a hose, working back from any existing pool.

2 Knock in the pegs about a metre (yard) apart along the route of the stream. Place a length of straight-edged wood and a spirit level on the pegs to identify any slight depressions or rises in the ground so that the surrounding soil can be adjusted if necessary. If the outlet point from the stream into the base pool is lower than the pool sides, there will be a flow when the pump is turned on. If this point is established first, then you can ensure that all the other edges are higher.

3 If the route of the stream is through a lawn, remove the turf and lay it elsewhere, if needed, or stack it upside down to rot down. Leave the pegs identifying the level in place.

4 Dig out the soil from the stream to a depth of 38cm (15in) in the centre. If the stream is wider than 60cm (24in), create shallow marginal shelves, 23cm (9in) deep, along the sides. Stack the soil on a *plastic* sheet to be used after the liner is inserted. Rake the stream bottom and the shelves to make them level, removing any sharp stones.

5 Place underlay along the stream length and drape the single length of liner into the stream contours. Use rocks to hold down the sides of the liner to stop them blowing about.

6 Create a spill point and prevent soil erosion by securing a thin, flat stone on the liner with a dab of mortar where the stream enters the pool.

7 Take some soil from the heap of topsoil and put it on the liner to form a shallow saucer shape inside the excavation. This will help to protect a cheap liner from ultra-violet light and provide a medium in which plants can grow. Top-dress the soil with rounded cobbles or river gravel to stop it from being washed away.

8 Bury a corrugated plastic delivery pipe along the side of the stream so that it runs from the base pool to the source. Cover the pipe with roof tiles before replacing the soil.

Above: *Winding streams are usually quite shallow, so care must be taken to disguise the liner at the edges, and cover the stream bed with varying sizes of gravels and cobbles.*

9 Position a few rounded boulders on the liner at the source to simulate a small spring.

10 Install a pump in the base pool and connect the outlet to the plastic delivery pipe. As the water will only trickle through this stream, a flow adjuster should be fitted to the delivery pipe to regulate the flow. Fill the pool with water and turn on the pump to check that the stream is running satisfactorily.

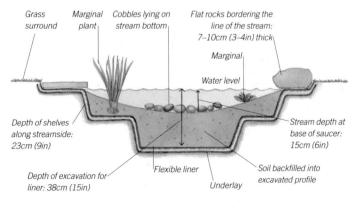

Grass
surround

Marginal
plant

Cobbles lying on
stream bottom

Flat rocks bordering the
line of the stream:
7–10cm (3–4in) thick

Marginal

Water level

Stream depth at
base of saucer:
15cm (6in)

Depth of shelves
along streamside:
23cm (9in)

Depth of excavation for
liner: 38cm (15in)

Flexible liner

Underlay

Soil backfilled into
excavated profile

Pond liners, pumps & filters

Pond liners and pumps are the invisible workers that enable you to create your Japanese water feature. They should never be seen, but are vital elements in the construction of a beautiful *tsukubai*, waterfall or stream. The pump ensures a constant supply of fresh, oxygenated water for fish, and special filtration systems help to keep water clear and process fish waste. The flow rate of a pump decreases over time so ensure you have spare capacity. Buy the best you can afford and you will be rewarded with a natural-looking water feature that lasts for years.

POND LINERS

Today's standard pond liner is made of black butyl rubber. It resists degradation by UV light and, being flexible, it is easy to fit and tolerant of stretching. It also resists puncturing and tearing. Undisturbed, good-quality butyl lining could last for thirty years. For naturalistic pools and ponds in Japanese gardens butyl is practical, versatile (fitting any irregular shape) and relatively easy to install compared to, say, a rigid fibreglass pond.

Butyl rubber comes in different grades, so discuss with your local aquatic garden specialist which will be suitable. For large ponds, liner made from one of the thicker grades could be very heavy and difficult to manoeuvre into position without several pairs of hands. The thickest grades are also less flexible and therefore trickier to lay or fold in tight bends and corners. Laying out the fabric on a sunny day allows it to warm up and become more flexible.

Above: *Wait a little while until the pond filters are mature before buying koi carp. Japanese koi are normally exported in November and December, but the best time to buy is in the spring when the water has warmed up.*

Below left: *The pool in this garden has been made with a flexible liner and is now being filled with water. The liner should not be exposed above the water line.*

Below: *This pool uses polythene (polyethylene) sheet as a flexible liner. Only trim the liner when you are certain the water level and edging are satisfactory.*

Above: *A unit with an even deep zone and ample shelves for marginal plants.*

Above: *Less digging out is required with this unit, which has a deep zone at only one end.*

Above: *Flexible liners are available in a variety of materials, thicknesses and colours. From left to right: 1 Butyl liner; 2 Butyl liner; 3 and 4 Low-density polythene (polyethylene); 5–9 PVC in different grades; 10 Underlay.*

Another option is to use a natural clay liner, made with compacted clay. There are also various artificial composite clay liners that are efficient replacements for conventional clay, ideal for long-term performance for large ponds or those in harsh climates (see pages 158–9 for how to line a pond with a soil liner). Mail-order companies specializing in pond liners or larger aquatic centres may offer a made-to-measure service.

Before you lay a flexible liner, you should use a geotextile membrane underlay to protect the butyl from being punctured by sharp stones and roots. You can use soft sand as an alternative, but the underlay is easier to keep in place over sharp corners and steep slopes. Use extra underlay and folded offcuts of butyl liner to provide a cushion beneath individual rocks and boulders laid on top of the liner (see pages 194–5 for how to line a pond with a flexible liner).

PUMPS

For moving water features, such as streams or waterfalls, you will need a pump. Designs vary depending on the task they have to perform and they have different power outputs, so ask a water garden specialist to advise you. The data needed includes:

• the distance over which the water is travelling around the circuit
• the gradient
• the height of the starting point
• the diameter of the pipe
• the flow rate, which affects the appearance of a waterfall and speed of filtration.

Large schemes will require a submersible pump running off the mains (utility) voltage and so, unlike pumps operating via a transformer, the electrical cabling must be run through protective ducting buried to a depth of 60cm (24in). Make sure that you fit residual current devices (RCDs) or circuit breakers for all pieces of electrical equipment, including lighting. This

safety feature ensures that if the device is accidentally earthed, the electricity supply cuts off. A waterproof outdoor switch can also be fitted.

FILTERS

For ponds containing fish, you will need a filtration system. This will either be a system submerged in the pond or, most efficiently, biological filters held in a header tank above the water. Fitting an ultra-violet clarifier causes green algae cells to clump together, making it easier for a biological filter to extract them. Fish and water lilies need a minimum pond depth of 45cm (18in) to overwinter, especially in colder regions. Consider installing a water heater for fish ponds, which keeps part of the surface ice-free.

Below and right: *Submersible pumps have an enormous range of outputs. Check the running costs if it is to be used continuously.*

This pump would be attached to piping.

A pump with a fountain attachment.

This pump has a fountain attachment and a flow adjuster.

Creating edges for a pond

The edges of most small ponds, especially those in small gardens, are best lined with rocks. Larger ponds in stroll gardens, however, often include stretches of cobbled beaches or grass rolling up to the very edge of the pond. The edges of ponds always need careful attention, as the water may run out or evaporate and this leaves an ugly view of the liner. Whichever kind of edging you choose, make sure that it covers the edge of the pond well and that it is a practical solution for the kind of pond you have made.

Above: *Cobbled beaches are popular around ponds, at times set loosely and at others set in mortar to create an even surface.*

CONCEALING A POND LINER

If you are using a butyl liner, make sure that you conceal 10cm/4in of the liner below the water line with rocks or gravel, and any part of the liner that might show above water level. Bear in mind that in summer, with increased evaporation, the pond level may drop and expose the liner. It is also worth noting that butyl liners deteriorate more quickly when exposed to sunlight and frost.

ROCK EDGING

The rocks around a pool should be partially submerged to achieve a natural effect. The rocks will also need to be supported on a foundation slab or concrete footing.
- If you are using a liner, pass it over the slab or footing and under the rock, embedding the liner into a layer of stiff mortar or concrete.
- You can use a sandwich of underlay above and below the liner to help protect it.
- Ensure that the liner finishes above the level of the water under the rock at the side of the pool.

COBBLE EDGING

The essential thing in introducing naturalness to a cobble edge is to arrange the sizes so that the main body of cobbles increases in diameter from below the waterline into the drier margins.

- Sort your cobbles into size before you lay them.
- To prevent the cobbles from rolling to the pool bottom, a concrete support should be constructed at the edge.

GRASS EDGING

An edging of grass is very easy on the eye and is suitable for larger pools and stroll gardens.
- The edge of the pool can become worn fairly quickly, which can cause the sides to crumble.
- Avoid this by underpinning the turf with a small foundation of stones or timber edging (see below right).

TIMBER EDGING

An alternative method of taking grass up to the water's edge is to construct a vertical timber wall, which will extend from below the waterline to just below the level of the grass. The timber wall looks most attractive if it is made with timber rounds, at a measurement of 5–7.5cm (2–3in) in diameter. These are placed tightly side by side to form a palisade-like barrier. Proprietary lengths of "log roll" could also be used

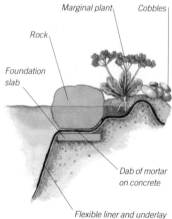

Rock edging A rock that is being used at the edge of a pool is best when it is partially submerged, and supported with a foundation slab under the liner.

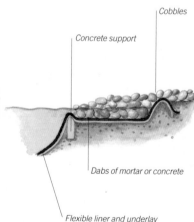

Cobble edging To prevent cobbles from rolling into the deeper zone of the pond, make a shallow shelf with a raised edge under the flexible liner in order to give extra stability.

Right: *Paving with a slight overhang around a pond edge can hide flexible butyl liners.*

instead of complete rounds, and these log rolls are already joined together by galvanized wire strands.

• To make either of these systems of timber edging stable enough not to crumble into the pool, a small trench, approximately 15cm (6in) deep and 10–15cm (4–6in) wide, must be dug out at the pool edge.

• A concrete support should be added in front of this trench.

• The pool liner is then run over the concrete support and into the trench, finishing above the waterline.

• A mix of stiff mortar is placed on the liner and the timbers bedded into the stiff mortar before it hardens. Make sure that the timber rounds are straight and tight together because they cannot be moved once the mortar sets.

• After a day or two, when the mortar has set hard, soil can be backfilled behind the timber edge and the liner can be wedged upright so it is held above the waterline.

• Turf can then be laid right up to the timber edge on the fresh soil, which is now supported by the concrete at the water's edge.

Right: Paving with a slight overhang around a pond edge can hide flexible butyl liners.

PAVED EDGING

Make a more formal and solid design for the pond edge with paving stones.

• Prepare the area by scraping away some topsoil. If the subsoil is not firm, replace it with 7.5–10cm (3–4in) of hardcore. Top this with about 5cm (2in) of damp sand, rake and level, then cover with the underlay and liner.

• Place the paving stones along the water's edge, checking that they overlap the water by 2.5–5cm (1–2in). Use the largest piece to give stability, with the straight edge overlapping the water.

• Mix some mortar on a board, then lay the first stones on to dabs of mortar trowelled on to the liner.

• Press the slab down on to the mortar dabs and bed it down firmly before laying the adjacent slabs.

• Check the slabs are level with a spirit level. To adjust the height, tap with a club hammer over a block of wood.

• The gaps between the slabs must be filled with a fairly wet mortar mix in order to hold each slab in place. Lay on a slight slope to reduce run-off from any adjacent paving or grass.

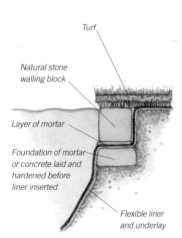

Grass edging *A grass edge is subject to heavy wear and tear. It should be supported by a natural stone walling block, which is placed on a deep foundation of stiff mortar or concrete.*

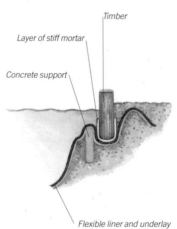

Timber edging *Log roll or timber rounds placed side by side make a good edge when mortared into a thin trench under the level of the water. Turf edging can then run up to the timber edging.*

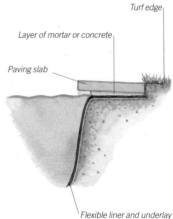

Paved edging *When using a paving slab to provide an edge, ensure that there is a small overlap above the water, and mortar the slab on to the liner above a foundation of hardcore.*

Tsukubai & shishi-odoshi

Some Japanese gardens contain very distinctive water features called *tsukubai,* or water basins. These water basins were often found in traditional tea gardens and were used for providing drinking water. They were usually fed by a natural spring. Taller basins, *chozubachi,* are sited nearer the house. Another traditional Japanese water feature, the *shishi-odoshi,* was designed as a deer scarer and uses running water to make a knocking noise with a bamboo pole against a stone basin, a sound loud enough to deter marauding animals from eating tender plants in the garden.

Above: *Water basins were traditionally made from stone and were fed with water from a bamboo spout called kakei.*

WATER BASINS

The principle of spiritual and physical cleanliness has been adapted for use in Japanese garden design from the earliest days. You will often find a water basin or other standing water feature in a Japanese garden, and sometimes even two or three such features.

Water basins are not always kept full, except those that are fed from a concealed bamboo pipe that is allowed to drip into the basin to keep the water fresh, rippling and constantly overflowing. Water basins that are not automatically filled will need cleaning out and topping up with fresh water. In addition, just as the path can be cleaned and damped down before the guests arrive, the sides of stone water basins may also be wetted to darken and intensify the natural colours and markings of the stone.

The water basin itself may be a simple rounded bowl carved from a single piece of granite, but traditional designs (copied from various historic shrines and temples in Japan) vary, and some are surprisingly geometric, cube-shaped or cylindrical, with carved patterns and designs around the outside. These intricate designs tend to stand out more than the rustic bowls, making a pleasing contrast to the surrounding rock forms and

Above: *A 17th-century crouching basin in the temple garden of the Ryoan-ji. This has been one of the most copied of all water basins.*

Above: *A cube-shaped water basin with regular square indentations in a private garden in Ohara. This design, made from granite which has* tarnished and discoloured over time, is copied from an original basin in the gardens of the Silver Pavilion, or the Ginkaku-ji Temple in Kyoto, Japan.

plantings. Nowadays, materials other than granite are often used, and the more porous they are, the more quickly they will develop a pleasing patina of age due to the moist environment.

There should be good drainage around a basin, as the fact that the basin is frequently topped up, and so overflows, could make the area swampy. If the basin is being refilled constantly from a pipe, a drain will also be needed to take the water away. The area around the water basin is often surrounded by cobbles or large-sized gravel to keep it dry. This combination of gravel and water basin is another opportunity to express artistry. You can place a special stone that does not get wet in the surrounding gravel area for people to stand on.

TALL WATER BASINS

Although tall water basins come in all shapes, sizes and materials, such as cut and natural stone, ceramic and wood, there are essentially two types: *chozubachi* and *furisode*.

Chozubachi basins are usually up to 1m (3ft) high and are placed on verandas where they can easily be reached from the house. These basins may have a slatted bamboo cover to keep the water fresh, to stop birds from drinking there and to prevent leaves and debris from falling in.

Furisode basins come in the form of a narrow, naturally rippled rock that is shaped like the long sleeve of a kimono. A bowl is carved into the stone, sometimes in the shape of a gourd. (The gourd is a symbol of good hospitality, being the traditional holder for the Japanese rice wine sake.)

A more elaborate tall basin can be found in some Japanese gardens, one example being the *ginkakuji*, which is named after the famous garden of the Silver Pavilion, near Kyoto, with tiled patterning on the sides.

LOW, OR CROUCHING, WATER BASINS

The *tsukubai chozubachi* is a low, or crouching, basin placed on or just off the *roji* (the path to the tea house). The act of crouching to reach the basin, like the bending needed for the middle crawl-through gate and the tea house's small hatch-like entrance, compels guests to humble themselves.

One famous anecdote recalls how the great tea master Rikyu had hidden the view of the beautiful inland sea in his tea garden with dense plantings. His guests and visitors could see the view only at the moment when they bowed down to cleanse themselves at the *tsukubai*. This is a perfect expression of Zen – that true beauty is available to us only once we have lowered our heads (and therefore our minds) lower than our hearts.

CHOOSING A WATER BASIN

Water basins were originally made of granite, which makes them very heavy and therefore expensive to transport. However, fake stone (fibreglass), glazed ceramic and concrete versions are easy to come by nowadays and may be found in garden centres, especially those that specialize in Japanese garden ornaments.

Above: *A simple* tsukubai *will work in naturalistic settings as well as in Zen gardens.*

Above: *Still quite simple, this flower-like* tsukubai *looks best in plain surroundings.*

Above: *This* tsukubai *is hewn out of a rock, a dramatic feature with a strong presence.*

Above: *This reproduction, like many others, is based on original Japanese designs.*

Above: *This cube-shaped* tsukubai *would make a good courtyard feature.*

Left: *Purification is ritualized by the Japanese. Outside all Buddhist and Shinto shrines there are water basins for cleaning the hands and mouth.*

Below left: *Two tall water basins (*chozubachi*) that can be reached from the veranda of Sanzen-in, in Ohara. These are square basins set on stone pillars.*

As well as this, pottery or stone urns can be used, and these make excellent alternatives.

Recycled materials are another option – maybe some hollow, second-hand architectural pillars, or old *stupas* (a feature in many Buddhist temples). So use anything that might take on a new life as a water basin, including old stone water troughs or a stone with a natural deep depression.

PLACING A WATER BASIN

A *tsukubai* should always be placed by a path and a *chozubachi* by a house, but apart from that there is no need to get too caught up in the idea that everything should be set exactly according to a pre-ordained plan. Japanese gardeners do not consider this to be in the true spirit of Zen. In fact, Rikyu, the master of the Japanese tea ceremony, would have

disapproved of an approach that meant everything was too rigidly correct. For instance, it is traditional to place the *tsukubai* on the sunny side of the path, so that guests do not have the sun on their backs and necks when they kneel down to take water from it. This kind of tradition is just respectful, intended to be attentive to the comfort of the guest, and it is therefore not necessary to copy it precisely. The key consideration here is that the exact placement depends on the conditions within the garden – if it is shady enough, your guests will not need to shelter from the sun.

There are often special stone arrangements around the basin, featuring worn, rounded cobbles and pebbles, with accompanying stones, a lantern, ferns and evergreen shrubs. Often a special flat-topped stone is placed to the side of the basin for guests to stand on or to rest their fan or bag.

In wooded wilderness settings, the arrangement can be quite lush and atmospheric, but as with so much that is connected with the tea ceremony, the *tsukubai* is full of symbolism. This gives the garden designer plenty of opportunities to take the concept of the *tsukubai* and the lantern that often accompanies it, to abstract it and give it a modern interpretation, as befits a contemporary garden.

The fact that water basins symbolize cleanliness and hospitality means that they are not only found in tea gardens or off the verandas of houses: they will also be found in courtyard gardens and along passageways to the house.

Below *A stone basin, or* tsukubai, *covered with moss in the gardens at Ten Juan Temple, Kyoto.*

Below: *Water basins are often filled constantly by fresh water, the excess draining away among rocks and pebbles. A sump could be built under the stones to collect the water, which can then be recycled using a submersible pump.*

Above *Visitors to the Meiji Shrine in Tokyo, Japan, use the traditional bamboo ladles provided for washing and purification.*

Below *This basin in the Seiryu tea garden at Nijo Castle is carved from natural rock.*

Above: *The water in a shishi-odoshi is circulated with a small pond pump, placed below water level in a bowl, and hidden with a metal grill and stones. One outlet makes the water surface ripple and the other trickles into the swinging arm.*

DEER SCARERS (*SHISHI-ODOSHI*)

Another traditional Japanese garden water feature, the *shishi-odoshi*, or deer scarer, is sometimes found in kit form in garden centres, but you are likely to find more authentic-looking *shishi-odoshi*, or the individual elements and raw materials for making your own, from specialist Japanese garden suppliers. This can be an enjoyable do-it-yourself project, and means you can choose the elements to fit with your garden.

The *shishi-odoshi* consists of a piece of bamboo 60–90cm (24–36in) long, drilled through to accommodate a pin on which it pivots. One end rests on a piece of stone called a sounding rock and the other end fills with water fed from a bamboo spout. When it contains enough water, the pivoting bamboo tips, releasing the water, and then flips back up, striking the stone and making a noise. This is very similar in basic construction to the *tsukubai*, with an underground, camouflaged reservoir containing a submersible pump and a length of plastic tubing that links the pump to the bamboo feed pipe.

Above: *This deer scarer was featured in Horoshi Namori's show garden at the Chelsea Flower Show, London, in 1996.*

Below: *A traditional Japanese fountain, the shishi-odoshi was originally used to deter deer from feeding on shoots in rice paddies.*

Making a *sui-kinkutsu*

A *sui-kinkutsu* is a water echo-chamber, or more literally a "water harp chamber". It is constructed so that you can listen to the dripping of water falling into an underground chamber by means of a hollow bamboo pipe held to the ear at one end and to a hole in the ground above the chamber at the other. The sound is like that of the traditional stringed Japanese musical instrument called the *koto*. This might also make you think of a stream in a mountain cave. In very quiet surroundings you should be able to hear the sound without the aid of a bamboo pipe.

Purists believe that a *sui-kinkutsu* should be constructed only in conjunction with a *tsukubai* arrangement (see pages 112–116), as it collects water dripping and draining away from the water basin, which is itself fed by a dripping bamboo pipe. However, a *sui-kinkutsu* may also be constructed as a separate feature, independently from a *tsukubai*, perhaps simply collecting water from a dripping hose that is switched on especially for visitors or at your personal discretion.

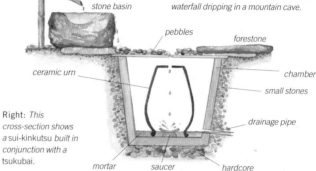

Above: *The idea behind the* sui-kinkutsu *is to create "music" from the sound of water, like a waterfall dripping in a mountain cave.*

Labels: bamboo pipe; stone basin; pebbles; forestone; ceramic urn; chamber; small stones; drainage pipe; mortar; saucer; hardcore

Right: *This cross-section shows a* sui-kinkutsu *built in conjunction with a tsukubai.*

You will need

- a piece of cylindrical shuttering or an old plastic barrel
- concrete mix, 1 part sand to 4 parts cement
- an Ali-Baba-style urn about 80–100cm (32–40in) high and 40cm (16in) in diameter with a single drainage hole in its base
- a small ceramic plant saucer
- rope to lower the pot
- a paving slab, 1m (40in) square, with a hole 4cm (1½in) wide drilled in the centre

1 Dig out a pit around 1.2m (4ft) deep and 1m (40in) wide. Create a circular shuttering around 70cm (28in) in diameter using an old plastic drum or some other mould that can be removed easily after surrounding it in concrete. Line the base of the hole and the outside of the mould with 8–10cm (3–4in) of concrete. Make sure the bottom of the hole is level. Make a drainage outlet 10cm (4in) above the bottom of the chamber to take the excess water away to a soakaway or an approved watercourse.

2 Leave the concrete to set for two days before removing the mould and proceeding with the next stage.

3 Place the ceramic saucer at the bottom of the hole. The saucer should be smaller than the rim of the vase.

4 Tie a rope around the rim of the Ali Baba vase and (with assistance to balance the weight) lower the upturned vase carefully into the chamber so that it completely covers the saucer, with the drainage hole directly above it.

5 Lay the paving slab over the chamber. Then direct your chosen water source to the hole in the paving slab.

6 You will need to disguise the paving slab and the water source (for example a hose). You can do this using small stones and cobbles. An alternative camouflage idea is to place a water basin over the slab, but position it off-centre so that the water spilling out of the basin finds its way into the hole above the chamber.

Constructing a reservoir

Water basins and deer scarers both need a reservoir and pump to make a circulating water system, unless they have a natural source of water. The reservoir for the water will sit immediately under the water basin (which is usually made from a hollowed-out rock, but any basin that is dignified enough, including a stone trough, could be used) or at the spilling end of the deer scarer, and it gives the illusion that the water feature is stream fed. If the site is in a windy location, check that all the water flows back into the reservoir, otherwise it can empty, causing the pump to burn out.

The amount of water that circulates around a water basin is much the same as that for a deer scarer (*shishi-odoshi*), where both require a mere trickle for best effect. Thus the reservoir need be no more than 100 litres (22 gallons). The reservoir can be set almost directly below the feature, but in a place where you can access it for cleaning, and where, if it were to overflow, there is some suitable drainage around it.

The small amount of water spillage likely from the basin will not need an extensive drainage system, but it is a good idea to cover the immediate area around the reservoir with loose stones and gravel to aid drainage. This will also give a more authentic appearance.

Above: *Ladles are laid over or by the side of the basin supported by a rack of bamboo. Guests use them to cleanse their hands, mouths and faces before entering the tea house.*

Below: *The* shishi-odoshi *reservoir differs little from that of a water basin. Always ensure that the spillage goes back into the reservoir.*

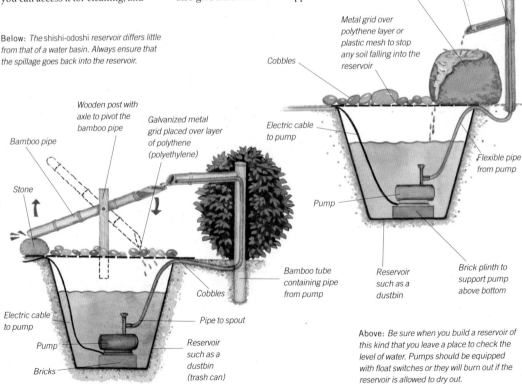

Hollowed-out stone basin that overflows into grid

Pipe inside bamboo tube

Shorter piece of bamboo tube

Metal grid over polythene layer or plastic mesh to stop any soil falling into the reservoir

Cobbles

Electric cable to pump

Flexible pipe from pump

Pump

Reservoir such as a dustbin

Brick plinth to support pump above bottom

Wooden post with axle to pivot the bamboo pipe

Galvanized metal grid placed over layer of polythene (polyethylene)

Bamboo pipe

Stone

Electric cable to pump

Pump

Bricks

Pipe to spout

Reservoir such as a dustbin (trash can)

Cobbles

Bamboo tube containing pipe from pump

Above: *Be sure when you build a reservoir of this kind that you leave a place to check the level of water. Pumps should be equipped with float switches or they will burn out if the reservoir is allowed to dry out.*

You will need

- a reservoir kit from a specialist supplier (see page 498), which should include a reservoir, a metal grid, a sheet of plastic mesh, a polythene layer, a small pump with a cable, and a length of ribbed hose to join the pump to the delivery pipe of the deer scarer or water basin

Or you can make your own kit using

- a strong plastic bin at least 60cm (24in) deep and 45cm (18in) wide, such as a cold-water storage tank sold for central heating systems
- a small pump kit from your local aquatic centre – the pump should have a variable pressure valve so that you can modulate the flow
- a polythene layer to cover the bin
- a sheet of plastic mesh
- a metal grid, which can be made of a piece of concrete reinforcing mesh from a builder's merchant

For both options, you will also need

- lengths of pre-drilled bamboo tubes to deliver water to the feature
- some cobbles or large gravel
- a spade to dig a hole
- some sharp sand
- a spirit level
- a waterproofed electrical source or socket for the pump

1 Choose a small, level site. The cobbles can extend as far as you wish, but the area need be no bigger than a circle of the diameter of the reservoir. Mark out the diameter and dig out a hole wider and deeper. Line the base and sides with sharp sand to protect the reservoir from stones and to make it level.

3 Backfill the gap between the reservoir and the hole sides with soil and ram it until firm with a piece of timber, such as a cut-down broom handle. Rake the surrounding soil and remove any stones.

5 Before lowering the submersible pump on to the plinth, attach a flexible delivery pipe to the pump outlet. Take the pipe over the side of the reservoir (or through a hole in the top edge) and push it through a tube of bamboo, 60–90cm (2–3ft) tall, next to the reservoir.

2 After placing a 4–6cm (1½–2½in) deep layer of sand at the bottom of the hole, lower the reservoir into the hole and check that the rim is just below the edge. Then check that the sides are level with a spirit level. If necessary, you will need to adjust the base of the hole until it is completely flat.

4 Remove any soil from inside the reservoir as, if it is left, this may silt up the pump and stop it functioning. Make a plinth in the reservoir with two bricks or a piece of broken paving.

6 Push the pipe through to a further bamboo spout positioned to spill into the basin. These can be made by cutting away the end of the pipe. Lay the polythene layer over the depression and the reservoir and cut out a hole 5cm (2in) smaller than the bin diameter.

7 Lay the galvanized metal grid on top of the reservoir. This should be larger than the diameter of the top of the reservoir. Fill reservoir with water.

8 Lay a sheet of plastic mesh over the grid to stop any soil falling into the reservoir. Position the spill basin at the side of the grid, but make sure that it slightly overhangs the reservoir so that it will overflow on to the cobbles.

9 Test the flow of water, adjusting the regulator on the pump or moving the position of the spout so that the water falls into the saucer part of the spill basin. Arrange the cobbles over and around the metal grid. Test the system to make sure there is minimal water loss through spillage or splashing, and adjust accordingly.

CONSTRUCTING A RESERVOIR 119

CREATIVE CONSTRUCTS

This chapter looks at the elements that are designed and created to fit within the Japanese garden. Manmade constructs such as paths, fences, bridges, lanterns and water basins add form, character and scale to a garden. When used well, these can contribute to its beauty. Such artefacts are not placed to be admired as sculpture as in Western gardens, but blended into their surroundings to form an intrinsic part of the whole composition.

The Japanese garden designer is deeply interested in the quality of these objects, choosing them very carefully so that they form part of the design of the garden. Most fences and garden buildings are built of raw timber, bamboo, sisal and reeds, exhibiting the pure natural qualities of those materials, while lanterns and water basins are often carved out of the finest stone and encouraged to weather. Paths and bridges should be designed with great care and creativity, using a combination of natural materials and balancing the gardener's deliberate artistry with nature's own perfection.

Above: *A path in a bamboo grove near the Tenryu-ji Temple.*
Left: *A Japanese garden, featuring a curved bridge, ablaze with the colours of autumn.*

Paths

Japanese garden paths have evolved from the simple surfaces of gravel and fine sand that were originally used for paths that circled around ponds, to the stepping-stone paths of the tea garden where each step carries a special significance for the traveller. Some of the path styles used today are simple and naturalistic whereas others use a highly sophisticated mix of materials and designs. The only requirement is that whichever kind of path you choose blends well with the natural style of your garden.

Above: *Ginkgo leaves fall on to a path. Paths are often edged in imaginative ways.*

THE PURPOSE OF PATHS

The main purpose of paths is to control the visual experience of the stroller, with each change of direction introducing a new view. From the earliest times, paths have suddenly stopped or turned abruptly – a device that encourages the stroller to hesitate and scan a view that was deliberately composed to be seen from a particular spot. Zigzag paths and bridges take this idea to a greater extreme.

Paths found their true significance in the tea garden and were originally known as dewy paths (*roji*). The tea path recalls the pilgrimages that philosophers, painters and Zen monks made on their visits to China in search of renowned Chinese artists and sages, who lived, often alone, in huts and hermitages in the hills and mountains. As the tea guest is drawn along the *roji*, they are made more conscious of each step they take through the use of stepping stones. These had previously been used only for practical purposes: to cross water and swampy, muddy ground. Their addition to the tea garden was initiated by Rikyu, who was one of the great Japanese tea masters of the 16th century.

The strategic placement of some larger stepping stones on a path gives the visitor the freedom to be less conscious of where their feet are falling. This means that they would be able to look up to take in a special view of the garden or cleanse themselves at a water basin. Stepping stones were always kept scrupulously

Left: *The formality of this path cutting through the dry garden of Tenju-an is softened by an enveloping carpet of moss. The path takes a sudden right-angled turn at the end, a black pine (Pinus thunbergii) grows alongside it.*

Above: *In some climates, moss will readily creep over gravel paths, and may create a desirable effect.*

Above right: *In the gardens of Rheinaue in Bonn, Germany, a naturalistic path of stepping stones set in gravel crosses a cobbled path, which gives way to more formalized paving set in grass.*

clean, brushed and even damped down to give the impression of mountain dew. Damping down paths is considered to be a very hospitable way to welcome guests into a tea garden or the tea house itself. However, great care must be taken to keep stepping stones free of slimy algae, which can become extremely slippery when wet.

In some Japanese gardens, especially dry ones – which were mostly designed to be viewed from one particular place, such as the veranda of a building – the paths of stepping stones might be set to weave right across the garden. In the past, these paths were rarely walked on, but were used by the garden designers of the day to suggest movement and to draw the viewer's eye across a particular scene. If a path was not

EDGING GRAVEL PATHS

Gravel is a loose material, so it is always best to contain it carefully within solid edges. If you don't edge these paths, the gravel will tend to get pressed into the surrounding soil or kicked around and will eventually disappear.

Edging materials	Where and when to use
Paving and cobbles	Paving stones or cobbles should be chosen for the appropriateness of their setting. Make sure the size and shape of paving stones complements the surrounding garden.
Granite setts	Near the house, more formal granite setts might be used.
Random stones and other materials	In more naturalistic areas you could choose to use random stones. In Japanese gardens it is common to find imaginative use of all kinds of "found" materials such as old roofing tiles, long strips of chiselled granite or even charred post tops. Such elements need to be placed with great sensitivity.
Wood and steel	The use of easy-to-install wooden boards and steel edging would be possible in any area, as these materials are subtle and will blend in with the surrounding shrubs or mossy areas, especially once they have weathered. Steel is best used sparingly for a more authentic design.
Bent bamboo	Paths in Japanese parks and some private gardens are edged in hoops of bent bamboo, which adds style and rhythm to the path, as well as discouraging visitors from stepping on the garden.

supposed to be taken, for reasons of privacy or in order to delay the tea guests from entering the inner tea garden, a small, round boulder bound with a knotted string, rather like a small parcel, would be left in the middle of a paving stone. This would indicate to any visitors to the garden that the path was not yet meant to be used for crossing the space.

SAND AND GRAVEL

By the Kamakura period (1185–1392), when the first stroll gardens were constructed, garden paths were likely to have been laid with a mixture of compacted fine sand and a light grit surface, similar to the one used for ceremonies in the courtyards of Heian residences. Both materials are readily available today. Although gravel paths need maintenance, they are one of the easiest and cheapest means of providing an all-weather surface in gardens, particularly in rainy climates such as that of Japan. The paths need to be topped up occasionally with fresh gravel, weeded and then raked or brushed with bamboo brooms.

PAVING AND COBBLING

Whole paths are frequently made with randomly or formally arranged paving or cobbling. There are numerous designs to choose from, as shown on pages 126–127. The joints between the paving or cobbling are usually filled with compacted sharp sand, which is a good medium for the colonization of moss. If the moss is left uncontrolled in damp climates, it may grow until it almost envelops the surface; this is not always discouraged, because moss is both natural and beautiful.

In many Japanese gardens, the paths do become soft and mossy and this is a perfect surface to wander on. You can

fill the joints of paved areas with a soft cement mix (1 part cement to 12 parts sand) to give a firm binding but also grow less vigorous mosses and other plants. To exclude all vegetation between the joints, use a stronger mix (1 part cement to 6 parts sand).

DRAINAGE

Even on loose gravel paths, make allowance for the run-off of surface water. This is best done by creating a slight camber to the path, by sloping one side or raising the middle so that excess water can run off to one or both sides. This will be important on sloping paths, where heavy rain can cause erosion. On solid paved areas, provision may need to be made with land drains and soakaways, especially on poorly drained ground.

WIDTH OF PATHS

You can make gravel paths as little as 1m (1yd) in width, but bear in mind that only one person will be able to walk down the path at one time. If paths are too narrow, rain-soaked shrubs will wet you as you pass. If you want to be able to walk two abreast, the minimum path width should be 1.5m (5ft), though a more comfortable width for two people would be 2m (7ft), which will allow for plants that have grown over the sides of the paths.

Tea paths that are made of stepping stones are designed for one person to pass along them at a time. The width of such a path will depend on the design effect and how comfortable you want the path to feel. Some tea paths in Japan can be quite tricky to negotiate. This is a deliberate device, used to make the guest much more aware of each step they take. If you want to achieve a more relaxed stroll, then place the stones about 70–80cm (28–32in) apart. You can experiment with this spacing by marking out where each foot falls at your own natural pace.

It is difficult to make any stepping-stone path without the walker having to be aware of where their feet land, but if you make the joints between them quite tight, no more than 10cm (4in), and level with the height of the stone, the transition between each stone will be easier. Most stepping-stone paths are placed higher than the

Below: Small stepping stones sunk in a carpet of moss wander through this private garden in Ohara. The small symbolic "lantern" by the tree is made of stones piled up on top of each other.

KEY CONSIDERATIONS

Materials	Sand and gravel are commonly used but need careful solid edging. Alternatively use paving stones or cobbles and encourage moss to grow between the stones.
Drainage	All paths will need to be drained by shaping the path with a slight camber or slope.
Width	Bear in mind how many people will want to walk along the path together, and the direction and shape of the path.
Purpose and meaning	Some paths lead to a destination; some require the visitor to wander and pause to look at the view; others are for show, not for walking on. Make sure you have thought about the purpose and meaning of your path before you lay it out.

surrounding soil, but this will depend on how thick your stepping stones are. You may find it difficult to obtain random stones of the quality and thickness that you could find in Japan. The use of substitutes such as logs, or concrete logs with strips of bamboo, is fine as long as you keep them clean of slimy algae. All stepping stones, especially those that are sawn rather than riven, can become slippery, especially in shady gardens, so be prepared to clean them occasionally to reduce their slipperiness.

Path styles

To the Japanese, a path is not simply a way of moving around the garden without getting your shoes muddy – it is a precisely designed element of the garden that directs you to certain points, where the view is carefully constructed to be seen from that point. A path can be of great spiritual significance, as in the stepping-stone paths of the tea garden, symbolizing the progress of the spiritual seeker. There are three specific styles of path used by the Japanese: informal (*so*) paths, semi-formal (*gyo*) paths and formal (*shin*) paths.

Above: *This* shin *path uses formal paving blocks that are combined with a formal pattern. Moss is used to link the two elements.*

INFORMAL AND FORMAL STYLES

Around the turn of the 17th century there was a movement away from pure naturalism in the use of stone paths, and towards a greater emphasis on the design element. A greater freedom of expression allowed designers to use a variety of materials and patterns and to exhibit more formalism. While the original tea paths were laid out with a series of informal stepping stones, natural slabs of stone or buried boulders, later paths tended to blend in more formal shapes.

The Japanese expressions for the varying styles of path are *so* (informal), *gyo* (semi-formal) and *shin* (formal). This was linked to a social means of determining the level of formality for greeting people of varying status.

Stepping-stone paths were designed to unite separate parts of a garden, areas often with different atmospheres. The path may start near to the house, being set with formal paving or cobbling, and then launch off across a sea of sand before entering a more earthy and mossy "forest" area planted with maples and shrubs. In each case a different style of paving can be used.

Informal (*so*) paths

These are paths that may be made of rough, uncut stepping stones set in a weaving motion. It also applies to straight paths made up of random stones, without well-defined edges.

Semi-formal (*gyo*) paths

This mixing of the rough with the smooth, the informal with the formal, can be expressed in different ways. Square stepping stones can be set in the

Left: *An interrupted line of formal rectangular granite slabs helps to contain a* gyo *path of mixed natural cobbles and stones.*

Above: *These formal paving stones combine with an informal surround of other stones.*

Above: *This* gyo *path through a rock garden uses formal materials in an informal pattern.*

Above: *A* so *path through a bamboo grove uses informal materials and an informal pattern.*

same weaving motion as rough uncut stepping stones, but being of a formal shape they will give a different impression. Rectangular or square paving set out in this manner could flow through planted areas or across areas of moss or a sea of sand. Another mixture might use informal

random stones bordered by straight-edged granite setts or long strips of paving. Other semi-formal paths might have square forms with sections of informal cobbles, roofing tiles set on edge and natural paving. The use of old roof tiles, mill stones and reclaimed relics is seen as a sign of good taste.

Formal (*shin*) paths

These paths may be made of square paving, bordered by long, rectangular granite setts, or paved in random but rectilinear patterns. This kind of path will look quite familiar to the Western gardener as it is commonly used in terraces, patios and driveways.

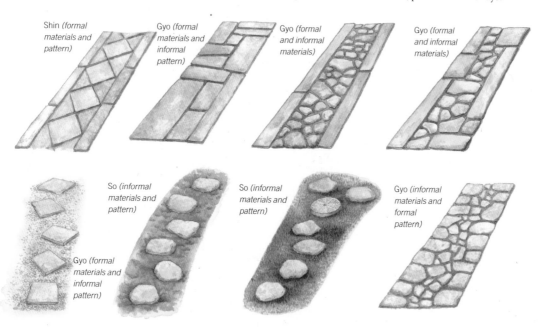

Shin *(formal materials and pattern)*

Gyo *(formal materials and informal pattern)*

Gyo *(formal and informal materials)*

Gyo *(formal and informal materials)*

Gyo *(formal materials and informal pattern)*

So *(informal materials and pattern)*

So *(informal materials and pattern)*

Gyo *(informal materials and formal pattern)*

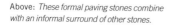

Tea houses & other buildings

Early Japanese gardens had Chinese-style viewing pavilions, designed to give a view of the pond and garden, often built at the end of a long covered corridor that was open to the sides. The introduction in the 16th century of the unique Japanese tea house would come to influence the style and character of Japanese garden buildings to the present day. Apart from the traditional tea house, other buildings can also be a feature of the Japanese garden, such as small pavilions and arbours surrounded by plants with a place to sit and look at the view.

Above: *Wisteria-covered arbours are popular in Japanese gardens. They are simple constructions of robust timbers to carry the weighty stems of wisteria, with very little, if any, ornamentation.*

THE JAPANESE TEA HOUSE

The tea house was originally conceived by the Japanese as "a mountain place in the city", and it was often built as a rustic hut that was thatched with grass, but later became increasingly sophisticated in design. Originally, the tea house was the place to which the tea garden path led, and it was a place of reverence and social intercourse; it was not a place from which to view the garden. However, by the 17th century, especially in the exquisite gardens of the Katsura Palace in Kyoto, the tea house had opened up its sides and front so that its visitors could look out over the new pond and stroll gardens.

If you want to build a tea house in your garden, then you can easily create a structure that can be used as an outdoor room, but still retains the key elements of the ancient style. Paying close attention to the design of the building and the materials will give your tea house an undeniable air of authenticity.

TEA HOUSE COMPONENTS

All the materials you might need to build a tea house are readily available. The main elements are:

• a mixture of natural raw materials blended with finely planed, high-quality timber;

• a floor consisting of a layer of straw mats (tatami) bordered by fabric;

• the supports for the buildings might be made using the whole trunks of small trees with the bark left on;

• the walls are often finished with plaster, lined with bamboo strips, or painted in weathered gold and pale blue.

Left: *This unusual tea house was shipped from Japan to the English garden of Heale House in the early 1900s, where it stands on stone pillars so that it can straddle a stream.*

TEA HOUSE INTERIORS

The essential elements of tea house interiors typically include the entrance hatch, which in 16th-century tea houses was a small 76cm (2½ft) square sliding-door hatch, so that guests were forced to enter on their knees and demonstrate a suitable level of respect for the ceremony to come. Other window-like openings are often round, like the moon, or rectilinear with sliding rice-paper panels. There is often a sunken hearth for heating the tea water, which is placed off-centre. Calligraphic scrolls might hang in a special alcove (*tokonoma*) in the back wall. There might also be a vase containing a simple, seasonal, "country-style" flower arrangement.

You may not wish to go to the trouble of building a sunken hearth in your tea house, but even if you are simply using the tea house as an outdoor shelter or gazebo, you might still include some classic Japanese design features to give the structure an air of authenticity. There is nothing ostentatious whatsoever about these tea houses, and they blend beautifully into the landscape.

OTHER BUILDINGS

Different types of building might include a small open-fronted waiting room, similar to a rustic shelter with benches, where guests can relax before being invited by the host to proceed to the tea house. There might also be outside toilets for a tea garden built in a similar style to that of the tea house. Raised boarded walkways are also

common in stroll gardens, used for viewing the cherry blossom, and these could lead to a thatched pavilion. You might find umbrella-shaped arbours, with a single pillar supporting a circular or square thatched roof, for viewing the garden, or Chinese-style hexagonal shelters, similar to modern Western gazebos. In and around such a shelter were often portable benches and tables, some in the style of Chinese porcelain tubs. These arbours and pavilions are often placed in more prominent places than tea houses, such as on a hill crest or other vantage point.

In some ancient gardens, the contrast of bright red paper umbrellas over tables draped in red cloth, set against dark green evergreen trees and shrubs, can be quite startling, an approach that would even suit a contemporary Japanese garden.

Above right: The waiting room alongside the tea path is often of the simplest design, such as this one at Newstead Abbey, England.

Right: A Japanese tea house gets an English touch in the form of a wicker chair. The Japanese usually sit directly on tatami mats.

Far right: The interior of a tea house at Toji-in. The materials are natural and simple, but the craftsmanship is detailed and refined.

Boundaries

Ever since Heian times (794–1185), when the city of Kyoto was laid out on a strict grid system, Japanese gardens have invariably had distinctive boundaries. This approach did not really change until the Edo period (1603–1867), when gardens became large enough for their perimeters to be of secondary importance to the overall design. Now that the average garden is fairly small, the walls, fences and hedges have once again become an important element in the design, and are made to be admired.

WALLS

The outer boundary walls of large houses and temple gardens that were constructed before the Edo period were designed as a reflection of the architecture of the buildings. They also became an important backdrop and could be seen from within the garden. These boundary walls were often built of clay and tiles, and were usually neatly plastered. With a stout wooden framework and bracket as a cornice, they were usually crowned with ornamental tiling, although they were sometimes thatched on the top with a ridge of protective tiles.

These walls were rather grand structures, suited to palaces and temples, but smaller residences used many of the same techniques and materials. Modern brick and stone were used more rarely in traditional Japanese gardens, although many garden boundaries on slopes were supported by stone retaining walls, sometimes with azaleas growing in their crevices. Incidentally, internal walls around courtyards were often kept lower than perimeter walls, giving views of trees or distant hills.

Walls in Japanese gardens tend not to be used for growing exotic plants or fruits, as they are in Western gardens. When climbing plants are grown, in large and small gardens, they are allowed to twine through light bamboo trellising.

If you would like to give a Japanese look to conventional brick or concrete block walls, including walls around a courtyard or Zen-style dry garden, the careful use of plaster, paint and some timber uprights at intervals can be effective. Top with large reclaimed or new terracotta pantiles for an authentic finish.

FENCES

Beyond the practicalities of privacy and security, fences were, and still are, considered an important garden feature. In the use of bamboo, in particular, the Japanese have excelled in their inventiveness. An ornate bamboo fence may be woven into wonderful patterns,

Left: *The wall surrounding the garden amid the sweeping roofs of the temple of Tofuku-ji is an intrinsic part of the overall design, with its vertical blackened timber supports and heavily tiled coping.*

Above: *The use of vertical boarding is generally seen as aesthetically the most pleasing and is very practical when changes of ground level require adjustments in the levels of a wall or fence.*

Left: *Vertical bands of reeds seem to mimic the trunks of the trees in this elegant bamboo fence found in the Nanzen-in temple, in Kyoto. The use of raw natural materials such as unpainted wood or bamboo allows a boundary fence to merge with the trees beyond.*

Below: *Horizontal bands of split bamboo, tied to the main fence with black jute, add strength and beauty to this fence. The Japanese use these bands to create many different designs.*

bundled together, tied with jute, or combined with branches, twigs, thatch or bundles of reeds, to flow alongside a path or to help direct the way.

Generally, timber fences are left raw and unpainted. At their most rustic, planks might be old and weathered or sometimes deliberately chiselled and charred to give an instantly distressed and aged effect.

A hybrid between a fence and a wall is the wattle-and-daub fence. The upright support timbers are often left exposed and stained black. Posts with horizontal, vertical or even angled boarding are also used, sometimes with the boards staggered to allow air and light through and occasionally with gaps that are wide enough to allow visitors to peep out.

Japanese bamboo fences can be expensive to buy or build but you can make suitable and more affordable fences using simple methods. Try rolls of bamboo tied to posts, and add superficial framing with other materials such as timber or pine. If you are unable to find authentic fencing for a traditional Japanese tea garden or pond garden, you can use willow or hazel hurdles, chestnut paling or rustic pole fencing. These alternative fencing materials are usually available from larger garden centres and fencing specialists, the latter often providing an on-site construction service if you require it.

SLEEVE FENCES (*SODE-GAKI*)

These are screens of bamboo and reeds that were, and still are, used for two reasons: firstly to deflect the view to another part of the garden, and secondly to create privacy. This is often the case in Japanese restaurants, where guests do not want to be aware of other diners, yet still wish to have a view of the garden, usually a courtyard (*tsuboniwa*). Sleeve fences are usually about 2m (6½ft) high by 1m (1yd) wide, often curved at shoulder level and pierced by an aperture. They come in different designs, from rustic to more formal, and work well in modern gardens.

Above: *A granite water basin and an artificial bamboo fence constructed in a fan shape with jute ties. There is also a Donald Duck figure, a popular feature in contemporary Japan.*

Below: *This main entrance gate to the Huntington Botanical Gardens needs to be secure so is built of more substantial materials such as timber and roofing tiles.*

Above: *Sleeve fences are a classic feature used to frame a view.*

Above right: *A bamboo panel tied with jute is framed between two branches. At the step, guests remove their shoes before entering the tea house.*

Above far right: *Brushwood, reeds and bamboo are combined in this sleeve fence.*

Below right: *These bamboo fence posts tied with jute give a dense, yet informal, barrier to this entrance gateway.*

TREATING NATURAL MATERIALS

The Japanese tend to leave fences unpainted to retain their natural look:

• achieve a blackened effect with several coats of dark wood stain;

• treat the base of posts that go into the ground with wood preservative;

• bamboo fences last longer painted with a layer of matt varnish diluted with white spirit;

• wooden fences can be preserved using linseed oil or oil-based stains.

SCREENS

Western-style brick walls, fence panels, wooden sheds and outbuildings can be camouflaged or blended into your Japanese garden by fixing on bamboo roll or other screening materials such as the darker, more rustic-looking heather screening. Rigid panels, made of framed sections of split bamboo, heather or willow, are also available to conceal pre-existing buildings.

Traditional Japanese screens, including curved sleeve or wing panels, come in a wide variety of designs made from bamboo or brushwood 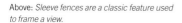 and feature many different knotting patterns and styles of construction. For more contemporary settings, plain square trellis panels, either bought off the peg or constructed from pressure-treated roofing laths, can also be used for creating screens and divides. By making trellises you can customize the panels to be more Japanese looking than the standard models that are available from garden centres and fencing specialists. Paint or stain them black and, for privacy, attach bamboo, heather or brushwood roll to the back using an industrial staple gun.

Except perhaps in the case of contemporary Japanese gardens, one desirable feature is that any constructions look attractively weathered even when relatively new. Though bamboo tends to take a couple of years to fade and lose its sheen, after washing and rubbing down it can be treated with stains, oils, waxes or varnish as required. Bamboo can also be effectively "aged" and blackened using a gas blowtorch.

HEDGES

Japanese box hedges (*Buxus microphylla*), evergreen oak (*Quercus ilex*), Japanese cedar (*Cryptomeria*), photinia and podocarpus are common. Where they thin near their base, they may be backed by bamboo fencing.

Japanese hedges are almost always evergreen, so plant a mixture for a varied texture. Camellias and other flowering plants can be used, especially the autumn-flowering *Camellia sasanqua*.

WATER AND PATH EDGINGS

Although on a smaller scale, these boundaries are also important in the Japanese garden, both practically and aesthetically. Water features and pathways will always benefit from neat but natural-looking edging. This approach is practical too, as a firm edge will help to retain and strengthen pond banks and define areas of gravel and other loose material. If you are making pond edgings, or outlining paths and raised beds, use lines of tanalized or pressure-treated logs or rounded posts set in a bed of concrete to hold them rigid. The advantage of this approach is that this edging is 100 per cent flexible, creating curves and following the rise and fall of the land as required.

GATES

Often at the main entrance to the garden, the gate is the threshold between the busy outside world and the calm and tranquil mood of the garden beyond.

The entry gate to a Japanese garden is often a low wooden structure with a roof. This has a humbling effect reminding visitors of their stature in comparison with the space they are about to enter. It may be simply an opening in the wall or fence or a hinged structure often made from latticed bamboo. Particular attention is given to the floor of the entry gate. Stones are carefully selected for this area and positioned with much care.

A classic *Torii* gate, consisting of two vertical posts joined with a double crossbar and often painted red, may be used to indicate that you are entering a sacred space.

can be found on the internet, through mail order firms advertising in specialist directories and in the classified sections of home and garden magazines.

In addition, a number of companies outside Japan manufacture structures either to catalogue specifications or as bespoke items. The best of these use traditional materials and methods such as split bamboo and black hemp for tying and knotting.

DO IT YOURSELF

If you like the idea of having your own construction project, build or adapt screens, fences and walls using a variety of raw materials. There are mail order and internet supply companies selling the basic materials, from bamboo poles to lengths of split bamboo and wooden roof shingles.

Gates were very popular in tea gardens, developing their most elaborate and ritualistic style by the early 17th century. The traditional tea garden is often divided into two or even three parts: an inner, middle and outer garden, linked by a *roji* (dewy path), featuring specially designed gates opening into each area.

The main entrance gate (*roji-mon*) may be a large tile-covered gatehouse or a simple thatch-covered bamboo gate. The second gate into the middle or inner *roji* might be a small crawl-through opening or stooping gate (*naka-kuguri*). One type has a door that is hinged at the top so that the guest has to push it forward and up to get through, being forced to bow in the process. This can be propped open.

You can simulate this effect with a series of sections, each with their own entrance, to enhance the feeling of deference as you approach the tea house, and give the garden authenticity.

You can buy ready-made Japanese gates, or make your own from natural materials, using a simple shape hinged at the side or top.

READY-MADE STRUCTURES

A wide range of traditional Japanese structures are available direct from Japan or through specialist importers. These include garden screens, fence panels and roofed gateways. Details

Right: *This gateway, with its thatched roof, is a symbolic statement as well as a physical entrance to the tea garden at Nijo castle. Such roofs can also be finished with wooden shingles.*

Making a tea-path gate

Small lattice bamboo gates are very lightweight and are easy to install. Gates are very common features throughout Japanese gardens, from the main entrance to key points within the garden or along the tea path. The gates that are sited on the tea path itself are often not meant to keep people or animals out of the garden, but are more of a symbolic feature, for example the middle crawl-through gate (see also page 178). In the case of the tea-path gate, it is quite usual for the gate to be found standing alone with no fence on either side of it.

Above: The semi-transparent nature of this jute-tied bamboo trellis gate gives a light and airy feel to a garden.

The simple design of this gate gives the garden an airy feel, especially when associated with live bamboo plants, maples and glossy evergreens, the kind of plants that you would find in a tea garden.

This system for hanging a gate is only suitable for very lightweight gates that are made of bamboo or light wood, as we have used light posts and heavy twine for the top hinge. For heavier gates, you will need to use stronger posts and a hinge at both top and bottom, but the methods of measuring and levelling will be the same. This bamboo gate is also hinged in such a way that gravity will ensure that the gate naturally swings to a close behind you.

As the gate is merely symbolic and not designed to be child or animal safe there is no latch, but a loop of twine could easily be attached to the top of the gate to keep it firmly shut.

You will need
- a lightweight lattice bamboo gate
- 2 x 7.5cm (3in) round softwood gateposts, ideally pressure treated or with wood preservative on the base
- an L-shaped gate hinge with a pin that will fit inside the bamboo frame
- a short length of black jute or nylon rope
- a hammer
- a crowbar
- a small sledgehammer
- a spirit level
- a hand saw
- dark ash black wood stain and a paintbrush (optional)
- an electric drill or hand wood drill

1 Having chosen the site, you must decide which way the gate will open and on which side the hinge should be. Now make the first hole for the post that the gate will hang on. This needs to be deeper than the "receiving" post. Prepare the hole with a crowbar, to a depth of at least 30cm (12in).

2 Prepare both posts for the gate by staining them, if you like, and making sure that the part below the ground is protected with wood preservative. Place the hinge post in the hole and check by eye that it is more or less vertical. If you have an assistant, ask them to hold the hinge post while you knock it into the ground with a sledgehammer. It is a good idea to protect the top of the post with a block of wood to prevent the top of the post from being damaged by the sledgehammer.

3 Using a spirit level, check that the post is upright. Check the distance to the other post by laying the gate in place. The receiving post can be at a slighter narrower width than the gate so that the gate will lean against it when closed. Prepare the second post hole with the crowbar and knock in the receiving post.

4 It is better that your posts are set a little too high, so that you can cut them off to the right height. The tops of the posts should line up with the top of the gate or can be slightly higher. Using a spirit level, check that the two posts are level with each other. If they need to be cut, mark the cutting line.

5 Cut off the tops of the posts with a wood saw if necessary to ensure they are level. If you have stained the post to give it the blackened and charred look that the Japanese love to create, you will need to paint some more wood stain on to the cut surface at the top.

6 Check the height of the gate against the post, positioning it so that the bottom of the gate will hang just off the ground, clearing any stones or paving slabs. Mark on the hinge post where the bottom hinge needs to be.

7 Select a drill-bit slightly smaller than the diameter of the hinge. Drill to the depth needed. Alternatively you can buy a hinge with a flat plate that can be drilled directly on to the side of the post.

8 Knock the hinge in firmly with a hammer. Drop the gate on to the hinge and tie a piece of black jute in a figure of eight around the post near the top. You may need to adjust this until the gate hangs and swings comfortably.

9 The gate can now swing until it just touches the side of the receiving post. If the gate hangs well, you may not need to secure it, but another loop of jute could be used to secure the gate to the receiving post.

Right: *The gate acts as a transition into the inner* roji *of a tea garden with its* tsukubai *arrangement of lantern and water basin.*

Bridges

Always a dominant feature, bridges tend to be particularly associated with Japanese gardens. One of the most well known is the Chinese-style bridge (*sori-hashi*), lavishly ornamented, high-arched and lacquered red or orange. While the islands in a pond represented the abodes of the immortals, bridges symbolized the crossing over to that world. These red-painted bridges are often closely associated with Japanese gardens in the Western mind, but they are in fact rarer in authentic designs than those made of more natural materials and unpainted wood.

Above: *A moss-covered log bridge in the gardens of Saiho-ji, the Moss Temple in Kyoto, where over 60 species of moss are said to grow.*

STYLES OF BRIDGE

In the garden of the Tenryu-ji, built in the 14th century, a Chinese-style, curved red wooden bridge was replaced by a series of flat, natural stone slabs, propped up on rock pillars. Later gardens used single pieces of wrought granite, supported by granite piles. Some of these granite slabs were carved with a gentle curve. This was the dominant style of Japanese bridges until Chinese high-arched bridges returned to favour in the Edo period (1603–1867). These semicircular bridges, known as full-moon bridges because their reflections in the water make up a complete circle, are so steep that the only way to cross over them is by means of steps going up one side and down the other.

YATSUHASHI BRIDGES

Especially designed for viewing iris beds, the *yatsuhashi* style of bridge, which is still popular today, is constructed from a series of single horizontal planks, which are supported by short wooden piles that are driven into the mud at the head of the pond, where the Japanese love to grow beds of irises. The planks cross the swampy beds in a zigzag fashion, forcing the visitor to loiter, watch the fish and admire the flowers. This simple style of bridge can easily be incorporated into today's Japanese garden, perhaps designed to sit in a boggy area in which moisture-loving plants such as irises and sedges can be grown. See overleaf for instructions for making a *yatsuhashi* bridge.

WATTLE AND LOG BRIDGES

Bridges were also often made from wattle (woven branches) then covered in earth, or from batches of logs bundled and laid across a timber frame and then covered with earth and gravel. These were designed more for effect because they were fairly fragile, and did not usually feature a hand-rail. Those that link up the islands at the famous Moss Temple, in Kyoto, for example, are quite rotten, but they blend in with the deep shady mystery of the garden. If you want to construct this type of bridge, consider how long you want it to last and whether the logs should be treated in order to improve their longevity. Nowadays, wattle is not easily available, so it is best to use bundles of logs that have been coated in a wood preservative, or use a good hardwood, such as oak, which needs no treatment.

WISTERIA BRIDGES

Sturdy wooden bridges with a trellised canopy to carry twining wisterias are popular in Japan. This style of bridge was immortalized by Monet in his

Left: *This style of red-painted bridge, seen here in the gardens at Heale House in England, is Chinese in origin, and became popular in Japan in the Edo period.*

paintings of his garden at Giverny, in France. The effect of the long racemes of the Japanese wisteria (*Wisteria floribunda*) is doubled when they are reflected in the water, and cascades of wisteria flowers create a shady, scented walkway to stroll on.

STEPPING-STONE BRIDGES
These bridges can be made of recycled pillars or natural rocks. Like the *yatsuhashi*, the stones zigzag across the water instead of taking a straight line, offering a variety of views as you cross streams, inlets and ponds, and possibly echoing the wandering nature of the path it joins at either end. If you

are lucky enough to have a large garden with an expanse of water, a stepping-stone bridge would make a delightful feature.

Top: *This massive curving slab of schist in the grounds of Nijo castle is a symbol of strength. The original garden was thought to have been designed as a dry garden with no water at all.*

Above: *Another style of bridge, borrowed from China. The high arch allows the passage of boats underneath but the sides are so steep they require steps to cross over them.*

Right: *This stepping-stone bridge in the garden of Tenju-an is made of unusually shaped piers – possibly recycled temple-pillar bases.*

Making a *yatsuhashi* bridge

The *yatsuhashi* bridge is a popular form in Japanese gardens. The origin of the name *yatsuhashi* is a poetic reference to a timber bridge made of eight planks that zigzag across a river. The idea is to delight the eye of visitors to the garden with unexpected sights as they make their way over the bridge and across a pond or swampy area filled with flowers. It should also encourage them to linger and admire an unexpected aspect of the garden. A *yatsuhashi* bridge is relatively simple to construct, as it requires only a few posts and planks.

This unique kind of bridge is mostly found in gardens where the inlet of a stream flows into a pond, or any other area that is similarly ideal for the growing of the Japanese water iris (*Iris ensata*). *Yatsuhashi* bridges do not have to have eight planks – they can be made up of as few as two planks, and whatever their size, they are an excellent addition to any small or large pond or stroll gardens. In some cases the device can simply be a design that is viewed but not actually used to walk on.

When constructing the bridge, make sure that your measurements are accurate, so the planks will be level. If possible, drain the pond water first.

Above: *Although appearing to be complex in design, the actual construction of a* yatsuhashi *bridge is relatively simple.*

If you cannot drain the pond or other water feature, it is still possible to construct a bridge but you may need to get professional help as setting the posts into water can present problems.

You will need
- planks or boards at least 5cm (2in) thick – the number and length of planks and posts will be determined by the span and depth of water you are working with, and the width of the planks can also be variable
- supporting posts, 7.5cm (3in) square or round
- cross beams, 7.5cm (3in) deep x 5cm (2in) thick – the length of these will be determined by the width of the planks
- bolts, minimum 1cm (½in) wide by 15cm (6in) long
- an electric drill with wood bits
- cement and concreting sand/aggregate
- metal post holders (for a butyl-lined pond)
- a shovel
- a spade
- a crowbar
- a coarse-toothed wood-saw
- a sledgehammer if you are driving posts into the ground or a clay-lined pond

POSITIONING YOUR BRIDGE

When considering the design of your *yatsuhashi* bridge, use the angles to encourage the garden visitor to take in varying views. You may even place a bench at a strategic position on the bridge.

1 Measure the exact span for the bridge and make a sketch of how many planks will be needed to cross your inlet, iris bed or pond, and the length of the planks. The directional changes do not have to be at 90 degrees – they can be at even sharper angles.

2 Measure how deep the water is at different points to calculate how many posts you need and how long they should be.

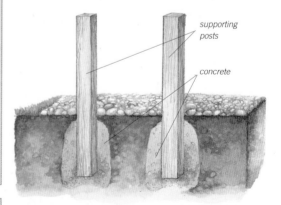

supporting posts

concrete

3 Start on dry land by setting two posts in the ground exactly the width of one plank apart, or two plank widths if you are laying two planks side by side. The posts need to be dug into the ground to a depth of 45–60cm (18–24in) and their bases set in two or three shovelfuls of concrete (1 part cement to 6 parts concreting sand or aggregate). If the first set of posts will be in the water, follow step 7 opposite.

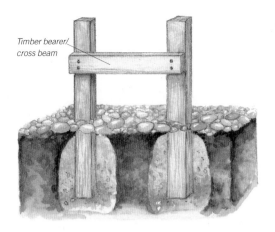

Timber bearer/ cross beam

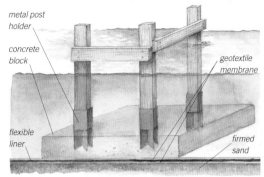

metal post holder

concrete block

flexible liner

geotextile membrane

firmed sand

4 Measure how high you want the bridge to be off the ground and make a mark on one of the posts. With a spirit level, mark across to the other post. Attach the cross beam on to the posts using bolts. Stout screws may suffice but bolts will be stronger and last longer. The first set of planks may overlap these first posts by up to 30cm (12in).

5 Drain off the water if possible, as this makes it much easier to construct the bridge. Driving posts into the clay base or mixing cement directly into water is very tricky and unreliable.

6 Measure across to where the next set of posts will stand. The first set of planks will overlap the second set of posts by the width of a plank, as the next set of planks will lie over the top of the first.

7 The second set of posts may be dug or driven directly into the base of a clay-lined pool, but in a pool with a butyl liner, they will need to sit in post holders and be set in a concrete base (1 part cement to 5 parts concreting sand). You can use fast-setting concrete that is specially designed for posts and will set in less than 15 minutes.

8 Leave the concrete to set for at least a day before laying the planks and two days before you walk on them. You only need three posts at each junction, but four will make the bridge more stable. If you prefer the look of three posts, include a fourth one for strength and trim it off flush to the top of the cross beam. Attach cross beams as in step 4 and continue one set of posts at a time, testing them for measurements as you go. On the far side you may need another pair of posts on dry land.

Below: A yatsuhashi *bridge of planks, resting on wooden piles, staggers past baskets of irises towards an impressive stand of cycads.*

Decorative artefacts

The addition of objects without any useful function is generally avoided in Japanese gardens. The garden is regarded as a completely integrated composition, and the introduction of unnecessary features can destroy the unity of the design. Many Japanese garden designs are either inspired by nature or reproduce famous views; they avoid distractions that might divert the eye from reading the composition as a whole. However, the useful objects such as water basins and lanterns that are found in gardens can be beautiful in their own right.

Above: *A pagoda stands in the middle of an island in the gardens of the Golden Pavilion (Kinkaku-ji), in Kyoto.*

In the Japanese garden, specimen plants, focal points, sculptures and statues are usually shunned, as are overt colour schemes, textural combinations, surprise effects and most of the elements that are the bedrock of many Western gardens.

This general emphasis still accommodates the more focused effect of sculptural forms with a religious connotation. These include garden stupas, pagodas, water basins, lanterns, or images of the Buddha. Although these artefacts are still integral to modern Japanese gardens, their religious significance can be more diluted.

PAGODAS AND STUPAS

These are structures of the Buddhist treasure houses where relics and scriptures were stored to commemorate a saint. Like lanterns, they were found close to temples, but when used in the garden they do not dominate because they are such familiar images that they readily blend into the scene. Indeed, both pagodas and stupas represent very recognizable features, from a Western viewpoint, of the Japanese garden and what it should contain.

WATER DEVICES

There are one or two playful devices found in Japanese gardens that recall a distant rural past. Deer scarers (*shishi-odoshi*) are the best known of these. They use water to make a noise intended to startle any deer feeding on plants in the garden (see page 116). A more unusual device is the *sui-kinkutsu* (see page 117). It literally

Left: *Carved reliefs and sculptures of the Buddha are sometimes placed in gardens, as many gardens are inspired by the philosophy of Zen Buddhism.*

Above left: *Many temple-style lanterns still carry Buddhist motifs, such as this one crowned with a lotus bud.*

Above centre: *Organic rock forms can be layered on each other to create a lantern shape. These naturalistic forms can add an unusually animistic quality to a garden.*

Above right: *The valley lantern has been specially designed to place by the water's edge where the light from the lamp, usually an oil wick, can be seen to reflect in the water.*

Left: *The introduction of the stone lantern into Japanese gardens came through the development of the tea garden, where they were used to light the path (roji) and water basins.*

Below: *Short and stocky lanterns are often placed near water or at the end of gravel spits to evoke lighthouses.*

STYLES OF LANTERN

Lanterns play such a large part in Japanese gardens that long ago they were classified into different types. Some were named after famous tea masters or gardens; the most well known and popular of these is the Oribe lantern. Oribe was an eccentric samurai tea master active at the end of the 17th century. The Oribe lantern often has a Buddha carved on the front of the pillar base. In some gardens this image was disguised and purported to be of the Virgin Mary, an image that was banned after the Christian

Above: There are many styles of Japanese stone lantern. This is a kodal rokkaku.

Westerners were evicted from Japan in the 17th century. The Oribe lantern is easy to install (see pages 184–5). Taller and statuesque lanterns such as the Kasuga sit on a round plinth, some of them with elaborate carvings of lotus petals. More squat stone lanterns and low lanterns that rest on a tripod or four feet are often placed by the sides of ponds.

In gardens with ponds designed to include a symbolic reproduction of the Amanohashidate Peninsula, a famous scenic spot on the northern coast of Honshu, a lantern is usually placed at the gravelled promontory. This is a classic example of *shakkei*, a small-scale version of real scenes or objects. Some of these poolside lanterns are designed to look especially beautiful when covered in snow, a regular feature of the Japanese winter.

Although most lanterns are made of stone, some are also made of wood and thatched with reed. Hanging lanterns made of bronze are also popular and can easily be moved around, hung from a tree or simply placed on a rock.

TSUKUBAI ARRANGEMENTS

The most popular way to use lanterns is as part of a *tsukubai* water feature in tea gardens (see pages 182–3), a

Above left: In some Japanese gardens, lanterns are the only architectural artefacts to be found. Most are never lit, but this one is. Rice-paper panels diffuse the light from the lit oiled paper.

Above: Lanterns were often designed to look dramatic within the larger landscape – this one is majestically placed within a pond.

classic arrangement that consists of a lantern placed near a water basin, with one or two paving stones in a sea of gravel at the base, and surrounded by ferns, camellias and sedges. Versions of *tsukubai* arrangements can also be found in courtyard gardens or along passages that lead to the front doors of houses and restaurant entrances. These often include a backing piece of bamboo fence, a water basin, and a pine or maple tree to provide shade and promote the growth of moss.

CONTEMPORARY USE OF LIGHTING

In the Muromachi and Momoyama periods, special platforms and gardens were made for "viewing the moon". Moonlight was especially revered and was considered to be at its most moving when seen across a dry garden. These days in Kyoto, many of the most popular gardens are open during the autumn months at night, when artificial lighting is laid out to highlight the main buildings, the reflections of water and the autumn colours of the maples. Modern dry gardens can also be lit in a surprisingly adventurous manner.

As traditional lanterns give off very little light, in a contemporary Japanese garden electric lighting could be used effectively. Low-voltage and wattage systems that are cheap to install and run are ideal. Many of the traditional stone lanterns and other Japanese-style garden lights that you can buy today can be fitted with low-voltage electric light. Another way to supplement the meagre light is to hang bronze lanterns or hurricane lamps from trees or posts.

In naturalistic Japanese gardens, small black uplighters are used to light rocks, plants and ornamental features. Other kinds of low-level lighting can be installed to illuminate a pathway or steps, and in decked areas, small LED or halogen lights can be recessed into the wood to great effect. Low-voltage garden lighting sets running off a transformer are relatively easy to install. Not connected directly to the mains supply, the cabling can lie close to the surface and does not have to be buried in armoured ducting, though great care must be taken to hide the fittings and wires so that they are not visible during the day, as this would spoil the romantic effect. It is advisable to use an electrical contractor to install lighting projects, however, and you must fit residual current devices, or circuit breakers, as a safety measure.

Right: *A low-level wall light is discreet and effective. Such lights can be fitted to help light the way to a door or gate.*

Far right: *LED uplighters can be set into wooden decking or into pathways that are paved with setts.*

CREATING A GARDEN

Japanese gardens will always include a selection of the classic components that we have so far encountered. When it comes to planning your own garden, start on an achievable scale. Choose either to plan a small garden, or focus on a specific area in a more spacious garden, the rest of which can be developed over time.

After an outline of how to plan a garden design, this chapter looks at the five main garden types – pond gardens, dry gardens, tea gardens, stroll gardens and courtyard gardens. Each section explains the style and presents a colour plan showing the typical elements. This is followed by a design proposal for a garden in this style. Three practical sequences showing the three stages for each one then show how to bring the design to fruition. Some of the features, such as constructing a pine island, involve detailed planning and logistics; others, such as setting a lantern or laying a paving stone path, are relatively simple. They can all be adapted to the requirements of individual schemes, and many can be used within other garden styles.

Above: *A "hillside" of clipped azaleas at Sanzen-in, Ohara.*
Left: *A turtle island in Huntington Botanical Gardens, Los Angeles.*

Making a plan

Once you have decided on the style of garden you want to make, taking into consideration all the criteria of space, type of site and natural features, you will need to make a rough plan of the layout. This need not be too sophisticated, but it should be accurate enough for you to position any pool or any new trees, for instance, in relation to existing items such as buildings, walls, trees and slopes. It is worth measuring the site as accurately as you can and making a sketch of your plan from various viewpoints, especially if the site is not flat.

Above: *Measurements need to be taken with some precision, especially when calculating pond levels and drainage requirements.*

WHAT TO INCLUDE IN YOUR PLAN

If you are planning to make new water features on different levels, and are considering the fall of water for waterfalls and streams and any drainage that may be required, you will need to take some fairly accurate levels. This can be done using a spirit level placed on a long straight board, which will be accurate enough for most of your requirements. Knowing the levels at different points in the garden is especially important with water features but will also help with your overall design. When you are preparing your plan, make sure that you include all of the features mentioned below before you even begin to consider anything exciting like future planting. It might seem laborious, but it will definitely be worth it in the end. Japanese garden designers pay special attention to detail, scale, viewing angles and ways of framing those views from different vantage points.

CHECKLIST FOR YOUR PLAN

Marking the features identified in the plan shown here will allow you to see the areas that might be problematic for planting (those in shade, those with underground service supplies and those in windy areas, for example) while identifying where you definitely do want plants (such as places in sun and those that can be appreciated from the windows of the house). Only when you have identified all the existing characteristics of your garden will you be in a position to get down to the creative planning.

Orientation
It is important that you do not forget to mark the position of the sun in relation to your garden, as this may affect the placing of plants.

Utilities
Identify and mark the position of all underground services, such as water pipes, gas pipes, electric cables, drains, sewer pipes and manhole covers. If you

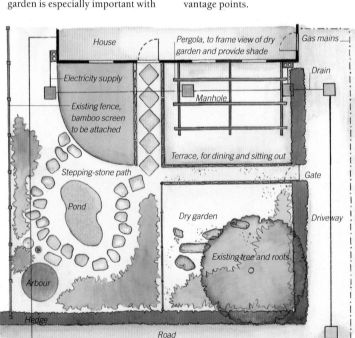

House

Pergola, to frame view of dry garden and provide shade

Gas mains

Drain

Electricity supply

Manhole

Existing fence, bamboo screen to be attached

Terrace, for dining and sitting out

Stepping-stone path

Gate

Pond

Dry garden

Driveway

Existing tree and roots

Arbour

Hedge

Road

Left: *Before you plan your garden you must familiarize yourself with the location of all the utilities. Your garden design should keep them accessible and prevent them from being damaged by excavations.*

are planning to excavate a pond, you should avoid these rather than have them diverted. Most of them are deeper than the average depth of an ornamental pond, but do not assume that this is the case. If you have no idea where they are, contact the utility company involved, which will have the equipment to trace the route of its pipes if no plan exists.

Trees

The position of existing trees will affect the siting of a pond or any new plantings owing to the shade they cast, the extent of their roots and their falling leaves. The leaves of some trees, such as yew, release toxins if they accumulate in water, so avoid placing a pond near such trees. Some trees, such as birch, rowan and pine, produce only light shade, but many, including beech, sycamore and horse chestnut cast dense shade, and any area under them that is in shade constantly, rather than for just a small part of the day, should be marked on the plan.

Boundaries, outbuildings and viewing points

Walls and fences, as well as outbuildings such as sheds and garages, should be marked on the plan because they, too, will cast shade. They also cause eddies of wind, which gust around the walls on an exposed site. The main ground-floor viewing windows are most important to include on your plan because they will help to identify view lines. Doors inevitably mean paths to various points, and in a new garden it is important to establish the route of paths early on in the planning process.

Wind tunnels

Suburban gardens are notorious for having wind tunnels between buildings and fences. Even if you cannot entirely avoid a wind tunnel, you can plant windbreaks or erect trellises in order to filter the wind.

Filtered wind, such as that which occurs in the area behind a hedge or trellis, causes much less damage than eddying wind on the leeward side of a solid barrier. In fact, wind strength will still be greatly reduced some distance away from a trellis – so it is actually a better, and usually cheaper, shelter option than building a wall or fence.

Top: *You can use spray marker paint or a trail of powdered lime to mark out the principal design outlines in your garden. Be sure that you plan a logical sequence of tasks, so that any heavy or disruptive work will not disturb plantings.*

Above: *Turfing should be left until last, as new turf should not be walked on for several weeks after it has been laid. Any loose stones and building rubble should be raked off the surface of the ground prior to turf laying.*

The pond garden style

Starting with the very earliest gardens influenced by the Chinese and developing over the centuries to the most up-to-date designs, pond gardens have always been enormously popular in Japan. The pond will, naturally, be the central feature, and should ideally be big enough for you to incorporate an island or two, and, for greater authenticity, to make a ride in a small rowing boat possible. For this you will need space – it is obviously not suitable for a small town garden – as well as the time and energy to plan on a large scale.

ELEMENTS OF A POND GARDEN

The pond gardens of Japan were originally found only in city complexes. Despite being surrounded by buildings, these gardens were very naturalistic and much less stylized than the later stroll gardens. Ponds (with pine islands) and streams are the main features, along with naturalistic planting and a strolling path.

Pond

The edges of the pond should have a varied and natural outline resembling a coastline, with coves, grotto-like caves and beaches. Rocks can be placed at the edges of ponds and by waterfalls so long as their shape is considered carefully, and also in the water, where they can be used as stepping stones or supports for naturalistic bridges.

Above: *At the Heian shrine, in Kyoto, the staggered stepping stones are made of recycled bridge piers and temple column bases. Borrowing old architectural fragments is known as* mitate *("to see anew").*

Below: *Chinese-style red-painted bridges, such as this one at the Tully Japanese Garden in Ireland, were popular in the early days of Japanese gardens of the Heian period. They were also used extensively in later Edo gardens and copied in Western versions.*

Island

There are many styles of island to choose from, but the most popular is the pine island, planted with one very picturesque pine, or a group of pines set in a tight group. In pond gardens the island is often reached by a bridge, especially an old-style Chinese wooden bridge that is painted red or orange. You may of course prefer a different style of bridge, perhaps aiming for a more minimal, neutral effect.

Stream

Another main feature of a pond garden is a winding stream that either feeds into or empties the main pond (or both). This would originally have been used for ceremonial purposes, but even without the ceremonies it makes an attractive addition. Again it should follow a naturalistic course, and be planted at its edges with hostas and other waterside plants.

Plants

Planting in pond gardens should be in naturalistic groups of trees and shrubs that celebrate the seasons. Groves of

cherries, maples and pines can be underplanted with azaleas, kerria and spiraea for contrast.

Path

A strolling path is the final essential feature that should be added, in order to encourage the visitor to experience every part of the garden by wandering around the pond, over the stream and through the groves of trees.

Above left: A valley-style lantern, typical of the type used to arc over the edges of ponds at Pureland Zen garden, England.

Above right: Stepping stone paths that continue across ponds help to create a unity of design within a garden.

Below: The use of large rocks and clipped evergreens gives this pond garden a sense of scale that is much larger than in reality. The waterfall design carefully observes the natural flow of mountain streams.

Garden plan: a pond garden

The design of this pond garden would suit people with a large garden. The main feature is the pond fed by a winding stream or by a spring spilling over a waterfall. Pine islands and rocky islets are artfully placed, some of them reached by Chinese-style bridges and viewed from a pavilion that might double as a boathouse. The overall feel of the planting and rock placement is naturalistic.

MAKING A TURTLE ISLAND

Turtle and crane islands were built to lure the immortals to earth and learn their secrets, especially the recipe for the elixir of eternal youth. These islands can be made anywhere in a pond, just from a few well-placed rocks.

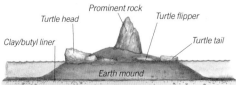

Turtle head · Prominent rock · Turtle flipper · Turtle tail · Clay/butyl liner · Earth mound

1 Make a rough sketch, then select rocks to represent the turtle parts. The island is the body of the turtle, made up of earth and a collection of supporting rocks. You also need rocks to represent the turtle's head and the four flippers. Just suggest the shape of the head and use wider rocks that reach out into the water at the four corners of the island for the flippers.

2 Construct the island before the pond is filled with water. You can build the island on a butyl liner, or add the liner after the island is complete, but if you are planning an elaborate arrangement then lay the liner first. If using machinery to transport the rocks and soil, you can roll back the butyl liner to avoid puncturing it. You can also lay out some extra layers of liner and underlay for protection.

3 Build the soil up in layers, making the base twice as wide as the island itself, so that the sides slope gently into the water. This will ensure that the rocks are sitting on stable ground. Place a ring of rocks just below water level around the soil to add stability.

4 Now place the rocks to signify the different parts of the turtle. Upright rocks will need to be buried by up to a third of their height to be stable and safe.

5 The island can then be planted with grasses and a pine tree. According to the myth, the turtle carries on its back one of the Isles of the Immortals. This could be represented by placing one particularly prominent rock on the "back" of the turtle.

Small hill with waterfall

Gravel path

Rocky

Small bridge over winding stream

Left: *Winding streams emulate a natural type of stream, with the rocks used to modulate the flow.*

Plant list
1 Black pine (*Pinus thunbergii*)
2 Cherry (*Prunus serrulata* varieties)
3 Japanese maple (*Acer palmatum*)

Rock groupings

Red Chinese bridge

Pine island with rocky shoreline

Rocky shoreline

Turtle island with Mount Horai

Rowing boat

Wooden boathouse

Left: *The arrangement of rocky islets is often taken from the myths of the Mystic Isles. This one is symbolic of Mount Horai.*

Left: *Heian garden buildings and bridges were often copies of those found in China at the time.*

How to make a pond garden

Pond gardens do not necessarily require a spectacular country setting. They were originally made in Japanese cities in large walled spaces, which means that the pond garden is a style that can easily be reproduced in Western gardens. However, a minimum of a quarter of a hectare (over half an acre) is required to make the style effective. Here is a suggestion for a pond garden created with a clay-lined pond, a pine island and a waterfall, all of which are key elements of the style. On the next few pages follow practical sequences on each of these three elements, with instructions on how to prepare and install them. This will give a good foundation plan for creating a pond garden and you can then vary these elements and introduce others in order to suit the needs of your own garden or your individual preferences.

Above: *The autumn colours of maple leaves are reflected in the pond at Tenju-an. Much of this garden dates back to the 13th century, with its simple design of two ponds, two islands and rocks arranged around a waterfall.*

Red pine

Cherry blossom

Japanese-style bridge

Pine island

Black pine

Japanese maple

Clay-lined pond

Grass

Waterfall

Above: *The most stable way to support the edges of a pond is to use rocks, even if you want grass to grow close to those edges.*

TYPICAL FEATURES

The following elements are the most important to include in a pond garden:

- ponds with rocks around the edges and cobble and sandy beaches shelving into the water;

- one or two islands, typically planted with pines and grasses among rocks;

- red-painted Chinese-style bridge;

- meandering stream or waterfall feeding the pond;

- boathouse with small boat;

- undulating hills around the pond;

- winding gravel paths;

- plants such as cherry trees, Japanese maples, kerria, azalea, spiraea.

PLANNING AND VISUALIZATION

First think about the site you are planning to use and how it might need to be adapted for a pond garden. A series of features such as these would have a minimum area requirement of 45 x 45m (147 x 147ft). The size, position and style of a pond will need to fit the location, and you may also want to imitate ponds you have seen in other gardens.

When you are choosing a site for a waterfall, find the most natural place in your garden for a fall, ideally a raised hill from which the waterfall flow can be created. If you want to build islands in the pond, these must be planned before you build the pond. Sketch your ideas for how the garden will look and what will be included (see also Making a plan on page 150). The coloured design opposite shows how an initial concept and visualization of this scene might work and how the elements will link together when everything is in place.

WATER PRACTICALITIES

Water sources It is obviously essential to have a source of water. If you own a natural source, such as a spring or a stream, make sure that it is sufficient to keep the pond clear and healthy in the dry summer months. If not, or if you have no natural source, consult a water garden specialist on what type and size of pump you will need for your pond. Remember that the power of the pump you need has a cost implication for running the electricity to drive the pump.

Loss of water You should also get advice on how to top up the pond from losses due to evaporation, and from inevitable leakages and splashing.

Draining excess water You will need to make provision for too much water from excessive rain, and also allow for drainage.

Making a pond with a soil liner

For creating a small pond the flexible liner method shown on pages 194–5 is the best option; this liner is easy to install and readily available at garden centres. Alternatively, a large-scale pond may be required, one to include in a pond or stroll garden with more generous dimensions. In this case you can use either a natural clay liner, or more conveniently an enhanced soil liner or geosynthetic clay liner, shown in the method below. Manmade liners such as these are now more commonly used than clay.

A natural clay liner needs to be created from naturally occurring clay within the garden site. It is also advisable to get professional advice for this type of pond because it has to integrate within the natural landscape of the site. Because of these requirements, if you want a substantial pond, especially one that won't be damaged by aquatic animals or other wildlife, an enhanced soil liner such as the one shown here is usually a safer choice, while having many of the advantages of a natural clay liner.

In the following method, a synthetic clay liner is combined with sodium bentonite crystals to produce a strong seal. For effective installation, the pond should be empty.

Sodium bentonite can be used either in the construction of a new pond, or to repair an existing pond. It is absorbed into the soil at the base of the pond and then swells to create a block so the moisture cannot escape. Treating a pond in this way will create a watertight seal

Above: Synthetic clay liners are the best method of sealing large ponds in areas where there is no natural clay subsoil to use for the job.

that will last for many years. What is more, it is environmentally friendly and safe to use. Make sure you use a high quality sodium bentonite, apply it following the manufacturer's instructions and use the recommended amount depending on your soil type and the area that is being treated.

You will need

- string, sand or canes for marking the outline of the pond
- 5 x 5cm (2 x 2in) stakes (for a pond more than 2m (6½ft) across)
- a laser level
- a spade
- rolls of synthetic clay liner that are sufficient to cover the sides and floor of the pond, allowing for a 15cm (6in) overlap between each sheet
- a sufficient quantity of sodium bentonite crystals to cover each of the overlapped joints of the liner to expand and seal it
- garden hose
- topsoil to overlap the liner by 30cm (12in)
- a tile or stone slab

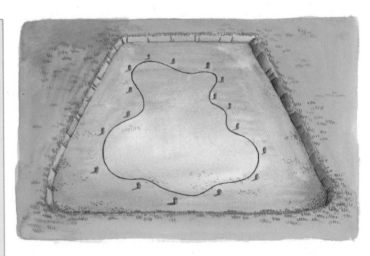

1 Remove at least 30cm (12in) of soil to a generous distance from the main working area and stockpile it for later use. If this excavation goes into the subsoil, keep the topsoil and subsoil in separate piles. Mark out the outline of the pond on the ground with string or sand or with a series of canes. With a large pond, drive in the stakes to indicate the level of water, as shown here.

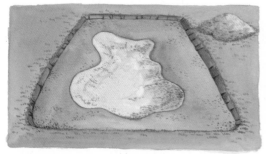

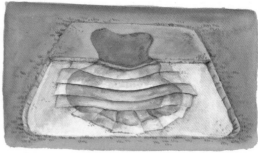

2 Excavate a saucer-shaped depression to a minimum of 60cm (2ft) and a maximum of 1.25m (4ft) at the deepest point. The sides should slope at no more than 30 degrees. Save the soil for replacing on the pond liner later and for grading around the sides.

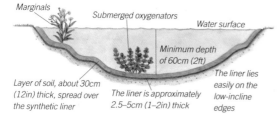

Marginals

Submerged oxygenators

Water surface

Minimum depth of 60cm (2ft)

Layer of soil, about 30cm (12in) thick, spread over the synthetic liner

The liner is approximately 2.5–5cm (1–2in) thick

The liner lies easily on the low-incline edges

Above: *A cross-section of a synthetic clay-lined pond.*

Below: *A large and complex pond like that at Syoki-ho-en could be lined using clay or a geosynthetic clay liner.*

3 Roll sheets of the liner over the excavation and over the edges of the pond, overlapping them by about 15cm (6in). Sprinkle sodium bentonite crystals between and over the joints: once they absorb water, they will swell to fill any cracks, so completing the seal.

4 Cover the liner with a 30cm (12in) layer of soil, avoiding soil with heavy levels of fertilizer. The liner expands when in contact with water to several times its original thickness. This process will reverse and the mat may crack if it is allowed to dry out, so once the mat is in contact with moisture, either from rain or from the soil layer, keep it wet by laying a plastic sheet over the completed areas or·by sprinkling it until you are ready to fill the pond.

5 Add water by resting the end of a garden hose on a tile or stone slab and letting the water in slowly. This prevents the freshly added soil from being dislodged.

6 Fine particles of debris, silt and clay suspended in the water may take several days or weeks to settle on the bottom, but the water will then begin to clear.

Making a pine island

A pine island can be one of the finest features of a traditional Japanese pond garden. This small rocky island would be planted with a twisted, weatherbeaten pine tree, and is reminiscent of the Matsushima islands off northern Japan (*matsu* means "pine" in Japanese). A pond of virtually any size could accommodate a small pine island, though obviously the pond and island will need to be in suitable proportions to achieve the desired effect. These islands are best surrounded by stones, which give a more natural look to the feature and can also be used to support the soil.

Above: *This pine island is located in the tranquil lake setting of the 19th-century Heian shrine, in Kyoto.*

Although it is possible to build an island after the pond has been made, it is always advisable to plan for an island during the pond-building process, rather than as an afterthought. Driving machinery or wheelbarrows across butyl-lined or clay-lined pools could damage the lining. If, however, the pond has been made, make a layer at least 30cm (12in) deep of protective soil, free of sharp stones, over a clay liner, or simply roll back a butyl liner.

Japanese black pines (*Pinus thunbergii*) are the best variety for pine islands as they can be easily shaped to give a picturesque windswept habit and they are also tolerant of wet roots. They do not like waterlogged soils, so build up the island to at least 60cm (2ft) higher than the water level to ensure that the pine roots have plenty of soil, not only to grow in but also to ensure they are sturdy enough to withstand winds.

PINE ISLAND PRACTICALITIES

Size The size of the island should be in proportion to the size of pond.

Shape Small islands should be simple in shape. Larger islands can have a more interesting outline.

Bridges If the island is close enough to the edge of the pond, you can link it to the mainland with a bridge.

Foundations Make sure that the foundations are at least twice the area of the exposed island.

Plants Pines do not like waterlogged roots, so make sure they have access to dry soil. Dwarf miscanthus looks good with pines and rocks.

Wild areas Leave some long grass to encourage wildfowl to nest.

Rocks Rocks blend well with pine trees. You can make a turtle or crane island by suggesting the shape with rocks.

You will need
- underlay and flexible liner
- scissors to cut underlay
- a number of rocks to support the soil
- interestingly shaped rocks to place on the pine island
- topsoil
- a spade
- a crowbar
- a wheelbarrow or small dumper truck
- a Japanese black pine tree (more than one in different sizes will also look good)
- grass seed or any ornamental grasses to decorate the island, including *Miscanthus yakushimenis* and *Molinia caerulea*

CONSTRUCTING A PINE ISLAND OVER A BUTYL LINER

1 Drain the pond, if necessary, then roll back the butyl liner and underlay. Make a large mound of soil where you want your island to be.

2 Lay the underlay and flexible liner over the top of the soil mound. Cut a hole in the underlay and liner so that an area of soil is exposed, but ensure that the liner is taken well above the waterline.

3 Add a further mound of soil on top of the foundation to create a gently curving island. Stack rocks on top of each other all around the edge of the island in order to hold the dry soil in place.

4 Plant the pine(s) and sow the grass seed, or plant grass plants. Keep well watered until established.

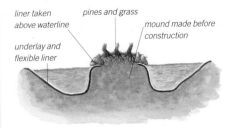

liner taken above waterline

pines and grass

mound made before construction

underlay and flexible liner

Above: *This method ensures that the pine roots do not become waterlogged.*

CONSTRUCTING A PINE ISLAND OVER A CLAY OR SYNTHETIC CLAY LINER

1 Drain the pond, if necessary, then protect the clay liner with an extra 30cm (12in) of soil. If draining is not possible, use a tracked vehicle to build the island. Alternatively, you could use a large digger with a long reach, if the island is made close enough to the edge of the pond.

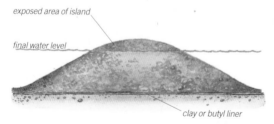

exposed area of island

final water level

clay or butyl liner

2 Build a mound of soil that will be the base of the island over the top of the liner. There is no need to roll the matting over the island. Make sure that the sides slope at no more than 30 degrees, which will keep the banks stable.

3 Keep building the island up with soil until it is 60–100cm (24–40in) above the water line. This will give the pine tree plenty of water-free root room in which to grow. There is no need to shape the mound at this stage.

Below: A good example of a well-shaped Japanese black pine on a rocky islet. The island is suggestive of a turtle, with the upright stones to the right of the island representing its head.

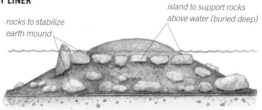

ring of rocks set around island to support rocks above water (buried deep)

rocks to stabilize earth mound

4 Bury rocks deeply all over the mound, from the base up to just below the water line. These will be the foundation for any rocks above water.

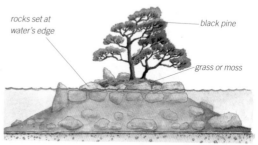

rocks set at water's edge

black pine

grass or moss

5 Build up an arrangement of rocks on top to imitate a rocky island. Shape the mound to look naturalistic. Add more soil between some of the rocks and use one of these crevices to plant a pine tree. Scatter grass seed over the soil areas in the autumn or spring and water well. Plant some ornamental grasses between one or two of the rocks.

Building a waterfall

Waterfalls were an important feature of Heian pond gardens. They were regarded as the abode of Fudo, an important personification of the Buddha, while the two main supporting stones were considered to be the Buddha's attendants. As a plentiful, natural, life-giving source, water was regarded as sacred, and waterfalls therefore tended to be well camouflaged in the landscape. The *Sakuteiki* says "There are many ways to make a waterfall, but no matter what, they should always face the moon, so that falling water will reflect in the moonlight."

First choose the "waterfall stone", the one that the water actually spills over. This will determine the height of the fall. You may decide to build a series of falls, but remember that a large amount of water does not necessarily mean a better effect. A small waterfall falling from a height of 1m (40in) into shallow water or on to a carp stone, a tumbling cascade or a plain sheet of water can be just as effective. Always follow the "desire" of the stones and the way they want to direct the water. If you are using a recycling system with an electric pump, try to minimize the amount of water that will be lost through splashing.

Above: *The sound of a trickling waterfall can create as much atmosphere as a torrent. A stone is often placed at the bottom, at the point at which the water falls, to make a feature of the sound. A notable example of this is the stone at the Dragon Gate cascade in Kinkaku-ji.*

WATERFALL PRACTICALITIES

Spillage Use a butyl liner to contain any potential water spillage.

Sound When planning, think of the sound effects as well as appearance.

Security Bed the base stones well into concrete to make a secure beginning.

Flow Test the water flow as you place stones using a hose to see the effect.

Control Be patient and flexible, water is difficult to manage when it is in freefall.

Flow rate The waterfall will change character if the flow rate is changed. If you are using a pump, make sure you buy one with a variable flow valve so you can manage the water flow to suit your waterfall.

You will need
- a good selection of large rocks to suit the shape of the proposed waterfall
- a spade
- a crowbar
- a large sheet of butyl rubber to fit the dimensions of the waterfall (note that you need to lay wider than the fall itself)
- a strip of liner sealing tape (optional if pond is clay lined)
- concreting sand and cement
- a wheelbarrow
- a concrete mixer (optional)
- machinery, such as a sack truck or skid loader for moving rocks if they are too heavy and awkward to move by hand (see moving rocks on page 76–77)

HOW TO CONSTRUCT A WATERFALL

1 First make an outline sketch of how you would like the waterfall to look. Then mark out the proposed position on the ground. If you have already made a selection of rocks, these will help to decide the design; otherwise, select special rocks to suit the intended shape of your cascade.

2 Dig out an area three or four times wider than the waterfall itself. This will give you plenty of room to work and to spread out a large sheet of butyl liner. The liner will lie under the whole structure of the waterfall so that any splashes and leakages will find their way back into the pond.

The liner is laid wider than the waterfall

Stones to weight down liner

The waterfall liner overlaps the pond liner, creating a sealed joint

3 If the pond has a butyl liner, lift up the edge of the liner and tuck it under the waterfall liner. The pond liner should be well above the pond water level. Seal the two liners together with the sealing strip. If the pond is clay lined, let the waterfall liner drop under the waterline.

4 Make a firm concrete base for the first foundation stones. These may be the two main supporting stones or simply the base from which you can build up a series of stones for a cascade-style waterfall.

5 Measure where you expect the water to fall and erect the main stone. Seal the joints between it and the main supporting stones.

6 You will need to build a header pool, even if the waterfall is being fed by a stream. The header pool will help to keep the flow of water constant.

Header pool or stream

Concrete base to support main stones

Flat-topped "fall" rock

Supporting stone

Rocks set around pond edge to conceal liner

7 Add more rocks to the sides and above the header pool to make a naturalistic setting and to help retain the soil on the steep sides. Make provision for some soil pockets to plant sedges, ferns and other waterside plants. Make sure all concrete joints are skilfully disguised.

Below: *With a natural water course and interesting contours, you can recreate the effects of a mountain stream. The Tully Japanese Garden has carefully observed the rocks and flow of natural streams.*

Cobbles and shingle at base of waterfall in shallow water

Fern

Concealed edge of liner

Hosta

Carp stone

8 Allow the waterfall base to open up by positioning a number of smaller stones and cobbles there. Having observed the flow of the water, place a "carp stone" at the base to receive the water, which will spill over and around it.

BUILDING A STREAM AND WATERFALL SYSTEM

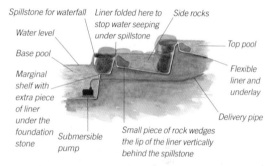

Spillstone for waterfall

Water level

Base pool

Marginal shelf with extra piece of liner under the foundation stone

Submersible pump

Liner folded here to stop water seeping under spillstone

Side rocks

Top pool

Flexible liner and underlay

Delivery pipe

Small piece of rock wedges the lip of the liner vertically behind the spillstone

The dry garden style

The dry garden is the most contemplative of all the Japanese garden styles. It is also the most abstract. You do need a fairly good understanding of the origins of this style to make one that is truly effective. Have a look at photos of the famous dry Zen gardens of Japan, and see if you think that your site would be suitable. You will also need to keep it tidy, so it's not an ideal choice for a large family garden. Dry gardens are especially well suited to courtyards and small enclosed spaces – even those areas that are inhospitable to plants.

Above: Dry gardens use gravel and rocks to suggest the flow and expanse of water in its different forms.

ELEMENTS OF A DRY GARDEN

As its name suggests, a dry garden's essential elements are dry materials in the form of sand and gravel, which are often raked into patterns, and carefully chosen and strategically placed rocks. Another important element is a flat site, as the extensive use of sand and gravel means that a level surface is highly preferable to a slope.

Sand and gravel

The "dry" aspect of the garden consists of sand or gravel spread to represent an expanse of water, either in the form of the sea or a lake. Dry gardens might also contain a dry "stream" and a dry "waterfall", although these are not essential. The use of all this dry material means that dry gardens need very little maintenance: the occasional raking of the gravel (and the trimming of any shrubs that might be included) is all that is required.

The sand and gravel will usually be contained within a rectangular frame. (In Japan, they are found in rectangular courtyards in Zen temples.)

Rocks

Once you have established that your garden is suitable, the key to a successful dry garden is in the arrangements of the rocks. There are many arrangements to choose from, for example a Buddhist grouping, where a central stone represents the Buddha or the sacred mountain Mount Shumisen; a grouping that represents different aspects of the Mystic Isles of immortals; or an arrangement simply placed with intuition and instinct – you will have to try this one out by moving your rocks until you are happy with the effect. All of these arrangements should be designed with a sense of the tranquil, and should avoid any excessive forms in shape or size.

Plants

If rocks are difficult to obtain, or you have decided not to use them, interesting arrangements can also be made with groups of plants clipped to the shape of distant hills or to represent sacred sites.

Left: Mirei Shigemori, in his finest work at Tofuku-ji, used bold groups of rocks and stylized gravel raking, to illustrate the ancient Chinese myth of the Mystic Isles.

Left: *Most dry gardens are designed in courtyards, where the rectangular shape in a sense represents the frame of a painting, while the spread of sand represents the white "unpainted" canvas. Despite this, they can be equally effective and suggestive in more naturalistic surroundings, such as this example in Kew Gardens in England, although it is more difficult to play with the sense of scale.*

Below: *Rocks set near the edge of an expanse of gravel can suggest a river or lakeside. Well-placed rocks need simple plantings to enhance their form: these rocks at Kew are set against a plain wall with a dramatically pruned pine.*

Garden plan: a dry garden

The best place for a dry garden is a courtyard enclosed by walls or fences. This contains the garden so it can be seen as a painting "hung" within its frame, and protects it from the elements. The deeper Zen meaning of these dry gardens is one of emptiness of mind – a goal of Zen meditation. The whole garden should possess an air of restraint and be a calm and spiritual place of sand, rocks and maybe a few plants.

TOPIARY IN THE DRY GARDEN

The use of topiary to represent a landscape can be seen in some of the great dry landscape gardens such as the Ryoan-ji or Shoden-ji. A weathered pine might suggest a mountain or a seaside landscape, and groups of clipped plants could symbolize a range of distant hills.

Shakkei (borrowed scenery)

Trees to frame view

White-painted plaster wall

Tile-topped wall

Clipped azalea

Raked gravel

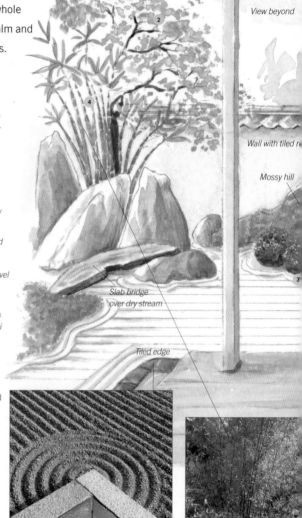

View beyond

Wall with tiled r

Mossy hill

Slab bridge over dry stream

Tiled edge

1 Make a sketch of the site and draw an outline of the landscape you want to reproduce. This kind of design typically incorporates *shakkei* (borrowed landscape), so look outside your garden to see if there is anything you could integrate. Get further inspiration by looking through a book on Chinese landscape painting. You may want to reproduce a favourite landscape that is familiar to you.

2 Decide whether to buy small, young plants, which are cheaper and easier to establish, but will take time to grow, or larger plants for a more instant result. Use plants that will be different sizes, as a variation in heights is effective. If you cannot obtain large azaleas, you should be able to buy large plants of cheaper unclipped boxwood, which you can clip to your own shape. Other evergreens could be used, such as varieties of camellia, photinia or osmanthus.

3 If the soil on your site is poor or of the wrong type for azaleas, which prefer acid soil, dig out generous holes for each plant. Make sure that the area is well drained or put some gravel in the bottom of the holes, then fill with the soil mix you require and plant your specimen plants.

4 Spread the gravel and sand for the raked "dry water" effect (see pages 174–5 for notes on gravel and drainage).

Above: *The interplay between the breaking waves of sand against the tiled "frame".*

Right: *Black bamboo is suitable as it does not get too big or spread around.*

Plant list

1 Japanese black pine
(*Pinus thunbergii*)
2 Spring plum (*Prunus*
species)
3 Clipped azalea
4 Black bamboo
(*Phyllostachys nigra*)

Dry waterfall

Mossy hill

Plaster wall

Turtle island

Raked sand

Veranda

Right: *Mossy
mounds may need
frequent watering in
order to keep them
fresh and green.*

Right: *Clipped
azaleas can have the
same solid presence
as standing rocks.*

How to make a dry garden

Dry gardens are generally best sited on level ground, unless you intend to include a dry waterfall, but even this can be built up in one corner of the garden. A garden called the Daisen-in in the Daitokuji Temple in Kyoto portrays an entire mountain landscape and has almost all the elements of a dry garden: rocks and bent pines, dry streams, a dry waterfall, a natural stone slab bridge and even a block of stone "floating" on the sea of sand. Here is a suggestion for a dry garden design that incorporates these key features, all contained in a defined rectangular area. The planting is restricted to a pine and some bamboo, interspersed with stones and rocks and surrounded by raked gravel. The three stages of creating this garden are shown in the following pages: positioning rocks, placing edging stones and improving drainage.

Above: *While dry gardens are popularly known as Zen gardens, the Japanese name is kare-sansui, which translates as "dry mountain water", with sand or gravel representing water and the rocks the mountains.*

pruned pine

bamboo

tiled wall capping

painted plaster wall

rock set in line of stone edging

cobbles

raked gravel (concentric ripple pattern)

main rock arrangement

raked gravel (parallel lines or stream current)

stone edging

TYPICAL FEATURES OF A DRY GARDEN

A dry garden should be a rectangular level courtyard within three walls, the fourth side used as a viewing platform and including the following:

• a rectangle of edging stones or tiles to frame the garden;

• rocks of interesting shapes;

• gravel, preferably a light silvery grey;

• moss around the bases of rocks to make them look like islands;

• stepping stones and lanterns ;

• bent pines and small-leaved evergreens to tuck around the rocks;

• clipped azaleas to imitate hills;

• dry waterfalls and landscapes with dry streams and bridges.

PLANNING AND VISUALIZATION

Before you start you must have a good idea of the elements you want to introduce and be certain that you can get all of them to the site. Rocks are especially difficult to move in narrow confines, but mini-diggers can get through openings of around 1m (1yd) wide, which might be sufficient. If you are contemplating growing plants in your dry garden, make sure the soil is right for them. If there is no soil on site or the drainage is poor, you can build up planting areas between rock arrangements or dig trenches to improve the drainage.

ROCKS, EDGING AND GRAVEL

The first priority is to get the rocks in place as this will be the most awkward and messy job. After this, you can frame your "picture" with edging stones that will contain the area of gravel and will set off both the gravel and the rocks. In Japan these edges are often quite elaborate, using a combination of tiles, strips of granite, and a row of cobbles that doubles up as a drainage channel. Even if you are using a more contemporary design, unconfined in an open space, it will still be necessary to build an edge to contain the gravel or sand.

The gravel will need to be spread around 5–6cm (2–2½in) deep if you intend to rake it into patterns (see pages 84–85). It can be less deep if you want the gravel to be a practical element that can be walked over. However, the spiritual, Zen quality of a dry garden is more effectively achieved by the creation of elements for both viewing and contemplation.

Positioning rocks

Rocks are seen as important natural symbols of strength. They are used in many Japanese gardens, with the order and positioning seen as key to the balance of the garden. They can vary from monumental sizes that need digging in and cementing to stabilize them, to smaller rocks that can be moved by hand. Rocks should always be placed in a naturalistic manner, so that they look balanced in relation to each other. Traditional Japanese gardeners, attributing a living spirit to rocks, described this as "following their desire".

Above: *Rocks with interesting grain patterns and markings are ideal for dry gardens.*

The placing of rocks is a crucial aspect of Japanese gardening. You may choose to employ professional landscapers, but with some guidance it is possible to organize it yourself, so that you understand the process, from hiring the right equipment to all the safety issues. Once you have established how you are going to move them, you will need to know how to position them both safely and artistically. Establish the rough weight of the rocks so that you can be advised on the right size of machinery and correct gauge of lifting straps. See also pages 76–77 on moving rocks.

You will need

- two people to carry the rock
- protective clothing (e.g. hard hat, gloves and boots)
- strong straps (from a hire shop)
- a scaffolding pole and shackle
- a spade and a crowbar
- smaller propping stones
- a fencing stake
- a sledgehammer
- loose soil for backfilling

ROCK PRACTICALITIES

Finding rocks It may be hard to find rocks that match your artistic intentions exactly, so be flexible when arranging them.

Buying rocks Allow yourself one or two extra ones to give more choice.

Placing rocks Move back from time to time to a different vantage point. The rocks must look right from all possible viewing angles.

Adjusting rocks Take your time to make sure the rocks feel right. It may seem like hard work, but large rocks will be very difficult to move later, once the garden is established.

Leaving rocks Once you have set the rocks and finished the garden, it will be virtually impossible to move any of the bigger rocks without considerable disruption.

1 Decide which way round and up you want the rock to be. Then measure the amount of rock that will show above ground and how much needs to be buried. Tall upright rocks will need to be buried deep to ensure they are stable. The more angled you want the rock to be, the deeper the hole should be.

2 Draw a line with a piece of chalk to indicate ground level on the rock. Measure again so that you know how deep to dig the receiving hole, taking into account the extra 4–6cm (1½–2½in) of gravel that will be laid over the area.

3 Dig the hole, and lay a fencing stake, with a spirit level on it, across the top, raised to the height of the finished gravel.

4 Check the hole has been dug to the right depth. Digging too deep may make the soil loose below the rock and cause it to "settle" too much. Allow for plenty of room each side for packing and adjusting the angle of the rock.

5 Using a digger, lower the strapped-up rock very slowly into the hole. Two people should be in place to help to guide the rock as it is lowered, twisting it so that it is angled correctly.

6 With the rock safely strapped up and attached to the lifting gear, try out different angles and positions until you are satisfied that it is placed where you want it.

7 Keeping the rock still strapped up and attached to the digger, support the undersides and sides of the rock with smaller stones. These can also be used to wedge between two rocks for support.

8 Use a sledgehammer to ram the stones tightly into place. Then test the rock for its overall stability. The rock should be in a "rock solid" position even before you start to pack around it with soil.

9 Backfill the hole with a loamy or clay soil. Sandy soil will not pack well and is far too loose. With the butt end of a fencing stake, ram the soil between the stones.

10 Ram the final layers of soil firmly around the rock with a sledgehammer.

11 Rake the surrounding soil until it is level. Set the accompanying rocks in place. In this case they are smaller and lower, and therefore don't need such a deep and solid foundation.

12 The final stage of the process is to water the soil in around the rocks to remove all air pockets and to help compact the ground.

MOVING ROCKS

There are various practical considerations to bear in mind when positioning rocks:

• move large rocks with a mini-digger (see pages 76–77);

• use tough nylon/canvas fibre straps to minimize damage to the rock;

• so you can calculate the foundation depth, decide which part of the rock will be visible in the finished garden;

• dig the hole slightly deeper than you

need so you have the flexibility to adjust the position later;

• try the rock in different positions and angles before removing the straps;

• check the rock for stability and fill in tightly with soil.

Placing edging stones

Most dry gardens are set within a framed space, whether it be in the open with a fenced area or in a courtyard with existing walls surrounding the space. This framing serves both to contain the dry sand or gravel and to make the garden look more like a painting hung within a frame. In all the famous dry gardens, you will notice the considerable care that is taken in choosing the edging materials and how they are laid. Long pavers of granite or dark blue tiles, or both, can be used with a channel of cobbles between them as an aid to drainage.

In your own garden, you can use any native materials. For this project lengths of stone made of the same local sandstone as the rocks have been used. These edging stones are fairly uniform but by no means perfect rectangles. These stones are being used to separate a border of cobbles against the surrounding wall from the dry sea of gravel.

Above: Edging stones not only help to separate planting areas from gravelled areas but can also make decorative features of their own, such as this raised area in the Tully Japanese Garden. The Japanese pay close attention to detail in all parts of the garden.

EDGING MATERIALS

The following materials can be used for framing areas of the dry garden:

- local or salvaged materials;
- old, slightly misshapen bricks;
- old granite setts;
- old roofing or floor tiles set on edge;
- charred wooden post tops.

1 Set up a builder's line parallel to one of the walls and mark the level of the outside of the edging stones, using a tape measure to check that it is an equal distance from the wall at both ends. On a flat site, use a spirit level to check the line is level. On a sloping site, set the line up tightly at either end of the edging run. Dig out a trench for the edging stones, a little deeper and wider than the stones themselves, always keeping an eye on the line. Lay out your row of edging stones so that they are easily reached.

2 Make a concreting mix using soft or sharp sand mix, eight parts sand to one part cement (most cement will have mixture recommendations on the bags). Small amounts of concrete can be easily mixed in a wheelbarrow with a spade but larger amounts might require a concrete mixer. Towable concrete mixers, both electrical and petrol-powered, can be hired from plant hire depots. Shovel a small amount into the trench, enough to set 1m (1yd) of edging stones at a time.

3 Set one of the edging stones on to the cement bed so that it sits slightly higher than the builder's line.

4 Using the hammer, tap the stone firmly until it becomes level with the line. Repeat with the other stones until the path edge is complete. The stone ends should be close enough to prevent sand and gravel slipping between them.

5 Shore up the edging stones with the concreting mix, making sure that the mix will not show above the finished gravel.

6 Spread some soft sand between the edging stones and the wall. Remove any stones or blocks of earth that are still protruding.

7 Measure, cut and lay weed-suppressing fabric over the layer of soft sand and tuck in the edges well.

8 Spread a layer of cobbles over the fabric, keeping the level of the cobbles below the top of the stones.

9 For an unusual touch, place a natural rock, one that can be easily moved using a sack truck, into a pre-measured gap. Scoop out 6–10cm (2½–4in) of soil and spread a layer of 4cm (1½in) of sharp sand, then lay the rock directly on to the bed of sharp sand.

Improving drainage

Drainage requirements must be carefully considered in the early stages of planning a dry garden, especially if you are intending to grow plants. Dry gardens are most frequently created on level sites, and often close to buildings, where heavy machinery and ground works may have caused compaction of the natural texture of the soil. This is especially true of gardens built on clay soils or on a concrete base. In such situations, flexible drainage pipes may need to be laid to improve the drainage.

Poor drainage will kill plants and may cause damage to buildings and walls. If a dry garden is constructed over badly drained heavy clay soil, the water will stay on the surface after heavy rain once the rocks and edging stones are in place. To remedy this, the best solution is to lay a network of feeder drains and a main drain to ensure that the water can flow away naturally.

Above: *On some level sites you will need to make allowance for drainage. This can be set around the edge of the dry garden and made into a design detail of its own. A trench filled with large gravel or cobbles may be enough to disguise such areas.*

You will need
- 10cm- (4in-) diameter flexible perforated drainage pipe
- angled joints
- a sharp knife
- a spade and shovel
- a wheelbarrow
- a hose
- 10–20mm (½–¾in) pea gravel
- crushed stone with stone dust (known as scalpings or hoggin)
- coloured gravel or sand
- a roller or wacker-plate
- a rake

1 Mark the layout of the drains with marker paint. Then dig the main drain to a depth of at least 45cm (18in) and the feeder drains, closer to the surface, at 30–35cm (12–14in) deep. The trenches should slope to give a fall of at least 10cm (4in) per 20m (20yd).

2 Spread a layer of pea gravel (small, smooth, rounded stones) 4cm (1½in) deep in the bottom of the trench.

3 Lay the flexible drainage pipe in the trench and check that the slope allows an effective fall of water by filling with a hose at the top end. Cover the pipe with at least a further 10cm (4in) of gravel. Leave uncovered in places where the feeder pipes will join it.

4 Cut the main pipe at the places where the feeder pipes (from the planted areas) will join it. (The perforated drainage pipes can easily be cut with a sharp knife.)

5 At the junctions of the feeder drains to the main drain, you will need to fit angled joints. These joints are often designed to take different sized pipes; cut out the size that fits your chosen pipe sizes. Once again, cover over all the pipes with gravel.

6 Spread a 5–7.5cm (2–3in) layer of crushed stone/stone dust mix over the entire area of the dry garden where the raked sand or gravel will eventually be.

7 Spread the layer until it is level, filling in potholes and making sure the drainage trenches are filled in. The roller will not be able to firm in narrow trenches so these should be compressed with your feet. This will help to avoid any subsidence later on.

DRAINAGE PRACTICALITIES

Soak-away You will need to check for the nearest point for collecting storm water. If this is at some distance, you should construct a soak-away or French drain to collect the drain water.

Location Check the location for all services, such as sewerage pipes, electric cables, gas pipes and mains water pipes, before you dig any trenches and before you decide where to lay the main drain.

Flow Check how the drainage levels will work. The principle to follow is that the main drain must be dug to the lowest level, so that all the drains on the site can feed into it. This can be done by eye and by feeding a hose into one of the drains to check for flow, or by using levelling equipment for more precise measurements.

Fall The fall for a drain should be no less than 10cm (4in) in every 20m (20yd).

Capacity On large sites, a larger main drain of 15cm (6in) diameter may be required.

8 Using the mechanical wacker-plate or a roller, compact the surface. If any subsidence occurs in this process, fill in any depressions with more crushed stone and roll again, until the whole surface is perfectly level.

9 Spread the gravel or sand over the surface to the required depth and rake it level. For sand that will be raked in patterns the depth should be at least 6cm (2½in).

Right: *On this site, the subsoil was of solid clay so a drainage pipe was laid around the perimeter of the garden. Additional drains feed from the planting holes into the main drain.*

The tea garden style

This type of garden is characterized by pathways and thresholds, and represents a journey to a more spiritual world. You enter a tea garden through a covered outer gateway, or *sotomon*. Inside, the garden is divided into two halves: an outer area, where a small waiting room can be placed, and an inner area, where the tea house will be found. Linking the two areas is the path, or *roji*, which leads the visitor past shelter seats and through a stooping gate to reach the ultimate goal: the tea house itself and the host within who waits to welcome the guests.

Above: *Water basins and lanterns were originally set alongside the tea paths of Japanese gardens as part of the tea ceremony.*

ELEMENTS OF A TEA GARDEN

There are four important elements that make up a Japanese tea garden: the tea house, the path or *roji* (dewy path) and garden around it, lanterns to line the path, and a water basin.

Tea house

A tea house is traditionally a rustic building set within a tea garden. It can be quite small and hidden away in a secluded place, but in later Japanese gardens it became a more open building placed with a view over the garden. This makes it more like a tea arbour, or a gazebo. The original essence of the tea house was as a "mountain place in the city", a secluded rustic hermitage and retreat from busy lives.

Path

The path, usually a stepping-stone path, will pass by the waiting room and through a small "stooping gate" – encouraging visitors to be aware of the world they are leaving behind and the wilderness and realms of higher

Left: *Reaching the tea house is the ultimate goal of a tea garden. The route typically consists of gateways that mark significant stages of the journey, and the tea house itself can often not be viewed until the final stage.*

consciousness ahead. The wilderness does not need to be literal – it can be suggested by "mountain" plants, usually glossy-leaved evergreens such as camellias and aucubas, planted under a canopy of maples.

Lanterns and water basins

The path and the area around the main water basin should be lit by carefully positioned lanterns, originally because tea ceremonies were often held in the evening. The water basin is an important feature representing the need for cleansing before entering the tea house.

Right: *The veranda pillars at Hosen-in frame the scene from the tea house.*

Below: *Shelter seats are placed alongside the tea path for guests to wait in comfort before they are summoned to the tea house.*

Garden plan: a tea garden

The principles of making a tea garden can be adapted to almost any space. The main feature is the path of stepping stones inside the main gate that leads to the tea house via a waiting room, past lanterns and water basins, and through intervening gates. The garden should become wilder as the path approaches the tea house. This, as in so many of the Japanese arts, is achieved symbolically rather than literally.

THE MIDDLE CRAWL-THROUGH GATE

This gate is placed halfway through the tea garden between the inner and outer *roji*. In leaving the everyday world for the spiritual world, the guest is forced to bow their head, either under a low lintel or, as in the style of gate described below, by pushing their way under it.

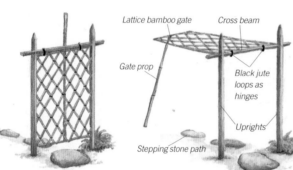

Lattice bamboo gate

Cross beam

Gate prop

Black jute loops as hinges

Uprights

Stepping stone path

7

1

Waiting room

Outer *roji*

Stepping stone path

5

4

Entrance gate

1 Using the gate as a guide, mark where the two upright posts will be. They should be 7.5–10cm (3–4in) square or round and 2.5m (8ft) long.

2 Dig holes 60–70cm (24–28in) deep for the posts. If the soil is firm, simply firm the two posts in around the bases. In loose ground, you should concrete the base of the two posts.

3 Measure the height of the gate, and trim off the tops of the two posts to the right height.

4 Fix the cross beam (which should be the same width as the posts and 1m [1yd] long) on top of the posts, creating mortise-and-tenon joints, by drilling holes for a piece of dowelling and pushing it through, or by screwing the crossbeam down with two 15cm (6in) screws on to each post.

5 Hang a lightweight bamboo gate, 1.5–2m (5–6½ft) high, on to the cross beam using some thick black jute for hinges.

6 Attach a bamboo pole 4cm (1½in) in diameter and 2.5m (8ft) long to the base of the gate. This pole will be used to prop the gate open.

Left: Guests rest in a waiting room before the host invites them to go into the tea house itself.

Lavatory

Tied rock

Bamboo fence

Well

Inner roji

Moss

9

Tsukubai

Rock
Moss
Rock

Lantern

Moss

8

6

3

2

Plant list

1 *Enkianthus perulatus*
2 Clipped azalea
3 Autumn-flowering
   camellia (*Camellia sasanqua*)
4 Sedge (*Carex*)
5 Domestic bamboo
   (*Nandina domestica*)
6 Red pine (*Pinus densiflora*)
7 Japanese black pine
   (*Pinus thunbergii*)
8 Japanese maple (*Acer palmatum*)
9 Fern (many species)

Left: *A fence and gate along the tea path divide the garden into two halves. This one is a hinged bamboo gate, but could equally be a middle crawl-through gate.*

Left: *The* tsukubai, *or "crouching basin", is always accompanied by a lantern.*

How to make a tea garden

The art of creating a Japanese tea garden is not just in placing the features: it requires some understanding of the philosophy behind the tea ceremony. Once familiar with this, you can combine the elements of the stepping-stone path, lanterns, water basins and plants into a style that is both unified and unique to your own tastes and culture. The tea garden adapts well to small areas: the essential wandering path can be as short as 5m (around 16ft), though in a large garden it could be 30m (100ft) or more. The practical sequences that follow you will show you how to create the main features of a tea garden: arranging a *tsukubai*, setting a lantern and laying a stepping-stone path. The example shown below combines all the elements; there is room for a tea house, but the path will lead to a "tea room" in the house itself.

Above: *A tall water basin of this type would commonly be found next to a veranda in a courtyard garden, or as a self-contained unit on the "spiritual" journey to the tea house through the tea garden.*

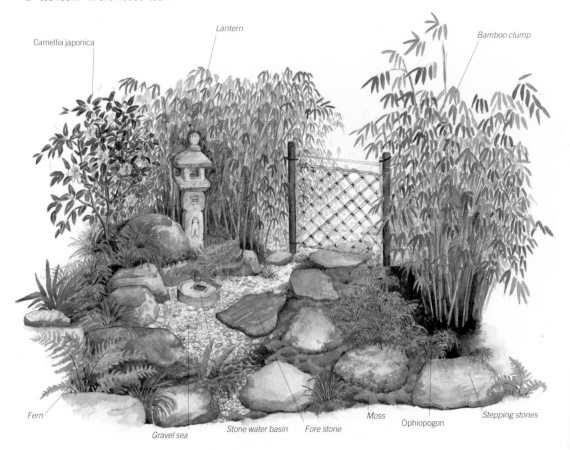

Camellia japonica

Lantern

Bamboo clump

Fern

Gravel sea

Stone water basin

Fore stone

Moss

Ophiopogon

Stepping stones

PLANNING AND VISUALIZATION

Once you have established the goal of the tea path (i.e. the tea house or tea room), you will want to work out an intriguing journey for the path to take. At some point on the path, look for a suitable place to create the *tsukubai* arrangement – the combination of the water basin and lantern. If your tea garden is large, you might want to divide the garden into two halves – an inner and outer *roji* – placing a waiting room in the inner garden and a middle crawl-through gate (see page 178) to divide them. Build up the planting to suggest a wilderness, with rocks informally placed at the sides of the path, using ferns and sedges and also including other plants tucked in among them.

Even if you have only a very small space, try to place all the elements to create the sense of a journey that leaves the busy world behind, so that you and your guests can feel you are entering a place of spiritual purity.

TYPICAL FEATURES OF A TEA GARDEN

In addition to the tea house or tea room, the following are usual elements:

- an entrance gate;

- a winding stepping-stone path;

- a water basin with cobbles around it;

- lanterns to light the path and basin;

- a waiting room or bench for guests;

- a middle crawl-through gate;

- woodland planting of camellias, maples and bamboos, and low planting of ferns and sedges around rocks.

WATER BASIN

The simplest system is to source an attractive basin and fill the basin by hand, as you would a bird bath. But if you want your water basin to be constantly topped up, you will need to build a reservoir under the basin to receive the spillage. The water can then be drained to a soak-away, a pond or a mains drain, or be recycled by a small pump placed in the base of the reservoir (see pages 118–119). If you use an electric pump, and if you want an electric lantern, you will need a source of electricity that is both safe and fully weatherproofed.

Arranging a *tsukubai*

The *tsukubai* is one of the key ingredients of the tea garden. The term *tsukubai* means a low crouching basin that guests use to wash their hands and face, a spiritual cleansing before they enter the teahouse. It has also come to refer to the whole arrangement of the low water basin and its accompanying lantern, the paving stone that the guests stand on when they use the water basin, and the sea of gravel and cobbles around it. The paving stone, or laver stone, on which visitors stand, results in the lowering of the body before water, indicating humility.

The water basin is replenished with fresh water each time the tea guests arrive. This can be done either by manually emptying the basin and refilling it with a jug (pitcher) – the easiest method – or by having a constantly dripping flow of water fed from a tap or natural spring via a bamboo pipe, which then overflows into the reservoir below, where the water is either drained away or recycled by an electric pump.

Above: *Water can be fed to the basin through a bamboo pipe. Allowing a tap to drip slowly but steadily at the source will ensure that you keep a constant supply of fresh water in the basin. Cleanliness and purity are viewed as sacred, and are crucial aspects of the Japanese tea ceremony.*

SETTING UP A *TSUKUBAI*

The elements that accompany the *tsukubai* are as important as the water basin itself for an authentic setting.

Rocks Place two or more flat-topped rocks on either side of the *tsukubai*. These are useful to stand a lantern on and for guests to place their personal effects on while they are washing themselves.

Cobbles Arrange a sea of cobbles around the *tsukubai*. While not essential, this makes an attractive surrounding for the basin as well as helping to keep the surface area around it dry.

Ladle Keep a bamboo ladle near or laid over the basin for guests to scoop up water to wash with. The ladle will need to be kept clean, as bamboo becomes mouldy quickly when it is left damp; alternatively you can place it by the basin only when guests are expected.

Drainage Provide a drainage outlet for larger basins (see pages 118–119).

You will need
- a spade
- a wheelbarrow
- a reservoir kit (optional; see page 118)
- a water basin
- rocks
- a flat stepping stone
- large-diameter gravel or cobbles
- a bamboo spout (optional)

1 Having selected the position of your *tsukubai*, first dig a hole with a spade to accommodate the reservoir you have chosen. The hole should be made deep enough in order to leave the rim of the reservoir approximately 4cm (1½in) proud of the soil level.

2 Place the reservoir in the hole, check that it is level, backfill with sand and then firm it in place.

3 Level the surrounding soil for the area that will represent the "sea". If you are not recycling water from the reservoir (see pages 118–119) you could use a large plastic pot that can be filled with gravel to help with drainage. If you do this you will need to make sure there are adequate holes in the base of the pot for the water to drain through.

4 Spread a layer of sharp sand 4cm (1½in) deep over the soil area, so that it lies level with the rim of the reservoir. The sand will help both to keep the site clean and to act as a free-draining medium on which to lay the cobbles. Place the metal grill over the reservoir and then lay a piece of fine plastic mesh over that. The mesh should be fine enough to prevent debris, soil or sand falling into the reservoir; this is especially critical if you intend to use a recycling pump, which can easily become blocked by debris.

5 Place a few cobbles to secure the mesh in place and lower the water basin on to the middle of the grill.

6 Spread a layer of cobbles or large gravel over the area to a depth where there is no soil, sand or mesh visible.

7 Collect the cobbles around the basin. Place your stepping stone next to the basin and firm it in so it is surrounded by cobbles or gravel.

8 Place the surface layer of cobbles by hand, arranging them so that they fit snugly together and lie in an attractive but natural manner.

Right: *Plant some ferns, sedge or ophiopogon close to the basin as well as around the surrounding rocks.*

Setting a lantern

Lanterns are integral to any Japanese tea garden. Originally they were found only outside Buddhist temples, but they were later introduced to the tea garden as the tea ceremony became influenced by Zen Buddhist symbolism. The lamps were lit as an offering to the Buddha, and early ones accommodated an oil lamp. Lanterns were also needed to light the tea path, as tea ceremonies often took place in the early evening. The stone lantern is an important connecting factor in the Japanese garden, as both a raw material and a manmade element.

Once you have placed the *tsukubai*, you will need to choose a position for the stone lantern. If only one lantern is used in a tea garden, this should be placed to accompany the water basin, ostensibly to light the *tsukubai* arrangement and the path. In many Japanese gardens these lanterns are rarely lit – they are designed more for their artistic and sculptural quality. We have chosen the Oribe-style lantern, with a carved image of the Buddha on the pillar. This lantern is both easy to assemble and

Above: *Although most lanterns are placed as sculptural features in the tea garden, they are sometimes lit. This light is often very subdued.*

easy to install by burying the base of the pillar in the ground and securing it with concrete.

You will need

- a lantern set
- a spade
- a spirit level
- concreting sand or aggregate
- cement
- a shovel
- water for concrete and cleaning
- mastic (optional)
- low-voltage electrical supply (optional)

1 Lay out all the parts of the lantern to show the correct sequence of assembly. This lantern arrived from the supplier with pencilled-on numbers. Notice the rough granite base on the main lantern pillar: once the lantern is buried, this rough area will be covered.

2 Dig a hole to accommodate the base of the lantern. This should be 15cm (6in) wider than the base of the pillar and 10cm (4in) deeper than the height of the pillar that is to be buried.

3 If the base of the lantern is small, for example just 15cm (6in) deep, you will need a wider concrete base to make it more secure. Prepare a concrete mix made up of one part cement to six parts of concreting sand or aggregate. Add enough water to the mix to make a firm concrete. (A sloppy, wet mix will make it difficult to level the pillar base.) Place a shovel or two of the concrete mix in the hole.

4 If you are intending to light the lantern, thread an electric wire through the base before you lower the pillar into the hole. With the pillar in the hole, stand back and check that the front of the pillar is facing in the right direction. Using a spirit level, check that the pillar is standing vertically straight. If not, adjust it before the concrete sets.

5 Now check that the pillar is level horizontally by placing the spirit level across the top. After making any adjustments to the pillar position, check the level once again both vertically and horizontally until you are happy that it is straight.

6 With a concreting trowel, smooth concrete around the base, making sure it slopes away, and that no concrete will show once you have levelled the soil around it.

7 Leave the concrete mix to set for at least six hours before you add the remaining parts of the lantern. It is vital that the base is held firm before more weight is added.

8 Add each remaining part of the lantern in turn. Their weight gives them stability, but for absolute safety, secure the individual parts with some mastic.

9 Once the main box for the light is in place, position the two final elements: the roof of the lantern and the carved top.

LANTERN PRACTICALITIES

The following information will help you create an effective lantern feature:

• pick predrilled granite lanterns so an electric light can be inserted easily;

• ensure that you have a safe source of electricity (preferably low-voltage);

• LED lights consume little electricity.

Right: *In time, this lantern will weather and develop a surface of algae and moss.*

Laying stepping stones

The popularity of stepping stones in all Japanese gardens comes as a result of their introduction into the tea garden centuries ago. The stones themselves can vary in size and shape but are mostly natural and very thick, sometimes even whole rocks buried with just their tops showing. You can add formal paving, millstones or the occasional large stone beside the *tsukubai* or in any good place to stop and look around. Very large stones can lie on the ground just on a bed of sand, while smaller stones may need to be more firmly installed on a bed of concrete.

When planning a stepping-stone path, avoid using very smooth stones, as these can become slippery and dangerous, especially in damp shady areas. Naturally riven paving is safer and much more attractive to look at. Growing moss between the paving stones is the best approach for a Japanese garden to give the stone a distressed, timeworn quality, or alternatively you can try growing a few ground-hugging plants such as dwarf ophiopogon or ajuga to soften the paving edges.

You will need
- sharp sand
- a wheelbarrow
- a shovel
- a rake
- paving stones
- a sack truck
- cement (optional)
- a concreting trowel
- a rubber-headed hammer
- a spirit level
- a stiff broom

Above: Stepping stones in Japanese gardens are often very thick and substantial, and are designed to sit proud of the surrounding area of gravel or moss.

PATH DESIGN

Design your stepping-stone path as a weaving line of stones. This will add mystery to the garden as the path leads through the wilderness, past shrubs, trees and hills, towards the tea house itself.

1 Choose the line that your tea path will take and remove a layer of topsoil at least the depth of your stones. Collect some sharp sand in a wheelbarrow and pile it along the path. Use a generous amount – the eventual depth needs to be 4–7.5cm (1½–3in).

2 Spread the sharp sand along the path, ensuring it is flat, and even it out. Move the paving stones into place at the side of the path, preferably using a sack truck. You may need two people to handle any heavy, awkward stones.

3 Lay out the pattern of stepping stones before you finally set them. Stand well back from the pattern to assess the effect. In fact, it is advisable to leave them for an hour – even a day – and come back to look at them afresh. Then walk along the path to check that it is an easy and interesting route. Stones should be laid no more than 20cm (8in) apart, and at a regular distance from each other.

4 Heavy stones can be set directly on to the sand, but lighter stones will need a cement base. Make up a dry mix of eight parts sharp sand to one part cement. A dry cement mix is easier to use. Make four or five piles of the mix, 4–6cm (1½–2½in) higher than the desired height of the base of the stone.

5 Lower a paving stone on to the piles of cement. With the rubber hammer, tap the stone down until it is in position. Thin stones can easily break if not well bedded down. Repeat with the remaining stones.

6 The edges and corners of the stones are the most liable to break and tip over because they will take the pressure if the stone is unevenly supported, so shore up any hollow corners with some wet mix.

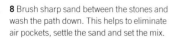

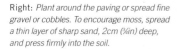

7 On a flat site, check the level of each stone, or if you are aware of the overall fall of the path, make allowances for this. If you don't have a spirit level, use builder's string laid along the length of the path, or you can simply lay a long length of timber down to make sure there are no snags that could trip someone up. Check the level from one stone to the next.

8 Brush sharp sand between the stones and wash the path down. This helps to eliminate air pockets, settle the sand and set the mix.

Right: *Plant around the paving or spread fine gravel or cobbles. To encourage moss, spread a thin layer of sharp sand, 2cm (¾in) deep, and press firmly into the soil.*

The stroll garden style

A stroll garden, just like a pond garden, should be set around a pond as its main feature. The pond is usually stocked with fish and circled by a winding path. The garden should be designed to be seen from various vantage points along this path, where special views are composed. These views can be of a single well-placed pine tree or of a whole scene of the pond with small hills beyond it, maybe with trees that act both as a backdrop and to frame a "borrowed view" or *shakkei* (using elements outside the garden).

ELEMENTS OF A STROLL GARDEN
A stroll garden is made up of many of the elements of pond gardens, dry gardens and tea gardens: a pond, a dry area, lanterns, buildings, fences or statues and decorative planting.

Pond
The garden should have a pond with a varied outline, or one that might correspond to a Chinese ideogram for water or heart. The inlet to the pond may include an area for water irises.

Dry area
An area between the main building and the pond can be made of sand, rocks and clipped shrubs. It can also include a tea arbour, stepping-stone paths, lanterns and water basins.

Above: Stroll gardens usually had large ponds as the focus of the garden. Fishing pavilions such as this one would have been used for boating parties. It would also have given attractive views of the pond from the paths around the garden.

Below: Stroll gardens evolved in the Edo period, and incorporated many aspects of earlier styles. Paths circulate around the garden arriving at points with specially contrived views.

Above: *Paths can be narrow or broad, cobbled or gravelled and may pass groups of trees.*

Right: *Most stroll gardens circle around ponds that are crossed by bridges, such as this one made with a curved stone.*

Lanterns
These can also be placed on the side of slopes or beside the pond – wherever makes the most pleasing composition.

Structures and statues
A rustic wisteria arbour, handsome stretches of bamboo fences, pagodas and statues of Buddha may all feature.

Plants
The planting can be varied and have something for every season. Many stroll gardens include a grove of cherries, but if space is limited, a single tree will do.

Garden plan: a stroll garden

A stroll garden can be made in a relatively small space. If you start with a flat site, small hills can be built up using the soil dug out when the pond is made. The path can wander around these hills and by the edge of the pond. The weaving path will lure the strolling visitor to arbours and vantage points to view cherry groves, waterfalls or iris beds, or to entice them over a natural stone bridge.

Hexagonal thatched arbour

Clipped hedge

Stepping-stone path

HOW TO BUILD NATURAL STONE STEPS

Steps can be created from naturally found rocks or large stones. When building the steps, always start from the bottom and work uphill. Design your steps to follow the natural shape of the garden, allowing them to change direction from time to time. Over long stretches, add the occasional platform or bench as a resting place.

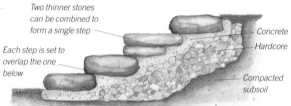

Two thinner stones can be combined to form a single step

Each step is set to overlap the one below

Concrete

Hardcore

Compacted subsoil

1 Measure the vertical and horizontal distances that you need the steps to climb. If you take the average of each stone you have available you can work out the number you will need. The steps should be flat, and the ideal dimensions are 10–15cm (4–6in) risers and 40–100cm (16–40in) treads. With Japanese-style steps these dimensions can vary with each step to make them appear more natural.

2 Dig out to a depth of 10cm (4in) below the lowest step, and lay a 10cm (4in) thick layer of concrete (one part cement to six parts concreting aggregate). Lay the first stone on this concrete slab.

3 If the ground is solid and the hill is not constructed artificially, you may not need the concrete mix, but you will need to firm the soil well as you go. On made-up ground, dig out all the loose soil to a depth of at least 30cm (12in) and backfill on to the compacted subsoil with hardcore, leaving enough room to add the 6–7.5 cm (2½–3in) depth of concrete for each step. Make sure the hardcore is rammed solid.

4 The front edge of each of the stones that you add should rest on the back of the previous one. This will ensure greater stability and will also appear more natural.

5 Set one step at a time, but be careful not to stand on them as you build the next one. For a long stretch it is advisable to build five or six steps at a time, then leave the concrete to set over two days before continuing. If you are building without concrete this will not be necessary.

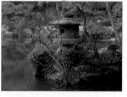

Above: *Lanterns may be placed on promontories as the watchful symbol of the lighthouse.*

Above: *Recycled materials (mitate) such as these millstones make beautiful stepping stones.*

Plant list

1 *Iris ensata*
2 *Wisteria floribunda*
3 Clipped azaleas
4 Weeping cherry trees (*Prunus subhirtella pendula*)
5 Japanese maple (*Acer palmatum*)
6 Bamboo
7 Red pine (*Pinus densiflora*)
8 Japanese black pine (*Pinus thunbergii*)

Cherry grove

Flowering wisteria arbour

Moss

Mixed hedge

Waterfall

Carp stone

Pebble bottom

Rocks

Millstone stepping stones

Water

Iris beds

Solid granite slab bridge

yatsuhashi bridge

Dry sand garden

Pond outlet

Hooped bamboo strips

Right: *Waterfalls and pond inlets in stroll gardens are built with naturalism and artistry.*

Left: *There are many styles of bridge in wood or stone. A single slab of stone looks very natural.*

How to make a stroll garden

The stroll garden evolved as a style to combine many aspects of the tea garden, dry garden and pond garden. The central feature is usually a pond, with a gravel path that weaves around it, wandering through the garden and reaching vantage points to view specially composed scenes. Stroll gardens can range dramatically in size from park-like gardens to relatively small spaces; in small gardens, it may be possible to increase the sense of space using the technique of *shakkei* (see page 36). The layout shown below is suitable for a reasonably large garden. A gravel path leads to a tea house, then over some stepping stones to a planted area almost surrounded by the pond. A wisteria has been trained over an arbour here and the trailing purple flowers reflect attractively in the water. The process of making this garden is shown in the following pages.

Above: A path's "flow" is linked to the quality of the surface. Smooth gravel or neat granite pavers will enable easier movement than uneven, narrow paving stones. But the latter can contribute to the atmosphere of the garden.

Wisteria arbour

Natural stone steps

Japanese red pine

Tea house

Stepping stones

Pond

Iris ensata   Lantern   Rocks around the edge

Ferns   Gravel path   Hydrangea

PLANNING AND VISUALIZATION

To plan a stroll garden you need some kind of vision of a scenic landscape so that you can sketch out the general contours and outline of the pond. From the house you may also compose a scene that will be framed by a window or an arbour. In a stroll garden you may have some open grassy areas, some hills, a bridge and one or two good vantage points from where a variety of scenes can be viewed. Ponds should have some shady, deeper areas for fish to shelter from the heat. Paths can be made in any style but the main strolling path should be surfaced in gravel and wide enough for two people to be able to stroll side by side.

THE POND AND PLANTING

The main challenge is how to keep the pond water healthy. Unless you are lucky enough to have a natural stream, you will need to circulate the water with a pump. Drainage will be necessary to collect the overflow. You will need to be sure you can keep an adequate water supply going so that the water will be well aerated, so get advice on the size of pump required. Otherwise you might have a stagnant, half-empty pond by midsummer.

Make sure that your site is large enough to spread out the soil that is removed when you dig out the pond. This soil can be used to construct small hills, making the site more interesting and intriguing for people using the main gravelled path to wander around visiting tea houses and arbours.

Any fairly open site with good soil, some sunshine and good access can be used. Shady areas can be adapted to grow azaleas and hydrangeas, but cherry trees need an open aspect to grow and flower well. Wisteria too needs at least half a day in full sun to flower abundantly.

TYPICAL FEATURES OF A STROLL GARDEN

- a pond;

- a stream and cascade or waterfall;

- stone or wooden bridges over the stream or to an island on the pond;

- rocks among the plants on pond edge;

- small hills with dwarf or pruned pines;

- a strolling path in gravel or paving stones;

- gates into the tea garden;

- stepping-stone or paved tea paths;

- a wisteria arbour;

- a waiting room or bench;

- a tea house or tea arbour for viewing;

- fences surrounding the garden and bordering the tea path;

- shakkei, or "borrowed scenery";

- lanterns;

- water basins near tea house and on path;

- a dry garden near the house or in an enclosed courtyard;

- extensive plantings including: groves of cherries, plums and maples; groups of clipped azaleas, bamboo and hydrangeas; evergreen trees, especially pines, cryptomeria and hinoki cypress; herbaceous plants such as grasses, anemones, tricyrtis, platycodon, asters.

Making a pond with a flexible liner

The versatility of flexible (butyl) liners has made them the most popular of materials for a variety of applications for holding water, such as lining ponds and streams, and for backing around waterfalls. They certainly provide the greatest scope for small pond design. (For larger ponds, you will need to use a clay or synthetic clay liner; see pages 158–159.) They can also be used with natural stone, concrete or walling blocks to stabilize the sides of an excavation and have the advantage that they will not dry and become brittle if the water level should drop in dry weather.

To calculate the liner size, measure a rectangle to enclose the pool. After measuring the length and breadth, measure the depth and add twice that measurement to each dimension.

The measurements for length and width represent the minimum of liner required. Add about 30cm (12in) to each measurement to provide a small overlap of 15cm (6in) on each side. For brimming pools, where the surface of the water has to be level with the edge,

add a little more than the width of the paving or bricks that will edge the pool to provide enough liner to extend beneath and behind (the end of the liner will finish by being held vertically behind the edging material).

One rectangle of liner can be used for a variety of pool shapes, including designs with narrow waists. Where the wastage would be excessive for narrow sections, smaller joining pieces of some types of liner can be welded together

Above: *When laying out a pond with a butyl liner, make sure that the liner is not visible, especially around the edges of the pond.*

or taped together on site using proprietary waterproof joining tapes. Large creases in the corners of rectangular pools or sharp curves in informal shapes are inevitable, but they can be made to look less conspicuous if the liner is carefully folded before the pond is filled.

You will need
- a garden hose, rope or sand
- a spade
- plastic sheet
- a rake
- a spirit level
- a straight-edged piece of wood
- sand or underlay
- flexible liner (calculate the dimensions as described above)
- bricks or heavy stones as temporary weights
- large scissors
- paving for the pool surround
- ready-mixed mortar
- a mortaring trowel

1 If the pond is to be sited in a lawn, remove the turf by stripping off the grass to a depth of 5cm (2in) in squares of 30cm (12in) and stack the turf upside down for later use. Dig out the hole to a depth of 23cm (9in), angling the sides of the hole slightly inwards. The soil from the top 23cm (9in) can be stored on a plastic sheet nearby if it is to be used for any new contouring of the surrounds. Rake the hole base to a rough level finish after the first layer of soil has been removed and mark with sand the position of any marginal shelves around the sides.

2 The inner or deeper zone, avoiding the marginal shelf outlines, can now be dug out to the full depth of the pond. The soil from this deeper zone will be subsoil and can be used later if it is placed underneath any fresh topsoil. It should not become mixed with the freshly excavated topsoil. Marginal shelves around the sides of the hole should be 30cm (12in) wide and be positioned where you anticipate having the shallow water plants.

3 Rake the bottom of the pool to level the surface and remove any sharp stones, protruding roots or sharp-edged objects. Gently firm the surface by patting. Line the pool with about 1cm (½in) of damp sand – it should stick to the sides if they slope slightly. If the soil is stony, drape a piece of underlay across the hole and shelves, to overlap the edge of the pool by about 30cm (12in).

4 Lay the flexible liner over the sand or underlay. Once you have done this, place temporary weights, such as bricks or heavy stones, on the edges of the liner to keep it securely in place. Make sure that there is enough liner width above the edge of the pool all the way round. Then use a hose to start filling the pond with water.

5 Wait until the water has almost filled the pool, then remove the bricks or stones temporarily holding the edges of the liner. Replace any turf you want around the edge, and complete any edging finishes before the water is filled to the final level. Trim the surplus liner only when you are completely sure that the water level and edging are working satisfactorily.

6 Cut away the surplus liner and underlay, leaving an overlap around the edge of about 15cm (6in) to be covered by the paving.

7 If you want edging paving, bed the paving on mortar, covering the edge of the liner. The paving should overlap the edge of the pool by about 2.5cm (1in). Finish off by pointing the joints with mortar using the mortaring trowel.

8 If there is ample surplus liner, features such as bog gardens can be made around the sides. When a kidney-shaped pool is created, a small bog area can be achieved using the corner piece of a rectangular liner. Instead of cutting off the surplus, place soil on the liner and prevent it from spreading into the main pool water by a small submerged retaining wall of inverted turfs, rocks or walling stones.

Right: *This small pond is surrounded with gravel and provides a home for koi carp.*

Making a gravel path

The Japanese stroll garden is specially designed for taking a walk around the scenic environment and for this you will need a suitable path. A gravel path may seem simple to make, but it must be done properly or all sorts of problems will ensue. The edging of gravel paths is vital, as it prevents the gravel from drifting on to beds, grass or mossy areas. In Japanese gardens this edging is often made of stone or granite blocks. When choosing suitable blocks you should always aim to achieve a balance between the natural and the artistic.

Above: *The minimum width of a path for two people to stroll side by side is 1.5m (1½yds). As well as this practical role, paths also play an important part in linking garden elements and creating fluidity in the design.*

The most common mistake made by gardeners is to dig out a trench and fill it with pea gravel. However, deep gravel is very spongy, making it awkward to walk on, and almost impossible to push a wheelbarrow or wheelchair over. For a successful path, follow the guidelines below.

You will need

- a spade
- a shovel
- a rake
- a wheelbarrow
- edging stones
- concreting sand and cement
- a concreting trowel
- a rubber-headed hammer
- weed-suppressing landscape fabric
- scissors
- "scalpings" or a mix of crushed stone and stone dust
- gravel
- a roller or motorized wacker plate

1 Mark out the edges of the gravel path you are planning. Using a shovel, dig out the area of the path down to a depth of 10–15cm (4–6in) and remove the soil. Lay out the edging stones informally.

2 Position the stones so that you can see what they look like before you actually fix them in place.

3 Fix the edging stones in place using a concreting mix of one part cement to eight parts sand. Firm them in place with a rubber hammer and check that they are level.

4 The concrete mix on the inside edge should fall below the stones by at least 4cm (1½in). Allow the concrete to set for a day before proceeding. Collect some soft sand in a wheelbarrow and bring it to the path.

5 Lay a thin layer of soft sand over the path area. This will protect the landscape fabric from being punctured by small stones.

6 Lay out the landscape fabric so that it tucks in around the edging stones. Cut the fabric to shape with sharp scissors.

7 Spread a layer of "scalpings" or crushed stone/stone dust mix to a depth of 10–12cm (4–5½in), raking it evenly so that the top level is 2–4cm (¾–1½in) below the top of the edging stones. Do not roll this layer.

8 Spread a single layer of gravel over the "scalpings" base, and rake it out evenly.

9 Roll the single layer of gravel so that it is pressed well into the base layer. Now spread another single layer of gravel over this pressed surface and roll again. (Do not spread more than 4cm (1½in) of gravel in total. You can always top it up later.) Test the surface for firmness and comfort before adding any more gravel. Rake out the gravel around the edges of the path so that it works in nicely around the edging stones.

GRAVEL OPTIONS

Type of gravel	Advantages	Disadvantages
Very fine gravel	Easy to deal with, attractive to look at	Can get caught in the soles of shoes and can easily be kicked around the garden
Sand/stone mix	Gives a firm, well-drained finish	Expensive
Stone chippings	Attractive and interesting to look at	Can be uncomfortable to walk on in soft-soled shoes
Pea gravel 10–20mm (½–¾in) in diameter	Ideal for general use, beds down well and tends to stay in place	Will need raking and topping up from time to time

Below: *Gravel paths should be raked and brushed regularly to keep an even layer of gravel.*

Making a wisteria arbour

The native Japanese wisteria, *Wisteria floribunda*, can be seen cascading out of trees on hillsides and valleys in some parts of Japan. Wisteria is ideal for festooning wooden arbours, constructed so that the long scented flower racemes hang down between the rafters. The pendulous flowers look especially wonderful when reflected in water, so arbours are often constructed near to or even leaning out over ponds. In Japan, wisteria arbours are very simple constructions that can be easily assembled from round poles or branches with the bark still on them.

Although rustic poles are ideal for an arbour, it is sometimes difficult to find ones of sufficient strength. (Indeed, some arbours are built using concrete "logs".) This project gets around this problem by using square posts and beams locked together using mortise-and-tenon joints that are fixed by a dowelling peg. The rafters can then be made of rustic poles laid across the beams or lighter-weight poles can be simply fixed in place with screws.

Above: *The two most popular species of wisteria are* W. floribunda, *the Japanese species with very long racemes, and* W. sinensis, *the Chinese species whose flowers are half the length. You will need to allow plenty of headroom in an arbour for these trailing flowers to hang.*

You will need

- posts and beams, 10–14cm (4–5½in) square, made of green oak, cedar or treated softwood
- rafters, 7.5–10cm (3–4in) in diameter, made of rustic poles
- a post-hole digger
- a crowbar
- a spade
- concreting aggregate and cement
- metal post fixers (optional)
- a hammer and chisel to make mortise-and-tenon joints for the upright posts
- 10mm (½in) diameter dowelling
- an electric drill and 10mm (½in) wood drill bit for dowelling
- 7.5cm (3in) screws

1 Mark on the ground where the arbour posts will be placed, making sure they are square.

2 Dig the post holes 25cm (10in) wide and 4cm (1½in) deeper than the post will be. The posts should be set at least 45cm (18in) deep if set in concrete. Make sure the posts are upright and in line.

3 Lightly nail the rafters at an angle from one post to another to make the structure secure.

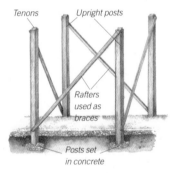

Tenons   Upright posts

Rafters used as braces

Posts set in concrete

4 Set the posts in a concrete mix of one part cement to six parts concreting aggregate. The rafters should ensure that the arbour stays square as the concrete sets. This process requires precision.

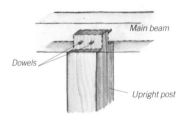

Main beam

Dowels

Upright post

5 Lay the main beams on the mortise-and-tenon joint uprights (at the top of the posts). From the side, drill twice through the beam and the tenon of the post, and hammer in two lengths of dowelling.

6 The dowelling should be tight but it will swell up and tighten more once it gets wet. Set the holes around the posts in the same concrete mix that was used in step 4, ensuring the joints line up snugly, and leave the structure to set for at least 24 hours. You may need to adjust the joints during this time, especially if you are using green oak, which can warp quickly. Once the concrete is set, further bending of the oak will add to the pergola's natural charm.

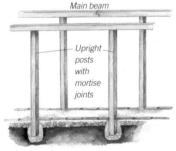

Main beam

Upright posts with mortise joints

7 Remove the brace rafters. Rest the rafters on top, across the main beams. They can be notched to fit over the beam to hold them in place. One or two screws drilled from above down into the main beams should fix them. The arbour is now ready as a structure over which wisteria can be planted and trained.

ARBOUR DESIGN

Timber A mature wisteria plant has twisting stems that can exert a stranglehold on any structure, so any timber you use must be of sufficient strength and thickness to withstand its grip. Green oak is both strong and long-lasting.

Height Japanese wisteria flowers can be more than 50cm (20in) long, so the roof of the arbour should be high enough for a person to stand in comfort beneath the flowers – a recommended 2.5m (8ft).

Posts Set the posts no more than 2m (6½ft) apart along the sides, and at least 1.5m (5ft) apart across the width of the path.

Fixings You could construct an arbour using screws, bolts and nails, but it may not last as long as a mortise-and-tenon jointed construction.

Joinery You may be able to ask a timber merchant to cut the pieces of wood for you and to make the mortise-and-tenon joints. It will then be simply a case of assembling the arbour.

Above right: *This sturdy wisteria arbour draws the viewer into the garden. Arbours are best placed at transition points in a garden.*

Rafter

Overlapping beam

Upright post

Gravel

Stone edging

Stepping-stone path

Wisteria

EXTENDING A BEAM

Dowel

If the main beam requires extending to give the arbour the length you require, create an L-shaped notch in the two pieces of wood, and secure with wood glue. Then drill a hole through both parts and insert a dowelling rod through. When the wood becomes wet, the dowel will tighten.

The courtyard garden style

The form of a courtyard garden has many variations. The main criterion is that it is a small, sometimes minuscule, space contained within a building or the narrow passage that leads from a street to the main door of the house. The courtyard might be viewed from more than one room, so it should look good from more than one angle and is an excellent opportunity to experiment in miniature landscapes or with abstract design, mixing the many elements that make up the various styles. You may find this style of garden in a Japanese restaurant, a hotel or even a temple garden.

ELEMENTS OF A COURTYARD GARDEN

Most courtyard gardens are dry gardens, often laid out with a spread of gravel, sometimes with a stepping-stone path crossing over it. Although the space is limited, there may be room for a very small pond, but in courtyards where no soil is available and light is poor, a purely "dry" garden is ideal.

Lanterns and water basins, along with minimalist planting, are key features.

With enough space, you could combine rocks and plants, a waterfall and a small pond, but more often a courtyard may have only enough space for an island of greenery in the middle, decorated simply with a few rocks, ferns, a water basin and lantern.

Above: A chequered pattern of moss and gravel on the Brunei Gallery roof garden in London evokes the one used by Mirei Shigemori at Tofuku-ji in the 1930s.

Below: Dry gardens suit roof gardens well, where the weight of soil and invasive plant roots might damage the building. This dry courtyard garden contrasts natural rock forms with carved blocks.

Lanterns and water basins

Most courtyard gardens include a lantern and water basin arrangement, similar to that found in a tea garden. A taller water basin, or *chozubachi*, can also be placed where it can be easily reached from the veranda of a nearby room or passage, and where the eaves of the house help to protect the water.

Plants

In a very shady courtyard, some plants do not grow well, and you will have to choose shade-loving plants such as aucuba, camellia and bamboo. With more light, a single pine tree or cherry tree might provide a point of focus and possibly some welcome shade in the heat of summer.

Left: *These raised paving stones give a sculptural quality, as well as leading up to the veranda.*

Below: *Courtyard gardens can be made in almost any enclosed space. They are typically bordered by the walls of the house.*

Garden plan: a courtyard garden

Courtyard gardens, or *tsubo-niwa*, can be made in the most unpromising sites, in narrow passages or in places where little light can reach. They often include elements from other garden styles, such as sand and rocks from the dry garden, or stepping-stone paths, lanterns and basins from the tea garden (with careful consideration of the miniature scale). Plants could include a clipped pine, an azalea, bamboo and a few ferns. The gardens are usually enclosed within walls or fences.

CREATING A *SHUKKEI*

The art of *shukkei*, which literally means "concentrated view", is most often found in courtyard gardens, especially in the form of a *kare-sansui* (dry-mountain-water) design made up of stones, gravel and clipped plants. The aim is to reduce an entire landscape scene to a miniature scale.

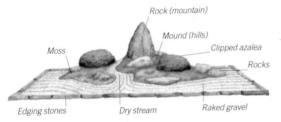

Rock (mountain)
Mound (hills)
Moss
Clipped azalea
Rocks
Edging stones
Dry stream
Raked gravel

Glass

Above: *Sleeve fences are used to deflect or to help frame a view.*

1 When choosing and planning your location note that *shukkei* should be laid out over a level site. The scenery can then be built up using small amounts of soil and rocks to suggest mountain and hill ranges. To do this, make small mounds of earth into which you will "plant" your rocks. Choose rocks that have credible mountain shapes. Some of these rocks can be almost buried, leaving exposed areas to look like escarpments.

2 Re-work the soil after placing the rocks to create a realistic undulation of hills and valleys, leaving indentations around the edges at ground level where you might expect seas and rivers to have eroded the natural forms.

3 Plant azaleas or boxwood, which can be clipped into mound or hill shapes, around the rocks and on the mounds. You can also add a wizened old pine to suggest an open weathered mountainside. Plant the earth with pieces of moss if you can find some, or with dwarf "dragon's beard" (*Ophiopogon*).

4 Spread gravel and sand around the level area to suggest an area of sea or a lake, drawing some of the sand into the scenery you have created where rivers might flow.

Veranda

Right: *Tall water basins (chozubachi) are often placed where they can be reached from the veranda. Long-handled ladles of metal or carved bamboo are usually laid across them, along with a bamboo lattice to prevent leaves from falling in.*

Lantern

Bamboo fence

Sleeve
fence

Large rock

Stone

2

3

Mossy mound

Stepping stones

Sand

Water basin

Step down

Plant list

1 Clipped bamboo
  (*Phyllostachys nigra
  henonis*)

2 Soft shield fern
  (*Polystichum
  setiferum*)

3 Clipped azalea

4 Hart's tongue fern
  (*Asplenium
  scolopendrium*)

5 Red pine (*Pinus
  densiflora*)

Left: *Stepping stones
across sand look
effective when
surrounded by moss.
These paths may be
used for tea ceremonies,
where guests will leave
the house by one door,
and walk along the path
into a specially prepared
tea room.*

Left: *This high bamboo
fencing gives a clear
definition to the edge
of the courtyard.*

How to make a courtyard garden

The courtyard garden is any small area in an enclosed space that incorporates traditional features found in other Japanese garden styles. Some are dry gardens with just a spread of sand and one or two rocks, while others might include elaborate paths that cross over the space, using plantings that evoke a distant but miniaturized landscape. Here is a suggestion for a courtyard garden in a level space. A mound (middle back), which represents a hillside, is planted with a dwarf Japanese red pine, ferns and *Ophiopogon japonica*. The space itself is walled on one side and has a bamboo screening fence on two other sides. Crossing the space is a semi-formal stone path leading from a door in the house to a side gate. Like most courtyard gardens, this one also includes a lantern and a water basin – elements borrowed from the tea garden. The process of making this garden is shown on the following pages.

Above: *Defined as a closed-off external area, the courtyard garden is an excellent style to use for controlled drama. The minimalism and simplicity of this design, a view from a Japanese restaurant, creates an attractive, peaceful pictorial composition of the enclosed garden beyond.*

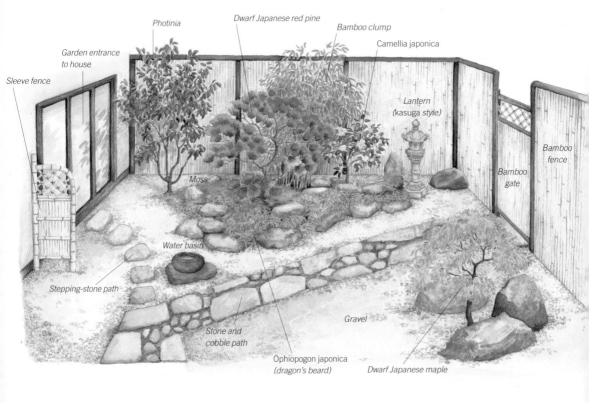

Photinia

Dwarf Japanese red pine

Bamboo clump

Camellia japonica

Garden entrance to house

Sleeve fence

Lantern (kasuga style)

Bamboo fence

Moss

Bamboo gate

Water basin

Stepping-stone path

Stone and cobble path

Gravel

Ophiopogon japonica (dragon's beard)

Dwarf Japanese maple

COURTYARD GARDEN: TYPICAL FEATURES

The following features would normally be found in a courtyard garden:

• sliding screens, small fence panels and bamboo blinds for private areas;

• dry-garden elements with one or two rocks and a "pool" of raked gravel;

• stone paving bordered by lanterns;

• stepping stones;

• clipped evergreens such as azaleas, mahonias, nandinas and bamboos;

• glossy evergreen shrubs, such as aucubas, fatsias and camellias, as well as shade-loving ferns, bamboos and farfugiums;

• a carpeting of moss;

• lanterns, basins and small bridges.

PLANNING AND VISUALIZATION

Before making a courtyard garden, you need to think carefully about your design. If you want to include a number of features, then you must have an overall composition that is coherent. Is your garden going to act as a path from one room to another, or is it simply going to be viewed from one or two points?

Your next consideration is a question of scale. A *shukkei*, or condensed landscape, for example, should not have too many features, as this might make it appear too busy. Make a plan, and stand back from time to time to check the view over the garden as you construct it.

As courtyards are, by their very nature, enclosed, access to them can be tricky, so make sure you can get all the materials into the space (some may have to come through the house, which could be difficult). Also, being so close to a house, the space may have water, electricity and gas services crossing underneath, so check before doing any excavation. Generally, deep excavation is not necessary in courtyard gardens except to ensure that the site is well drained before planting anything.

Courtyards may not have a great deal of light, so plants should be carefully chosen to suit the amount of light available. Remember that you will need a source of water to irrigate the plantings, to maintain any water feature and to keep the space clean. Electricity may be required for lighting or for any water pumps, but neither of these is essential for a successful courtyard garden.

Building a bamboo screen fence

The design and construction of bamboo fences in Japan has developed into a highly specialized and elaborate art, and if you are interested in developing the skills to make your own traditional fence, there is no shortage of information available. If you prefer a more instant solution, however, you can buy sections of these beautiful bamboo fences ready-made from specialist suppliers. In this project, rolls of bamboo canes, held together with wire and supported with a frame, were used, which required a fence on two sides that would act as a screen.

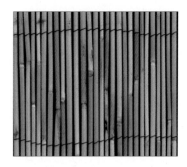

When using bamboo in rolls, you will need to build a suitable frame against which to support the bamboo. Every one of the timber elements in the frame should be made of durable hardwood or treated softwood. You should also remember to apply an additional coat of preservative to the parts of the posts that are going to remain underground.

Above: *A detail of bamboo fence supplied in a roll. This economical form of fencing is often used, even in authentic Japanese gardens. Bamboo of this type will usually need replacing after five to ten years, depending on the weather and how well it is cared for.*

You will need

- 10cm (4in) square posts, 2.5m (8ft) long
- a 5 x 7.5cm (2 x 3in) supporting baton, ideally just one length measuring the length of the fence
- temporary supporting batons to hold posts in position
- 4 x 5cm (1½ x 2in) cross batons, in 1.5m (5ft) lengths
- capping timber 14 x 4cm (5½ x 1½in), the length of the fence
- vertical strips 2.5 x 7.5cm (1 x 3in) and 2m (6½ft) long for facing boards to hold the fence in place
- a roll of bamboo fencing, 2m (6½ft) high – these are usually available in 3m (10ft) lengths
- a wood saw
- an electric drill
- 6cm (2½in) screws
- a screwdriver
- a spirit level
- concrete mix of aggregate using 1 part cement to 6 parts aggregate
- a chisel
- a shovel
- a wheelbarrow
- thick black jute twine

1 Identify your fence line with builder's twine. Mark out the position of the posts, around 1.5–2m (5–6½ft) apart. Dig holes for the posts up to 45–50cm (18–20in) deep by 20cm (8in) wide. Stand the posts upright in the holes. Screw on the lower supporting baton, which should be 4cm (1½in) off the ground and perfectly level. This will help to keep the posts square.

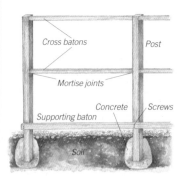

Cross batons   Post

Mortise joints

Concrete   Screws

Supporting baton

Soil

4 Once all the posts have set, remove the temporary supporting batons. Chisel out shallow mortises in the uprights to receive the cross batons (see mortise-and-tenon detail shown on page 198). The cross batons, and therefore the joints, should be positioned half way up the posts and at the top of the posts. From the side, drill through and screw the mortise-and-tenon joints into the posts.

2 For extra stability, erect some temporary supporting batons to help hold the posts perfectly upright while the concrete sets.

3 Make up a mix of concrete and fill the holes, tamping it in firmly around the posts. Using a spirit level, check again that the posts are in line, and are square and upright. Leave the concrete to set for at least 24 hours.

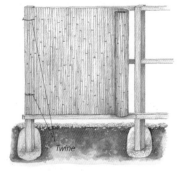

Twine

5 Stand the roll of bamboo fencing on the lower supporting baton, temporarily attaching one end of it to a post with some twine. Unroll the fence, attaching it to the cross batons with twine as you go and as necessary to hold it in place. You can leave the twine in place attaching the bamboo roll to the cross batons as additional support, particularly if you weave it in a way that makes it an attractive addition to the design.

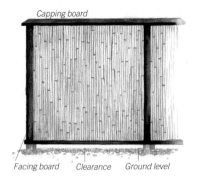

Capping board

Facing board   Clearance   Ground level

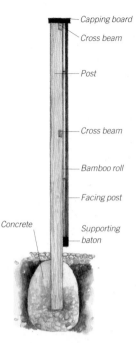

Capping board
Cross beam

Post

Cross beam

Bamboo roll

Facing post

Concrete

Supporting baton

6 To hold the bamboo roll securely in place, screw facing boards on to the posts. Cut off the tops of the posts so that they are level with the top of the bamboo fence roll. Lay the capping boards over the tops of the posts and then screw them down on to the posts. Either stain all the exposed timbers ash black or leave them to weather naturally.

Below: *The neutral colour and quality of bamboo fences make them excellent backdrops to many styles of Japanese garden.*

Left: *Cross-section of a bamboo fence.*

MAINTAINING THE FENCE

If you maintain your bamboo fence well, it will last much longer. Bamboo will eventually become brittle and attract mould if left untreated, so, every year or two, scrub off the mould and apply either some light teak oil or a matt varnish diluted 1 part varnish to 3 parts white spirit. (There are special wood preservatives formulated for willow and hazel fences that would be equally effective on bamboo.) To make maintenance easy, make sure that you attach the bamboo roll to the fence in such a way that it will be easy to remove. For example, don't use heavy nails as these will be hard to pull out without damaging the frame.

Note that some bamboo rolls are made of heavier cane than others – the larger the cane, the longer they will last.

Laying a paving-stone path

There are many styles of stone path to choose from in the Japanese garden (see pages 126–127 on path styles), but they almost all use natural materials in a combination of formal and informal shapes. Your choice of design may be determined by the availability of materials. This courtyard garden uses a combination of local paving stones, most of which have at least one straight edge, and large cobbles from a local quarry. Using the straight edge to act as a border to the path, the cobbles are set out to weave a thread through the path, unifying the design.

Above: *A randomly paved path makes a bold entrance to the Huntington Botanical Gardens. The guardian dogs are a Chinese inspiration.*

It is advisable to lay a path with a complex design such as this on a level site over a concrete base. You should make sure that the surface allows rainwater to drain off, because stones that stay wet will become slippery and therefore dangerous.

To keep the stones clean, lay them on a dry mix of cement and moist sand, rather than using a wet cement mix. This mixture can also be easily brushed into joints between the stones. The mixture will then set either from the moisture in the sand or from rain. If the weather remains dry, hose down the paving stones with water after they have been put in place to make sure that the cement sets properly.

There is a danger of the stones becoming stained by the cement while laying. For any persistent stains, use a stain remover, such as muriatic acid, which will dissolve cement. Always follow the manufacturer's instructions carefully when using chemicals.

You will need
- hardcore for the base
- a wheelbarrow
- a sack truck
- different sizes of natural paving stones
- large rounded cobbles or smooth, flat-topped stones
- marker paint or powdered lime
- white chalk
- concreting sand and cement
- a shovel
- a tape measure
- a bricklaying trowel
- a rubber-headed hammer
- a stiff broom
- stain remover (muriatic acid)
- old rags
- builder's twine

1 Prepare a level site with a solid hardcore base and lay out the stones and cobbles on the ground to establish the pattern you want. Mark out the outline of the path with marker paint. This type of paint comes in spray cans, and is available from most builders' merchants. Alternatively, sprinkle a line of powdered lime which will dissolve after a few days.

2 Number or code each stone with white chalk so you remember which stone goes where in the path. Then remove all the paving stones to one side of the path. Obviously some variations may occur when you replace the stones, but try to keep the main dynamic of the design within the marked eges of the path.

3 Dig out the base to a depth of 10–16cm (4–6¼in), allowing 5–7.5cm (2–3in) for the concrete mix and 3–5cm (1¼–2in) for the paving thickness, and 2–4cm (¾–1½in) for the gravel. If you want the paving to sit proud of the ground, reduce the depth to allow for this.

4 Make a mix of 1 part cement to 8 parts sand. Lay the paving slabs first, spreading this mix (dry or wet) to a depth of 5–7.5cm (2–3in).

5 The mixture should be heaped up in the corners so that each stone is laid higher than its intended level, as its weight will press the mix down.

6 Once the stones have been laid and the mortar mix is set, fill in over the mortared areas with a dry mix of 1 part cement to 8 parts sand and brush it level. Tamp the stones down gently with the handle of a hammer. Use a spirit level to check that the stone is level.

7 Lay out the cobbles on top of the dry mortar mix, push them down and tamp them into position. Here, the cobbles sit proud of the mortar mix, which has hardened from the ambient water and some rain.

8 Once the stones and cobbles have nearly set, apply some water to the surface to check it flows away from the path. Brush or scrape out any excess mortar that may be preventing water from draining off the surface of the path.

9 After two or three days, wash off any stains from the path using stain remover and a rag.

Right: *The deep-set pointing of the path will encourage moss to grow after a few years, particularly in dark, damp areas. You can encourage it by adding leaf mould or compost in the gaps and keeping it damp, but it is best to keep the stones themselves clean and dry – otherwise they may become slippery with algae.*

Building a mound

Courtyards are often contained on level sites within buildings or compounds where there is little or no soil, and where a complex web of underground services may be running beneath the garden. In this courtyard garden, building up a mound of earth answered this practical issue, and also added to the artistry of the garden, because the mound of earth takes on the representation of a landscaped hill, or even a mountain. Planted with a dwarf Japanese red pine, and laid with rocks, the garden has the feeling of a condensed landscape.

As moss can be tricky to establish in many climates, planting the lower level with dwarf ophiopogon helps to give the appearance of a grassy hillside, while ferns soften the outline of the rocks. Finally an authentic Japanese touch is achieved by placing both a lantern and a water basin just off the paved path that crosses the courtyard to the gate.

Above: *Mounds of moss represent the Mystic Isles in this courtyard garden. Rocks in a large expanse of raked sand complete the picture. The mounds form dramatic shapes in the space and give structure and balance to the created landscape.*

You will need

- 2–3 tonnes of screened topsoil
- a wheelbarrow
- a shovel
- a selection of small rocks
- a sack truck to move rocks
- plants: a dwarf Japanese red pine, a clump of *Ophiopogon japonicus*, a *Camellia sasanqua*, two *Polystichum setiferum* (ferns)
- a planting trowel
- a paving stone
- sharp sand
- a rubber-headed hammer
- a water basin
- a lantern
- gravel
- a rake
- a broom

PRIOR PLANNING

- Assess the site access before ordering materials such as soil and rocks.

- If you are building a mound on a rooftop, ask a building engineer to assess the load that the building can carry.

1 Add a heap of screened topsoil to the area, surrounding it with a ring of stones to prevent soil spilling on to the gravel. The stones can be moved later, so put them into temporary positions for now. Then start shaping the mound so that it has natural contours.

2 Plant large shrubs first. Placed at the highest point, the dwarf Japanese red pine anchors the mound, accentuates the shape of the hill and gives a central feature. Place more rocks on the banks of the mound to create the escarpments and rocky outcrops.

3 Partly bury the rocks so that only a third remains exposed. Simply placing rocks on top of the soil will look unnatural. Reshape the mound and build up soil behind the rocks for planting pockets and to create a more uneven shape. Stand back to check the result.

4 If you already have a clump of ophiopogon or have bought a large pot, you can divide the plant up by simply pulling it apart. Firmly gripping the base of the plant, tease it apart gently, taking care not to break too many of the roots.

5 Plant your ophiopogon divisions around the slopes of the mound at a distance of approximately 15cm (6in) apart, tucking them under the rocks. The plants will spread until they knit together eventually to form a carpet. Plant the ferns underneath the pine.

6 The next stage is to lay a well-shaped paving stone on to which you will place the water basin. The paving stone can be simply laid on a bed of sharp sand, without any cement. Spread the sand out evenly and then raise it up in small ridges.

7 Lay the stone on the sand base. Tamp the stone down with a rubber-headed hammer.

8 Place the water basin on the stone. Leave space at the side for a ladle, for guests to drink from and clean themselves.

Below: *The underplanting of Japanese mondo grass (Ophiopogon japonicus) will knit together to form a solid carpet over the next few years.*

9 Follow the step-by-step guide to installing a lantern on pages 184–5. Place some more rocks artistically around the lantern and in other places on the flat area.

10 Spread an even layer of gravel over the entire flat area to create a dry garden effect. Clean the paving and brush out any gravel that has strayed into the joints of the paving.

PLANT DIRECTORY

The Japanese have planted beautiful trees and shrubs ever since they first started making gardens. Although initially many plants were brought over from China, gardeners soon harnessed the potential of the native plants. Japan has exceptional and enviable flora, including many species of cherry, azalea, camellia and magnolia, which blossom in the mountains in spring, while in the autumn, maples and oaks give a display of fiery reds, yellows and oranges. Evergreen trees such as cedars and pines are considered symbols of longevity and resilience.

Wisterias, peonies and hydrangeas feature in many Japanese gardens, in natural groupings or massed in orchard-like groves rather than in formal beds. Herbaceous and bulbous plants, such as platycodons, lilies, hostas or Japanese anemones, are usually planted naturalistically with ferns in individual clumps near the base of a rock, in a carpet of moss, or scattered in small groups. Irises are grown in swampy areas or in formal beds near the inlet of ponds, while sedges and ferns are used to soften the edges of streams. This chapter will show you many of the best plants to use, along with seasonal highlights and care instructions.

Above: *The stunning autumn foliage of* Acer palmatum *'Sango-kaku'.*
Left: *Wisteria is a classic plant in Japanese gardens.*

How plants are named

All living things are classified according to a system based on principles that were devised by the 18th-century Swedish botanist, Carl Linnaeus. The method used a two-name method of classification, where all plants were given two Latinized names to determine their relationship to all other living things. This system states that a particular plant genus (plural: genera) is a group of plants containing similar species. Beyond that there may be plants that are simply a slight variation of a species, or are a hybrid (cross) of different species or variations.

Above: Camellia sasanqua *is a species native to Japan. It starts to flower in late autumn, with more flowers opening throughout the winter.*

SCIENTIFIC NAMES

Under this internationally adopted system, plants have botanical names, which are often Latin but are also derived from other languages that consist of the genus name (for example, *Prunus*), followed by the name that denotes the particular species (for example, *serrulata*). Some genera contain a number of species that may include annuals, perennials, shrubs and trees, while others contain just one species. While all members of a genus are assumed to be related to each other, this is not always visually obvious.

A species is defined scientifically as consisting of individuals that are alike and tend naturally to breed with each other. Despite this system, botanists and taxonomists (the experts who classify living things) often disagree about the basis on which a plant has been named. This is why it is useful for a plant to retain its synonym (abbreviated to syn. in the text), or alternative name. Incorrect names often gain widespread usage, and in some cases, two plants thought to have separate identities, and with two different names, are found to be the same plant.

VARIATIONS ON A THEME

Genetically, many plants evolve over time to adapt to a changing environment. In the wild, natural random mutations will survive and reproduce only if they are well adapted. The average garden is a controlled environment, so variations can be grown within a species that have small but pleasing differences such as variegated leaves and double flowers. The terms for these variations are subspecies (subsp.), variety (var.), form (f., similar to variety and often used interchangeably) and cultivar (cv.). A cultivar is a variation that would not occur in the wild but has been produced by deliberate cross-breeding. Cultivars are given names in single quotes, for example *Prunus mume* 'Beni Chidori'.

HYBRIDS

When plant species breed with each other, the result is a hybrid. Rare in the wild, crossing is very common among plant-breeders, and is done to produce plants with desirable qualities such as larger or double blooms, variegated foliage and greater frost resistance. A multiplication sign (x) is used to indicate a hybrid, and the name will often give a clear idea of the origins of the hybrid.

GROUPS

A plant group is a grouping of similar variations. Their names do not have quotation marks, for example *Tradescantia* Andersoniana Group.

Callicarpa japonica

Deutzia

How to use the plant directory

Within the plant directory, the plants are split into sections relating to seasons and particular types of plants, such as Spring Trees and Shrubs, Autumn Foliage or Evergreen Shrubs. Each main entry within these sections features the botanical name, the Japanese name, the common name and the plant's family. This is followed by a general introduction to that genus with a description of the plant, including the leaves, flowers and growth habit. There are also brief notes on methods of propagation, flowering time, average size, preferred conditions, as well as a guide to the plant's hardiness. Entries in the directory often also suggest a selection of closely related species that may fulfil a similar role in the garden.

Paeonia suffruticosa

Genus and species name
This is the internationally accepted botanical name for a group of related plant species. This starts with the current botanical name of the plant, and this can refer to a species, subspecies, hybrid, variant or cultivar. If a synonym (syn.) is given, this provides the alternative name(s) for a plant. A common name may be given after the botanical name.

Japanese name
The Japanese name for each plant is given.

Common name
This is the non-scientific, vernacular name, so it is different in each language.

Propagation
This gives the best method of producing more plants by seeds, cuttings, grafting or other methods.

Flowering time
This indicates the season of flowering, where applicable.

Size
The average expected height and spread of a genus or individual plant is frequently given, although growth rates may vary depending on location and conditions. Metric measurements always precede imperial ones. Average heights and spreads are given (as H and S) wherever possible and appropriate, and more consistently for perennials and bulbs, although it must be noted that dimensions can vary a great deal.

Paeonia suffruticosa
Botan, moutan
Tree peony
Family: Paeoniaceae
The tree peony flowers at exactly the same time as the wisteria, and both are associated in Japan with beautiful women. There are many cultivars of *Paeonia suffruticosa*, known as the "flower of prosperity" and the "king of flowers" because of its luxuriant blooms. It is not easy to cultivate in Japan, and the flowers are too gorgeous and blowsy for the subtle refinement of most of their gardens, so it is usually grown in pots. The most prized colours are white, pale pink and red. It is often represented on painted screens with lions, tigers and bamboo plants.
Propagation grafted
Flowering time late spring to early summer
Size shrub to 2.1m (7ft)
Pruning by removing over-long and crossing shoots in late winter
Conditions full sun or partial shade; deep, rich soil
Fully hardy/Z 4–8

Photograph
A large number of entries feature a full-colour photograph that makes identification easy.

Caption
The full botanical name of the plant in question is given with each photograph.

Family
This shows the larger grouping to which the plant belongs and can reveal which plants are related to each other.

Pruning
Indicating the most effective method of pruning and at which time of year this should take place.

Conditions
This section gives the level of sun or shade that the plant either requires or tolerates, with advice on the best type of soil in which they should be grown.

Plant hardiness and zone
A plant's hardiness and zone are given at the end of this section. Zones give a general indication of the average annual minimum temperature for a particular geographical area in the USA. The smaller number indicates the northernmost zone it can survive in and the higher number the southernmost zone that the plant will tolerate. In most cases, only one zone is given. (See page 511 for details of hardiness ratings, zone entries and a zone map.)

Spring trees & shrubs

The first signs of spring are a cause for celebration throughout the temperate world, but especially in Japan. In spring gardeners enjoy the bright green of new buds and the blossoms of the azaleas. Camellias and some azaleas are evergreen; some varieties flower very early, and they lend themselves well to being clipped. Kerria has been grown in Japanese gardens since the 11th century and often flowers early, as do many species of magnolia, some of which are native to Japan. You will also find many varieties of rhododendron in full bloom.

Above: *The red flowers of* Chaenomeles japonica, *the Japanese quince, open almost as soon as winter ends.*

Camellia japonica
Tsubaki

Camellia

Family: Theaceae

This evergreen shrub, native to the warm temperate coasts of Japan, is planted in gardens together with species and hybrids from China. *Camellia sasanqua* has smaller, narrower leaves than *C. japonica*, and the pale pink single flowers appear sporadically through winter before dropping when spent.

Camellias are now common, but in the past they were found mainly in Buddhist temples. The simpler, paler coloured, single-flowered forms with glossy foliage, known as *wabi-suke*, were planted in tea gardens. Two types of camellia can be grown as hedges: the dense, glossy foliage of *C. japonica* or the tea plant *C. sinensis*, with smaller leaves than other species and white flowers in autumn, often clipped to give a compact, dense shape.

Propagation semi-ripe leaf cuttings
Flowering time mid- to late spring
Size shrub or small tree to 10m (30ft); keep to 2m (6½ft) by restricting the roots in a tub, or by regular stem pruning
Pruning by thinning out stems after flowering
Conditions light shade and away from early morning sun; moist, acid soil
Fully hardy/Z 6–7

Chaenomeles japonica
Boke

Japanese quince, japonica

Family: Rosaceae

The Japanese quince, or japonica, is loved for its early spring flowers, which range in colour from the deepest scarlet to pale pink and white. They appear before the leaves, clustered close to the bare, spiny stems. It can be pot grown, when it tends to take on a wizened habit of growth.

Propagation semi-ripe cuttings
Flowering time spring
Size shrub to 1m (3ft)
Pruning by cutting back hard after flowering to encourage a compact habit, or training against a frame or wall
Conditions sun or partial shade; well-drained, slightly acid soil
Fully hardy/Z 5–8

Kerria japonica
Yamabuki

Jew's mallow

Family: Rosaceae

A deciduous shrub native to Japan, kerria has been grown in gardens since the 11th century. Its simple, five-petalled, orange-yellow, star-like flowers are a welcome sight in spring. The double-flowered form is most common in the West, but Japanese gardens tend to use the single form, usually planted as part of a broad scheme.

Propagation hardwood cuttings
Flowering time mid- to late spring
Size shrub to 2m (6½ft)
Pruning by thinning out old stems after flowering
Conditions full sun or partial shade; any soil
Fully hardy/Z 5–9

Camellia japonica

Kerria japonica

Magnolia

Magnolia spp.
Mokuren

Magnolia

Family: Magnoliaceae

Native magnolias have been planted down the centuries and include the deep purple-pink, lily-flowered *Magnolia liliflora*, known as mokuren; the familiar white, star-flowered *M. stellata*, hime-kobushi; and its taller close relative, *M. kobus*, kobushi. The large *M. obovata*, to 15m (50ft), is a hardy, deciduous tree with highly scented, cream-coloured flowers in midsummer. In more recent years the bold American evergreen species, *M. grandiflora* (bull bay), growing to 18m (60ft), has proved popular, with its large, cream-coloured flowers appearing in late summer. Magnolias are usually planted in large stroll gardens.

Propagation seed and grafted
Flowering time mid-spring to midsummer
Size large shrub or small tree, 3–12m (10–40ft)
Pruning by removing over-long shoots in late winter; best left unpruned
Conditions partial shade; rich, acid soil
Fully hardy/Z 5–9

Paulownia tomentosa
Kiri

Foxglove tree

Family: Scrophulariaceae

Although strictly a native of China, the foxglove tree has been cultivated in Japan since the 9th century. Planted as specimen trees in the courtyard gardens of aristocrats, they became associated with the military leader, Hideyoshi. Paulownias have two notable features: the fabulously large leaves and the beautiful, lavender-blue, foxglove-shaped flowers. It may take a few years and some mild winters before a *Paulownia* will establish a strong stem, but once a trunk has been developed, the tree will form a handsome and perfectly hardy crown.

Alternatively, the stems may be coppiced in spring to encourage the production of massive leaves, up to a metre (40in) wide. This eliminates the flowers, but when combined with bamboos, palms and cycads, it has a bold, tropical look.

Propagation seed
Flowering time mid- to late spring
Size tree to 12m (40ft)
Pruning none needed unless grown as a pollard
Conditions sheltered position in full sun; any soil
Fully hardy/Z 6–9

Rhododendron spp.
Satsuki (small-leaved);
hirado (large-leaved)

Rhododendron, azalea

Family: Ericaceae

Evergreen and deciduous azaleas belong to the genus *Rhododendron* (Tsutsuji), of which 50 species are native to Japan. The two main kinds of azalea are the kirishima (*R. obtusum* type) and the slightly later flowering satsuki (*R. indicum*). There is also the large-leaved azalea, called hirado. Most of the thousand or more hybrids are of mixed parentage and have flowers that span the colour spectrum from purple to pink, salmon and white. Flower sizes vary, as does the growth.

Azaleas, most of which flower after the cherries and wisterias, have no symbolic significance in the Japanese garden. Kirishima azaleas have been grown in gardens since the 11th century, though they are often seen on treeless mountainsides in drifts and mounds. This natural habit has made azaleas the perfect subject for clipping for centuries; they lend themselves to being rounded into mounds that imitate hills, trimmed down to echo the shape of a stream, or used in a clipped form with rocks or at the edge of small pools to add shape and contrast. The clipping also reduces the number of flowers, which, to the Japanese, is a bonus because too much colour over-stimulates the senses. Left unclipped, their flowering is so profuse that the leaves are completely obscured.

The art of *o-karikomi* (similar to the representational forms of topiary) is often practised on blocks of azaleas and camellias. In the garden at Shoden-ji, three groups of clipped azaleas have been planted as part of a dry landscape (*kare-sansui*).

Propagation seed, softwood cuttings
Flowering time spring to early summer
Size shrub 1–3m (3–10ft)
Pruning by shaping after flowering and, if necessary, again in the autumn
Conditions full sun or shade; moist, acid soil
Fully hardy/Z 6–9

Paulownia tomentosa

Rhododendron

Spring blossom

The end of winter is signalled by the plum blossom (mume) whose flowers, appearing as the last snows melt, are regarded as brave and resilient. The delicate pink flowers of the peach tree (momo) are the next to open after the plum, but it is for the sakura or cherry blossom that Japanese gardens have become famous the world over. Indeed, their first flowers entice people out to celebrate spring. Cherry trees are relatively shortlived and are only lightly pruned, while the longer-lasting plum is tolerant of hard pruning.

Above: *The kikuzakura (chrysanthemum cherry), flowering in late April/early May, has as many as one hundred petals per blossom.*

Prunus mume
No-ume
Japanese plum or Japanese apricot
Family: Rosaceae
Like the European sloe (*Prunus spinosa*) and the damson (*P. damascena*), the deciduous Japanese plum has a pure white blossom, which may open in some areas while snow is still on the ground. The earliness of the blossom makes it one of the most popular flowers in Japan. The flowers of some forms are pale or deep pink, covering whole valleys with a haze of colour. The round fruit is often pickled or candied.

Prunus mume

Unlike cherry trees, which are relatively short-lived and resent being pruned, venerable plum trees may be pruned hard. Old trees with their branches covered in lichen are revered more than vigorous young trees; the gnarled trunks might need to be propped up and bandaged like an old soldier, with ropes, jute and hessian, and should still bear a few branches with blossom.

The festivals of plum-blossom in Japan lack the boisterous aspect that you often find later in spring under the boughs of cherry blossom. Plum blossom appears when the weather is often quite cold and is viewed with quiet solemnity, touched with a hint of sadness. A symbol of purity and hope, it is revered as the prophet of spring. *Prunus mume* is also seen as the epitome of integrity and fidelity, "as virtuous as a true gentleman", and its resilience marks it out as one of the "three excellent plants" that bear the winter so bravely (the others are pine and bamboo). It was said to be a courageous tree, releasing its scent from leafless branches while the last of the winter cold persists, which is why it was popular with warriors, who might carry sprigs of plum blossom into battle. According to Japanese legend, when a warbler (the equivalent of a nightingale) sings in the branches of the plum tree, the two join together to become the spirit of the awakening spring.

The most common variety of *Prunus mume* in cultivation in Western gardens is the deep pink form called 'Beni Chidori',

which is sweetly scented. It is an upright shrub to 3m (10ft). The variety 'Omoi-no-mama' is white. Suitable substitutes for damsons include *P. cerasifera* (cherry plum, myrobalan), which grows to 10m (30ft) and has white flowers in early spring (but avoid the purple-leaved form, 'Nigra'); *P. cerasifera* 'Princess' is suitable for a small garden. *P. glandulosa* is a shrub, to 1.5m (5ft), with white to pale pink flowers followed by red fruit.
Propagation budded or grafted
Flowering time early spring
Size small tree to 9m (9yd)
Pruning by thinning out old stems after flowering
Conditions full sun; any soil
Fully hardy/Z 7–9

Prunus persica
Momo
Peach
Family: Rosaceae
The deciduous Japanese peach is the next flowering tree, after the plum, to be honoured in spring. Peaches were planted in great numbers on the sides of Kyoto's Momo-yama (Peach mountain) as an emblem of longevity and perfection. It was on this same mountain that the great shogun Hideyoshi built his Fushimi castle in the late 1500s; his reign was later referred to as Momoyama.

Prunus persica

Peach blossom is a soft, vibrant pink, and the flowers appear just as the leaves unfurl. The peach was thought to win over the spirits of the dead, and was also a sign of new life. Concoctions of peach were taken at the first sign of pregnancy and were administered as a cure for morning sickness. Peach blossom festivals, originating in China, are still celebrated at the beginning of March. They are a special favourite with children, especially girls, who decorate themselves and their dolls in silk and lacquer.

Peach trees are generally rather short-lived (as little as 15 years) and are prey to a number of pests, including the disfiguring peach leaf curl.

Propagation budded or grafted
Flowering time early spring
Size tree to 8m (25ft)
Pruning by removing dead, diseased and damaged branches in midsummer
Conditions full sun; rich, well-drained soil
Fully hardy/Z 7–9

Prunus serrulata
Sakura
Japanese cherry
Family: Rosaceae
It is for the sakura, or cherry blossom, that Japanese gardens have become famous the world over. Their first flowers bring people out in celebration, and there are huge spring festivals for three weeks in April. The length of Japan, "The Land of the Cherry Blossom", friends gather in gardens and public parks to have picnics and sip sake well into the night, as the ephemeral clouds of blossom float above them. People also tie red paper lanterns in the branches, while children run around in the early evening, clapping to the music of drums and *shamisens*, a lute-like instrument.

The classic Japanese cherries mostly date from the late 19th-century Meiji period. These trees often have fully double and profuse blossoms that derive from the Japanese hill cherry, *Prunus serrulata*. The best-loved forms are those with white flowers and dark, unfurling leaves that are revealed as the petals fall.

Before the 19th century Japanese gardeners mainly grew the species *P. incisa* (Fuji cherry), *P. serrulata* (the Japanese hill cherry) and *P. jamasakura* (formerly *P. serrulata spontanea*), when their more subtle elegance was in keeping with the aesthetics of the times. These trees were the object of veneration and celebration, their short-lived blossom being viewed by the samurai as a reminder of their own fragile mortality, and a symbol of chivalry and loyalty to their lords and masters.

The first of the cherries to flower, from late autumn to spring, is *P.* x *subhirtella* (Higan cherry, rosebud cherry). Its weeping forms, 'Pendula Rosea' and 'Pendula Rosea Plena', are very popular in Japan, the cascading branches being propped up by cedar poles and bamboo frames. *P. incisa* flowers soon after, just before its leaves appear, and makes a small, spreading, attractive tree to 8m (25ft), ideal for the smaller garden.

The next to flower is the hybrid *P.* x *yedoensis* (Yoshino cherry), which is named after Mount Yoshino. The white flowers appear just as the leaves break from their buds, and the spreading tree has a lovely, weeping form, 'Shidare-yoshino'. Around the Arishyama district of Kyoto and the gardens of the Tenryu-ji, hundreds of Yoshino cherries have been planted and admired for over 800 years.

The foliage of *P. incisa* also turns beautiful shades of yellow, orange and red in autumn.

In the last 200 to 300 years, especially during the early 19th century Edo period when plant breeding became very popular in Japan, innumerable hybrids and forms of *P. serrulata* were raised. These have become known as simply "Japanese flowering cherries" or Sato zakura (literally "domestic cherries").

Japanese flowering cherries are very easy to grow in almost any soil type that is neither too wet nor too dry. The roots are often very shallow, sometimes lifting to the surface. In general they are short-lived trees, some living less than 50 years. They do not flower all at the same time, so it is possible in a large garden to make a selection from these hybrids and the other species that extend the flowering season from very early spring to late spring.

Propagation budded or grafted
Flowering time early to late spring
Size tree 3–8m (10–25ft)
Pruning only by removing dead, diseased and damaged branches in midsummer
Conditions full sun; rich, well-drained soil
Fully hardy/Z 7–9

Prunus x yedoensis

OTHER CULTIVARS OF CHERRY OFTEN FOUND IN JAPANESE GARDENS

'Amanogawa'

'Shirofugen'

'Ukon'

- 'Amanogawa', a columnar tree with dense clusters of lightly fragrant pink flowers. This is ideal for the small garden or town garden as the tree only spreads to 2m (6½ft) wide and grows only to 8m (26ft) high. Flowers in mid-to late spring.
- 'Beni-yutaka', with semi-double disc-shaped flowers of a unique sugary pink with a dark central eye. Flowers in early to mid-spring.
- 'Hanagasa' (Pink parasol), a tree with a broad spreading habit that bears heavy clusters of long-stemmed blooms in pale pink surrounding a crown of green. Flowers in mid-season.
- 'Ichiyo', a tree with ascending branches with double shell-pink flowers set against bronze green unfurling leaves. Flowers in mid-season.
- 'Kanzan', a classic broad vase-shaped tree often seen in Western gardens, with its densely double, deep purplish-pink flowers. The colour of this popular tree would be too strong for most Japanese garden settings.
- 'Kiku Shidare Sakura' (Cheal's weeping), a charming small weeping tree whose branches cascade vertically down. The flowers are double rose-pink and held in dense clusters.
- 'Pink Perfection', a strong growing vase-shaped tree with bronze unfurling leaves that contrast with the rose-pink flowers. A very dwarf form of this

variety called 'Little Pink Perfection' would be perfect for the small garden or even for growing in a pot.
- 'Shirofugen', one of the oldest and still one of the very best varieties. It makes a vigorous wide spreading tree with large double white fragrant flowers that open late in the season.
- 'Shirotae' (Mount Fuji cherry), another very old variety that almost went extinct in Japan but was rescued by an English plantsman 100 years ago and reintroduced to cultivation. This tree has remarkable branches that spread out almost horizontally and slightly weeping. The very large single and semi-double white fragrant flowers burst in drooping clusters amid soft green emerging foliage. Mid- to late season.
- 'Taihaku' (the Great white cherry), a stunning hybrid that makes a vigorous spreading tree with very large white flowers. Mid-season.

- 'Ukon', an unusual tree for its clusters of pale yellow to sulphur-green flowers that hang from wide spreading branches. Mid- to late season.

Hybrids from some of the other species also have particular properties that are worth considering:

For the small garden:
- *P. incisa* (Fuji cherry) 'Kojo-no-mai', with curious zig-zag growth, and *P. nipponica* var. *kurilensis*, brilliant colour with large open pink flowers.

For autumn colour:
- *P.* 'Amanogawa' (Japanese flowering cherry), *Prunus avium* 'Beni-yutaka', *P.* 'Taihaku' (Great white cherry), *P. sargentii* (Sargent cherry) and *P. incisa*. *P. sargentii* turns bright red while the others turn a mix of orange, yellow and red.

'Taihaku'

Prunus sargentii

Late spring & summer trees, shrubs & climbers

As the last of the cherry blossom falls, the wisteria unravels its pendulous, perfumed flowers. Alongside the wisteria, the tree peony unfurls its fabulous frilly petals. This is a plant with sumptuous flowers, which was highly regarded by the Chinese long before the Japanese introduced it to their gardens. Other plants are grown for their shape and foliage as much as for their flowers, and small trees such as *Styrax japonicus* (Japanese snowbell) continue their blossom season into the summer. Clematis are popular in Japan but are mostly grown in pots.

Clematis spp.
Tessen
Clematis
Family: Ranunculaceae
Some species of large-flowered clematis, such as *C. patens*, are native to Japan. While rarely grown as climbers over arbours as in Western gardens, the colourful hybrids of *C. patens* are often planted in containers and placed near the main house entrance.
Propagation seed, all cuttings, layers
Flowering time summer
Size climber up to 4m (13ft)
Pruning prune regularly for strong growth
Conditions sun and part shade
Fully hardy/Z 4–9

Cornus kousa
Mizuki
Japanese flowering dogwood
Family: Cornaceae
A handsome deciduous large shrub or small tree up to 10m (33ft), native to Japan and China, with wide spreading tiered branches that carry flowers with four white bracts in early summer. They open green and steadily change to pure white, or pink in the variety 'Satomi'. The best form is *Cornus kousa* var. *chinensis*, which freely bears larger and whiter flowers than the straight species. *Cornus kousa* and its forms are outstanding plants, not only because they are very hardy and can be grown in most soil

Clematis patens

types, but also because they flower in midsummer when few other trees or shrubs are blossoming. There are some hybrids between this species and the American flowering dogwood, *Cornus florida*, which flower earlier in the spring.

Cornus kousa

Above: Deutzia gracilis. *This small shrub is smothered with flowers in late spring and has an attractive fine texture.*

Cornus kousa and *C. florida* both turn tones of red and purple in the autumn, keeping their display for up to a month.
Propagation grafted, layers, seed or softwood cuttings
Flowering time early summer
Size small tree to large shrub, up to 10m (33ft)
Pruning remove dead wood after flowering
Conditions sun or part shade
Fully hardy/Z 5–8

Deutzia spp.
Unohana, utsuki
Japanese snowflower
Family: Philadelphaceae
The Japanese grow many species of deutzia in mixed plantings. The shrub's white or pink flowers are borne later than those of other spring-flowering shrubs and can be used to bridge the gap before the summer. *Deutzia crenata* and *D. gracilis*, both native to Japan, have clusters of star-shaped white flowers.
Propagation stem cuttings
Flowering time late spring to early summer
Size shrub 1m (3ft)
Pruning by cutting out old flowering stems after flowering
Conditions full sun; any reasonable soil
Fully hardy/Z 5–9

Paeonia suffruticosa

Paeonia suffruticosa
Botan, moutan

Tree peony

Family: Paeoniaceae

The tree peony flowers at exactly the same time as the wisteria, and both are associated in Japan with beautiful women. There are many cultivars of *Paeonia suffruticosa*, known as the "flower of prosperity" and the "king of flowers" because of its luxuriant blooms. It is not easy to cultivate in Japan, and the flowers are rather too gorgeous and blowsy for the subtle refinement of most of their gardens, so it is usually grown in pots. The most prized colours are white, pale pink and red. It is often represented on painted screens alongside lions, tigers and bamboo plants.

Propagation grafted
Flowering time late spring to early summer
Size shrub to 2.1m (7ft)
Pruning by removing over-long and crossing shoots in late winter
Conditions full sun or partial shade; deep, rich soil
Fully hardy/Z 4–8

Sophora japonica
Enju

Japanese pagoda tree

Family: Papilionaceae

Sophora japonica belies its name. It is not native to Japan, but, like so many garden plants, was introduced from China around 1,000 years ago. This fine stately tree, growing ultimately to 20m (65ft), has elegant pinnate leaves and produces large panicles of small white flowers in late summer.

The weeping form *S. japonica pendula* is often seen in Japan, which needs support as even its main stem has a serpentine nature and is unable to form a straight trunk. The tree may become self-supporting, making an umbrella-shaped mound. While hardy, *Sophora japonica* and its forms need hot summers to ripen the wood and flowers.

Propagation seed (weeping form is grafted)
Flowering time late summer to autumn
Size medium-sized tree up to 20 (65ft)
Pruning prune to remove deadwood
Conditions sun
Fully hardy/Z 7–9

Spiraea nipponica
Shimotsuke

Nippon spiraea

Family: Rosaceae

Several species of spiraea are native to Japan, most small to medium-sized shrubs. They make a round or spreading shape, with arching growth, decked with bunches of tiny flowers. *S. nipponica* has dark green leaves and white flowers.

Propagation semi-ripe cuttings
Flowering time midsummer
Size shrub to 1.2m (4ft)
Pruning by cutting hard back after flowering to remove old flowering stems
Conditions full sun; any soil
Fully hardy/Z 5–9

Sophora japonica

Spiraea nipponica

Stewartia pseudocamellia
Hatsutsubaki

Japanese stewartia

Family: Theaceae

Grown for its small, white-cupped, camellia-shaped flowers (which bloom in mid- to late summer), mottled bark and autumn tints (with yellow, red and purple leaves in the autumn), this small to medium tree is often planted among mixed blocks of evergreen shrubs or as a specimen near a gateway.

Propagation seed
Flowering time midsummer
Size tree to 20m (65ft)
Pruning none needed
Conditions full sun or light shade; moist, acid soil; does not tolerate wind or drought
Fully hardy/Z 5–7

Stewartia pseudocamellia

Styrax japonicus
Storax
Japanese snowbell
Family: Styracaceae
The Japanese snowbell is a small, broad, deciduous tree, with glossy, dark green leaves and masses of small white flowers.
Propagation seed
Flowering time early to midsummer
Size tree to 10m (30ft)
Pruning none needed
Conditions full sun or partial shade; moist, neutral to acid soil
Fully hardy/Z 6–8

Ulmus parvifolia
Akinire
Chinese elm
Family: Ulmaceae
A graceful medium-sized tree, native to both Japan and China. It has relatively small leaves, which are not dropped until well into winter, and hop-like flowers late in the summer. It has given rise to some dwarf forms, such as 'Yatsubusa' and 'Hokkaido', which have extra dense growth and very small leaves and would make ideal companions to other Japanese plants in a very small garden. These dwarf forms could also be pruned to give the appearance of an older, larger

Ulmus parvifolia 'Yatsubusa'

tree in a *shukkei*, or "condensed landscape" arrangement.
Propagation seed (dwarf forms from hardwood cuttings)
Flowering time late summer to autumn
Size medium-sized tree up to 20m (65ft)
Pruning tolerant of heavy pruning
Conditions sun
Hardiness/Z 4–8

Wisteria spp.
Fuji
Wisteria
Family: Papilionaceae
As soon as the cherry blossom has fallen in mid-spring, the long racemes of wisteria start to unravel. *Wisteria floribunda* is native to Japan, where it can be seen in the wild, tumbling out of tall trees and creating blue cascades on steep hillsides. *W. floribunda* has much longer racemes than its cousin from China, *W. sinensis*, and in the cultivar 'Macrobotrys' (formerly 'Multijuga') the racemes of lilac-blue flowers can reach 1.2m (4ft) long. Wisterias were revered for their longevity and were the only climbing plants to have been cultivated seriously in Japanese gardens. They have been grown through pines since the 1600s, but are now more often planted on frames, arbours and tripods. Wisterias also look terrific when they are draped over a specially constructed bridge, with the long racemes reaching down to the water beneath to meet their reflection. Another wisteria grown in Japan is *W. brachybotrys* 'Shiro-kapitan' (syn. *W. venusta*), which produces attractive, beautifully scented white flowers a few weeks before the leaves appear.

Wisterias may also be trained against a firm stake as standards, to stand alone as specimens, or grown more as a shrub, by simply allowing them to spread along the ground. To keep wisterias within bounds, they need to be pruned quite hard. Pruning is done in two sessions, the first in midsummer, when the long wands of growth are reduced by two-thirds, and the second in midwinter, when growth is further reduced to 10cm (4in) spurs. The plant's tolerance of pruning makes it suitable for pot growing as well as bonsai treatment.

Wisteria

Propagation mostly grafted, seed
Flowering time early summer
Size to 9m (30ft)
Pruning in midsummer and in midwinter
Conditions full sun or partial shade; rich, moist soil
Fully hardy/Z 4–10

SPRING FOLIAGE

Early spring is not just about flowers, because Japanese gardeners try to avoid using too much colour. *Salix babylonica* (weeping willow) has been planted around ponds and lakes in Japan since its introduction from China in the 9th century. The soft green of its unfurling leaves is much admired. The young foliage of *Acer palmatum* is quite varied, with tints ranging from soft green to salmon pink. In general, purple, golden and variegated foliage is not found in traditional gardens, because the colours are too unnatural and detract from the overall design.

Summer flowers

Japanese summers often bring heavy rain, which few flowers can endure. However, hydrangeas continue to flourish in these conditions, and in recent years they have gained in popularity. Apart from hydrangeas, two flowers are often grown as Buddhist symbols of mortality and immortality: the annual morning glory for its fleeting existence, and the lotus, a symbol of purity as it emerges out of the wet mud in ponds. The iris is also planted in or near water, and is a plant celebrated for its power to ward off evil spirits.

Above: *The mop-headed* Hydrangea macrophylla *here grows profusely in a shaded woodland.*

Hydrangea spp.
Ajisai
Hydrangea
Family: Hydrangeaceae
Hydrangeas were first mentioned in Japanese gardens as early as 759, but they did not become instantly popular. The four petals and rather gloomy purple colours were thought to represent death. The common name, ajisai, means "to gather purple". They were also called shichihenge, which meant "to change seven times", alluding to the way in which the flower colour changes through the season.

Three of the most important species of hydrangea are native to Japan, *Hydrangea macrophylla*, *H. petiolaris* (climbing hydrangea) and *H. serrata*. The great round mop-head hybrids originated here and are found in a number of Japanese gardens. Among their useful attributes are their late-summer flowering and their ability to withstand heavy summer downpours. On acid soil with plenty of moisture, the blue varieties are intensely blue. The lacecaps, which come closer to the species in their flower form, are also very elegant and suitable for planting in light woodland shade, where their mysterious beauty can be almost bewitching, especially when the flowers are moist from the rain. Varieties of *H. macrophylla* can be grown in pots, if regularly fed and watered. The other species that is native to Japan is *H. paniculata*, which has cone-shaped flowerheads in late summer. It is ultra-hardy and can be grown in full sun. All these hydrangeas come in a multitude of forms to suit every taste, and they have become very popular in Japan in recent years, with some towns and districts making the hydrangea their special flower.
Propagation semi-ripe and hardwood cuttings
Flowering time mid- to late summer
Size shrub to 2m (6½ft)
Pruning by removing dead and over-long shoots in early spring
Conditions sun or partial shade; moist, rich soil
Fully hardy/Z 4–9

Ipomoea
Asagao
Morning glory
Family: Convolvulaceae
During the Nara and Heian periods, when poets typically sang of the fleeting condition of human life, they latched on to morning glory as an ideal symbol: as one flower fades after a day of glory, it is quickly replaced by another. But it was in the 18th and 19th centuries that the morning glory became fashionable among the *daimyos*, who helped to create a new array of colours. Morning glory is usually grown in pots over lightweight bamboo trellises and fences. While so many flowers tend to wilt at the onset of summer, the morning glory revels in the heat.
Propagation seed
Flowering time summer to autumn
Size climber to 6m (20ft)
Pruning prune climbing species in spring
Conditions full sun; any soil
Tender/Z 8–10

Hydrangea

Ipomoea

Iris laevigata

Iris spp.
Hanashobu

Iris

Family: Iridaceae

The iris is a great favourite in Japan. *Iris laevigata*, known as kakitsubata, grows naturally in the swamps around the ancient capital of Nara, where it was collected to be made into a dye, its blue colour used to decorate the robes of the imperial family. In *The Pillow Book*, an 11th-century novel, the author writes of the iris festival when men, women and children warded off evil spirits

Iris ensata

by adorning their hair and clothes with iris flowers and roots. The festival still takes place in late May and early June.

I. laevigata is cultivated in gardens in swampy, but not waterlogged, ground, often near an inlet to a pond. *Yatsuhashi* or zigzag plank bridges weave over the beds, forcing the visitor to slow down and admire the plants from different angles. The flowers are said to have a "naive neatness" that needs no improvement; they are narrower and smaller than the larger and flatter *I. ensata* var. *spontanea*, known as hanashobu.

Hanashobu is more spectacular than kakitsubata and has been bred intensively. It now comes in all shapes and colours, from white and pink to deep purple, and is often cultivated in large beds in slightly ridged rows or in pots, so that it can be admired as an individual against golden folding screens.

In parts of Japan where they cannot cultivate either of these irises for lack of water, the European *I. germanica* is often grown in the same way, in large beds exclusively devoted to irises. Other irises grown are *I. tectorum* (roof iris) and the shade-loving *I. japonica*, whose wild look is perfect for the tea garden.

Propagation division
Flowering time summer
Size to 80cm (32in)
Pruning only when dividing
Conditions full sun or partial shade; slightly acid soil
Fully hardy/Z 4–9

Nelumbo nucifera
Hana-basu

Lotus

Family: Nymphaeaceae

By high summer the glories of the spring blossom have long faded, and it is time for the lotus to bloom. The lotus is the flower most closely associated with Hinduism and Buddhism, and the Buddha is often portrayed in statues and images sitting on a lotus, in his state of perfect enlightenment. The lotus symbolizes the evolution of the human spirit, with its roots in the mud, its growth passing through water and air and into the sun, to

open, pure and unsullied. The wheel-like formation of the petals is also said to represent the cycle of existence.

A succession of flowers opens over six weeks, the buds opening at dawn with an indescribable sound. The white flowers of *N. nucifera* 'Alba' have an especially powerful and sweet perfume. Lotus flowers close in the heat of the day and after a couple of days gracefully fall, one petal at a time, leaving their distinctive honeycombed seed pods. The lotus is also an important source of nourishment. The seeds, roots and leaves are all eaten, but varieties grown as food rarely flower. The lotus is not reliably hardy, and some climates are simply not hot enough in the summer to stimulate its flowering. In these circumstances *Nymphaea* (waterlily) is a good substitute, although the flowers sit closer to the surface of the water and are not held on erect stalks, like the tall flower stems of the lotus.

Propagation division
Flowering time summer
Size 1.2m (4ft) above water
Pruning Remove dead, faded or damaged components
Conditions in full sun; in water to a depth of 60cm (24in)
Half hardy/Z 4–11

Nelumbo nucifera

Autumn foliage

Plants that celebrate autumn with their colourful leaves were known collectively as *momichi*, but in time the term became synonymous with the beautiful tones of *Acer palmatum*, the first entry here. Traditional Japanese gardens do contain other trees and large shrubs, although the *Acer* varieties will always be favourites for autumn colour. Some of these trees and shrubs also turn beautiful colours in autumn, while others are more valued for their glossy evergreen leaves as a foil to the bright foliage of the *Acer* and other plants. A few are scented or bear edible fruits.

Acer palmatum
Kaede
Japanese maple
Family: Aceraceae

The Japanese maple is perhaps second only to the cherry blossom in popularity in Japan, and it has become a tradition to take special trips to view the flaming autumn tints of their wild maples. *Acer palmatum* is native to Japan, where it can be seen mingling on hillsides with cedars, bamboos and pines. Although there are hundreds of fancy types of Japanese maple, some with finely cut leaves and others with variegated and purple foliage, the species *A. palmatum* is the chief focus of all the celebrations in gardens and in the wild. *A. micranthum*, *A. tataricum* var. *ginnala* and *A. japonicum* are also native, and all turn beautiful colours, but in November the temples and gardens of Kyoto are ablaze with the fiery red and orange leaves of *A. palmatum*.

Some very beautiful forms of Japanese maple have foliage that is salmon-tinted in spring, while some turn bright yellow rather than red in autumn, and others have bright red or green stems in winter. The dwarf and cut-leaf forms may be more suitable for the smaller garden, but it is better to try and avoid the purple-leaf forms, which tend to distract from carefully composed, harmonious arrangements.

Propagation seed and grafted (all named varieties will need to be grafted, although to raise just one or two plants you can layer them)
Size small tree to 8m (25ft)
Pruning best left unpruned; can cut out over-long stems in late winter
Conditions full sun or partial shade; moist soil; occasionally the young growth can be injured by late frosts or cold winds
Fully hardy/Z 5–8

Other species of maple, native to Japan:

Acer buergerianum
Buerger-kaede
Trident maple
Family: Aceraceae

This small oval tree is often seen in larger Japanese gardens but in a mild autumn holds on to its leaves well into the winter, and will not always colour as reliably as some of the other species. It has a multi-stemmed habit and medium-fine, glossy dark green leaves. The bark exfoliates to expose an orangish under-bark.

Above: Acer palmatum *can be grown as a single or multi-stemmed small tree. In the autumn its leaves turn to shades of scarlet, yellow or orange.*

Acer cissifolium
Mitsude-kaede
Ivy-leaved maple
Family: Aceraceae

This barely looks like a maple at all with its three-lobed leaves. It is one of the very first to colour in autumn, but keeps those leaves for a remarkably long time as they turn a patchwork of oranges, yellows and reds.

Acer ginnala
Amur-kaede
Amur maple
Family: Aceraceae

An upright but eventually broad spreading small tree that has handsome leaves. The form *A. ginnala* 'Flame' has been selected for the brilliance of its autumn colours.

Acer palmatum 'Linearilobum'

Acer buergerianum

Acer japonicum
Momji

Full moon maple

Family: Aceraceae

Second only in popularity to *Acer palmatum*, *A. japonicum* has much larger leaves. While rarely cultivated in gardens it has produced the two forms of 'Aconitifolium' and 'Vitifolium', bold and fine garden plants which are easily grown, slowly becoming medium-sized trees. 'Vitifolium' has leaves like grape vines while those of 'Aconitifolium' are deeply incised. Both come into leaf very early and turn fiery red in autumn. The golden-leaf form, which turns more or less green in summer, is now classified as *Acer shirasawanum* 'Aureum'. Another form of this latter species is *Acer shirasawanum* 'Ogurayama', with smaller leaves and a more upright habit. *Acer sieboldianum* is similar to both these and makes a small tree.

Acer micranthum
Komine-kaede

Komine maple

Family: Aceraceae

A small-leaved maple that grows in native forests in central Japan with *Acer palmatum*. It forms a delightful small wide spreading tree that colours brilliantly in autumn.

Acer rufinerve
Uri hada kaeda

Redvein maple

Family: Aceraceae

This snake-bark maple has long white striations in the bark and beautiful leaves that turn a mix of yellow and red.

Acer japonicum

Acer palmatum var. *dissectum*

SUITABLE CULTIVARS OF ACER PALMATUM

• *A. p.* 'Chitoseyama' has a hint of purple in the foliage as it unfurls in the spring, and then turns purple-red in autumn.

• *A. p.* var. *dissectum* (Dissectum Viride Group) is a small, rounded shrub with deeply cut leaves and fine autumn colour. There are many purple cut-leaf forms of this type that are sometimes planted in contemporary Japanese gardens but their colour intensity is too distracting for more refined and traditional styles.

• *A. p.* 'Ichigyoji' has bold green foliage similar to the species itself but turns an especially bright yellow in autumn.

• *A. p.* 'Katsura' has bright pink young foliage in spring, which turns red in autumn.

• *A. p.* 'Linearilobum' has deeply cut linear leaves that are bright green in spring and summer, turning rich tones of yellow and orange in autumn.

• *A. p.* 'Omurayama' has finely cut leaves that become elegantly pendulous with age. The leaves turn orange and yellow in autumn.

• *A. p.* 'Osakazuki' is a rounded tree with large leaves that turn bright orange and red in autumn.

• *A. p.* 'Seiryu' is a wide spreading small tree of exceptional beauty and an excellent maple for small gardens or for groups. It has elegant, finely cut leaves which unfurl as a soft green and turn a mix of flame colours in the autumn.

• *A. p.* 'Sango-kaku' has salmon spring tints, and the leaves turn yellow in autumn. The stems are red and stand out well in the winter landscape.

Cercidiphyllum japonicum
Katsura

Katsura tree

Family: Cercidiphyllaceae

Thought to resemble the moon, this medium-sized tree has ascending branches and beautifully rounded leaves that colour up in the autumn. As the leaves fall they give off an aroma akin to burnt, crushed sugar.

Propagation seed

Size tree to 20m (65ft)

Pruning by removing over-long or crossing branches in late winter

Conditions sun or light shade; slightly acid soil

Fully hardy/Z 5–9

Acer cissifolium

Cercidiphyllum japonicum

Diospyrus kaki
Kaki
Persimmon
Family: Ebenaceae
A fine autumn tree with yellow to orange fruits. The most edible of date plums, it is grown for its handsome leaves, which turn yellow, orange-red and purple before they fall. In cold areas this frost-hardy plant is best grown against a wall.
Propagation grafted
Flowering time summer
Size tree to 10m (33ft)
Pruning by removing over-long or crossing branches in late winter
Conditions sheltered position in full sun; rich soil
Fully hardy/Z 4–8

Enkianthus perulatus
Dodan
White enkianthus
Family: Ericaceae
A member of the heather family, this large shrub has clusters of small cream- and pink-tinted bells in spring, but is more often grown for its bright red and golden-orange autumn foliage. When pruned hard it produces few flowers, although judicious pruning can enhance its tiered branching. Grow as a hedge or mix with evergreens. An alternative is *E. campanulatus.*
Propagation semi-ripe cuttings
Flowering time mid-spring
Size shrub to 2m (6½ft)
Pruning by cutting out crossing or over-long shoots in early spring
Conditions sun or partial shade; moist, slightly acid soil
Fully hardy/Z 5–7

Enkianthus perulatus

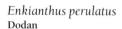
Ginkgo biloba

Ginkgo biloba
Icho
Maidenhair tree
Family: Ginkgoaceae
The ancient maidenhair tree dates back to the time of the dinosaurs. It is unique with no close living relatives. Its leaves, curiously shaped like webbed feet, turn to shades of bright butter yellow in autumn. Originally native to China, ginkgo is now found all over Japan, especially in Kyoto, where trees can be seen growing to an immense size and the ground under them in autumn is smothered in blankets of yellow. They produce an edible but unpleasant-smelling fruit in autumn. *Ginkgo biloba* 'Annie's Dwarf' would be suitable for smaller gardens or pot culture.
Propagation seed and grafted
Flowering time (catkins) spring
Size tree to 30m (100ft)
Pruning by removing diseased or dead branches in late winter or early spring
Conditions full sun; any soil
Fully hardy/Z 5–9

Nandina domestica
Nanten
Sacred bamboo
Family: Berberidaceae
Native to Japan, the nanten is a close relative of *Berberis.* In midsummer, small white flowers are carried in large open panicles, and they are followed by red berries, which lie above the glossy, pinnate foliage. In a good autumn the leaves turn bright red, especially if the shrub has been planted in full sun, although they are tolerant of some shade. In very cold areas

many of the leaves tend to fall by late winter, but the plant is considered to be evergreen.
Propagation seed
Flowering time midsummer
Size shrub to 2m (6½ft)
Pruning by trimming back over-long shoots in mid- to late spring
Conditions full sun; moist soil
Fully hardy/Z 7–10

Stewartia pseudocamellia
Hatsutsubaki
Japanese stewartia
Family: Theaceae
Each leaf of this plant turns a mixture of yellow, orange, green and red. It also has small white flowers in high summer.
Propagation seed
Flowering time midsummer
Size tree to 20m (65ft)
Pruning none needed
Conditions full sun or light shade; moist, acid soil
Fully hardy/Z 5–7

Styrax japonicus
Storax
Japanese snowbell
Family: Styracaceae
This, combined with various cherries, adds lovely shades to the autumn garden. Its leaves are dark green and it bears masses of small white flowers in summer.
Propagation seed
Flowering time early to midsummer
Size tree to 10m (30ft)
Pruning none needed
Conditions full sun or partial shade; moist, neutral to acid soil
Fully hardy/Z 6–8

Nandina domestica

Autumn flowers

The "seven grasses of autumn" have been known and used in Japan since the 11th century. The selection of these seven herbaceous plants has varied over the centuries and from region to region, but in general they are the ones that flower after the summer rains and during the autumn leaf colour season. Included here are some of the original seven, together with a few others that have since gained in popularity. Except for *Miscanthus* none of these are grasses, and the remainder can be categorized as meadow flowers.

Above: *Potted hybrid chrysanthemums outside a Japanese temple.*

Anemone spp.
Shuumeigiku
Anemone

Family: Ranunculaceae

Plants known as Japanese anemones have been developed from the Chinese import *Anemone hupehensis*, which has been extensively hybridized. This tall herbaceous plant with vine-like leaves is often seen in shady gardens, planted in clumps of moss and beside streams. The finest form is the single, pure white *A.* x *hybrida* 'Honorine Jobert', but there are many cultivars, with colours ranging from white and pale pink to a deep purple-pink, some with double flowers. In fertile soil it can be invasive and may need to be kept under control.

Propagation division

Flowering time late summer to mid-autumn

Size perennial to 1.2m (4ft)

Pruning cut back in the autumn

Conditions sun or partial shade; rich, moist soil

Fully hardy/Z 5–8

Callicarpa japonica
Murasaki shikobu
Japanese beauty berry

Family: Verbenaceae

Named after the author of the great 11th-century novel *The Tale of Genji*, the Japanese species *Callicarpa japonica* (beauty berry) is a low-growing, arching, deciduous shrub, which bears beautiful purple berries in autumn and winter. It has delicate pink flowers that arrive in the early summer (which precede the purple berries) and simple, medium blue-green leaves. Its larger cousin, *C. bodinieri* var. *bodinieri* 'Profusion', is more frequently planted in Western gardens but is a much larger shrub.

Propagation semi-ripe cuttings

Flowering time late summer

Size shrub to 1.5m (5ft)

Pruning cut back close to ground level in early spring

Conditions sun or light shade; rich soil

Fully hardy/Z 5–8

Chrysanthemum spp.
Kiku
Chrysanthemum

Family: Asteraceae

Almost all chrysanthemums have now been reclassified as members of the genus *Dendranthema,* but most gardeners still use the old name. The plant was long associated with the imperial Japanese family, and its mythological status has made it the subject of fairy stories and legends. Extracts and essence of chrysanthemum were believed to possess miraculous powers for a longer life.

The large, ball-shaped flowers are rarely seen in Japanese formal gardens, but are often grown in pots, outside temples and in domestic gardens. Great pride is taken in the cultivation of the artificial giants, but more modest species are grown in gardens. The related *Leucanthemum* x *superbum* (formerly *Chrysanthemum* x *superbum,* shasta daisy), with white, yellow-centred flowers, like a large marguerite, might flower in late autumn. These, and some wild asters, are suitable for wilder parts of the tea garden.

Propagation cuttings and division

Flowering time early to late autumn

Size perennial to 1.5m (5ft)

Pruning for fuller blooms pinch the tips several times in early summer

Conditions sheltered position in full sun; rich soil

Fully hardy/Z 4–9

Anemone

Callicarpa japonica

Eupatorium

Eupatorium spp.
Fujibakama
Hemp agrimony (UK)/Joe Pye weed (US)
Family: Asteraceae
The Japanese species *E. chinense* and *E. lindleyanum* are tall herbaceous plants with flattened heads of fuzzy purple or white flowers, which are adored by bees. The subdued colouring and upright habit make them excellent for semi-naturalizing.
Propagation seed and division
Flowering time autumn
Size perennial 1–2m (3–6½ft)
Pruning prune in early summer
Conditions full sun or partial shade; any moist soil
Fully hardy/Z 4–9

Lespedeza bicolor
Hagi
Shrubby lespedeza
Family: Papilionaceae
The purple-flowered bush clover is a lax and arching shrub, which comes into leaf

Lespedeza bicolor

late in the season. Its purple, broom-like racemes of flowers, up to 15cm (6in) long, appear in autumn at the ends of shoots and side-shoots on wand-like stems 1–3m (3–10ft) long.
Propagation seed and division
Flowering time mid- to late summer
Size shrub to 2m (6½ft)
Pruning by cutting down to ground level in early spring
Conditions full sun; well-drained soil
Fully hardy/Z 4–6

Miscanthus sinensis
Obana, susuki
Fountain grass or Eulalia grass
Family: Poaceae
Because *Miscanthus sinensis* colonizes waste ground in Japan it is rarely used as a garden plant. When it is, it is used with restraint. The silvery plumes, which appear in autumn, reach 2–4m (7–13ft) high. *M. sinensis* 'Yakushima Dwarf' is a low-growing form from Yakushima, the volcanic island off the south coast of Japan, which makes a rounded clump 1m (3ft) high and across. The old flower and leaf stems turn to shades of fawn, persisting into the New Year before being dispersed by the wind. Eulalia grass covers many of the hills in Japan, where it waves elegantly in the wind.
Propagation division
Flowering time autumn
Size grass to 4m (13ft)
Pruning cut back before new spring growth
Conditions full sun; well-drained soil
Fully hardy/Z 5–9

Platycodon grandiflorus
Kikyo, asagao
Balloon flower
Family: Campanulaceae
From the campanula family, the balloon flower has inflated and pleated flower buds. The flowers, which eventually open to a wide cup, are mostly blue, but can also be pink or white. This compact, herbaceous plant with blue-green leaves will do well if planted near the edge of a stream.
Propagation seed and division
Flowering time late summer
Size perennial to 60cm (24in)

Miscanthus sinensis

Pruning Cut back stems after flowering and cut down leaves to base in autumn
Conditions sun or partial shade; moist soil
Fully hardy/Z 4–9

Tricyrtis
Hototogisu
Toad lily
Family: Convallariaceae
The old Chinese name for this plant means "oil spot plant" and its flowers are freckled with maroon to purple spots. Its Japanese name, hototogisu, also means cuckoo, a bird with a freckled chest. This genus has become popular in Japan, where its wild forms with their modest and mysterious colours are suitable for planting in moist shade beside a tea garden path or near a stream.
Propagation division
Flowering time late summer to mid-autumn
Size perennial to 80cm (30in)
Pruning remove faded flowers
Conditions shade; rich, moist soil
Fully hardy/Z 7

Tricyrtis

Evergreen shrubs

Japan's flora is rich in native evergreen shrubs. Many are grown in and around the gardens of Kyoto. The following selection has been made for the plants' hardiness and general availability. Camellias and azaleas have already been discussed under spring-flowering shrubs (see pages 216–217), but they need to be mentioned again because they form the backbone of most evergreen schemes in Japanese gardens, especially as they can be well pruned and shaped. Many of these evergeen shrubs can be grown in the shade of trees and buildings.

Above: Buxus microphylla *var.* japonica *is a dense evergreen shrub that can be used to form small hedges and topiary.*

Ardisia japonica

Ardisia japonica
Senryo
Marlberry
Family: Myrsinaceae
Seen in many gardens in Kyoto and in the south of Japan, marlberry is a delightful evergreen shrub which is only hardy in sheltered spots. *Ardisia japonica* is a small shrub with white or pale pink flowers, which are followed by red or yellow berries. They last from autumn into winter.
A. crenata (coralberry, spiceberry), which is known as manryo, is a larger shrub, to 2m (6½ft), with white or pink flowers followed by scarlet fruits.
Propagation seed
Flowering time summer
Size shrub to 1m (3ft)
Pruning by removing over-long shoots in mid-spring
Conditions sheltered position in shade; moist, rich, acid soil
Half hardy/Z 4–8

Aucuba japonica
Aoki
Japanese laurel
Family: Cornaceae
The spotted laurels are reliable evergreen shrubs with glossy foliage. They love shade and tolerate the dry soil among the roots of large trees. In the autumn female shrubs bear small clusters of large red berries, so they are sometimes called Japanese hollies. There are forms with yellow-spotted leaves and others with orange or yellow berries, but in Japanese

Aucuba japonica

gardens the most popular plant is the species or its narrow-leaved form, 'Salicifolia'.
Propagation from cuttings or seed
Flowering time mid-spring
Size shrub to 3m (10ft)
Pruning by removing crossing or over-long shoots in late winter or early spring
Conditions shade or partial shade; any soil
Fully hardy/Z 7–10

Buxus microphylla var. *japonica*
Asama tsuge
Japanese box
Family: Buxaceae
The Japanese box is a small evergreen shrub up to 2m (6½ft) high and wide. Hardier than *Buxus sempervirens* (the European boxwood), it has longer, narrower leaves and a more compact habit. Many hybrids and forms exist in rounded, dwarf forms, such as 'Compacta' and 'Green Pillow'. It is easily grown in sun or shade. Like all box, this species can be clipped into almost any shape and this makes it an excellent plant for Japanese gardens, especially in soils of high alkalinity where azaleas are not able to grow.
Propagation hardwood cuttings
Flowering time spring
Size shrub to 2m (6½ft)
Pruning twice a year in autumn and spring
Conditions sun or shade
Fully hardy/Z 5–8

Cleyera japonica
Sakaki
Japanese cleyera
Family: Theaceae
This slow-growing evergreen shrub with upright rigid growth is sacred to the Shinto religion. Boughs of its scented leathery foliage are presented at special ceremonies and it is often planted near Shinto shrines and in gardens in Japan. *Cleyera japonica* is not fully hardy, so it should be grown in a sheltered spot on an acid soil.
Propagation seed, semi-ripe cuttings
Flowering time early summer
Size to 10m (30ft)
Pruning twice a year
Conditions sun to light shade; moist, well-drained acid soil
Half hardy/Z 8

Daphne odora
Jinchoge
Winter daphne
Family: Thymelaeaceae
This small evergreen shrub carries its deliciously sweet-scented, pink-white flowers in late winter to early spring. It is often seen in the form 'Aureomarginata', which has gold-edged leaves, and is a lovely plant to include in a mixed planting, but is not long-lived. Note: it is highly poisonous.
Propagation seed or semi-ripe cuttings
Flowering time late winter to early spring
Size shrub to 1.5m (5ft)
Pruning best left unpruned
Conditions sun or partial shade; rich, moist, slightly acid soil
Fully hardy/Z 8–10

Elaeagnus x ebbingei

Daphniphyllum macropodum
Yuzuri-ha
Family: Daphniphyllaceae
A handsome large-leaved shrub, bearing long strap-like leaves with red leaf stalks. This Japanese native plant, which can be grown in almost any moisture-retentive soil in sun or part shade, makes a good substitute for rhododendrons on alkaline soils where bold foliage is required. It will grow into a large shrub. While its flowers are insignificant they release a pungent scent.
Propagation seed, semi-ripe cuttings
Flowering time spring
Size shrub to 8m (26ft)
Pruning after flowering, if necessary
Conditions sun or shade
Fully hardy/Z 7–8

Elaeagnus spp.
Gumi
Silverberry
Family: Elaeagnaceae
Popular species of elaeagnus include *Elaeagnus pungens, E. glabra* and *E. macrophylla*, but the most common green-leaved form is the hybrid *E. x ebbingei*, with dusty green leaves, which are silvery beneath. In autumn small, creamy-white, bell-shaped flowers are borne in the leaf axils, almost out of sight, but their scent can carry far.

This is a wonderful evergreen for mixed hedges, when it can be pruned to maintain a neat shape, and as a general evergreen backdrop. Variegated forms are available, but are not appropriate for a Japanese garden. The growth of *E. x ebbingei* can be a bit rangy and will need some tidying.
Propagation semi-ripe cuttings
Flowering time autumn
Size shrub to 4m (13ft)
Pruning by cutting back over-long shoots in mid-spring
Conditions full sun or partial shade; any soil
Fully hardy/Z 7–9

Euonymus japonicus
Mayumi
Japanese spindle tree
Family: Celastraceae
A handsome and cheerful evergreen, native to Japan, euonymus is often planted

Daphniphyllum macropodum

in coastal areas owing to its resistance to salt-laden air. It is a variable shrub up to 4m (13ft) tall that has produced many variegated forms, but also a large-leaved variety called 'Macrophyllus' and a dwarf form with minute leaves called 'Microphyllus'. This dwarf form would be suitable for smaller gardens but is on the tender side and may need the shelter of other plants. As with most of this species, *Euonymus japonicus* is easily grown on most soil types. A similar species, *E. fortunei*, is much hardier and has given rise to countless cultivars, many of which, like *E. fortunei* 'Coloratus', can be used as ground cover in dry shady areas.
Propagation hardwood cuttings
Flowering time insignificant
Size shrub to 3m (10ft)
Pruning in autumn or late winter as a shrub or in midsummer if grown as a hedge
Conditions sun or shade
Fully hardy/Z 6–8

OTHER NATIVE JAPANESE EVERGREENS

- *Leucothoe keiskei*, which is a small shrub, to 60cm (24in), with slender, glossy, dark green leaves. It must have acid soil.
- *Nandina domestica* (sacred bamboo; see page 228), which is evergreen in mild areas. It is an upright shrub, to 2m (6½ft), with white flowers in summer and bright red fruit.

Fatsia japonica

Fatsia japonica
Yatsude

Japanese aralia
Family: Araliaceae

Native to the forests of Japan, the Japanese aralia has distinctive large, glossy, divided leaves. The flowers, which resemble those of ivy, are like small explosions; they are initially pale cream-green but turn almost black. A hybrid between *Fatsia* and *Hedera* (ivy), *Fatshedera lizei* (tree ivy), is a rather sprawling but smaller plant, to about 2m (6½ft).

Propagation seed, cuttings
Flowering time autumn
Size shrub to 4m (13ft)
Pruning not needed
Conditions sheltered position in full sun or partial shade; slightly acid, humus-rich soil
Fully hardy/Z 7–9

Ilex crenata

Ilex crenata
Inu tsuge

Japanese bush holly
Family: Aquifoliaceae

The Japanese holly, which can grow up to 6m (20ft) high and as wide, looks more like a box than a holly, especially as its leaves are small and spineless. It can be clipped into almost any shape. *Ilex crenata* is hardier than *Buxus sempervirens* and *B. microphyllus*, so could be grown as a substitute for these and azaleas in cold regions. When unclipped the species will grow into a large wide shrub with long narrow leaves, but is variable when grown from seed. There are a number of selected forms, such as 'Convexa' with small leaves and a low bushy habit, and 'Helleri' with very small leaves and a dense and flattened habit. The berries are black and not as attractive as those of many holly species.

Propagation seed, semi-ripe cuttings
Flowering time spring
Size shrub to 5m (16ft)
Pruning Prune young plants to promote growth and older plants to maintain shape
Conditions sun or shade
Fully hardy/Z 5–8

Ilex integra
Mochi-no-ki

Japanese tree holly
Family: Aquifoliaceae

There are a number of *Ilex* species native to Japan that appear as part of a general mix of background evergreens. *Ilex integra* (mochi-no-ki) is a large shrub with spineless broad leathery leaves that carries red berries in autumn, while *I. rotunda* (see above right) has rounder leaves. In Western gardens, *Ilex aquifolium* 'J.C. Van Tol' would be a suitable substitute as it also has spineless leaves and red berries. *Ilex* x *altaclerensis* 'Camelliifolia' is another variety with more rounded and very glossy leaves and would make an ideal tall background evergreen for larger gardens. These species and varieties can also be clipped as hedges.

Propagation seed, semi-ripe cuttings
Flowering time spring
Size shrub to 7m (23ft)
Pruning late winter to early spring
Conditions sun or shade
Fully hardy/Z 5–8

Ilex rotunda
Kurogane-mochi

Japanese tree holly
Family: Aquifoliaceae

Propagation seed, semi-ripe cuttings
Flowering time spring
Size tree to 23m (75ft)
Pruning cut back annually
Conditions sun or shade
Fully hardy/Z 7–8

Ligustrum japonicum
Nu-zhen-zi

Japanese privet
Family: Oleaceae

A rounded bushy shrub with shiny, black-green leaves. In late summer (if not clipped), it produces pyramidal panicles of small white flowers with a strong, sweet fragrance, which some find disagreeable. The Japanese privet is a useful dense evergreen that will need some protection from hard frosts and cold winds. It could form a part of evergreen mixed plantings used as a background in stroll gardens. *Ligustrum japonica* 'Rotundifolium' has dense blunt foliage that is thick and leathery, and is often found in Japanese gardens.

Propagation hardwood cuttings
Flowering time summer
Size shrub to 4m (13ft)
Pruning shear annually to shape, will take hard pruning
Conditions sun or shade
Fully hardy/Z 6–8

TOPIARY AND HEDGES

• Mixed groups of camellias, azaleas, pieris and photinias as well as evergreen oaks and hollies are often clipped into *o-karikomi*, the Japanese equivalent of Western topiary (see pages 94–97).

• These plants can also be grown as hedges. Low hedges of *Camellia sinensis* (tea plant) are often planted in tea gardens; tea plants have much smaller leaves and flowers than the more ornamental camellias and they are less hardy.

Magnolia grandiflora
Taizen-boku

Evergreen magnolia
Family: Magnoliaceae
While this evergreen species of magnolia is native to the USA, it was introduced to Japan by the end of the 19th century and has been extensively planted in gardens. It suits the larger Japanese-style garden due to its bold and glossy foliage. In summer it produces huge creamy white cupped blooms that yield an intoxicating fragrance.
Propagation seed, semi-ripe cuttings, grafted
Flowering time summer
Size tree or large shrub to 10m (30ft)
Pruning best left unpruned; cut back in late winter if necessary
Conditions sun
Fully hardy/Z 7–8

Mahonia japonica
Bealei

Japanese mahonia
Family: Berberidaceae
An erect, pinnate, holly-like plant related to berberis, this mahonia has a strong, architectural shape, and bears spikes of sweetly scented yellow flowers in winter and early spring. When it becomes too woody and overgrown, prune the plant hard, removing the old stems first, immediately after flowering.
Propagation semi-ripe cuttings
Flowering time late autumn to early spring
Size shrub to 2m (6½ft)
Pruning by cutting back over-long shoots after flowering
Conditions sheltered position in partial shade; any reasonable soil
Fully hardy/Z 6–8

Osmanthus fragrans

Mahonia japonica

Osmanthus fragrans
Kinmokusei

Tea olive
Family: Oleaceae
A popular shrub in Japan, the fragrant olive or sweet tea is famed for its creamy autumn flowers, but it is not very hardy. A hardier species, *O. fortunei*, is more suitable for most gardens, or try *O. heterophyllus*, known as hi-ragi, a broad, holly-leaved shrub.
Propagation semi-ripe cuttings
Flowering time autumn
Size shrub to 6m (20ft)
Pruning by cutting back to maintain shape in mid-spring
Conditions sheltered position in sun or partial shade; any reasonable soil
Fully hardy/Z 8–9

Photinia glabra
Kaname-mochi

Red-leaf photinia
Family: Rosaceae
Photinias are mostly handsome, broad-leaved evergreen trees and shrubs, often planted to create a backdrop or shade. White flowers are carried in loose panicles from spring to summer, followed by the rosy-red flush of young foliage, evident in hybrids such as 'Red Robin' and 'Birmingham'. Photinias are pretty hardy and can be kept at a manageable height through pruning. They can also be grown as a hedge.
Propagation semi-ripe cuttings
Flowering time late spring to early summer
Size shrub to 5m (16ft)
Pruning by cutting out crossing and badly positioned stems in early spring
Conditions full sun/partial shade; moist soil
Fully hardy/Z 7–8

Photinia glabra

Pieris japonica
A-sebi

Japanese Andromeda
Family: Ericaceae
A-sebi means "horse-drunk", relating to its poisonous effects on animals. This compact shrub is reasonably hardy, with pendulous clusters of white lily-of-the-valley-like flowers in early spring. The young growth is tinted pink. The Chinese species, *P. formosa*, has brilliant red-bronze young growth but is not as hardy. The American species, *P. floribunda*, is hardy. Pieris prefers acid soil and plenty of humus but can withstand quite dry conditions in late summer. More commonly seen as a large shrub, it can grow into a small tree. Small-leaved and dwarf forms include 'Green Heath', which grows to 60cm (24in).
Propagation seed, semi-ripe cuttings
Flowering time late winter to spring
Size shrub to 3m (10ft)
Pruning remove dead shoots after flowering
Conditions full sun or light shade; acid soil
Fully hardy/Z 6–8

OTHER NON-JAPANESE EVERGREENS

- *Arbutus unedo* (strawberry tree), a spreading small tree or shrub, to 8m (26ft), with creamy white flowers followed by red fruits.
- *Ilex meserveae* (blue holly), a vigorous shrub or small tree, to 5m (16ft), with sharply spined, glossy, blue-green leaves.
- *Prunus lusitanica* (Portugal laurel), a dense shrub or tree, to 20m (66ft), with large, glossy, dark green leaves.

Evergreen trees & conifers

The general Japanese name for conifers is *shohaku-rui*, and the tall, straight pines in particular were said to draw the gods down to Earth, while the Shintoists beat wooden planks to attract them. Such evergreen trees have been regarded in Japan as symbols of chastity, consistency and loyalty. The Hinoki cypress and Japanese cedar are two of Japan's most important timber trees, their naturally resilient wood being used in many of their buildings and garden structures. Two of the native species of pine are the most popular of conifers in Japanese gardens.

Above: *Cryptomeria japonica has a dense habit and thick, spreading branches. The foliage is scaly and finely dissected.*

Cephalotaxus harringtonia

Cephalotaxus harringtonia
Inu-gaya

Japanese plum yew

Family: Cephalotaxaceae

C. h. drupacea, also known as the cow's tail pine, is a medium shrub up to 3m (10ft) high with a dense compact habit. Its short upright needles are quite soft and form a V-shape on the upper side of the branches. As they age, the plant develops into a large mound with elegant drooping branchlets. *C. h.* 'Fastigiata' is quite different with its stiffly upright habit that bears a striking resemblance to the Irish yew.

Propagation seed or hardwood cuttings
Flowering none
Size tree to 10m (30ft)
Pruning cut back in early spring
Conditions sun or part shade
Fully hardy/Z 6–8

Chamaecyparis obtusa
Hinoki

Hinoki cypress

Family: Cupressaceae

Often planted in forests alongside the Japanese cedar, the Hinoki cypress is a valuable timber tree. It is more commonly seen in gardens in its dwarf forms: *C. obtusa* 'Nana Gracilis' grows to 3m (10ft) high and *C. obtusa* 'Pygmaea' reaches only 1.5m (5ft) high. These smaller versions have more character than most cypress-like trees, with their twisted whorls of vivid young growth. Exceptionally hardy, all these plants can tolerate exposed situations. They can also be successfully clipped into hedges and topiary-style (*o-karikomi*) shapes.

Chamaecyparis obtusa

Propagation hardwood cuttings
Size tree to 20m (66ft)
Pruning not needed, but remove dead or diseased branches
Conditions full sun; slightly acid soil
Fully hardy/Z 4–8

SACRED PINES

Pines (*matsu* in Japanese, which means "waiting for a god") were regarded as the king of trees in Japan and are an important image in Japanese poetry. One of the most famous natural Japanese landscapes is Matsushima Bay, in northern Honshu, which is dotted with more than 800 pine-clad islands.

There are few Japanese gardens that do not contain a pine tree. Together with azaleas and maples, they are one of the fundamental ingredients. Many hours of loving care are spent plucking their needles and pruning their boughs, creating shapes that deliberately evoke trees bent by the winds on mountains and seashores. Pine boughs are often draped with decorations for the moon-viewing celebrations, weddings and New Year.

Chamaecyparis pisifera

Chamaecyparis pisifera
Sawara

Sawara cypress

Family: Cupressaceae

This handsome "false cypress" makes a large tree with spreading branches and flattened sprays of dark green foliage. Its main attribute, however, is the number of sports and varieties that have derived from it. The thread cypress, *C. pisifera* 'Filifera', with its long drooping whip-like shoots and broadly shrub-like growth is planted widely in Japanese gardens. In contrast, *C. pisifera* 'Squarrosa' has soft sprays of dark green foliage, and it has a number of dwarf forms such as 'Intermedia' which forms a dense mound of congested bluish foliage. This is an easy tree or shrub to grow in most soil

Cryptomeria japonica

types and will tolerate a certain amount of shade, especially under the canopy of large deciduous trees.

Propagation hardwood cuttings
Flowering none
Size tree to 20m (66ft)
Pruning trim new growth of current season
Conditions sun or shade in any well-drained soil
Fully hardy/Zones 4–7

Cryptomeria japonica
Sugi

Japanese cedar

Family: Taxodiaceae

After the pine, the most important and sacred conifer in Japan is the Japanese cedar. Capable of living for more than 2,000 years, it is often planted as a sign of virtue and as a guardian at the entrance of Buddhist and Shinto shrines. Cryptomerias are planted in most of the commercial forests in Japan, as it is an easily worked timber and is used extensively in the building industry. Its aroma makes the wood prized for sake casks. The cryptomeria is a towering, conical tree, with finely dissected, scaly foliage. It is often coppiced in gardens, and new growth is pruned into tiers with shaped, pompom-like foliage at the ends. It can also be planted on its own or as part of a mixed hedge. There are many cultivated varieties, but most are merely curiosities.

Propagation seed, hardwood cuttings
Flowering none
Size tree to 25m (82ft)
Pruning not needed
Conditions full sun or partial shade; deep, moist, slightly acid soil
Fully hardy/Z 6–9

Juniperus chinensis
Ibuki

Chinese juniper

Family: Cupressaceae

The Chinese juniper is popular for clipping into "cloud pruning". It is a highly variable species that has given rise to one particular form, 'Kaizuka', popular in Japan and the USA where it is also called 'Torulosa'. Its unusually angular branches, clothed in dense clusters of bright green foliage, give it a picturesque outline, ideal for creating a

Juniperus chinensis

windswept look. *Juniper chinensis* and its cultivars are very hardy and easy to grow in almost any soil type, even tolerating salt-laden winds. They are best planted in full sun.

Propagation hardwood cuttings
Flowering none
Size tree to 20m (66ft)
Pruning little, if any, required
Conditions sun
Fully hardy/Z 5–8

Pinus densiflora
Aka-matsu

Japanese red pine

Family: Pinaceae

A tree with pinkish-red bark and a rounded head, the Japanese red pine is often pruned to accentuate its soft crown and show its

Pinus densiflora 'Umbraculifera'

Pinus densiflora

Pinus parviflora
Go-yo-matsu

Japanese white pine

Family: Pinaceae

The Japanese white pine has shorter, grey-green needles and is slower growing and more manageable than *P. densiflora* or *P. thunbergii*, but it will eventually make a large, multi-stemmed, mounding tree. There are many dwarf forms, including 'Glauca Nana' and 'Hagaromo Seedling'.

Propagation seed, grafted
Flowering none
Size tree to 20m (66ft)
Pruning needs little pruning to develop a strong structure
Conditions full sun; any well-drained soil
Fully hardy/Z 4–7

Pinus thunbergii
Kuro-matsu

Japanese black pine

Family: Pinaceae

More rugged and darker in leaf and bark than *P. densiflora*, the Japanese black pine is generally pruned into more horizontal and dramatic windswept shapes. It is the most popular bonsai pine.

Propagation seed, grafted
Flowering none
Size tree to 25m (82ft)
Pruning during the early growing season
Conditions full sun; any well-drained soil
Fully hardy/Z 6–8

elegant, branched structure. *P. densiflora* 'Umbraculifera', known as tanyosho, is a compact, rounded or flat-topped bushy tree, reaching 2–3m (7–10ft). This dwarf pine can be planted in groves over small hills, giving the impression of a larger landscape.

Propagation seed, grafted
Flowering none
Size tree to 20m (66ft)
Pruning needs little pruning to develop a strong structure
Conditions full sun; any well-drained soil
Fully hardy/Z 3–7

Podocarpus macrophyllus

Podocarpus macrophyllus
Kusamaki

Maki

Family: Podocarpaceae

While most *Podocarpus* species are not very hardy, this one is fully hardy down to -20°C (-4°F). It forms a shrub or small tree with leaves, bright green above and pale beneath, up to 18cm (7in) long and arranged in spirals around the stems. It is grown in China and Japan as an unusual hedge, but only suits acid soils. There are many fancy forms, but the straight species is sufficiently interesting to be grown in its own right.

Propagation seed for species and hardwood cuttings for special forms
Flowering none
Size tree to 15m (50ft)
Pruning Pinch back new growth as necessary
Conditions sun
Fully hardy/Z 7-8

POPULAR PINES IN JAPANESE GARDENS

- *Pinus densiflora* (red pine)
- *Pinus thunbergii* (black pine)
- *Pinus sylvestris* (Scots pine), especially *P. sylvestris* 'Watereri'
- *Pinus mugo* (dwarf mountain pine), which grows to only 3.5m (11ft) high and is suitable for very small gardens

Pinus parviflora

Pinus thunbergii

Sciadopitys verticillata

Thujopsis dolabrata

Sciadopitys verticillata
Koya maki

Japanese umbrella pine

Family: Pinaceae

This distinctive conifer forms a perfect cone shape and retains its bright green foliage right to the ground. Its most unusual feature is the cool leathery feel to the long pine-like leaves, which stand out from each other like the spokes of an umbrella. It grows slowly when young, enjoying a moisture-retentive acid soil but tolerating a neutral soil. It will grow in light woodland shade, but it is more likely to keep its perfect shape in full sun. It is rare in the wild but is found in temple gardens, especially high in the mountains.
Propagation seed for species and hardwood cuttings
Pruning may need training to maintain a central trunk
Size tree to 20m (66ft)
Flowering none
Conditions sun or part shade
Half-hardy/Z 4–5

Taxus cuspidata
Ichii

Japanese yew

Family: Taxaceae

Taxus cuspidata is hardier than *T. baccata*, the common European yew that is popular for hedging. There are numerous forms of the Japanese yew and hybrids between it and *T. baccata*; some, like 'Hicksii', are quite upright, while others like 'Minima' and 'Nana' form small dense shrubs, and could be planted and clipped in *o-karikomi* style.

Propagation seed or hardwood cuttings
Size tree to 15m (50ft)
Pruning carry out after spring growth begins
Conditions sun or part shade
Fully hardy/Z 5–8

Thujopsis dolabrata
Hiba

Japanese elkhorn cypress

Family: Cupressaceae

Thujopsis dolabrata, with its shiny dark green flattened scaly fronds that are silvery on the reverse, is the most interesting of a group of conifers including species of *Thuja, Calocedrus* and *Chamaecyparis* that share many similar characteristics. All these evergreens form medium to large trees

Taxus cuspidata

that are ideal as background planting, for screening or as individual specimens. They all thrive on most soil types and are very hardy. Some have given rise to dwarf forms, such as *Thujopsis dolabrata* 'Nana', which would be more suitable for the smaller garden.
Flowering none
Propagation seed, hardwood cuttings
Size tree to 20m (66ft)
Pruning bushy forms need no pruning
Conditions sun or part shade
Fully hardy/Z 6–8

Tsuga
Tsuga

Hemlock

Family: Pinaceae

A genus of elegant, large trees with fine soft-needled foliage. There is a Japanese species, *Tsuga sieboldii* (Southern Japanese hemlock), but for gardens there are a slow-growing and dwarf forms of the American species, *T. canadensis* (Canadian hemlock). Those with weeping habits such as *T. canadensis* 'Pendula', or dome-shaped varieties such as *T. canadensis* 'Nana', would be suitable for Japanese gardens.
Flowering none
Propagation hardwood cuttings or grafted
Pruning during the summer
Size tree to 10m (30ft)
Conditions sun or part shade
Fully hardy/Z 4–8

Tsuga

Ferns

Japanese ferns are regarded as excellent, shapely plants for softening the hard edges of groups of rocks and for providing a sympathetic foil to glossy evergreens, which are planted to give a wooded, wilderness effect around the path in tea gardens. Ferns are often found tucked around the *tsukubai* and other water features, where they can take advantage of the extra moisture. Camellias with light pastel colours and simple plants such as aucubas, nandinas and maples combine well with ferns.

Ferns vary from the largest tree ferns to tiny species that creep around in crevices, such as *Blechnum penna-marina* (Alpine hard fern). *Athyrium nipponicum pictum* (Japanese painted fern) is native to Japan, and is unique among ferns for its maroon stalk and fronds with a silvery cast. *Athyrium trichomanes* (lady fern) is a finely cut small-leaved fern for tucking into small spaces.

Above: Asplenium scolopendrium, *the hart's-tongue fern, has a distinctive leaf shape.*

Propagation separated by root division
Size from 4–6cm (1½–2½in) to 10m (30ft)
Conditions most species need shade and moisture, and most like humidity
Hardiness dependent on species/Z 4–9

Onoclea sensibilis

USEFUL NON-JAPANESE FERNS

- *Asplenium scolopendrium* (hart's-tongue fern) has strap-like leaves and thrives in deep shade but must not be allowed to dry out.
- *Dryopteris felix-mas* (robust male fern) and its forms could be used under trees or in gardens which are very dry.

Polystichum setiferum

Matteuccia struthiopteris

- *Matteuccia struthiopteris* (ostrich fern), *Onoclea sensibilis* (sensitive fern) and *Osmunda regalis* (flowering fern) are all excellent for ground that is damp or swampy.

- *Polystichum setiferum* (soft shield fern) is an ideal all-round fern species as it is more or less evergreen. It is best to remove all the old fronds in spring just before the new fronds unfurl. This species will grow in shade and full sun in any reasonable soil as long as it doesn't become too dry. The various forms such as 'Dahlem' with simple plain leaves and 'Herrenhausen' with curly edges to the fronds are excellent for planting along the tea path, and under camellias and aucubas.

Athyrium trichomanes

Bamboo

Most Japanese gardens are cultivated in temperate climates, where plants such as azaleas, cherries and plums grow well, but in more tropical or subtropical climates it is best to grow plants that are better suited to the heat. However, if you want to create a "tropical look" in a temperate climate, there are various hardy plants that can be used, and bamboo is ideal. Bamboos can be highly invasive plants, so site them carefully. The bamboo species listed below like full sun or partial shade and rich soil, unless stated otherwise.

Pleioblastus humilis
Nakai
Dwarf bamboo
Family: Poaceae
A fairly low-growing bamboo with dark green canes and light green leaves. It can be invasive, so contain the roots.
Propagation division
Size to 1.5m (5ft)
Conditions sheltered in sun or partial shade
Hardy/Z 1–3

Pleioblastus pygmaeus
Nakai
Pygmy bamboo
Family: Poaceae
This can be planted as ground cover and clipped down to 5–10cm (2–4in) high. It makes a good substitute for lawns or moss.
Size to 40cm (16in)
Conditions semi-shade or full sun
Hardy/Z 6–11

Phyllostachys aurea
Kosan chiku
Fishpole bamboo or golden bamboo
Family: Poaceae
These mid-green canes age to golden-brown. It will spread, so contain the roots.
Propagation division
Size to 10m (33ft)
Conditions moist soil and tolerates drought
Hardy/Z 6–8

Phyllostachys aureosulcata
Ousou chiku
Yellow-groove bamboo
Family: Poaceae
This has brown-green canes, attractively ribbed with yellow.
Propagation division
Size to 6m (20ft)
Conditions full to partial sun
Hardy/Z 5–10

Phyllostachys edulis
Kina mousou chiku
Moso bamboo
Family: Poaceae
This evergreen bamboo is often harvested for its huge stems. In colder climates it will not reach its full growth dimensions, which are only seen in the southern half of Japan. *P. edulis heterocycla* has fascinating tortoiseshell-shaped internodes.
Propagation division
Size to 6m (20ft) or more
Conditions Full sun; medium drought tolerance, intolerant of shade
Hardy/Z 7–11

Above: Pleioblastus humilis *or dwarf bamboo. This fast-growing bamboo makes a good low hedge or screen.*

Phyllostachys nigra
Kuro chiku
Black bamboo
Family: Poaceae
This dramatic bamboo is popular for its polished black stems, especially in the form 'Munro'. The distinctive canes become black with age.
Propagation division
Size to 5m (16ft)
Conditions full sun or partial shade; well-drained soil
Hardy/Z 7–9

Phyllostachys vivax
Madake
Vivax bamboo or Chinese timber
Family: Poaceae
This makes a good alternative to *P. edulis*.
Size to 25m (82ft)
Conditions full sun to light shade; well-drained soil
Hardy/Z 6–10

Pseudosasa japonica
Kishima yadake
Arrow bamboo
Family: Poaceae
A tough and rather invasive bamboo with dark green leaves on pale beige stems.
Size to 6m (20ft)
Conditions requires well-drained soil
Hardy/Z 6–11

Pseudosasa japonica

Palms

As long as they are grown in sheltered positions, many palms are surprisingly hardy; like bamboos, they can be used for a tropical look in a temperate climate. Their growth is reliable and they are also appealing because they are low-maintenance. Although Japanese gardens tend to be associated more with temperate flora, it is not inappropriate to use palms and other exotic plants, providing that the same design principles are followed. In cold areas, cycads are often wrapped up in winter with straw to protect their leaves and crowns from frost.

Above: Trachycarpus fortunei, *distinctive for its huge fan-shaped leaves, is a very hardy palm and thrives in mild coastal gardens.*

Cycas revoluta
Cycas nana
Sago palm
Family: Cycadaceae
This ancient plant is native to the southern islands of Japan. It is a beautiful glossy evergreen, which looks like a cross between a palm and a fern. It is only marginally hardy, and is rarely seen in gardens north of Kyoto. Even in Kyoto the sago palm has to be wrapped up in winter, and like many other aspects of Japanese gardens, this elaborate wrapping has been raised to the level of an art form.
Propagation seed
Size to 2m (6½ft)
Conditions requires full sun and moist, rich soil.
Half hardy/Z 8–10

Rhapis excelsa
Shuro
Miniature fan palm
Family: Arecaceae/Palmae
Native to China, the miniature fan palm was introduced to Japan in the 19th century. Stockier and spinier than the Chusan palm, but not quite as hardy, it is still a valuable addition to the tropical look in a temperate garden. With shiny dark leaves, the fronds of the miniature fan palm stretch out from an upright furry trunk. The plant can be used as group plantation. It is good for planting in shaded areas.
Propagation sucker division
Size to 5m (16ft)
Conditions requires a sheltered position; light shade and any soil.
Fully hardy/Z 8–11

Trachycarpus fortunei
To-juro
Chusan palm
Family: Arecaceae/Palmae
This hardy palm was originally grown for its yield of fibre, and it has since become naturalized in many parts of the country. It grows quite erect and has fan-shaped leaves. Dwarf forms include 'Compacta' and 'Green Pillow'.
Propagation seed
Size full size to 20m (66ft); dwarf forms to 1m (3ft)
Conditions full sun or shade; any soil
Fully hardy/Z 7–10

Cycas revoluta

Trachycarpus fortunei

Other plants of interest

This selection includes plants that can be placed beside the tea path or grown in shady courtyards. Many of them have hundreds of interesting, even quirky, variations, and they are often specially grown in pots so that they can be highlighted. They are not usually grown for planting out in the garden, where they might disrupt the overall scheme. Hollyhocks, popular in English cottage gardens, originated in the Orient, and are often grown against house walls. Mondo grass is the most popular ground cover in Japan, its glossy leaves forming a dense, impenetrable mat.

Althaea rosea

Althaea rosea
Tachia-oi
Hollyhock
Family: Malvaceae
The hollyhock has been popular in Japan since Heian times and is still common, especially in gardens of small houses.
Propagation seed
Flowering time early to midsummer
Size perennial to 2.4m (8ft)
Conditions full sun; any soil
Fully hardy/Z 6–9

Equisetum hyemale
Tokusa
Small tufted mare's tail
Family: Equisetaceae
In Western gardens this is a pernicious but attractive weed that likes wet soils. Japanese

forms are less invasive. The vertical, leafless stems of *E. hyemale* are an arresting sight.
Propagation division
Size perennial to 1.5m (5ft)
Conditions sun or partial shade; moist soil
Fully hardy/Z 4–9

Farfugium japonicum
Tsuwa-buki
Leopard plant
Family: Asteraceae/Compositae
The yellow flowers of this evergreen perennial with scalloped leaves are similar to those of *Ligularia*. Many variegated forms have been developed, the most common 'Aureomaculatum', which has random yellow spots on the leaves.
Propagation division
Flowering time autumn to early winter
Size perennial to 60cm (24in)
Conditions partial shade; moist soil
Fully hardy/Z 7–9

Hemerocallis

Above: Farfugium japonicum *is a perennial native to Japan, grown for its attractive foliage and its autumn flowers.*

Hemerocallis
Kisuge or kanzou
Day lily
Family: Hemerocallidaceae
H. fulva is native to Japan and has given rise to hundreds of varieties. In its natural state its flowers are a buff orange, rising up on stalks in summer from a deciduous herbaceous perennial that will colonize large areas in shade or full sun. Day lily flowers last only one day but a succession are produced over several weeks in mid- to late summer. The species *H. flava* produces a lovely fragrance from its yellow flowers in the spring.
Propagation division
Flowering time spring to late summer
Size 90cm (36in)
Conditions sun or shade in most soil types
Fully hardy/Z 4–8

Hosta
Giboshi
Hosta
Family: Hostaceae
Hostas, or plantain lilies, have been planted in Japanese gardens since Heian times. *Hosta sieboldiana*, one of the hostas with the largest leaves, can be seen growing at 1,000m (3,280ft) at the foot of Mount Fuji. *H. plantaginea* has white, scented flowers, while *H. montana* and *H. tardiva*, both native to Japan, are grown for their handsome foliage. *H. ventricosa* is particularly striking,

Hosta

Houttuynia cordata

Lilium

with beautiful violet flowers and strong, green-ribbed foliage. Hostas were selected for their variety of leaf forms during the 19th century. Plants with variegated and twisted leaves were grown as specimens for display, rather than as part of the garden scheme.

Propagation division
Flowering time summer
Size perennial 25–90cm (10–36in)
Conditions sheltered position in sun or partial shade; moist soil
Fully hardy/Z 4–9

Houttuynia cordata
Dokudami

Chameleon houttuynia
Family: Saururaceae

Houttuynia is grown in many Japanese gardens, especially near water, but it can be invasive. The heart-shaped leaves have a strong odour when crushed, while the small white flowers are picked to make herbal tea. There are a number of variegated forms, but the plain green kind is the most popular.

Propagation division
Flowering time spring
Size perennial to 30cm (12in)
Conditions full sun; moist soil
Fully hardy/Z 5–9

Lilium
Yuri

Lily
Family: Liliaceae

Lilium auratum is the golden-rayed lily of Japan. Its large, white, trumpet-like flowers

have freckles and golden streaks inside. It is a fussy plant that needs acid soil with plenty of humus. Hybrids between *L. auratum* and *L. speciosum* are much easier to grow. In Japanese gardens lilies are grown in pots and put out on seasonal display.

The unscented but vibrant *L. lancifolium* (tiger lily), with its orange and yellow, heavily spotted, reflexed flowers, has been grown extensively as a food (where the bulbs are eaten) and is only rarely allowed to flower.

Propagation seed, scales, offsets
Flowering time late summer to early autumn
Size bulb to 1.5m (5ft)
Conditions full sun; acid soil
Fully hardy/Z 4–9

Musa
Musa basjoo

Hardy banana
Family: Musaceae

This will survive frosts as low as -10°C (14°F). Grow it in a sheltered position as its huge leaves tend to get shredded and blackened when exposed to cold winds. In cold areas you can wrap the whole stem up with fleece or straw to protect it in winter. Not really suitable in more "temperate" style gardens, *Musa* could be planted with palms and bamboos for a tropical effect.

Propagation division
Flowering insignificant, may fruit in warm climates
Size shrub to 3m (10ft)
Conditions sun or part shade; sheltered spot
Half hardy/Z 7–9

Ophiopogon japonicus
Ja-no-hige or ryo-no-hige

Japanese mondo grass
Family: Convallariaceae

This leathery, grass-like plant can colonize whole gardens. It has dark green leaves, which curve over. Carpets of it can set off larger plants, such as groups of maples, azaleas and bamboos. The flowers are white or pale blue, followed by small black berries. The dwarf, tufted *O. japonicus* 'Minor' is better in small gardens.

Propagation division
Flowering time summer
Size perennial to 60cm (24in)
Conditions full sun or partial shade; slightly acid soil
Fully hardy/Z 6–10

Ophiopogon japonicus

Growing Bonsai

Bonsai, like Japanese gardening, has strong roots within Zen Buddhism and is linked to both meditation and creative expression. Bonsai specimens are housed in a pot surrounded with soil, and are seen as spiritual, independent entities that also form part of nature – they have been described as "heaven and earth in one container".

Features integral to bonsai include an asymmetrical arrangement and a triangular form to create a dramatic and balanced visual effect. Many classic specimens are centuries old, but there is also great excitement in starting a new bonsai from a seed, cutting or young tree.

This section provides all you need to become familiar with the art of bonsai – basic principles, practical techniques, different styles and a comprehensive directory of suitable plants. Bonsai does not require a large budget, but it does need time, dedication, skill and persistence. It will not always work as you have planned, but if you keep trying then you will be amply rewarded.

Opposite: *Various species of beech (*Fagus spp.*) can be used for bonsai although* F. sylvatica *and* F. crenata *are the most popular.*

Above: *Japanese white pine (*Pinus parviflora*) is a classic bonsai specimen with twisted needles and blue/green tufts on the tips.*

BONSAI ESSENTIALS

To take your first steps in the fascinating art of bonsai, you will need some gardening knowledge, some common sense, some practical ideas, a little bit of artistic feeling and, most importantly of all, the will to succeed. You may already grow container plants or trees that need some control of their growth combined with regular repotting, so you will probably, albeit unknowingly, have already mastered some of the basic techniques required for bonsai culture.

This chapter gives you a background knowledge and understanding of the art of bonsai, starting with a history explaining its rise in popularity. It also shows a selection of inspirational trees that we find around us that can give us shape templates to work from. It also discusses which trees and shrubs are most suitable to work with. Sections on bonsai size, aesthetics and proportion give you the standard parameters for what you should be aiming to achieve. Finally, a short section on buying bonsai explains what to look for when making your first purchases.

Above: *The colourful leaves of the Japanese maple* (Acer palmatum). **Left:** *Cascade-style Chinese elm (*Ulmus parvifolia*) displayed on an elegant Chinese stand in a domestic situation.*

The history of bonsai

Almost certainly, the very first examples of *penjing* (which is the Chinese version of bonsai) and bonsai were made from trees and plants that had been collected from the wild mountainous areas of China and Japan. Indigenous, naturally stunted trees were arranged and planted in ceramic pots and containers and kept in or around the collectors' homes, tended carefully and eventually regarded as natural works of art. These trees and plants would have been formed by nature's elements, often into contorted and extremely interesting shapes. Men would have risked their lives to collect very old, gnarled trees from high mountain areas, such as sheer rock faces, and other types of inhospitable terrain, in order to acquire the very best material for study and display.

Above: *Late 19th-century Japanese woodblock print of a* Chrysanthemum *bonsai in the twin-trunk style.*

EARLY ORIGINS

Penjing appears to cover a very wide range of different styles that includes rock plantings and tray landscapes. When literally translated, *penjing* means roughly the same as bonsai: that is, a plant which is grown in a container. This fascinating art form is believed to have originated in China some 1,500–2,000 years ago. In Japan, there are records of the cultivation of bonsai that go as far back as 1,200 years, many of which include simple descriptions and drawings of bonsai, leading up to more recent woodblock prints and screens. These show how Japanese interiors looked in the past and clearly feature bonsai plants.

During the Chin dynasty (221–206BC), China and Japan started to make social and spiritual contact with each other when Buddhism was introduced into both countries via Korea. It would appear that many of the Buddhist priests encouraged the ceremonial use of potted plants as a part of their religious rituals.

Just as with cars, cameras and computers (among many other technical products), the people of Japan seem to excel in recognizing the potential of an idea and then developing it into a serious piece of engineering. This precision and attention to detail also applies to art forms such as bonsai. They develop, improve and mass-produce the product until it is perfected. Bonsai may be regarded as one of these products, one which the Japanese have developed into a recognized art form.

Left: *A late 19th-century Japanese lacquer screen depicting a Japanese winter scene with Mount Fuji in the distance. The pine shown is typical of those used to influence bonsai styling.*

LATER DEVELOPMENTS

A very early piece of Japanese documentation is a scroll dating back to 1195. This is entitled the *Saigyo Momogatari Emaki*. A priest named Saigyo apparently used a potted plant as an important symbol of his status, and this scroll depicts an example of this type of plant. There are other early mentions of bonsai in Japan shown in the Kasuga Shrine records of the Kamakura period (1192–1333) and in Heian period scrolls dating back to AD794–1191. These show scenes of household activities, including the displaying of potted plants and bonsai in and around the home. There are also drawings originating from the same time which give absolute evidence that bonsai were being created and cultivated throughout this period in Japan. This, of course, tells us that the

Above: This is the central panel of an antique Japanese triptych woodblock print by Kunisada II which dates from the 1860s. The delightful print shows Prince Genji, probably in a teahouse. This panel of the triptych includes two women, with a bonsai specimen clearly displayed in a tokonoma behind them.

art and culture of bonsai growing existed in Japan as far back as 1,300 years ago.

▷

The popularity of bonsai increased in the late nineteenth century, and the introduction of much improved techniques enabled many growers to produce commercial quantities of these miniature trees. Bonsai arrived in London in 1901 via the Japan Society of London, and was mentioned in *Cassell's Encyclopedia of Gardening* as early as 1905.

Windsor Castle appeared to have a collection of bonsai in 1907, and the first bonsai went on exhibition in London in 1909. Bonsai were shown at exhibitions in several major cities, including Paris, and caused great excitement and interest wherever and whenever they were seen.

THE WORLD OF BONSAI TODAY

For more than 50 years, these exciting miniature trees have become very popular around the world, and it would be extremely difficult to find a country where there is no interest in the art and culture of bonsai.

This international interest has meant that there are now many bonsai societies operating locally, nationally and internationally. These societies work together to advance bonsai culture worldwide. Consequently, there are many excellent nurseries

that specialize in growing bonsai plants, as well as operating as wholesale and retail suppliers.

Most of the world's growers and suppliers operate in Japan, China and Korea, and many are still small, family-run businesses, sometimes working in small growing areas. These growers often specialize in single-species production and then only for part of the bonsai-growing process.

Some growers will start their plants from seed, while others prefer to produce plants from cuttings or by grafting. Some still collect plant material from any source that makes available suitable varieties for bonsai.

Above: *Original antique Japanese triptych woodblock print by the artist and printmaker 'Gekko' c.1897 depicting a Japanese plant nursery displaying 'Morning Glory' plants arranged on timber benches. On the left of the print there are two rock landscapes.*

Each bonsai grower handles one part of the production process and then sells their product on to another nursery for the next stage and so on, until the bonsai trees suitable for sale have been completed. These trees, which come in lots of different sizes, are then sold around the world as a wholesale product or to individual purchasers who may already have large collections.

Left: *This is an ivory Netsuke of a seated man tending a bonsai. These are very unusual but are historically important artifacts.*

Right: *Late 19th-century Japanese woodblock print of a Chrysanthemum bonsai in the cascade style.*

Inspirational trees

Old trees develop some of the most beautiful shapes and forms that can be seen, both in the countryside and in mature and very old parks and gardens. Some of the most spectacular natural tree forms can be seen in rugged mountainous districts of the world, where they have been subjected to the ravages of time and weather. These old trees are looked upon in the bonsai world as inspirational trees, as it is through the study of these natural forms that the bonsai grower, designer and artist can produce bonsai of high quality. Every last detail of mature trees growing naturally is important because it is the study of these details that will make or break your progress into the real and sometimes compulsive world of bonsai. It should never be forgotten that all bonsai, however large or small, must resemble full-size natural trees.

Above: *Scots pine* (Pinus sylvestris) *collected from the wild and undergoing initial training as a literati-style bonsai.*

Most people do not notice trees in their natural habitat, but once you become interested in trees in general, or develop a more refined interest in trees such as bonsai, you will find that trees in their natural forms become noticeable. Mature trees of all species almost always grow into spectacular shapes, as can be seen upon closer inspection. Some species, such as pines, develop very gnarled trunks and thick, plate-like bark, while others retain very smooth bark growing into very elegant or gentle styles, whatever their size.

Very large, mature, full-size trees can often be seen to have hundreds of branches making up a very complex structure. When cultivating and developing a bonsai that is perhaps only one twentieth or even one fiftieth of the height of a full-size tree, it becomes clear that the smaller the tree, the fewer branches are needed (maybe only nine or ten) in order to impart the same impression of size but in a very

Above: *A Himalayan cedar (Cedrus deodara). The drooping branches are often emulated when growing similar species as bonsai.*

Above: Fagus sylvatica *'Laciniata' planted in 1955, here growing naturally in a style of bonsai known as broom. The tree is multi-branched from low down on the trunk, with a very fine, twiggy structure that radiates outwards from the trunk.*

Above: *Douglas fir (* Pseudotsuga menziesii*), giant redwood (* Sequoiadendron giganteum*) and a Japanese red cedar (*Cryptomeria japonica*), all inspirational for bonsai growers.*

much smaller form. Therefore, the intricate examination of full-size trees will play a very meaningful part in the bonsai learning process.

Bonsai, although produced by the human hand, must always look like mature trees. The species or variety is of little importance when the tree's structure is studied in terms of its artistic or aesthetic form. Mature trees can vary so much in shape and size that it is almost impossible to classify them into any sort of groupings, but this has been done in bonsai.

Right: *Old Scots pines (*Pinus sylvestris*), in a natural literati style. These trees are sparsely branched with a weathered canopy at the apex.*

Suitable trees & shrubs

Pine, juniper, larch and cedar are some of the most popular coniferous trees that are turned into bonsai, and there are, of course, many more species from which to choose. It should be remembered that larch is a deciduous conifer and will therefore lose its foliage (needles) in the winter. There is also a wide variety of deciduous trees to choose from, including maple, elm, beech, hawthorn, hornbeam, Judas tree, pomegranate, crab apple, wisteria and many more. The last three also bear flowers and fruit, and it should be noted that flowers and fruit produced will always be their natural size even when a tree is grown and trained as bonsai. Virtually any tree or shrub can be grown as a bonsai as long as it is able to produce suitably small foliage, flowers and fruit when it has undergone bonsai training and is mature.

Above: *Close-up of the trunk and buttress of a 55-year-old Japanese maple (Acer palmatum) showing the excellent roots and trunk flare.*

When deciding which type of plant material to use to grow and develop into a bonsai, a visit to a good garden centre or plant nursery will probably be the best place to start. Any establishment of this type should stock a wide variety of suitable species and varieties suitable for both beginners and more experienced growers. (To help you, a detailed list of the large range of plants available is provided in the plant directory section on pp.440–461.)

If you are not sure what type of tree to choose or how to differentiate between certain specimens, follow the golden rule of looking for a plant that exhibits a woody trunk structure with a reasonably chunky appearance. This will give you a head start when shaping your tree, as you will have something with a semi-mature appearance right from the start.

If you want a flowering bonsai, some of the most spectacular examples can be grown using rhododendrons and azaleas, of which there is a wide variety available.

INDOORS OR OUTDOORS?

Whether these subsequently become known as indoor or outdoor plants depends on the area of the world in which they are going to be grown. If, for instance, you wish to grow a tropical species as a bonsai in a temperate climate, you will need to keep it indoors for at least part of the year. Similarly, trees from temperate regions may need to be kept indoors if grown in a tropical or sub-tropical area.

Left: *A typical small needle juniper (Juniperus rigida) which is available from many bonsai nurseries and normally imported from Japan.*

PLANTS SUITABLE FOR OUTDOOR BONSAI

You can use a range of different plants for developing into beautiful bonsai specimens. The ones pictured below are just a selection of trees that you might already have growing in your garden. These can be collected and then trained into a wealth of different bonsai styles.

Cotoneaster

Cryptomeria japonica

Juniperus chinensis

Juniperus davurica

Juniperus procumbens

Juniperus squamata

the most popular are the many varieties of *Ficus* or fig, the most common of these being *F. benjamina* and *F. microphylla*. Other species frequently used are *Crassula arborescens*, *Nandina domestica*, *Serissa foetida*, *Punica granatum*, as well as *Sageretia theezans*, *Aralia elegantissima*, *Myrtus communis*, fuchsias, gardenias and many more. Trees grown indoors may need more frequent checking of the climatic conditions. Make sure the soil is always kept moist. Spray the foliage regularly to maintain a fairly high humidity and keep the leaves healthy.

Whether you are growing or buying plants for indoor or outdoor bonsai, they must always be healthy, and insect- and disease-free. By achieving this, you will give your bonsai a good start and it will be much easier to work with during repotting, root pruning, shaping and general maintainance.

When purchasing from nurseries or garden centres, always check for any sort of problem and reject plants if you find anything that looks suspicious in terms of leaf problems, such as spots, holes or infestations by insects, or root problems such as being too wet or generally loose in the pot.

This book generally deals with trees that are hardy when kept outdoors in a temperate climate. In any event, bonsai should not be subjected to deep-freezing – below -4°C (25°F) – which is why in cold winter regions they need the protection of a cold greenhouse or frame. When trees are referred to as indoor trees in this book, it means that they must be kept in a more controlled environment, such as in a house or greenhouse. These so-called indoor trees usually need extra warmth and humidity to maintain a healthy growth pattern. They may also be kept outside during the summer when, and if, the climate comes close

to the original conditions in which the plant would be grown. Suitable material for indoor bonsai can be bought at almost any garden centre or supermarket. Tropical or sub-tropical plants that are used as houseplants can often be turned into bonsai. These plants are normally those that have a wealth of green leaves as their dominant feature, but you should always check the trunk to consider whether it would look good when transformed into a tree-like form. You will have to use your imagination to decide if your choice will be suitable as a bonsai. Species used for indoor bonsai vary considerably, and some of

BONSAI SUITABLE FOR GROWING INDOORS

- Bird plum cherry *(Sageretia theezans)*
- *Bougainvillea*
- Dwarf myrtle *(Myrtus communis)*
- Finger aralia *(Aralia elegantissima)*
- *Fuchsia*
- Indian laurel *(Ficus microcarpa)*
- Money tree *(Crassula arborescens)*
- Pomegranate *(Punica granatum)*
- Sacred bamboo *(Nandina domestica)*
- Tree of a thousand stars *(Serissa foetida)*
- Weeping fig *(Ficus benjamina)*

PLANTS SUITABLE FOR INDOOR BONSAI

There is a wealth of exciting plants that can be grown and kept indoors. Those shown here are some of the most popular plants from the list on page 256. Any of them will make a decorative feature in the home, but it is important to ensure that the environmental conditions in the room in which you keep your bonsai are correct for each plant.

Ficus benjamina 'Wiandii'

Aralia elegantissima

Crassula arborescens

Myrtus communis

Sageretia theezans

Bonsai sizes

A bonsai can be virtually any size as long as it is a potted plant that takes on the appearance of a full-size, mature specimen tree as would be seen growing anywhere in the wild or in a parkland situation. Basically, if it can be carried it could probably be referred to as a bonsai even if it takes several people to actually do the carrying. At all times the pot and tree should complement each other, so much so that whatever their size they always take on an air of extreme maturity and elegance. It could be said that the smaller the bonsai the easier it is to look after; however it is most likely to be the opposite because very small trees are in reality quite difficult to style and maintain. This is because there is so little material in a small plant with which to work.

Above: Mame *English elm (Ulmus procera), only 15cm (6in) high, with a very mature trunk and branch structure.*

Sizes of bonsai can range in height from no more than 2.5cm (1in) up to about 1.2m (4ft), although in reality there is no prescribed limit. They are generally classified under three categories, but in some cases there could be seen to be four, which is how they are described here.

Below: *Three bonsai, from left to right: Mame elm, shohin juniper and chumono hornbeam. The three different sizes are clearly shown here.*

The very smallest size is known as *mame* (pronounced "ma-mey"). These tiny trees, which can vary in size from just a few centimetres up to about 15cm (6in) in height, create a fascinating image but are not easy to shape and care for because of their small size. Obtaining true tree-like images at this size can be very difficult, but a compensatory factor is that their diminutive size makes them easy to move around.

The next size is now commonly known as *shohin* (pronounced "sho-hin"), and can be 15–30cm (6–12in) high. Being larger than *mame* means that more detail can be incorporated into the design, and so a more tree-like form can be achieved. Once again this size of bonsai can be easily moved

about. This can prove especially useful if you are intending to move your display or exhibit it at bonsai shows.

From about 30cm (12in) upwards in size to about 1m (40in) the trees are known as *chumono* bonsai. These can generally be carried by most people unaided. Some, especially those that include a piece of rock, may need to be carried by two people. These larger trees are relatively easy to look after, as the watering situation may not be so critical as for *mame* or *shohin* trees, whose smaller pots mean that they require more frequent watering.

The final grouping includes trees up to 1.5m (5ft) or more. Although trained as bonsai, these are normally displayed as patio plants in much larger pots to suit the size of the tree. Once in place, they are moved only very occasionally.

Trees that are trained in the same way as bonsai but grown in the ground are not generally classified as bonsai.

Above: *A medium-sized, clump-style bonsai Japanese maple (Acer palmatum), showing good balance between the pot, root structure, trunks and canopy.*

Left: *An excellent example of two extremes of bonsai size, showing how maturity can be achieved from as little as 15cm (6in) to 90cm (36in) tall.*

Bonsai proportions & aesthetics

The words "proportions" and "aesthetics" are probably two of the most important words to bear in mind when growing, designing and styling plants into bonsai. The relationship between the overall height, width and depth of a bonsai is extremely important just as the relationship between the density of foliage and thickness and taper of the trunk must be complementary. The thickness of the base of the trunk compared with the size and shape of the pot is equally crucial, and when all these elements are combined and related to each other a truly magnificent bonsai can be the result. Features such as the position of the first branch and whether it is on the left or right of the trunk can make or break the final appearance of your bonsai, so careful consideration of all these aspects is of the utmost importance.

Traditionally, bonsai are usually seen as beautiful, graceful and pleasing-to-the-eye artistic creations, but some examples can appear to be rather contorted or artificial for some people's tastes. It must be appreciated that bonsai could just be considered to be an illusion of grandeur, because nowadays these trees are almost totally human-controlled creations throughout the entire production process. It should be understood right from the beginning that there is no real finished product with a bonsai. Bonsai are, of course, living works of art, and by their very nature they do not stand still, but are always evolving and need to be cared for correctly for their entire lifespan. If these important points are not fully understood and observed, then any bonsai can lose its shape completely within a very short period of time.

Throughout the process of growing a bonsai, there are some rules about design and aesthetics that should be

Above: Acer palmatum 'Deshojo' buttress, showing the excellent trunk flair and surface root structure.

constantly borne in mind. These very basic rules, which relate to the relationship between the trunk structure and branch positioning, are for guidance only and can be varied to suit each individual tree. This flexible approach will ensure that the best design for that particular specimen can be achieved.

Above: *Buttress of a Japanese white pine bonsai showing the surface root structure, taper and angle of the lower trunk.*

Above: *Detail of a European larch bonsai showing superb bark texture and a dead branch stub known in bonsai terms as a "jin".*

Above: *This is the same tree as the one on the left, but showing a larger part of the trunk with three jins and how they are spaced.*

- The height of the first branch up from the base of the trunk should be approximately one-third of the total height of the tree.

- The width of the trunk should be roughly the same as the depth of the chosen pot or container.

- The overall shape of the branch structure should generally be an irregular triangle, with all three sides of different lengths and the bottom side being slightly off the horizontal.

- Branches should alternate in their position going up the trunk, with the first being on the left or right, the second on the opposite side to the first and the third at the back of the tree. This layout should be followed right up to the top of the tree, so that when viewed from the top, the branches radiate out in a regular pattern. At no time should two branches be immediately above or covering each other.

Above: *This is a Japanese black pine (*Pinus thunbergii*) showing the early stages of styling into a slanting bonsai and the basic branch structure in relation to the trunk. The young bonsai specimen has also been wired to shape the basic branch structure.*

Above: *Trunk and buttress detail of an* Acer palmatum *'Deshojo', showing the relationship between the trunk and the main branches.*

Above: *Trunk and buttress detail of a* Chamaecyparis pisifera *bonsai. The trunk and root structure is very realistic.*

Above: *Buttress detail of a European larch (*Larix decidua*). This clearly shows the strong tree roots as they enter the soil.*

Buying bonsai

Bonsai can be very expensive, as it can take many years of dedicated work to produce a good-quality tree, but you need not spend vast sums of money to acquire your first tree. Realistically, you could be throwing money down the drain if you buy a very expensive tree before you have the knowledge to look after it, so it is always better to begin with an inexpensive tree from which you can learn as you go along. Begin with something that is relatively easy to look after, such as Japanese maple for outdoor use or a Chinese elm for indoors. Acquire some plants specifically for use as learning material on which you can practise pruning, wiring and repotting techniques, and remember that you will have failures in the early days. Do not be too hasty to desert a project, as plant development can be slower than expected.

Above: *A crab apple (Malus cerasifera) bonsai entered by a member in the Bonsai Kai Members' Competition at an RHS flower show.*

A so-called "finished bonsai" can easily be purchased from a garden centre, nursery or supermarket, but if you are looking for a better-quality first tree, you should visit a good bonsai nursery or shop. Here, you should be able to obtain expert advice on the type and size of tree that would be most suitable for your particular situation, as well as guidance on care.

The first thing to check is that the store or nursery looks good, is clean and tidy, and has good, healthy plants for sale. If you are buying from a bonsai centre, be sure to ask as many questions about the trees as possible, as bonsai growers are always pleased to share their extensive knowledge with you, whereas if you go to a garden centre or supermarket there is usually no advice available at all.

The tree that you buy should be firm in its pot. If it is not, then it has either been recently repotted or has very little root system, and it should be left alone. Check the soil to see that it is a good, open, free-draining mix and is not waterlogged. If the tree has wire on its trunk or branches, check that it is not cutting into the bark. If it is, this shows that the wire has been left on the tree for too long.

Thoroughly check the condition of your intended purchase, as it could be too late once you have taken it home.

Left: *Typical display benches at a bonsai retail outlet, showing a wide range of bonsai of various sizes, styles, species and varieties.*

Above: *A varied collection of both indoor and outdoor bonsai shown in an indoor environment. The outdoor varieties can only be kept inside for about one day.*

Right: *An exhibit of bonsai/penjing landscapes at an RHS Spring Show in London, showing a variety of styles and designs.*

EASY BONSAI PLANTS

- Beech (*Fagus*)
- Chinese elm (*Ulmus parvifolia*)
- *Cotoneaster*
- Fig (*Ficus*)
- Japanese maple (*Acer palmatum*)
- Juniper (*Juniperus*)
- Larch (*Larix*)

BONSAI GALLERY

Bonsai are seen at their best only when displayed correctly, which is normally against a plain background, usually white, off-white, or any similar natural shade. In this section, a slightly different approach has been taken, which incorporates a variety of different background colours and textures. A range of different types of stand, including various styles and textures of matting, have also been incorporated to give as wide a range of appearances as possible. Each illustration has its own caption, which includes the botanical and common name, style, size and approximate age of each tree as well as the type of pot and its maker. Also included is a short biography of each tree from its origin, through its known or possible history and a final description as it is seen in this chapter.

Above: *Japanese maples such as this one (Acer palmatum 'Deshojo') are favourites with bonsai growers.*
Left: *A very old – approximately 145 years – Japanese white pine (Pinus parviflora), with a well-balanced and refined branch structure.*

INFORMAL UPRIGHT

Chamaecyparis pisifera
Sawara cypress

◁ Imported from Japan in 1990, this
bonsai has been refined since then using
some minor wiring and shoot pinching.
The original pot was replaced by the one
shown in 1998.
Height 62cm (25in)
Pot English (Derek Aspinall)
Approximate age 90 years

INFORMAL UPRIGHT

Fagus sylvatica
Common or European beech

◁ This plant, shown here with summer
foliage, was collected as a very small
seedling, approximately 53 years ago, and
grown as a bonsai by the collector for
50 years before being handed on to Ann
and Ken Norman.
Height 70cm (28in)
Pot English (Joey Connolly)
Approximate age 55 years

TWIN TRUNK

Acer palmatum 'Ukon'
Japanese maple

▷ This bonsai was imported from Japan
in 1990 and the original pot replaced by a
more suitable design in 1997.
Height 83cm (33in)
Pot English (Denis O'Neil)
Approximate age 45 years

INFORMAL UPRIGHT

Pinus sylvestris
Scots pine

▷ The Scots pine is common throughout Europe. This particular example was collected from the wild in England in 1988. It was reduced in height by two-thirds, with the section above the two lowest branches resulting from a repositioned small side branch.

Height 68cm (27in)
Pot English (Gordon Duffett)
Approximate age 65 years

INFORMAL UPRIGHT

Ulmus procera
English elm

◁ Collected from beside a footpath as a sucker, this is now a very beautiful, small bonsai tree.

Height 16cm (6¼in)
Pot Japanese
Approximate age 20 years

CLUMP

Acer palmatum
Japanese maple

▷ This bonsai was imported from Japan in 1990, and the diameter of the trunk base of the tree has almost doubled since that date. It was possibly started as shown in the clump section or as a multiple grafted trunk.

Height 80cm (32in)
Pot English (Bryan Albright)
Approximate age 55 years

INFORMAL UPRIGHT

Acer palmatum 'Nomura'
Japanese maple

◁ Purchased from a Japanese supplier in
1987 and transferred into its current pot
in 1997, this is a very difficult tree to
maintain because of its large leaves and
long internodal growth.
Height 65cm (26in)
Pot English (Gordon Duffett)
Approximate age 50 years

DRIFTWOOD

Larix kaempferi
Japanese larch

▷ The living part of this tree which is
attached to the rear of the driftwood gives
a realistic impression of a very old,
naturally formed tree.
Height 52cm (21in)
Pot English slate
Approximate age 25 years

FORMAL UPRIGHT

Fagus crenata
Japanese beech

▷ This tree was imported from Japan and
has developed well as a result of constant
pinching out of shoots during late spring
and early summer. Bronze autumn leaves
remain in place throughout the winter.
Height 83cm (33in)
Pot Japanese
Approximate age 40 years

SAIKEI

Nandina domestica
Sacred or Heavenly bamboo
◁ This is a simple design made up of a relatively young specimen planted into a piece of Japanese *ibigawa* rock with a planting hollow. The rock is volcanic, is very hard and has interesting textures.
Height 45cm (18in)
Pot Japanese *ibigawa* rock
Approximate age 6 years

ROCK LANDSCAPE

Ulmus parvifolia
Chinese elm
▷ This rock formation is constructed of several small pieces of rock that are cemented to the pot for stability. The elm is planted artistically within the rock arrangement.
Height 45cm (18in)
Pot Chinese crackle glaze
Approximate age 20 years

ROOT-ON-ROCK

Picea mariana 'Nana'
Black spruce

△ The two spruce trees are attached with copper wire to shallow hollows on the sides of this very heavy piece of quartz.

Height 33cm (13in)
Pot Japanese
Approximate age 32 years

INFORMAL UPRIGHT

Pinus parviflora
Japanese white pine

◁ This tree originally had a second heavy low branch opposite the lowest right-hand branch. It has been removed and "jinned" to give a better balance to the tree. Compare this with the image of the same tree taken in 1995, on page 10.

Height 75cm (30in)
Pot English (Derek Aspinall)
Approximate age 80 years

ROOT-OVER-ROCK

Acer palmatum 'Deshojo'
Japanese maple

◁ This is an unusual composition using a Japanese maple whose roots have been trained over an interesting piece of Japanese volcanic rock.

Height 58cm (23in)
Pot English (Derek Aspinall)
Approximate age 39 years

SLANTING

Rhododendron obtusum 'Amoenum'
Kirishima azalea

◁ Collected as a very large garden plant in 1992 when it was approximately 62 years old, this plant was transformed into a very beautiful bonsai in only 13 years.

Height 85cm (34in)
Pot English (Derek Aspinall)
Approximate age 75 years

GROUP OR FOREST

Cryptomeria japonica
Japanese red cedar

△ These trees were imported in 1989 and arranged as a group at the FOBBS National Bonsai Convention hosted by the Sussex Bonsai group.

Height 50cm (20in)
Pot English (Petra Engelke-Tomlinson)
Approximate age 20–35 years

GROUP OR FOREST

Carpinus laxiflora
Japanese hornbeam
◁ Many trees with slim trunks
planted close together can make a
very lifelike natural forest. It is
realistic to have a suggestion of a
footpath running roughly through the
centre of the group.
Height 80cm (32in)
Pot English (Derek Aspinall)
Approximate age 31 years

INFORMAL UPRIGHT

Acer palmatum
Japanese maple
▷ An interesting surface root structure
gives this tree a very powerful
appearance. The pot glaze is designed
to blend with the shape of the roots.
Height 70cm (28in)
Pot English (Bryan Albright)
Approximate age 55 years

INFORMAL UPRIGHT

Pinus thunbergii
Japanese black pine
◁ The relatively heavy nature of this
pot and the squat appearance of the
tree beautifully complement the
powerful root structure.
Height 33cm (13in)
Pot Japanese
Approximate age 33 years

CLUMP

Acer palmatum 'Kiyohime'
Japanese maple

△ The trunk base has trebled in diameter and the branch structure improved beyond recognition over the past 25 years.

Height 40cm (16in)
Pot English (Derek Aspinall)
Approximate age 46 years

BROOM

Zelkova serrata
Japanese grey bark elm
▷ A very good example of the broom style, showing that a simple, shallow pot is ideal for this style of bonsai.
Height 52cm (21in)
Pot English (Yew Tree Potters)
Approximate age 45 years

ROOT-OVER-ROCK

Acer buergerianum
Three-lobed or Trident maple
◁ In this composition, the rock blends beautifully with the container, but the appearance of the roots could be improved using grafting techniques.
Height 68cm (27in)
Pot English (Gordon Duffett)
Approximate age 36 years

INFORMAL UPRIGHT

Pinus parviflora
Japanese white pine
◁ This is a very interesting, well-balanced bonsai that has a very refined branch structure and a subtle jin about half way up the trunk.
Height 95cm (38in)
Pot Japanese
Approximate age 145 years

INFORMAL UPRIGHT

Acer buergerianum
Three-lobed or Trident maple
◁ A thick, heavy trunk with well-defined branches gives this bonsai a very mature feeling. It would be advisable to defoliate this specimen in late spring.
Height 68cm (27in)
Pot Japanese
Approximate age 36 years

INFORMAL UPRIGHT

Rhododendron indicum 'Komei'
Satsuki azalea
▷ A beautiful Satsuki azalea which was imported from Japan. It produces multi-coloured, deep pink through to white flowers in the spring.
Height 90cm (36in)
Pot Japanese
Approximate age 40 years

GROUP OR FOREST

Zelkova serrata
Japanese grey bark elm

◁ This picture was taken in the autumn of 1992, six months after the group was first constructed using seven trees. The overall length of the display was then 80cm (32in).
Height 65cm (26in)
Pot English (by Ken Potter)
Approximate age 32 years

BROOM

Olea europaea
European olive

◁ A very young, small bonsai that is within easy reach of most beginners to the art form. Styled from a plant which is freely available from most plant centres, this tree will produce delicate creamy white flowers, followed by green fruits that will eventually become black olives.
Height 30cm (12in)
Pot Japanese
Approximate age 8 years

INFORMAL UPRIGHT

Acer buergerianum
Trident maple

▷ This tree has a massive trunk that
initially was quite uninteresting. It is
now undergoing a transformation by
hollowing out parts of the trunk to give
the tree more character and a more
aged appearance.

Height 68cm (27in)

Pot English (Gordon Duffett)

Approximate age 45 years

INFORMAL UPRIGHT

Rhododendron indicum 'Komei'
Satsuki azalea

▷ A beautiful Satsuki azalea which was
imported from Japan. In the spring, this
azalea produces multi-coloured, deep
pink through to white flowers.

Height 90cm (36in)

Pot Japanese

Approximate age 40 years

CLUMP

Acer palmatum
Japanese maple
▷ An unusual Japanese maple, styled into a clump, with a well-defined branch structure and foliage which turns rich red in the autumn.
Height 58cm (23in)
Pot English (Bryan Albright)
Approximate age 35 years

INFORMAL UPRIGHT

Malus cerasifera
Nagasaki crab apple
◁ This small, well-proportioned bonsai crab apple has small flowers and very small, cherry-like red fruits in the autumn.
Height 35cm (14in)
Pot Japanese
Approximate age 20 years

ROOT-OVER-ROCK

Acer buergerianum
Three-lobed or Trident maple
▷ This is a superb example of a style of bonsai that has very mature roots clinging tightly to a very interestingly shaped piece of rock.
Height 68cm (27in)
Pot Japanese
Approximate age 36 years

INFORMAL UPRIGHT

Acer palmatum 'Deshojo'
Japanese maple

△ The brilliant carmine-red spring
foliage of this maple fades to
red/green in the summer and changes
to brilliant deep red in the autumn.

Height 70cm (28in)
Pot English (Derek Aspinall)
Approximate age 50 years

BROOM

Acer palmatum
Japanese maple
▷ This is an interesting broom-style Japanese maple with an unusual buttress formation that is sometimes seen in plants that were originally grown in pots.
Height 47cm (19in)
Pot Japanese
Approximate age 55 years

GROUP OR FOREST: 23 TREES

Zelkova serrata
Japanese grey bark elm
▽ The very mature trees in this group vary considerably in height, but work well together on this very well-proportioned two-piece slab.
Height 70cm (28in)
Pot English (Brian Albright)
Approximate age 25–45 years

INFORMAL UPRIGHT

Acer palmatum 'Deshojo'
Japanese maple

▷ The good buttress and structure of
this bonsai blend perfectly with the
well-chosen pot. The proportions of
the height relative to the width, as
well as the branch placement, pot
size, colour and shape, work very well.

Height 80cm (32in)

Pot English (Derek Aspinall)

Approximate age 55 years

INFORMAL UPRIGHT

Larix kaempferi
Japanese larch

▽ This is an example of a small tree,
grown from seed, and painstakingly
developed into an excellent small bonsai
that exudes great maturity.

Height 30cm (12in)

Pot English (Bryan Albright)

Approximate age 44 years

SEMI-CASCADE

Ulmus parvifolia
Chinese elm

▷ This is an interesting variation of
the cascade style planted in a Chinese
pot and displayed on a tall stand that
was imported from Taiwan. This tree
has good aerial roots that lead into a
very rugged, thick trunk that gently
curves down and away from the pot.
The branches are well arranged and
terminate in densely foliated pads
that require close shoot pinching
throughout the growing season from
spring to late summer.
Height 40cm (16in)
Pot Chinese
Approximate age 25 years

LITERATI

Larix decidua
European larch

◁ Grown from seed that was sown 28
years ago, this tree spent 12 years
growing in the ground to develop its
excellent trunk formation before
being lifted and trained into a bonsai.
It was initially envisaged as a formal
upright but when it was discovered
that the trunk was not straight, some
of the lower branches were removed
and turned into jins that clearly give
the tree a lot more character.
Height 60cm (24in)
Pot English (Susan Threadgold)
Approximate age 28 years

BONSAI TECHNIQUES

There is a range of techniques that are essential for the successful development of any plant into a bonsai. These techniques include work at the very beginning when the plant is propagated right through to the final minute details that are required to achieve a mature, but miniature, representation of a full-size tree. Along the way, you will need a variety of tools and pieces of equipment that will enable you to achieve a satisfying result. Everyday tools, such as scissors and chopsticks, will be very useful and inexpensive parts of your toolkit, but, inevitably, you will want to acquire some better-quality tools as your experience grows. Under no circumstances should you try to reach your goal too quickly as the result may not be as good as you would expect. Take your time and plan your work very carefully before you embark on complex procedures. Stick to the simple methods and techniques first and slowly graduate to more complicated designs.

Above: Cotoneaster x suecicus 'Coral Beauty'.
Left: *Several bonsai techniques, such as tight shoot and branch pruning, as well as trunk carving and hollowing, have been applied to this trident maple (Acer buergerianum).*

Tools & equipment

There is a wide range of specialist bonsai tools designed for specific purposes when pruning bonsai, but a few very basic gardening tools will suffice at the beginning of your bonsai career. These tools, which will enable most pruning jobs to be carried out with minimum expense, are a pair of scissors and secateurs (pruners). As you become more experienced, however, you will find that specialist Japanese tools will start to appeal to you more. Given the ability and experience, it is possible to make some tools inexpensively or even purchase general everyday tools that will suffice for the beginner. However you begin, you may well find it useful to keep your bonsai tools separate from any other gardening tools, as well as keeping them in a special tool container.

Above: *This shows the correct use of branch or side cutters, with the cutting edges held horizontally to the trunk.*

TOOLS FOR PRUNING

For small-scale pruning, involving trimming shoots and leaves, the most useful tool is a pair of pointed scissors. Normal secateurs can be used for pruning branches, but they will leave a short stub. This will not only appear unsightly, but will also leave a wound that may never heal correctly. To carry out a much better, cleaner job, therefore, you should purchase some bonsai side or branch cutters. Using these cutters will enable you to make a clean concave cut close to the trunk, which results in a more rapid healing of the wound and so gives a much cleaner appearance to the tree. These cutters have a single curve to the cutting edges.

Possibly the next most useful tool to buy for your collection is a pair of "wen" or "knob cutters". These are mostly used to remove a branch or a branch stub close to the trunk. They have concave cutting edges in both directions, resulting in a small concave hollow that will heal much more quickly. By leaving such a hollow, you will help the callusing bark to "roll" into the hollow and leave only a slight trace of the pruning cut.

TOOLS FOR WIRING

Wiring is an important part of the shaping process and requires different tools for the job. The wiring process is dealt with in detail later on, but the

tools and equipment required are described here. The three main items normally used during the process of wiring a bonsai are wire cutters, pliers and the wire itself.

Wire cutters are available in several sizes, normally small, medium and large, but they can be very expensive if you buy the genuine Japanese article. You can, however, execute just as good a job with a standard pair of electrician's wire cutters, which can be purchased at a much lower price. The Japanese wire cutters are superior

Left: *Wire can be used to shape your bonsai as well as pruning. Here, the wire is being placed in a trunk and branch junction.*

Right: *You can prune the roots of your bonsai plants with vine pruners or with ordinary household scissors.*

Above: *You will need to use wiring techniques when styling some bonsai plants. If this is the case, it can be easier to have a special dispenser containing wires of different gauges.*

Above: *When potting up or repotting your bonsai, you will need a good-quality container, as well as a suitable soil for the bonsai. Here, akadama is being used.*

because they have longer handles in proportion to the cutting blades, which makes the process of cutting through thicker wires much easier than with the electrician's version. They also enable you to cut the wire close to the trunk or branch of the tree without damaging the bark.

A good pair of pliers can also be a very useful part of the wiring toolkit. Normally these would be the Japanese variety, called jinning pliers, which double up here for holding and bending thicker gauges of wire. These specialist pliers are normally used for the forming of jin (areas of removed bark, revealing heartwood below), but they can also be a very valuable asset as a general-purpose bonsai item to add to your bonsai toolkit. Jinning pliers may also be needed for repotting, as is shown in more detail later on. Once again, a more economical alternative to the Japanese pliers would be a standard pair of engineer's pliers.

Traditionally, annealed copper wire, which needs to be heated to soften (or anneal) each time it is reused, can be used in the styling process. The special appeal of copper is that it oxidizes

quickly and soon blends with the bark of a tree to become inconspicuous. In recent years, however, anodized aluminium wire has become more popular because it is easy to use and can be reused without being heated. Nowadays, only more experienced growers use copper.

The wire is available in many gauges, from 1mm (¹⁄₂₅in) up to 6mm (¼in) in diameter, and in rolls weighing 500g–1kg (1lb 4oz–2lb 4oz). The gauge of wire used must be thick enough to enable the branch or trunk to be held in place after it has been

bent into shape. If you use a wire that is too thin to do the job properly, you will simply have to replace it.

SPECIALIST TOOLS

Other special tools are available and you will doubtless add them to your collection as you gain experience. Make sure you keep your tools sharp for good cuts and also clean, so that the chances of introducing disease into a wound are kept to a minimum. You can also purchase a specialist turntable on which you can place your bonsai while you work.

Right: *You may find it easier to work on a specialist turntable when styling and caring for your bonsai.*

RANGE OF TOOLS

A large variety of specialist equipment is available for bonsai, but, just a few basic tools are all that is required to get started. You will find that all you need to begin are a large and small pair of scissors, secateurs (pruners), wire cutters, old chopsticks and an old household fork. These tools will do most jobs, but, as you gain experience, you will need to buy some specialist Japanese tools. These will make a much better job of all the tasks that need to be performed when training and styling a bonsai. You will probably invest in these tools over a period of time. The essential ones include a sharp pair of pointed scissors and a pair of heavy-duty scissors for pruning roots. Branch cutters and knob cutters may well be your next purchase. The other tools shown here are useful, but not essential to begin with. Tools should be sharp for making clean cuts, and free of dirt, so that the possibility of introducing disease into pruning cuts is reduced.

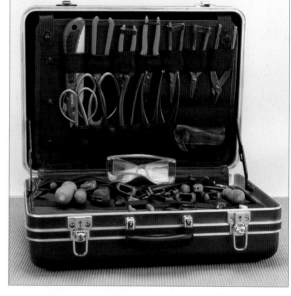

Right: *A comprehensive bonsai tool kit that includes all the tools required for bonsai culture.*

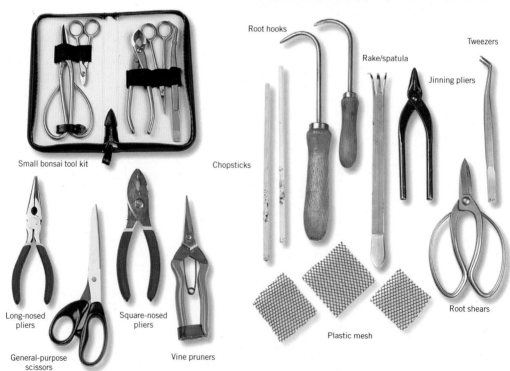

Small bonsai tool kit

Long-nosed pliers

General-purpose scissors

Square-nosed pliers

Vine pruners

Chopsticks

Root hooks

Rake/spatula

Jinning pliers

Tweezers

Plastic mesh

Root shears

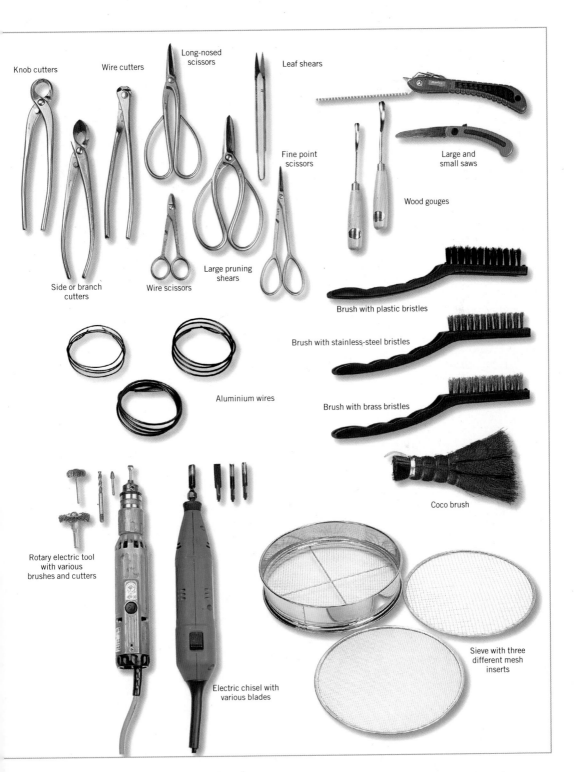

Knob cutters

Wire cutters

Long-nosed scissors

Leaf shears

Fine point scissors

Large and small saws

Wood gouges

Side or branch cutters

Wire scissors

Large pruning shears

Brush with plastic bristles

Brush with stainless-steel bristles

Aluminium wires

Brush with brass bristles

Coco brush

Rotary electric tool with various brushes and cutters

Electric chisel with various blades

Sieve with three different mesh inserts

Collecting plants from the garden

Plants that have been growing vigorously for many years, whether in your own garden or in an area of countryside nearby, can produce some of the best-quality bonsai, as they will almost certainly have thick, mature trunks, including well-developed root structures. It is therefore always worth checking trees and shrubs in your own garden, and those of family and friends, for suitable candidates. If you see an ideal specimen growing wild somewhere, you will need to seek authorization before digging it up. You will often find a plant that is no longer needed in its current place in a garden that would be ideal for training into a bonsai. Check it out thoroughly to ascertain if it is possible to remove and make sure that it is dug up in early spring to be sure of the maximum chance of survival.

Above: *This Satsuki azalea, a garden plant for about 50 years before being trained as a bonsai, shows the all-important mature trunk.*

It may require more than one season to prepare an old plant for removal from the ground. As a mature plant, it will have a substantial root system spreading several yards, and these roots cannot simply be severed and the plant removed in one operation. Cut through the roots with a sharp spade in spring by plunging the spade into the soil to its full depth. Complete a circle around the plant with the spade, about 30–45cm (12–18in) from the trunk base, and then undercut to sever any long taproots. Leave the plant for another season to allow it to develop a new, compact root structure, and remove it from the ground in the following spring just before any new growth begins. Before digging up the plant, carry out some basic pruning in order to aid the development of the basic structure.

When you have dug up the tree or shrub, plant it in a training container, using a gritty, open soil to encourage good root growth. Any type of container can be used for this initial growing period. You can make your own from timber pallets or even

LIFTING AND STORING A GARDEN PLANT

1 This is a good example of some suitable plant material for styling into a bonsai specimen, growing in the open ground. The tree can be prepared in advance by digging around the roots with a sharp spade during the season before lifting.

2 Remove the plant from the ground using a spade, cutting the roots as necessary with the spade or secateurs (pruners), but leaving a good fibrous root system. Having lifted the tree, prepare the roots by knocking away excess soil with the spade or a rake, and pruning any large roots so that it will fit into its training box.

3 This is the prepared training box. You will need to put a layer of coarse grit over the bottom of the box, followed by a layer of very gritty soil. You will also need to pass some wires through the holes in the bottom of the box, leaving sufficient length for "tying in".

4 Place the tree in the box, work the roots into the soil, and tie in by twisting the ends of the wire together until the tree is firmly held. Having filled up the box with more soil and watered well, the tree can now develop a new compact root system. Whatever container you use, it must have good holes in the base to allow free drainage of water.

COLLECTING AND STYLING A YOUNG PLANT

1 This Satsuki azalea, *Rhododendron indicum*, was removed from the open ground two years prior to this shot and then pruned, leaving only the roots and trunk. This shows two years of new growth.

2 Once the plant has been removed from its pot, remove most of the unwanted shoots.

3 There is an old branch stub that will need to be removed. Remove the unwanted stub, as well as some more small shoots. Wire the branches ready for shaping.

4 The potential bonsai has now been shaped and repotted in to a temporary pot.

5 Following twelve weeks of re-growth, a considerable amount of new growth has appeared which can again be shaped and pruned.

6 Select and remove any internal adventitious shoots, using a sharp pair of cutters.

7 Prune the tips of minor shoots in order to promote new, dense inner growth for the new season.

8 The finished bonsai following completion of the styling work. The young bonsai will take many years to reach maturity.

plastic washing bowls, storage boxes or anything that will contain your plant. Large drainage holes in the base of your container are very important in order to allow excess water to drain away freely. Always tie the plant into the container so that it is held firmly; this will allow the new roots to develop unchecked.

The Satsuki azalea shown in the sequence above was collected from a large plantation of unwanted material.

It had been previously cut back while in the ground, but required further work to turn it into a plant with some bonsai potential. Azaleas and rhododendrons grown in these situations make excellent material, as they will have a compact, fibrous root system and are easy to dig up and repot with minimal risk to the plant.

In addition to single plants, you should also look out for old hedges being removed by your neighbours,

and offer to relieve them of the best-looking plants; you may even be looking at a whole row of possible bonsai material. Check the plants closely to see if they have a compact habit. As a hedge, they will have been clipped for many years and would be ideal plants from which to start some new bonsai. Some species that are worth looking out for are azalea, beech, field maple, hedging honeysuckle, juniper and privet.

Propagating from seed

Growing from seed is a time-consuming way to produce any plant, let alone a bonsai, but it does have one benefit: it is the only way that you will be able to quote the exact age of your trees, which is always one of the first questions you will be asked about them. The seeds of some tree varieties, especially Japanese maples, can produce variable results. Leaf shape, size and colour can vary enormously, and this variety can, in many cases, enhance your collection of trees with a large range of interesting leaf shapes and colours. Only very basic equipment, such as pots, seed trays, chopsticks and some suitable soil, is required for the initial seed-sowing process. It is not a time-consuming exercise, but needs to be carried out correctly to obtain the maximum chance of germination taking place.

Above: *The European larch (*Larix decidua*) can be propagated from seed and grown on in plastic flowerpots.*

PREPARING SEED

When growing bonsai, it is best to choose seeds that grow into plants with naturally small leaves, needles, flowers and fruit. Make sure that any seeds you purchase or collect are fresh. Seeds with a shell or case may need to be cracked or chipped in order to aid germination. To crack them, gently squeeze the hard-shelled seeds with pliers until the seed coat cracks, which will then allow moisture to reach the kernel and so aid germination. To chip them, use a very sharp knife to cut a small chip from the seed coat for the same purpose.

An alternative method for aiding germination is to stratify seeds. To do this, you will need to mix them with a small amount of moist peat or sand, put this mixture in a covered container, and place the container in the salad compartment of a refrigerator for three to four weeks before sowing. This is a more natural way to break the dormancy of the seeds and speed up the germination process. The action of stratification normally takes place naturally when seeds either remain on trees or fall to the ground during winter. As they over-winter, the seeds will be repeatedly frozen or chilled, and the dormancy will be broken naturally.

SOWING SEED

Almost fill a seed tray or pot with some seed compost (soil mix) and gently flatten it, but do not compress it. With fairly large seeds you will need to place them carefully at regular intervals over the surface of the compost and finally

Left: *Seven Japanese larch (*Larix kaempferi*) of various ages grown from seed and arranged as a small forest in a shallow pot.*

1 Fill a seed tray almost to the brim with soil and lay the seeds on the surface, spacing them out evenly.

2 Cover the seeds with a layer of soil which is approximately the same thickness as the seeds you are sowing.

3 Press the surface down lightly to firm the seeds in place.

4 Spray with water that has had a fungicide added; this helps to prevent the seeds from rotting and also the "damping off" of the seedlings when they appear.

5 If the seeds are from hardy trees, the completed tray should be covered and placed outdoors; if they are from tropical or indoor varieties, they will need to be kept indoors in a warm place.

cover them with a layer of compost no deeper than the size of the seeds. Firm this top layer gently before watering from a watering can with a fine rose head. Following watering, it is a good idea to spray with a fungicide to guard against fungal attack.

Cover the tray of seeds to retain some humidity and warmth, and place in an unheated greenhouse until the seeds start to germinate. At this point, you can place them outdoors and remove the cover after a week or two so that the new plants can advance naturally.

Keep a close watch on your new young plants, because they are vulnerable to attack from a large variety of creatures, including slugs, snails and a wide range of insects.

Left: *Several one-year-old English oak (*Quercus robur*) seedlings growing in a seed tray and ready for transplanting into individual larger pots. These will enable the plants to develop freely for a few years before being styled.*

Propagating from cuttings

Since growing plants from seed is a slow process, you might prefer to speed up your journey into the world of bonsai by propagating from cuttings. Plants produced from cuttings will have exactly the same characteristics as the parent plant from which the cuttings originated. The process entails cutting small parts from the parent plant of your choice and inserting them into some potting compost (soil mix) that is specially formulated for growing cuttings. For this technique you will need some flowerpots or seed trays, some suitable soil, a chopstick, possibly a sharp knife, a pair of scissors and tweezers, as well as some rooting powder, although this last item is not always required. The soil should have a good, free-draining, granular structure in order to encourage young root growth.

Softwood and hardwood are the two types of material normally used when propagating woody plants for bonsai. Softwood, or semi-ripe, cuttings are taken in late spring or early summer, and hardwood cuttings in the autumn.

PROPAGATING BROAD-LEAF TREES

For broad-leaf trees, take a cutting with several nodes and remove the lowest leaves, as well as the growing tip. If the leaves are large, remove about two-thirds of each leaf using a pair of sharp scissors. This will reduce the rate at which the cutting will lose water through transpiration from its leaves by approximately two-thirds, so increasing its chances of survival.

PROPAGATING CONIFERS

For conifers, take heel cuttings by pulling down on shoots until they become detached. (The "heel" refers to the small amount of hardwood material from the branch that will come off with the shoot.) The amount of foliage should be reduced, as with broad-leaf cuttings, but not removed, as most cuttings will die without any foliage.

Fill a seed tray or flowerpot with some cuttings compost (soil mix), which is generally a more gritty mixture than that used for seeds. Make a small

hole for each cutting using a chopstick or something similar and insert the cuttings into the compost to about one-third of their length and firm in by hand. When the tray or pot is complete, water as for seed sowing and spray with a fungicide as a precaution against fungal attack. Cover the tray to retain humidity and place in a cool shady spot.

Above: *A four-year-old Chinese juniper (*Juniperus chinensis*) cutting propagated by the method described on these pages.*

Instead of using commercially available cuttings compost, you could use a Japanese potting soil called akadama. This is ideal for encouraging root production.

Left: *This* Acer palmatum *was grown from a cutting and is approximately ten years old. It is very difficult to raise Japanese maple cultivars from cuttings, as they do not freely produce roots.*

TAKING *JUNIPERUS* CUTTINGS

1 Remove the heel cutting – here from a Chinese juniper (*Juniperus chinensis*) – by pulling it down and away from the main stem.

2 After the cutting has been removed, you will be able to see the "heel" at the end of the cutting.

3 You can put several cuttings in each pot. Here, a heel cutting is being taken from a *Juniperus procumbens* 'Nana' shoot.

4 Make a suitable hole in the soil (this is akadama) using a chopstick.

5 Place each cutting into a hole in the soil and firm in using the chopstick.

6 Three different cuttings have been planted in this pot: *Juniperus chinensis*, *J. procumbens* 'Nana' and *Chaenomeles japonica*. All three are heel cuttings.

TAKING BROAD-LEAF AND CONIFER CUTTINGS

1 For broad-leaf trees, take a cutting that has several nodes and cut off the lowest leaves and the growing tip. Remove half of each leaf on the cutting to reduce water loss.

2 For conifers, take a heel cutting by pulling down on the shoot until it breaks free. Remove any excess long strands of bark that remain on the heel of the cutting.

3 Having filled a tray with very sandy soil, make a small hole with a chopstick for each of the cuttings.

4 Insert the cuttings into the soil for about one-third of their length. Spray with a mix of water and fungicide.

5 Cover the tray to retain humidity and place outdoors in a shady place.

Propagating by grafting

A graft is the name applied to a union made between two plants and also between two parts of the same plant. Grafting can occur naturally, such as when branches rubbing together over a period of time eventually produce wounds, and then calluses, before fusing together to form a graft. It can also be created artificially by making a wound with a knife into two parts of similar plant material, pressing the two together – making sure that the cambium layers come into contact – and binding them with raffia or other suitable material until the graft has formed. Grafting techniques are not commonly used by amateur bonsai growers but, as they can produce almost instant results in terms of adding a new branch or root, for example, they can be an invaluable asset.

Above: *The small round mark in the centre of the old wound is the cut-off end of a thread graft on an* Acer palmatum.

There are several types of graft used in horticulture that can easily be used to add branches or roots where they are required to improve the form of bonsai. The most common forms of graft used in bonsai work are root, thread and inarch grafting. Several other graft forms do exist, but these are normally used to produce plant material by propagating nurseries, and are not generally used by bonsai growers.

ROOT GRAFTING

This commonly used form of grafting in bonsai enables the grower to add roots to the base of the trunk. This improves the appearance of the root system and ultimately of the trunk buttress.

Root grafting consists of making a union between the main tree and a small plant of the same species, fixing them together securely and sealing the join to exclude water from the union. This will enable the union to bond together more quickly. The seal may be removed after about one season's growth, by which time the callus should have completely taken over.

THREAD GRAFTING

This is a relatively easy method of replacing or adding a new branch to a tree and is achieved normally by growing a long individual shoot on the plant needing the new branch. This can then be stripped of any side shoots and foliage before being passed

through a hole that has been drilled at the required place on the trunk of the tree. This is then sealed at both entry and exit points and allowed to grow and graft on to the main trunk.

INARCH GRAFTING

This technique is used to introduce a new branch into the trunk of a tree. Similar starting procedures are needed for this as for thread grafting, but the shoot is laid into a cut in the bark and tied in place with grafting tape or raffia. Any grafting technique will be described in detail in specialist books.

Left: *The right-hand branch of this* Acer palmatum *has been attached by a method of propagation known as thread grafting.*

Right: *The trunk base of a grafted Japanese maple. The lower part is the stock plant that will be* Acer palmatum, *while the upper section is the grafted scion of a Japanese maple cultivar.*

ROOT GRAFTING ON TO AN *ACER BUERGERIANUM*

1 Close-up of trunk base of a root-over-rock *Acer buergerianum* that needs an extra root grafted into place.

2 The main tree and donor tree side by side. The lower trunk of the donor tree will become the new root on the main tree.

3 Using a small saw, cut a suitably sized piece of root from the main tree.

4 Carefully remove the cut-out piece of soil and root.

5 Place a small amount of new soil into the bottom of the hole.

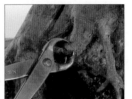

6 Using wen or knob cutters, cut a hollow into the side of the knobbly, unsightly root of the main tree.

7 Tidy the cut using a very sharp wood-working gouge. Remember to take great care when using extremely sharp tools.

8 Place the donor tree into the hole and mark on its trunk where it touches the main trunk.

9 Remove the donor tree from the hole and remove a piece of bark, using the gouge, so that the two areas of cambium on the donor and recipient tree match.

10 The points on each tree that will be in contact with each other are shown here. Remember that the cambium of each piece must come into contact with the other.

11 Place the donor tree back into the hole and press its trunk on to the main tree so that the cambium areas come into contact. Secure the donor tree to the main tree.

12 Apply wound sealer over the screw head and around the contact area between the trees. The sealer has been applied and the area topped up with soil.

13 The completed grafting procedure, showing the donor tree with its upper growth still in place. This will eventually be removed when the graft has successfully completed in about three months.

Propagating by air layering

This is a relatively straightforward method of propagation by which a plant is encouraged to produce roots from its trunk or from one or more of its branches. Some plants layer themselves naturally and produce roots when their branches droop and come into contact with the ground; this is known as ground layering. However, the most commonly used layering method for producing plants for styling into bonsai is air layering, which generates roots at any point above the level of the soil on woody plants. For bonsai purposes, this technique is mostly used to produce an annular root system around the trunk because, overall, annular roots give a better, and more realistic, impression than the odd individual root protruding from one side of the trunk base.

Above: *Damp sphagnum moss which is now ready for covering a bare stem when air layering. Soak in water and squeeze out any excess water by hand.*

Most woody plants can be layered, and, if you find propagating a plant from seeds or cuttings difficult, it is worth trying to propagate by air layering instead.

With a sharp knife, make two cuts, about 2cm (¾in) apart, around the trunk, through the bark and to the heartwood. Using the tip of the knife, prise the bark from the trunk as a complete band, exposing the heartwood beneath. Place about two handfuls of wet sphagnum moss around the exposed area of the trunk, making sure that it comes well above and below the exposed area. You can use your hands in order to squeeze out any excess water.

You should also aim to improve the stimulation of the roots by dusting the exposed ends of the cambium layer of the tree with some rooting powder or liquid.

Cover the sphagnum moss with a strip of plain polythene (plastic sheet) or even some bubble wrap, tying it close to the trunk with string or wire. The strip of polythene or bubble wrap should be tied both above and below the sphagnum moss in order to create a ball-like structure. The ties should be airtight to keep any moisture loss from the layered area to a minimum.

This operation can be carried out from early spring to midsummer, so that the layer has plenty of time to achieve good root development. This will be removed in late summer when the newly rooted plant will be severed from the parent plant. To do this, remove the polythene or bubble wrap and expose the area of removed bark. (Do not attempt to remove all the moss because you will be in danger of removing the delicate roots as well.) Carefully cut off just below the new root system. The new roots will be fragile at this stage, so take great care when potting this part of the plant into its new container. Use a good open soil mixture when potting and protect the delicate roots from frost over the first winter.

Left: *This layering only has roots on the lower side of the cut, so it is acceptable to remove the moss from where there are no roots.*

AIR LAYERING A *JUNIPERUS CHINENSIS*

1 This shows the area on the trunk of a *Juniperus chinensis* to be air layered.

2 Cut a ring through and around the bark using a sharp knife.

3 Make a similar second cut about 2.5cm (1in) below the first.

4 After making a vertical cut between the two ring cuts, remove the ring of bark using the tip of the knife.

5 The ring of bark is completely removed, so that the two areas of bark are separated.

6 Take a large handful of damp sphagnum moss and wrap it around the bare part of the trunk so that it extends about 5cm (2in) on either side of the cuts.

7 Squeeze the sphagnum moss tightly around the stem using your hand.

8 The moss will stay in place if it is wet and tightly compressed.

9 Wrap a suitable length of bubble wrap around the moss so that the wrap extends beyond the moss both on the top and on the bottom.

10 Secure the bubble wrap with two lengths of wire or string.

11 The preparation of the air-layering process is complete and it will now require two or three months for sufficient roots to develop so that the newly air-layered plant can be removed from the parent plant.

▷

REMOVING AND POTTING ON A LAYERED PLANT

Once an air layering has taken and produced sufficient roots, it must be removed from the parent plant as soon as possible. This can be carried out at any time of the year but preferably in midsummer so that the newly severed plant has a reasonable time in which to settle in to its new container and produce new roots before the winter. The new roots will be very tender so winter protection will be required.

You will need to plant your newly air-layered plant in a suitable training pot. The roots will be very delicate at this stage and, for this reason, they must be treated with the utmost care. Do not attempt to remove too much sphagnum moss because the newly formed roots will break away very easily. This will leave the air-layered plant with very little upon which it can survive.

AIR LAYERING AND REPOTTING AN *ACER PALMATUM*

1 This is a large *Acer palmatum* with air layering in progress. The wrapped area is covered with black polythene (plastic sheet).

2 A close-up of the wrapped air layering, showing how it has been tied in to create a ball shape.

3 Remove the black polythene wrapping in order to expose the sphagnum moss beneath.

4 Here, the new young roots can clearly be seen emerging from the surface of the sphagnum moss.

5 Using a sharp saw, cut through the base of the branch close to the main trunk of the parent plant.

6 The branch has been removed. Here, you can see the cut end and where it was cut from the trunk of the parent tree.

7 Part of the parent tree, showing the gap left, two-thirds of the way up on the left side of the trunk, by the removal of the branch.

8 The air layering only has roots on the lower side of the cut, so it is acceptable to remove the moss from where there are no roots. Leave the rest of the moss in place because the roots are very delicate and could be damaged if there is any attempt to remove it.

9 The air layering will need to be planted in an inexpensive training pot.

10 After inserting "tying-in" wires and adding some soil to the bottom of the pot, insert a piece of foam to prevent the wire from cutting into the bark.

11 Using a pair of pliers, twist the wire tightly over the foam until the plant is totally secure in the pot.

12 A wire support is added to prevent the trunk from resting on the side of the pot.

13 Top up the pot with akadama because this is an ideal growing medium for promoting good root growth.

14 Finished planting displayed on a round Chinese stand. This tree will need some winter protection and has the potential to become a very good cascade bonsai.

Left: *With the tree finally potted, all the leaves have been removed – a process usually known as defoliation – in order to help the tree to concentrate on the important task of producing a new root system. Within six weeks of this process taking place, a new set of leaves will begin to appear that will be slightly smaller than those that have been removed.*

Soils for bonsai

Bonsai can be grown in almost any type of soil, but if you wish to keep them in the best of health at all times, then they must be grown in the correct soil or potting mix. Soil for bonsai may consist of just one ingredient or a mixture of two or more different ingredients, all of which must be of a good quality in order to maintain the health and vigour of your tree for many years to come. All soils will also need to be dry to aid the mixing and potting processes. If the soil is wet, you will find that it can be very difficult to work into and around the root system of any tree when you are repotting, for example. If the soil is dry, however, it will flow freely in and around the roots of the tree. This will ensure that the roots are all in good contact with the soil at all times.

Above: *Sift all soils to remove the finest particles that could "clog up" the root structure of bonsai. Remove only fine dust and retain small granules for top dressing.*

The soil's function is to hold sufficient nutrients, water and air to provide a regular supply of these three vital components to the roots of your bonsai tree. If the soil stores too much water around the roots, it will encourage the roots to decay. It is therefore very important that the texture of the soil is open and free-draining to allow excess water to drain away. In fact, free-draining soil is one of the most important elements in the successful culture of bonsai. Any soil mixture must be open and incorporate as many air spaces as possible around the granules of soil, because it is these spaces that allow the root system to breathe.

The soil is also partly responsible for securing the tree into the pot and it needs to be firm enough to achieve this. The action of tying the tree into the pot with wire, using the holes in the base of the pot, is a standard bonsai procedure that will stop the tree moving around in the pot and therefore aid the formation of a good root system.

SOIL TYPES

A general-purpose soil mix can be one part sphagnum moss peat to one part loam to two parts coarse sharp grit. These ingredients can be bought from a garden centre or DIY store.

Coarse grit with angular particles measuring 3–6mm (⅛–¼in) will be ideal, but do not use grit that has very sharp edges, as it can cause severe damage to roots during repotting. There are many varieties of grit available, as well as other suitable substitute materials, and these can be added to the soil mix as you become more experienced in growing bonsai. A commercially prepared soil mix can

Right: *This tree has been potted in medium-grade akadama, with a top dressing of fine granules that look much better from an aesthetic point of view.*

be used to replace loam, but bear in mind that this mix already contains loam, grit and nutrients.

It is also important to make sure that the components of your soil mix are completely dry when you combine them, and pass them through a sieve in order to obtain particles measuring 3–6mm (⅛–¼in). Particles that are smaller than this will congest the air spaces in the soil and so will be detrimental to the development of the root system of your tree.

Other soils, which are imported from Japan, are available from good bonsai suppliers. While these soils are probably more suited to the experienced grower, they do provide excellent growing conditions for bonsai, as well as many other types of potted plants. Three varieties of soil for bonsai are obtainable: akadama, kanuma and kiryu. Akadama is a general-purpose clay granule soil and is suitable for most bonsai; kanuma is highly recommended for ericaceous

(acid soil) plants such as azaleas; and kiryu is good for pines (*Pinus*) and junipers (*Juniperus*), but is not always available to the average bonsai grower. These soils can be more expensive than normal ingredients, but they can be mixed with peat and grit to help keep the costs down.

It is not normal to mix fertilizers with any soil when you are potting, but they can be added as necessary at regular intervals throughout the growing season.

GROWING MEDIUMS

Various types of soil can be used for bonsai culture. They can be used on their own or mixed in different proportions to suit individual plants or growing conditions. Many bonsai growers develop their own special recipes but they will be mostly based on the materials described in this section.

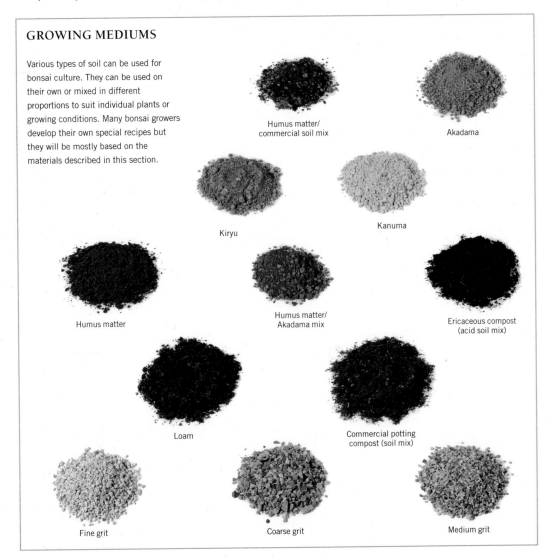

Humus matter/
commercial soil mix

Akadama

Kiryu

Kanuma

Humus matter

Humus matter/
Akadama mix

Ericaceous compost
(acid soil mix)

Loam

Commercial potting
compost (soil mix)

Fine grit

Coarse grit

Medium grit

Pruning techniques

All bonsai require some branches to be removed or pruned and other structural alterations to be made during their life. This may be necessary to improve the design or appearance of a tree or to style a tree during the initial training stages. Removing a branch, or part of a branch, is a straightforward process, but care should be taken to make a clean cut that will heal and leave little or no scar. Various purpose-made tools are available that allow bonsai growers to carry out pruning operations that will successfully achieve the required result. Gardening or household tools, such as secateurs (pruners) and scissors, are satisfactory for beginners, and require less financial outlay. As the various pruning techniques become familiar, you will find that proper tools will be a beneficial addition to your tool kit.

Above: *The difference between the scale-like adult foliage of the Chinese juniper (Juniperus chinensis) and the needle-like juvenile foliage is clear. Hard pruning will result in a proliferation of juvenile foliage.*

BASIC PRUNING TECHNIQUES

Using the correct type of cutters for the task in hand is vital. Also ensure that any cutters are clean and sharp. This will give good pruning cuts and reduce the risk of any infection to the tree or plant. Make the cut as close to the trunk as possible, placing the cutting edges at 90 degrees to the trunk. Using cutters with the edges vertical or parallel to the trunk can cause severe damage.

You can protect the wound left by the pruning process with a sealer specifically formulated for bonsai. Sealing the wound protects the cut bark edge, preventing it from drying out and accelerating the healing process. New

buds may appear around the pruned area. If too many appear, rub them off, leaving only those that may be in a useful position as future branches. You will need to feed the tree after pruning.

In all cases, care should be taken to ensure that flower-bearing growth is not pruned away before it blooms.

PRUNING DECIDUOUS TREES

Basic pruning of deciduous trees can be done using a pair of scissors. When removing a branch, cut as close to the trunk as possible. If you have a pair of concave branch cutters, you will be able to prune even closer to the trunk. If you are left with a small stub after

Left: *For beginners to bonsai, secateurs (pruners) will be adequate as a pruning tool.*

USING BRANCH CUTTERS

1 This is the correct use of branch or side cutters, with the cutting edges held horizontal to the trunk.

2 After removing the branch, it can be seen that the cut end is convex and the wound on the trunk is concave.

3 This is the incorrect use of branch cutters, with the cutting edges held vertical to the trunk. This usually results in a vertical split on the trunk that will slow down the healing process.

USING VINE PRUNERS

1 Removing a very long shoot on a Japanese hornbeam (*Carpinus laxiflora*) with vine pruners.

2 The long shoot has been removed and the cut end can be clearly seen.

3 Three shorter shoots also need to be pruned to correct the balance of the foliage.

4 One of the shorter shoots being removed with vine pruners.

5 Appearance of the foliage following the removal of all three shoots.

6 Backed by white paper, the foliage following pruning can be clearly seen.

pruning, this can be removed using a different tool called a knob cutter, which leaves a small hollow that also aids the healing process.

When pruning maples, particularly Japanese maples (*Acer palmatum*), do not cut back the shoots close to a bud as the branch or shoot will probably die back beyond that point. Leave about 12mm (½in) of shoot to allow for this die-back, as this can be tidied up later.

PRUNING CONIFERS

Most of the techniques used when pruning deciduous trees also apply to conifers, but there are one or two extra points that need to be considered. When removing a branch from a conifer, always leave a substantial length of the branch intact. This can be used to enhance the tree by creating a jin. A jin is where the bark is stripped from the stub, exposing the heartwood which

dries out to leave a natural-looking dead branch. This is often seen on full-size conifers in the wild.

When pruning conifer branches, you must always leave some foliage on the end of the branch so that there is something to draw the sap. This is not the case with deciduous trees because they will regenerate new shoots without you having to leave any foliage in place.

REMOVING UNWANTED SHOOTS

1 This rather long shoot on an *Acer palmatum* 'Deshojo' does not fit in with the tree shape and is spoiling the outline of the bonsai specimen.

2 Remove the shoot with a pair of vine pruners or even an ordinary pair of household scissors.

3 Following the removal of the offending shoot from the bonsai, this is how the outline of the bonsai looks.

PRUNING OUT SHOOTS AND NEEDLES

You will need to maintain the shape of your bonsai by pinching or cutting out the growing tips during the spring and summer. Broad-leaf trees generally produce shoots with pairs of leaves or single leaves on alternating sides of the branch. Conifers vary widely in the appearance of their tip growth, but the pruning technique is similar for each. Spruce (*Picea*) and some junipers (*Juniperus*) form small bunches of needles that can be removed using your fingers. Each week, remove the largest shoots, but make sure there is always some fresh growth remaining.

On maples and some other broad-leaf trees, you can remove all the leaves in late spring when they are fully developed. This encourages the tree to produce a second, smaller set of leaves, but should only be carried out once every two years, and then only if the tree is healthy. Always use clean sharp scissors for any pruning operation.

ANNUAL PRUNING

Every year your trees will produce an abundance of shoots from their leaf axils, which, if left in place, would eventually dominate the appearance of your bonsai.

For trees in training, you may be able to leave some of these shoots in place if you need to thicken the adjacent trunk or branch, but, in mature trees, remove them as soon as possible. You will need to cut back unwanted growth in the dormant season to allow the tree to develop the required shape. Prune out branches that are too thick for the design. The tree may look a little bald, but during the next season each bud will produce a new branch and leaves. Trim back any long shoots to a dormant bud and, where possible, to a bud pointing in the required direction of growth.

PRUNING DECIDUOUS TREES (*ACER BUERGERIANUM*)

1 An *Acer buergerianum* with extended shoots that require some radical pruning.

2 The tree has been wired and the branches positioned prior to pruning the shoots.

3 Prune the long shoots or branches to a suitable length.

4 Using wire cutters, cut any wiring back to suit the new branch or shoot length.

5 Bend the end of the wire back on itself in order to retain the end of the branch.

6 Following the restyling process, the tree has been transformed.

PRUNING CONIFERS (*CRYPTOMERIA JAPONICA*)

1 A *Cryptomeria japonica* group that requires some shoot pruning.

2 Close-up of foliage, showing the bright green young shoots that need pinching out.

3 Trim the long shoots using scissors, with the blades following the angle of the needles.

4 Close pruning is required on *Cryptomeria japonica* to encourage compact growth. Here, three branches have been completed.

5 Compare the pruned branches with those that are awaiting the pruning process.

6 The tree on the left shows how the trees in this group were initially trained.

SHOOT PINCHING ON *CRYPTOMERIA JAPONICA*

1 Hold the tip of the shoot between your thumb and first finger. Gently pull the shoot tip until it breaks free.

2 The same procedure can be carried out using a pair of tweezers. Pull gently to free the tip of the shoot.

3 If the shoots do not break using your fingers, use scissors. The scissor angle must follow the needle angle to avoid damaging the needles that are to remain.

4 The top of a *Cryptomeria japonica* following shoot pinching and showing the new buds beginning to grow.

PINCHING OUT "CANDLES"

1 Hold the "candle" to be removed with a pair of tweezers.

2 Snap the "candle" free by gently twisting the tweezers to one side.

3 The removed "candle" can be clearly seen in this shot.

Pinching out & defoliating

As bonsai trees develop, they produce a plentiful supply of new growth each year. However, during the main period of growth, which in both northern and southern hemispheres comes in mid-spring to late summer, the actual growth rate of some trees can be very high, so you will need to monitor their size and shape closely to stop them becoming too large. Both pinching out (removing shoots) and defoliating (removing all the leaves) encourage your trees to produce a tighter, more twiggy growth pattern, but note that defoliating applies only to deciduous trees: defoliating an evergreen conifer would kill it. The reason for any type of shoot and/or leaf pruning is to force the tree to produce more buds and thus more compact foliage, which will improve the appearance of any bonsai.

PINCHING OUT

Deciduous, or broad-leaf, trees need to have their shoots pinched out at the growing tips regularly during the spring and summer months. This encourages them to produce back budding – new buds within the branch structure which have been encouraged to grow by pruning the tip growth – and hence a more compact growth pattern.

Generally, broad-leaf trees will produce shoots consisting of pairs of leaves or single leaves on alternate sides of the shoot. Allow the shoots to grow several pairs of leaves before pinching them out, using your fingers or some scissors, to one pair of leaves.

DEFOLIATING

To improve the density of growth and assist with the size reduction of leaves, it is possible to remove all the leaves on a deciduous tree. This is generally known as defoliating, and its purpose is to deceive the tree into thinking it is winter. This process should be carried out only when the first set of leaves has matured, normally in late spring or early summer, and then only if the tree is in good health. If you have been following the correct watering, feeding and general care techniques for bonsai, your trees should be healthy enough for defoliating to take place. Complete defoliation of any deciduous tree should be carried out only every other

Above: This Acer palmatum *'Ukon' has been defoliated, leaving only the petioles to die back naturally. A full set of new leaves will be produced within six to twelve weeks.*

year so that your trees do not become unduly stressed. Some trees can be defoliated several times a year, but these are usually the very vigorous growers such as some varieties of maple.

The defoliation process entails removing all the leaves, leaving just the petiole, or leaf stalk, in each case. (The petioles are left in place to drop naturally, so that any goodness within them can drain back and feed the dormant buds at their base.) You will be left with a tree that looks rather

DEFOLIATING

1 Remove the leaf, leaving a complete petiole in place to die back naturally.

2 Petioles left on the plant die back and prompt dormant buds to break.

3 The remaining petioles following leaf pruning can be clearly seen.

COMPLETE DEFOLIATION

1 Commercial-style *Acer palmatum* 'Deshojo' that requires defoliation.

2 The defoliated tree, showing some petioles remaining on the plant and some that have fallen.

3 After about three weeks, the petioles will begin to fall from the tree.

4 Smaller, new leaves will soon begin to grow.

PARTIAL DEFOLIATION

1 Partial defoliation means that some old leaves are retained, allowing some smaller new leaves to develop.

2 Common beech (*Fagus sylvatica*) group that has been partially defoliated, giving a realistic impression of full-size trees.

"spiky", but the petioles will die back and fall away over the next three to four weeks. After a further three to four weeks, new shoots will begin to appear at the point where the fallen petioles were attached. As the new shoots grow, they will in turn need to be pinched back to one pair of leaves in order to maintain an even distribution of foliage.

Defoliation should result in the following crop of leaves being approximately two-thirds of the size of the first set.

Left: *Two small Acer palmatum 'Deshojo' bonsai, with the left-hand tree shown following defoliation and the right-hand tree before defoliation.*

Shaping by pruning

Some deciduous trees grow at an alarming speed during the four- to five-month growing season, and can easily grow completely out of shape in a very short space of time. Conifers are normally very much slower growers and are therefore not so likely to be in need of drastic pruning at any time of the year. There are, however, always exceptions to any rule, so keep a close watch on all your bonsai trees in order to make sure that they do not grow out of hand, and be prepared to start pruning to re-establish their shape. It is generally obvious which shoots need pruning because they will have extended well beyond the original form or outline of the tree. It is normally just a matter of cutting off the excess shoots until the outline of the tree has been restored.

Above: *This is a close-up of the long shoots at the apex of the literati-style Japanese larch (Larix kaempferi).*

The normal process of shaping a bonsai specimen is carried out using pointed scissors or branch cutters. Shaping of your bonsai tree has to be carried out at the right place, in the right way and at the right time of year. A good-quality pair of bonsai scissors, and possibly a similar quality pair of branch cutters, would be a great advantage when you are pruning any bonsai into shape. If you do not wish to spend a lot of money on tools, however, you could manage with a normal pair of kitchen or general-purpose scissors, though these must be clean and have sharp cutting edges.

Using scissors, cut each extended shoot back to the contour of the original pad-shaped foliage structure. Cut the shoots back so that only one or two needles or leaves remain, or even farther if you think it will benefit the overall shape of the tree. Continue this process of removing shoots until the whole tree has been tidied up and presents a pleasing profile once again.

Following each pruning cut, you may wish to seal the wound with a special bonsai wound sealer or a

PRUNING A FORMAL UPRIGHT LITERATI

1 This upright literati Japanese larch (*Larix kaempferi*) will benefit from shaping by pruning.

2 Using a pair of sharp scissors, carefully cut out the long shoots on the apex without cutting through any individual needles.

3 Remove one shoot at a time until all the excess shoots have been removed and a smooth outline is achieved.

4 Once you have pruned away excess shoots, the tree will start to look more mature.

PRUNING A TWIN TRUNK

1 This twin-trunk Japanese larch (*Larix kaempferi*) requires some minor pruning to improve its shape.

2 This shows the typical branch structure and good branch ramification of this type of bonsai style.

3 Individual needles may need to be removed in order to tidy up the overall appearance of the bonsai.

4 Gently pull out any downward-facing needles, using your finger and thumb.

5 The needles should come away by hand without too much effort.

6 After the minor shaping by pruning, the overall appearance of the bonsai has been greatly improved.

general-purpose sealer, which can be purchased from most good garden centres or bonsai specialists. Generally, this will be needed only on larger cuts, and it is not normally necessary if you are just trimming small shoots using a pair of scissors.

The two trees shown on these two pages have been trained as bonsai specimens for at least fifteen years, but they have been allowed to grow a little bit too much. The bonsai trees are both in good condition, but, in both cases, several shoots have been allowed to grow out of all proportion with the trunk and branch structure. This imbalance needs to be remedied through pruning.

When bonsai trees have developed into a mature shape over a number of years, they continue to produce plenty of growth every year. Maintaining these mature shapes requires constant pinching out of the growing tips during the spring and summer. In these two examples, neither of these operations has been carried out and therefore the time has come to rectify the situation. As a bonsai grower, you may often find yourself with this type of scenario and will have trees that have been allowed to grow too much between prunings.

Shaping by wiring

Shaping with wires is probably the most used, and certainly one of the most important, techniques in bonsai training, because it enables the bonsai grower to place trunks, branches and shoots accurately in the required position. This approach gives the bonsai artist total control over the design and shape of a tree, which, when complete, should resemble a full-size mature tree but in miniature form. Although this is a relatively straightforward technique, wiring can take a considerable amount of persistence and practice to master. It would be a good idea to practise applying some wire to branches of varying degrees of thickness – perhaps on plants growing in your garden – before trying to work on a serious bonsai styling project.

Above: *A completely wired* Cedrus atlantica *'Glauca', following the repositioning of all branches to achieve the required design.*

It is also advisable to practise handling various gauges of wire in order to get an idea of the flexibility of the different sizes and how easy or difficult they are to bend or manipulate.

CHECKING FOR FLEXIBILITY
Before applying any wire, check the flexibility of the branches because some plants are more brittle than others. Maples (*Acer*), for example, can be very brittle and could break easily, whereas junipers (*Juniperus*) and pines (*Pinus*) are much more flexible and therefore not so vulnerable to breakage.

You will find that young branches are generally more flexible than mature branches. Indeed, very old branches can be rather thick and stubborn, and may need the use of other techniques, such as wrapping with raffia, to aid the bending process.

APPLYING THE WIRE
You should begin by doing a trial run on a flexible branch that is not vital to the tree's final appearance. Use a piece of wire about half the thickness and about one and a half times the length of the branch to be wired, making sure that there is sufficient length of wire

for you to hold throughout the wiring process. Place the wire on the branch, holding it in place with one hand, and wind it around and along the branch with the other. The wire should run cleanly along the branch, at an angle of about 45 degrees to it, and should not be too tight or too loose. If it is too tight, then it is better to unwind it and start again.

Check the wired branch at regular intervals during the following year in order to make sure that the bark is not growing up and around the wire, giving the impression that it is cutting into the branch. If you see signs of "cutting in", it is very important to remove the wire immediately or the tree could be permanently damaged.

The branch should stay in place when the wire is removed, but, if it springs back out of position, then you will need to rewire it and leave it for a further period until the process is complete.

Left: *This is a newly planted and designed raft-style bonsai showing the wiring needed for the initial styling.*

HOW TO SHAPE A BONSAI USING WIRE

1 Push the wire into the soil in order to anchor the wire end.

2 Make the first turn of wire around the trunk.

3 This is the second turn of the wire.

4 Continue twisting the wire around the trunk right to the top.

5 If the trunk is particularly thick, it may need a second wire laid in parallel to the first.

6 The double-wiring process is now complete.

7 With the wire in place, the trunk can now be carefully bent into the required shape.

8 Place the wire in the trunk and branch junction when you are wiring a branch.

9 The wire is placed on one branch and taken on to the trunk for a good anchorage of the wire.

10 Next, run the wire on to the second branch.

11 Take the wire along the length of both branches.

12 Keep applying the wire until you reach the end of each branch.

13 Secure each wire by looping the end of the wire back on itself, as shown.

14 The finished wiring on two branches, which are now ready for bending into place.

15 Fully wired and shaped branch of a mature *Pinus parviflora*.

Creating jin

In bonsai, jin refers to a dead branch that has lost its bark. In the wild, dead branches are exposed to elements, such as rain and wind, and are eventually bleached by the sun until they turn silvery-white. This occurs naturally on many varieties of conifer, especially junipers and pines. Although jins do not appear on many deciduous trees, they are often seen on oaks. Jin plays a very important part in the final appearance of a bonsai because it creates that small, but often significant, detail that tells the story of an earlier part in the life of a mature tree. A bonsai tree can have as many jins as the grower thinks is necessary, but the total number should not overpower the living part of the tree in any way. Jins do not normally appear on the back of a bonsai, as they would not be seen when viewing the tree from the front.

Above: *You can break the jin back using side cutters to give a natural "weathered" or "torn" effect that blends with the size of the tree.*

The reason for creating jins by artificial means on bonsai is to create a feeling of substantial age. If this is carried out correctly, the effect can be dramatic. When pruning a branch on a conifer, always leave a stump several inches long, so that it can be converted into a jin. The best time to create a jin is during the summer when sap movement is at its greatest, as this makes the removal of the bark easier. When you have made the jin, you should leave it to dry in the sun before applying a coat of lime/sulphur, which will bleach and preserve the wood. This should be reapplied once or twice a year during the summer to maintain the weather resistance of the jin. The jin can then be refined by carving and smoothing with fine sandpaper until a truly natural effect is achieved. Ensure that the jin is always in proportion to the other branches that have foliage.

Above: *An equal-sized branch on the left of this tree has been turned into a jin to improve the balance of the bonsai.*

Right: *The jin on the left-hand side of this trunk reflects the appearance of the branches on the opposite side.*

HOW TO CREATE A JIN

1 A Chinese juniper (*Juniperus chinensis*) on which it would be suitable to create a jin on the lower left branch.

2 Close-up of the branch that is going to be turned into a jin.

3 To create the jin, all foliage on the branch will need to be removed using branch cutters and scissors.

4 Cut through the bark at the base of the branch with a sharp knife, making sure that the cut goes all round and penetrates through to the heartwood.

5 Using the tip of the knife, cut into the bark through to the heartwood from the trunk to the branch tip.

6 Squeeze and twist the bark with jin pliers, or any other suitable type of plier, to free the bark from the heartwood and remove all bark from the branch.

7 With the bark removed, the jin is beginning to take shape and look like a naturally occurring formation.

8 The branch can be split and torn back using branch cutters and pliers. This will give a more ragged, natural look to the finished jin.

9 The same process from a different angle shows how the natural look is achieved.

10 Close-up of the completed jin, showing how a naturally weathered look can be obtained using simple tools and just a few minutes of creative work.

Right: *The front of the tree, showing how the jin appears relative to the whole tree.*

Creating sharimiki

Sharimiki can be regarded as a bonsai technique that complements jin. It gives a tree an even greater appearance of age when used in conjunction with jin. A sharimiki is where a tree may have been struck by lightning and the bark on part of the trunk has been stripped off. This is commonly seen on pines and junipers, and often connects one jin with another, creating an even more dramatic effect. The technique is relatively straightforward and can be carried out using a few basic tools such as a gardening knife and a pair of electrician's pliers, but when you become more familiar with the technique, good-quality specialist tools will undoubtedly make the job easier to execute. Do not be afraid to experiment because this is the best way to learn what will and will not work.

In bonsai, sharimiki or shari are created by stripping the bark away from part of the trunk. This should be carried out with great care because the tree depends on its bark in order to survive. You should also ensure that you always leave enough bark on the trunk to enable the tree to support the branches that remain as removing the bark can weaken the structure.

Above: Stripping the bark from the trunk to reveal the heartwood which will become the sharimiki feature on the bonsai trunk.

The best time to create sharimiki is in the summer when the sap flow is at its greatest, thus allowing the bark to be stripped more easily.

Remember that you are trying to produce an artificial feature that would have normally been created by natural elements such as wind or a lightning strike. Think about how natural forces would have created this damage to the tree and which direction a branch would have fallen or how lightning actually strikes a tree.

Study trees in the wild that have undergone such traumatic events, and relate your observations to your work with your bonsai. When the work is complete, and the newly exposed heartwood has dried, you will need to treat the areas with a lime/sulphur solution to bleach and preserve the exposed wood. This initially gives a yellow appearance that soon fades to white and then to a natural grey.

Left: A shari or sharimiki in the early stages of the styling process of a mountain pine (Pinus mugo).

HOW TO CREATE A SHARIMIKI

1 The Chinese juniper (*Juniperus chinensis*) before styling has begun.

2 Mark the position of the proposed sharimiki on the trunk with a felt-tipped pen.

3 Cut into the bark through to the heartwood with a knife and peel away the bark from the trunk using the tip of the knife.

4 The area of trunk that is stripped of bark, the sharimiki, is linked to a newly created jin as well as any other old jins.

5 The stripped heartwood will have some fine hair-like elements on the surface. These can be burnt off with a small flame.

6 Any discrepancies on the jin or sharimiki can be dealt with in a similar way.

7 The whole tree begins to take on a much more mature appearance now that the jin and sharimiki are complete.

8 The newly formed jin and sharimiki can be toned down to look even more mature by slightly colouring the surface with charcoal or something similar.

Right: *The completed and textured sharimiki should blend well with the overall appearance of the bonsai tree.*

Root pruning & repotting

Maintaining a young and healthy root structure on a bonsai is the basis of producing a thriving and free-growing tree. What takes place in and around the root structure, and in the surrounding soil, is quite complex, as the roots are responsible for providing the tree with almost all necessary nutrients and water, without which it most certainly would not survive. Regular changes of soil, along with regular pruning of the roots, will produce a young, vigorous and fibrous root system, which should be largely free of disease and insect infestations. Root pruning is probably one of the most important and critical parts of the art and culture of bonsai, and one that has often been shrouded in mystery. The age, species and variety of the tree will dictate the frequency of the root-pruning operation.

Above: *A four-year-old cutting that is ready for some root pruning before being repotted into a new training container.*

ROOT PRUNING

Pruning of the roots followed by repotting with fresh soil encourages young feeder roots to multiply and develop. This eventually leads to healthy growth in the upper part of the tree.

The active root system should always be the youngest part of the tree, and root pruning should be carried out as soon as possible in early spring just before any buds begin to swell and break. Pruning the roots in spring means that any new roots will begin to form as soon as the temperature and weather conditions are suitable for growth to commence. It is not advisable to prune the roots of your bonsai in the autumn, as the freshly pruned roots may simply remain static throughout the winter. This could easily lead to the roots rotting rather than beginning to grow.

The first step is to remove the tree from its existing pot. If this proves difficult, use a knife to cut around the soil on the inside of the pot to release the tree. Once you have removed the tree from its pot, use a rake, root hook, chopstick or any other suitable implement to untangle and comb out the roots to remove the soil from most of the root-ball (roots) so that any long roots can hang down freely. A single root hook is ideal for untangling thicker, more complicated mature roots, while a fine rake would be more suited for combing out finer roots.

Using sharp clean scissors, trim the roots on all sides of the root-ball as well as from the underside, so that you are left with a flat circular pad of roots. You should aim for a neat and tidy appearance, while at the same time leaving sufficient fibrous roots to support the tree when it is finally repotted. When all the roots have been pruned satisfactorily, repot the tree.

Left: *The roots of a mature Japanese white pine (*Pinus parviflora*), showing the mycorrhiza, a beneficial symbiotic fungus.*

USEFUL TOOLS FOR ROOT-PRUNING

- A pair of long-nosed scissors for trimming fine roots.
- A pair of heavy-duty scissors for cutting heavier and larger roots.
- A small folding saw for dealing with even larger roots.
- A root hook (which has a single steel or brass, heavy-duty hook attached to a handle) for separating out a tangled and congested root system.

If you are planning major pruning of the roots and top growth at the same time, you should ensure you take a balanced approach to the exercise. In other words, if you need to cut away half of the roots, you may also need to remove half or more of the foliage. This allows the tree to balance its root and top growth activity, and recovery following the repotting process will be much more rapid than if the tree were left unbalanced.

ROOT PRUNING A *JUNIPERUS CHINENSIS*

1 This Chinese juniper (*Juniperus chinensis*), taken from a cutting, has been grown in a flowerpot for four years.

2 Remove the plant from the pot and untangle the roots using a rake.

3 The roots can grow very long and will need to be shortened. Cut the roots short, using a pair of sharp scissors.

4 A good dense set of roots should be left on the cutting. The cutting is now ready to pot on into its training pot.

PREPARING POTS

All pots and containers should be clean and dry. If you are reusing old pots, it is important to clean them with a stiff brush using water to which a small amount of washing-up liquid has been added. This helps to dislodge stubborn dirt, but you will need to rinse the pots thoroughly afterwards.

Cover the drainage holes in the bottom of the pots with a piece of plastic mesh of the type that is usually sold as greenhouse shading material. This prevents soil from falling through the holes, as well as stopping most pests from entering the soil. This type

of mesh is ideal because it is very thin and takes up a minimal amount of space in the bottom of the pot. If the traditional method of covering the holes with pieces of broken terracotta pot is used, a substantial amount of space will be taken up, especially in a shallow pot.

Hold the plastic mesh in place with what is loosely described as a wire "butterfly". Taking a short length of wire, bend it carefully into a loop at each end and subsequently bend the two ends up at right angles to produce a "butterfly". Pass the two ends through the holes, with the looped

part under the bottom of the pot, and through the square of mesh. Bend the wire ends over to secure the mesh over the holes. This is necessary because when the tree is placed in the pot you will need to move it around to settle it in place, which could disturb the mesh from its position over the holes.

In most cases, bonsai trees will need to be anchored into their pots using a reasonably substantial gauge of wire. So, pass a longer length of wire along the bottom of the pot, thread the ends up through the holes and pull up tight. This tying-in wire will secure the tree within the pot at the repotting stage.

PREPARING A POT FOR POTTING OR REPOTTING

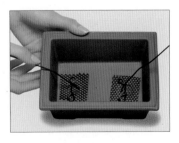

1 Twist a short length of wire into the shape of a butterfly.

2 Place a piece of plastic mesh over each hole. Push the free ends of the "butterfly" through the mesh and drainage hole, bending them back beneath the pot to secure the mesh.

3 Large pots may have special holes in the base for securing the tree with wire. If the pot does not have these holes, pass the wire through the drainage holes. ▷

POTTING AND REPOTTING

Whether you are planting a new tree in a pot or repotting a tree from a smaller pot to a larger one, make sure that the tree is placed correctly and held securely. You also need to use the right type and amount of soil to firm it in place. Repotting often follows on from root pruning and, in such cases, take extra care over watering and feeding.

Prepare the pot as described, then cover the mesh with a layer of coarse grit or akadama. This acts as a drainage course for the soil and root system.

If the pot is rectangular or oval, position the tree so that it is slightly to the rear and to one side of the centre lines of the pot. If it is round, square, multi-sided or any other regular shape, place the tree in the centre.

A very useful tip is to place a small mound of soil in the centre of the pot so that the tree will have plenty of soil under its root-ball (roots). Spread out the roots and rotate the tree carefully both clockwise and anti-clockwise while pushing it down into the pot. This will ensure that the central roots make good contact with the soil.

Bring the two ends of the wire together, cross them over each other, and use pliers to twist the two ends, pulling at the same time, until the tree is firmly secured within the pot.

Add soil until the pot is full, working around the roots with a chopstick. The soil, if completely dry, should filter down among the roots. Never use wet or damp soil, as it will not be possible to achieve good soil-to-roots contact. Carefully brush away any excess soil, so that the soil finishes just below the rim of the pot. Water well with a fine rose on a watering can or submerge the pot in water until the soil is soaked.

Remember that if major pruning of root and top growth is also carried out, you need to retain a balanced structure. So, if you cut away half of the roots, you may need to remove half or more of the foliage. This helps the tree balance root and top growth activity.

Following repotting, keep the soil just moist. Do not apply fertilizer to a root-pruned and repotted bonsai as the nutrients will burn the freshly cut roots. Wait a few weeks before starting any sort of feeding programme.

USEFUL TOOLS FOR REPOTTING

- Chopsticks for working the new soil down and around the roots during the repotting process and also for separating the roots of small trees.
- A stainless-steel sieve, with three different-sized mesh inserts, for separating out particle sizes when preparing soil mixtures for different sizes or species.
- A coco brush, or something similar, for brushing the soil surface evenly when finishing off a repotting session.
- A miniature rake for untangling and combing out fine root systems. To purchase a genuine Japanese item would be quite expensive, but you can make a very good, but simple, substitute for this by using an old dinner fork. Simply bend half the length of the prongs to about 90 degrees to form a simple rake.

REPOTTING A BONSAI

1 Use a sharp knife to cut around the edge of the pot and release the tree root.

2 Carefully lift the bonsai – here an *Acer palmatum* 'Ukon' – from the pot.

3 Rake the root-ball (roots) to remove the old soil.

4 The raked root-ball washed clean using a hose and showing the fibrous root structure.

5 The shallow form of the root structure can be clearly seen.

6 A close-up of the fibrous root formation and large surface roots.

7 This long root will need to be removed from the root-ball.

8 Trim the root system using a pair of scissors.

9 Prepare the pot with drainage mesh and "tying-in" wires.

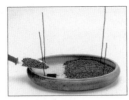

10 Spread a layer of medium akadama over the bottom of pot.

11 Add more soil to create a mound in the centre of the pot.

12 Place the tree slightly off centre in the pot.

13 Work the tree down into the soil with a circular, backward-and-forward motion, using both hands.

14 The soil will push up through the gaps between the roots.

15 Thread the ends of the wire through the roots and then twist them together.

16 Use a pair of pliers to pull the wire taut.

17 Twist the two ends of the wire together, pulling at the same time.

18 Cut off the excess wire with wire cutters.

19 Push the twisted end of wire down into the soil.

20 Fill in around the roots with more soil. If the soil is dry, it will flow down between the roots.

21 Work the soil into the roots until all the gaps are filled.

22 Tidy the surface with a brush and water the soil thoroughly.

23 Completed repot, showing the ideal, off-centre positioning of the tree. The pot should be the same depth as the diameter of the trunk base.

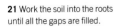

BONSAI STYLES

Styles of bonsai range from single-trunk designs through multiple-trunk to group and forest plantings. The style you decide upon will, to some extent, depend on the plant specimen you have chosen. Indeed, each tree will suggest a particular style, and you should follow that natural suggestion to obtain the best result.

One of the most important points to remember is that all styles of bonsai are based on the way trees grow in the wild. A natural-looking design is therefore the real test of a good bonsai, rather than how well it fits into any particular bonsai category. By observing full-size trees, you can soon start to appreciate how trees grow and into which styles your bonsai may fit.

When styling any tree, the first feature to look for is a good surface-root system. This will give the base of the trunk a more mature look. Rake the soil away from the trunk, exposing the roots to enhance the look of the trunk-to-soil junction.

All bonsai have a best angle, which is usually referred to as the front of the tree, but ideally every bonsai should look good from all angles.

Above: *The distinctive large yellow flowers of the witch hazel (Hamamelis x intermedia 'Pallida') appear in mid- and late winter.*
Left: *Pruning a Chinese juniper (Juniperus chinensis) using bonsai scissors. Care must be taken to cut only the shoots and not the foliage.*

Formal upright – *chokkan*

The name of this style is self-explanatory, being upright, straight and very rigid and formal in appearance, a shape that occurs frequently in nature when a tree is growing in ideal conditions. This means that there are no severe or adverse weather conditions and a constant source of suitable nutrients, as well as a good sustainable supply of water. In this bonsai style, the trunk of the tree should ideally have a very even taper from soil level right up to the apex. This straightness and taper create a very elegant and statuesque design which is not apparent in any other style of bonsai. Although these trees can have a symmetrical appearance, this is not so in every case, as a certain amount of asymmetry will give a much more pleasing and natural look.

Above: This Cedrus libani *subsp.* atlantica *'Glauca' is typical of the plant material that is available from garden centres or nurseries and is approximately 1.2m (4ft) high.*

The tree's final shape should be well balanced and centred on the formal, vertical emphasis of the trunk. The branches will be mostly horizontal, which will help to accentuate the formal appearance of the trunk.

Suitable plants for styling as formal upright bonsai include many coniferous species such as pine (*Pinus*), larch (*Larix*), spruce (*Picea*) and juniper (*Juniperus*). Trees that normally develop an informal habit, such as fruiting and flowering varieties, are not very suitable for this style.

If the trunk is not completely straight, apply a piece of wire of suitable thickness and manipulate the trunk until it is straight when viewed from the front. Viewed from the side, the trunk should be angled very slightly to the rear as it rises from the soil, and again very slightly to the front in the upper part of the tree, giving the overall appearance of being vertical.

Assess which branches are best suited for the design. Choose a thick branch as the lowest one and then cut out any insignificant shoots, leaving enough branches to complete the design. Apply wire to the branch, then, after running the wire around the trunk once or twice, wind it along the next branch up the trunk. Continue to wire the rest of the branches and arrange them so that they all complement each other. Finally, trim back the tips of the branches to give a balanced tree.

CREATING YOUR FORMAL UPRIGHT BONSAI

You will need
- branch cutters
- vine pruners
- wire cutters
- pliers
- rake
- pot
- mesh
- wire
- soil
- scoop
- chopstick

1 Remove the top of the plant, leaving the thickest part of the trunk, which will give the future bonsai more "character".

2 Using a pair of branch cutters at an angle, remove the top of the plant to leave a tapered top to the trunk.

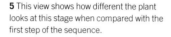

3 Following the removal of the top of the plant, it can be seen that the plant is beginning to show much better proportions as a future bonsai.

4 After the removal of one right-hand branch, a second similar branch is reduced in length, by approximately one-half, using side cutters.

5 This view shows how different the plant looks at this stage when compared with the first step of the sequence.

6 There are now too many minor branches still in place which will need pruning out using side or branch cutters.

7 One small branch has been removed, but there are still three more that must be cut off to give the plant a more open feeling.

8 There is still a long branch high up on the trunk that needs to be removed in order to give a better overall appearance to the tree.

9 This picture shows the plant after pruning, wiring and basic shaping has been completed, prior to being repotted into a suitable bonsai pot.

Right: *This is the completed tree, planted in a suitable pot and now ready for many years as a bonsai.*

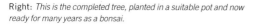

Informal upright – *moyogi*

This style is probably the most commonly seen style both in the natural environment and in bonsai. In the wild, an informal upright tree will have a trunk that bends and curves, and has changes of direction due to competition from other trees or buildings situated close by. These changes could be linked to the prevailing weather conditions surrounding the tree through the seasons. This is probably one of the easiest of bonsai styles to create, which makes it ideal for beginners. Many trees grow naturally with slightly bending or informal trunks, and you will find that working with these natural curves can create a pleasant bonsai design. Remember that any branches should appear to grow from the outside of a trunk curve in order to give a natural look to the finished tree.

Above: *A* Pinus sylvestris *'Jeremy' plant should be easily obtainable from a conifer nursery or garden centre.*

The trunk of an informal upright bonsai should be upright, but not absolutely straight, standing somewhere between the vertical and an angle of 15 degrees to the vertical. It should flow gently from one side to the other with a graceful, fluid form.

Examine the base of the trunk closely before carrying out any work. Carefully study the tree and try to decide on a preferred best side or front. It may be that it would be better viewed from a totally different angle to the one from which it has been seen in its original pot. Any curvature in the lower trunk as it rises from the soil should go in the rearward direction, as any forward bulge tends to look ugly. The trunk may then undulate from side to side and from front to back, finally finishing with the apex just forward of the trunk base. The branch structure is then designed around this informality, with branches coming from irregular points on the trunk and alternating from side to side and around the back. The front of the trunk should not have any branches pointing straight at the viewer unless they are small and near the top of the tree, where they become part of the crown. The informality of this design means that it is possible to style an informal upright bonsai using only pruning techniques and no wire at all.

CREATING YOUR INFORMAL UPRIGHT BONSAI

You will need
- rake
- scissors
- branch cutters
- tweezers
- wire cutters
- pliers
- wound sealer
- pot
- mesh
- wire
- soil
- scoop
- chopstick

1 Use a rake to clear excess soil from the top of the root-ball until the roots can be seen growing from the lower trunk.

2 Loose surface roots exposed by the raking process can now be identified and the "flair" of the trunk base can now be clearly seen.

3 Remove loose roots with sharp scissors, leaving a soil surface that shows a clean trunk base and some thicker surface roots which will become features in the future.

4 Using branch cutters, remove the central upward-pointing branch in order to open up the structure of the tree.

5 This is the central shoot following removal with a pair of branch cutters.

6 All excess branches should be eliminated until a basic tree shape begins to emerge.

7 Using a pair of tweezers, pull out the old, dark, stiff needles on the trunk and main branches, leaving only those on the shoot ends. ▷

8 You can also remove the needles by gently pulling them out with your fingers.

9 The amount of needles remaining can be clearly seen and the tree is now ready for shaping by wiring and tip pruning.

10 Apply the wire, as described in the section on wiring techniques.

11 The tree is now fully wired and ready for careful manipulation into shape using gentle bending so that you do not break any of the branches.

12 The wire can be applied to two branches and anchored to the trunk between the two branches.

13 This detail of the lower right branch clearly shows how the branch has been bent into a zigzag shape which will eventually enhance the appearance of the tree by giving it greater maturity.

14 The shaping is finished and the tree is now ready to be planted into a suitable bonsai container.

Right: *A Japanese white pine (Prunus parviflora), after many years of bonsai training.*

Slanting – *shakan*

This bonsai style is based on a tree growing in the wild that has been exposed to strong winds and very stormy weather, so that it has blown over at an angle slanting away from the prevailing wind. The natural reaction of the tree after this has happened is to redirect its branch growth to suit the new growing angle of the trunk. Most species of tree can be grown in this style and examples in nature can be seen on cliff tops and in mountainous areas where there is a prevailing wind that pushes the tree over to one side. When this becomes more pronounced, it generally falls into the windswept category, but it is difficult to draw a distinction between these two styles.

Above: *This is a hybrid* Rhododendron *that is commercially available from any good supplier of this type of material and measures 65cm (26in) from the top of the pot to the apex.*

The slanting style of bonsai should have its trunk leaning to one side, usually by about 45 degrees from the vertical, although it can be as much as 60 degrees. The trunk need not necessarily be straight – it can have some movement in its shape – but the apex should always take on the same angle as the one formed where the trunk rises from the soil.

Following the slant of the trunk, the roots will normally be extended on the side away from the slant, while those on the side under the slant will be compressed. This gives the impression of the roots stabilizing what would otherwise be an unstable-looking design.

The basic steps described previously to ascertain the trunk angle and root structure should be followed so that the angle of the trunk looks as natural as possible. The position of the branches must relate to the trunk so that a mature shape is obtained. Should a branch need to be placed in a drooping position, ensure the junction with the trunk bends down as soon as it leaves the trunk to achieve a natural effect.

When you are styling a bonsai from scratch, make sure that all of the branches are properly positioned, including the smallest twigs. The degree of attention to this type of detail in the early stages of styling can make or break the appearance of the end product. A suitable type of pot can be seen in the final picture.

CREATING YOUR SLANTING BONSAI

You will need
- stiff brush
- branch cutters
- wound sealer
- scissors
- wire cutters
- pliers
- rake
- pot
- mesh
- wire
- soil
- scoop
- chopstick

1 The moss that has grown on the lower part of the trunk of the *Rhododendron* should be removed using a stiff brush, so that the plant has a completely clean trunk. The soil of bonsai trees is always just moist and this provides the ideal conditions in which moss will grow. The lower parts of the trunks can quickly become covered in moss, which should be removed regularly.

2 The lower part of the tree trunk has now been completely cleared of unwanted moss and the beautiful texture and colour of the bark can be clearly seen.

3 There are two branches growing from the same point on the trunk, one of which must be removed in order to improve the tree's structure. Using branch or side cutters, remove the branch with a clean cut close to the main trunk.

4 Following the removal of the excess branches and some thinning out of the twigs and foliage in the upper part of the plant, the shape is now much improved. This tree has a long way to go before it becomes properly shaped with an aged-looking branch structure. Several years of shoot pinching, refinement, repotting and correct feeding will produce an excellent flowering bonsai.

Right: *The tree is planted in a temporary pot because it is not known, at this stage, exactly what colour, shape or design of pot should be chosen. When the bonsai specimen is finally developed, it may need a slightly different glazed or semi-glazed pot for display purposes.*

Semi-cascade – *han-kengai*

This style reflects the effect of extreme growing conditions on a tree. It is designed to give the appearance of a very old tree growing from the side of a quarry or rock face, or perhaps on a riverbank, where all the tree's efforts have gone into growing towards the light. Although the trunk line may initially have been upright, in natural conditions it could have been bent over into a nearly horizontal position by falling rocks, stones or soil. Ideal material for training as semi-cascade bonsai are prostrate-growing plants, such as cotoneaster and juniper, which can be bought from plant nurseries.

Semi-cascade is the name that is usually given when a bonsai leans over to one side or the other from 45 to 60 degrees from the vertical, even as low as just below the horizontal or the rim of the pot. Some people think that it should not go below the rim, while others think that going just below this point often gives a better and more appealing appearance.

Most types of tree can be grown in the semi-cascade style, except for those that normally have a very powerful vertical growth habit which

will overcome the forces of nature. It is important to note that if a tree leans so far that it droops over the edge of the pot and down the side, it should then be classed as cascade-style bonsai.

Just as with the slanting style, there needs to be some root exposure in order to give the feeling of a stabilizing structure at the base of the trunk. Following the initial steps for the formal upright and informal upright bonsai styles that we have already described, assess the structure of the

Above: *The widely available creeping juniper, Juniperus horizontalis 'Green Carpet', is ideal material from which a semi-cascade bonsai can be developed.*

roots, as well as the line of the trunk. Work with the natural flow of the tree, if possible accentuating any of those natural features.

A suitable container would be square, hexagonal or any other regular shape, and it should be of a medium depth so that it is in balance with the tree.

You will need
- branch cutters
- wound sealer
- scissors
- rake
- pot
- mesh
- wire
- wire cutters
- pliers
- soil
- scoop
- chopstick

CREATING YOUR SEMI-CASCADE BONSAI

1 Remove the plant from the original plastic pot and remove any adventitious foliage to expose a clean trunk base. This will provide a better insight into the styling possibilities of this particular plant.

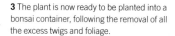

2 Remove the left-hand branch, using a pair of branch or side cutters in order to obtain a clean concave cut.

3 The plant is now ready to be planted into a bonsai container, following the removal of all the excess twigs and foliage.

4 After repotting into a suitable container, the tree is now in the early stages of becoming a fully styled bonsai specimen.

Below: *The finished styling exercise is shown here displayed on a flat slab of sandstone. This shows the basic shape following initial styling. With regular shoot pinching, the foliage area will bulk up over the next few growing seasons.*

Cascade – *kengai*

Once again, this style of bonsai represents a tree that has been growing in very difficult circumstances, such as out of the side of a rock face or somewhere similar. In fact, this style is intended to represent a tree in the wild that has been subjected to heavy winter snowfall, rock falls, avalanches and, indeed, its own weight, all of which would cause it to lean and fall vertically from wherever it is rooted. This particular design can be obtained by repositioning various parts of the trunk line and branches, so that a cascading and mature outline is achieved.

In this style, the trunk line will fall well below the horizontal, with its trunk tip resting level with the bottom of the pot or even lower. Just as with the semi-cascade style, the trunk line generally begins by growing almost vertically from soil level before cascading over and down the side of the pot.

This style is not easy to produce and would normally be considered an advanced project if one wished to achieve a satisfying result. A suitable plant to use would be one that has a long, flexible trunk that can be easily manipulated with wire into an interesting cascade design. Such a plant need not already be cascading at the time of acquisition – it can be vertical or any other shape – but it is essential that the trunk is long and flexible.

All the usual initial procedures should be followed, such as looking at the base of the trunk and the formation of the roots, before deciding on the best way forward. Be careful when applying wire and with the subsequent bending because there is a

Above: *This is a typical, young* Cotoneaster horizontalis *that, due to a flexibility, is highly suited for styling as a cascade bonsai.*

risk of breaking the trunk. Should this happen, however, you could always use the tree for a totally different style.

Cascade bonsai require relatively deep pots to show off the cascading characteristics that you have designed. The pot shape should be regular but can, in some circumstances, also be natural and primitive in appearance to match the rugged look of the tree.

CREATING YOUR CASCADE BONSAI

You will need
- branch cutters
- scissors
- wire cutters
- pliers
- wire
- rake
- pot
- mesh
- soil
- scoop
- chopstick

1 When working on a cascade bonsai, it may be helpful to work with the plant positioned on its display stand or post. The first part of the trunk should be cleared of growth, so remove any unwanted material in this area.

2 Begin wiring the trunk by pushing the end of the wire deep into the soil for anchorage.

3 Carefully wind the wire around the trunk to the length that is required, as described in the wiring section, and cut the wire ends cleanly when the process is complete.

4 If the trunk is extra thick, a second run of wire may be needed which can be applied alongside the first. This gives twice the bending power of one run of wire.

5 Using both hands, and your thumbs as levering points, carefully shape the trunk until a full cascading effect is achieved.

6 Continue the process further along the trunk until the whole of the trunk has been shaped satisfactorily.

7 Remove the excess growth, once you have decided on the final length of the trunk.

8 Here, the leading shoot is being removed in order to balance the length of the trunk.

9 Following the full wiring of the trunk and side branches, the tree is now ready to be placed in a decorative bonsai pot.

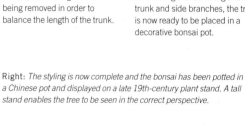

Right: *The styling is now complete and the bonsai has been potted in a Chinese pot and displayed on a late 19th-century plant stand. A tall stand enables the tree to be seen in the correct perspective.*

Twin trunk – *sokan*

The twin-trunk style is a very popular arrangement of two trees. This occurs naturally when a tree grows with two trunks from ground level. A twin trunk such as this may be the result of seeds germinating close together. As the two plants grow, they combine by natural grafting into one joined at the base. A bonsai twin-trunk tree can be created either by planting two or more trees very closely together or by starting with a plant that already has two or more trunks. If you are starting with a plant that has more than two trunks, then clearly any other trunks will need to be removed. The choice of which trunks to remove depends upon the shape and position of all the trunks on the plant. You will need to select the best pair of trunks in terms of their relationship with each other to achieve a balanced final appearance.

Above: *'Ginny Gee' is a* Rhododendron racemosum *hybrid and is ideal for bonsai by virtue of its small leaves and flowers.*

The simplest way to begin is to buy a twin-stemmed plant from a nursery and convert it into bonsai following the steps shown here. If, however, you have two trees from which to work, tie them tightly at the base with raffia or grafting tape so that they graft together at this point as they grow. Avoid tying with wire, as this has no flexibility and can create a rather unsightly union, especially with smooth-bark species. Check the junction regularly during the early part of the process to ensure that it is going according to plan.

If there had been a space between the two plants in the early years of growth, the expansion of the trunk girths would have been so large that a natural twin-trunk specimen would be the end result.

Always use two plants of the same variety, so that the leaf shape and colour are the same. Also ensure that the two plants have different-sized trunks: the main trunk should be taller with a larger girth than the other trunk. If the two trunks are identical in girth, or almost identical, then the

bonsai will look too regimented. If you want to find a suitable twin-trunk tree in the wild, then remember to look for one with unequal-sized trunks.

When considering the viewing angle of this style, arrange the smaller trunk so that it is alongside the main trunk, but slightly to the rear or to the front of it, as this will give a much better appearance.

CREATING YOUR TWIN TRUNK BONSAI

You will need
- rake
- branch cutters
- scissors
- pot
- mesh
- wire cutters
- pliers
- wire
- soil
- scoop
- chopstick

1 After removing the plant from its pot, gently rake away the surface of the soil until the base of the trunk and any surface roots begin to show, and cut out any excess lower shoots until a clear tree image is formed.

Right: *Following pruning and styling, the tree has been planted in a deep rectangular pot and displayed on a simple oak stand. Compared with the off-centre placing on the stand in the picture above, it can be seen that a central placing is best.*

2 Clear away any excess internal shoots and minor branches until the required shape emerges.

3 The finished tree after the pruning and styling process has been completed.

Triple trunk – *sambon-yose*

Multiple plantings should consist of three, five, seven and so on as a well-balanced group is difficult to achieve with even numbers except two. Here, we will be looking at the approach to a triple-trunk planting that can often be seen growing naturally in the wild. Any species of tree may be used to create this style of bonsai, but you will discover that it is largely conifers that have this type of growth formation. The plant material that you choose will need to include three plants with trunks of varying thicknesses, as well as of different heights. However, bear in mind that the heights of the trunks can be altered easily by pruning. Trees that have one-sided root systems would also be highly suitable because the bases of the trunks will need to be placed very closely together to create a satisfactory final design.

Above: *Three European larch plants,* Larix decidua, *in plastic flowerpots, which can be purchased from nurseries or garden centres.*

The trees chosen for this grouping are European larch (*Larix decidua*), and have been growing in individual pots for several years. They are about 20 years old and have trunks of varying thickness, which is very important when you are putting a group of this type together.

The traditional approach is to select the tree with the thickest trunk as the main tree which should then be placed towards the front of the grouping, with the subsequent positioning of the other two trees also being extremely important. Each tree must be securely attached to the pot and to the bases of the other two trees in order to encourage them to grow even more closely together as they mature alongside each other.

When cutting the roots back to enable the trees to be placed close together, it must be remembered that sufficient roots need to remain on each tree to enable them to survive the process and to grow on in the future. When the roots have been cleaned of soil, it is also necessary to keep the roots moist to prevent the trees from suffering dehydration. Use a fine atomizing spray to apply a fine mist of water to the roots if they appear to be drying out.

Once the trees are secured and the soil topped up and watered, the branches will need to be wired and manipulated into place to give the trees a mature overall design.

CREATING YOUR TRIPLE TRUNK BONSAI

You will need
- pot
- mesh
- wire
- soil
- wire cutters
- branch cutters
- scissors
- pliers
- rake
- scoop
- chopstick

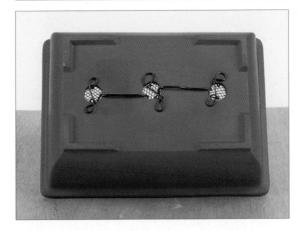

1 Prepare the bottom of the initial training pot with "butterfly" mesh retainers and "tying-in" wire.

2 This is the inside of the training pot showing the drainage mesh and "tying-in" wires in place.

3 Place a layer of coarse akadama over the bottom of the pot in order to improve drainage, followed by some medium akadama which will be the main soil ingredient.

4 Cut away the roots of the two largest plants on one side in preparation for placing them close together.

5 Place the two plants next to each other, with their roots pushed closely together.

6 Using 3mm (⅛in) wire, tie the first tree into the pot by twisting the ends of the wire tightly together with a pair of pliers.

7 Tie the second tree in place, close to the first, so that their bases are almost touching. ▷

8 After cutting the roots to fit, tie in the third tree, making sure that it is very closely positioned alongside the first two.

9 Wire all the trees firmly into the pot, so that they are all very secure because new roots will easily break if the trees are loose in the pot.

10 Here, all three of the trees have been securely wired into place.

11 Top up the soil using a scoop and then work the soil in and around the roots with a chopstick until the pot is completely filled.

12 The three trees are now finally planted and secured in the pot.

13 Prune out any unwanted shoots and branches, thus creating a pleasing shape.

14 After careful wiring and shaping, the triple trunk now looks relatively mature.

Right: *When complete, the group of trees should look like a full-size natural group of trees. Here, the triple-trunk planting has been improved by displaying it on a good-quality mahogany stand.*

Group or forest – *yose-uye*

This style of bonsai planting is intended to create the appearance of a copse, spinney, small wood or even a large forest, only in miniature. A group or forest can be created using anything from five to fifty or more trees; in fact, you can use as many trees as can be satisfactorily handled. The only stipulation is that there should be an odd number of trees in order to lend a more balanced appearance to the final design. Your aim should be to create a group that gives the viewer the feeling of being within a wooded area, while being aware that it will be viewed from the outside. It may take several plantings to achieve this effect. Most types of plant are suitable, but, by keeping to the same species and variety for each group, you will achieve a more natural appearance.

Above: *A pot of beech plants – here* Fagus sylvatica *'Purpurea' – which are usually supplied for planting a hedge and are normally very inexpensive to purchase.*

Aim for a feeling of authenticity by obtaining a good sense of depth and perspective. Preferably, the group should not include any straight line of three trees or more, and no trunk should be hidden behind another when viewed from the front or side.

Make sure there is good mix of sizes to achieve a natural look. Also, choose one tree that is larger than the rest to act as a focal point. Note that branches may need to be removed from all the trees so they can sit closely together and not become confused with each other.

Starting with the largest tree, remove the lowest branches before positioning it in the prepared pot, just to the right or left of the centre and about halfway back. Place the second largest tree close to the first tree, removing branches as necessary. Then, position the rest of the trees, preferably one at a time, close to each other so that they form a natural-looking group or forest. Place the smaller trees on the outside of the group, but generally not at the front, so that the group appears to have been growing for many years.

Secure the trees into the container as you work, and fill in with soil by working it around the roots with a chopstick. Water thoroughly to settle the soil and trees into the container. Trim any remaining long shoots to give a balanced appearance, then place the completed group outdoors in a shady spot to acclimatize.

CREATING YOUR GROUP OR FOREST BONSAI

You will need
- scissors
- branch cutters
- wire cutters
- pliers
- rake
- pot
- mesh
- wire
- soil
- scoop
- chopstick

1 One individual beech plant, showing the slim trunk, which is so suitable for group plantings, and with a good root system.

2 Remove any insignificant roots high on the trunk, thus creating a clean lower trunk.

3 Now, cut off the remainder of the tap root, leaving a cluster of fibrous roots near the required trunk base.

4 Tidy up the remaining roots in order to leave a small, neat set of roots. The roots of all the plants to be used in the group should be treated in the same way.

5 Prepare a shallow pot and add some initial soil. The first two beech plants will be placed to the right of the centre and at about the half-way point from front to back.

6 Plunge the two plants into the soil and then work in some soil around them.

7 The plants may not be very stable at this stage, but when all the plants are in place, they will support each other.

8 Add three more beech plants, making a total of five in all, and again work the roots down into the soil.

9 Using a scoop, add some extra soil around the roots of all five of the plants. It should be noted that the plants are inserted very close to each other. This needs to be done to make the final bonsai group look realistic.

10 When all fifteen plants have been introduced, more soil is added until the pot is full. The plants in this group are roughly arranged in two closely related sub-groups, with all trees set very close together.

11 Use a chopstick to work the soil thoroughly around the roots of the plants, so that there is good contact with the soil throughout the root system.

12 The appearance of the top of the group can be improved by carefully selecting and removing any unsightly shoots that may be too long and look out of place.

13 The final grouping shows the close relationship of all the plants. This positioning is necessary if you are to achieve a natural-looking group or forest.

Right: *When complete, the group will begin to look like a small mature copse. The pot shown is temporary to encourage the trees' root development. Pots for bonsai groups must be shallow, and either oval or rectangular in shape.*

Windswept – *fukinagashii*

On clifftops or mountains, trees grow in many different ways, but mostly in a windswept style caused by constant exposure to the prevailing winds coming from just one direction. Such trees will generally have a slanting trunk, with branches only on the leeward side of the trunk where the forces of nature are less harsh. Many trees in these situations have straight trunks with only the top part curved over away from the direction of the wind. Virtually any plant is suitable for creating a bonsai in the windswept style, although one with a leaning trunk would be easier if you are a beginner.

Above: *This* Juniperus chinensis *has been grown as a bonsai for several years and is now suitable for styling as a windswept-style bonsai.*

A straight trunk may be used, but it would have to tilt to give the impression of a wind-battered tree. The main interest of a tree like this is that the branch structure sweeps in one direction, which is the same direction as the one in which the trunk is leaning.

Suitable trees for the windswept style are pines, junipers, or tough deciduous trees such as hawthorn. These varieties are capable not only of surviving in a harsh natural habitat, but also of being manipulated, pruned and wired to form a windswept bonsai.

When selecting a suitable plant, check the root structure to find a plant which has strong roots on one side. This will then become the side that is opposite to the lean of the trunk because, in nature, the roots would develop a stronger structure on that side in order to support the leaning tree.

Remove the branches on what will appear to be the windward side of the trunk, along with any other insignificant branches. Position the remaining branches using the wiring techniques outlined earlier to obtain a

mature windswept feeling. Once the tree has been prepared, plant it in a suitable pot, tie it in place, top it up with soil and water in well.

Pots for this style of bonsai are generally round and shallow, but may have a rough, primitive finish, reflecting the fact that natural trees of this style would often exist in similarly rough surroundings.

CREATING YOUR WINDSWEPT BONSAI

You will need
- branch cutters
- scissors
- wire cutters
- pliers
- rake
- pot
- mesh
- wire
- soil
- scoop
- chopstick

1 When viewed from a lower angle, it can be seen that the branches are all growing in one direction, indicating that a windswept design is possible.

Right: *The bonsai is displayed on a suitable base and against a sympathetic background so that the final design can be fully appreciated. The tree will need several years of work before it is fully developed.*

3 Following the process of wiring and positioning all of the branches, the windswept form is even more accentuated.

2 When the pot is tilted slightly to the rear and left using a suitable block, the potential of the windswept design for this particular specimen becomes even more apparent.

4 The tree has been repotted at a different angle to complete the windswept design.

Raft – *ikadabuki*

The raft or straight-line style is based upon a natural phenomenon that occurs when a tree is blown over. Although the trunk of the tree lies flat on the ground, it may survive if some of the roots remain attached and viable. Many of the branches will have been broken off when the tree hit the ground, leaving that side of the trunk in contact with the soil. Eventually, roots will emerge from here, while the remaining branches begin to grow into a vertical position. After many years, the original broken roots will have rotted away, and what remains will look like several trees growing together.

Above: *This is a Chinese juniper (*Juniperus chinensis*) that has been previously grown as a bonsai and is ideal for styling as a raft-style bonsai, as can be seen from the fact that the branches are all on one side of the trunk.*

When looking for a suitable plant, ideally choose one that has a one-sided branch structure, which will mean less pruning to achieve the raft style. If this is not possible, purchase a tree that has a good set of branches, and remove all the branches on one side of the trunk.

Lay the tree down on the branchless side of the trunk, and use scissors to remove the roots that are now revealed at the base of the upper side of the trunk. Removing half the root system will not harm the tree, as half the branches have already been removed.

In fact, this equal pruning of branches and roots will ensure a balanced regrowth of the plant. If you need to remove more than half the root system for aesthetic purposes, then you should also remove a roughly equal number of branches to balance the plant and so ensure its survival.

Next, select the best remaining branches to be the new set of trunks, removing any that will not suit the shape. You will probably have to wire all the branches and place them in a more suitable, near-vertical, position

to create a group-like appearance. Finally, select the most suitable secondary branches (removing the rest), position them with wire and trim branch tips where necessary.

The most widely used pots for this style are long, narrow and oval. Thin slabs of slate or rock may also be used.

CREATING YOUR RAFT

You will need
- rake
- branch cutters
- scissors
- knife
- wire cutters
- pliers
- wire
- scoop
- chopstick
- wound sealer
- pot
- mesh
- soil

1 The congested root system is apparent and needs to be raked, untangled and pruned so that a manageable amount of root remains.

2 Having raked away most of the soil and untangled the roots, cut back the roots until a compact pad of roots remains.

3 It is necessary to remove squares of bark on the lower side of the trunk. When this side of the trunk is beneath the surface of the soil, roots will grow around the edges of the removed squares of bark.

4 Cut into the bark using a sharp knife and then peel away the squares of bark in order to leave exposed areas of the heartwood.

5 Six pieces of bark have been removed. This should result in six areas of root growth on the underside of the trunk following planting in the soil.

6 Begin the shaping process by wiring the trunk and all of the main branches of the tree.

7 In this close-up, it can be seen that some of the wires run from one branch to another. This will ensure that the wire is properly anchored, so that the branches remain in the desired position.

▷

8 The initial wiring is complete and the relationship between the old trunk, which will form the new root system, and the old branches that will be the new trunks, is now becoming clear.

9 A long, shallow pot has been prepared with securing wires and a base layer of soil. The tree is then lowered into position.

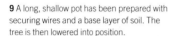

10 Press the tree into the surface of the soil using gentle side-to-side movements. Bring the ends of the wires together in pairs.

11 Twist the ends of the wires together with a pair of pliers, pulling at the same time, so that you can be certain that the tree is securely fixed in the pot.

12 Make sure that the pairs of wire ends are twisted and pulled tight because this will enable the new roots to grow without disturbance.

13 Top up the pot with soil using a scoop and work the soil into and around the existing root system, as well as the old trunk that is now below the surface of the soil.

14 Water the completed raft arrangement thoroughly, using a watering can that has been fitted with a fine rose attachment. This will ensure that the soil is not disturbed.

15 This is the completed raft arrangement following the tidying of the surface of the soil and careful watering.

Above: *The smaller branches have now been wired and carefully manipulated into their final position. What was once a rather* *insignificant-looking plant has been transformed into a root-connected group that is commonly known as a raft.*

Root-in-rock planting – *ishizuki*

Throughout the world, there are many places where trees can be seen growing on, over or in rock formations. It will have taken many years for the roots, often exposed over parts of the rock, to have grown into extremely interesting formations. It is these naturally occuring forms, when reproduced for the purposes of bonsai, that can create a very natural and inspirational design. Three variations of rock planting are commonly used in bonsai. These are "root-on-rock", "root-over-rock" and "root-in-rock". The name for each style aptly describes the placing of the roots relative to the piece of rock.

Achieving this style relies upon finding a suitable plant, as well as a matching piece of rock. The roots will be on the surface of the rock and covered with soil and moss; they will not necessarily carry on down to soil level. The roots grow in an artificially created or natural hole or crevice in the rock, which contains all the roots as well as the soil in which they grow.

Start with a piece of tufa (a porous sedimentary limestone that is easy to carve with a chisel or spatula), and make a hollow for the plant's roots.

Choose a small plant with a compact root-ball (roots) that will fit inside the hollow. Place a layer of soil in the cavity, then plant the tree in it, firming it in and topping up with extra soil until the plant is secure. Trim the plant and remove any unwanted branches to give the appearance of a naturally formed composition.

You may need to feed this type of bonsai more often than is normally the case because rain and regular watering will wash away the nutrients quite quickly.

Above: *This piece of tufa already has one hole in a suitable position for growing a cascade-style tree. You will need a couple of plants; here, Juniperus procumbens 'Nana' has been used. The first plant has had its roots trimmed ready to fit the hole.*

Tufa retains water for some time, but does not waterlog the roots growing in the rock. Stand the tufa in a shallow basin of water so that the water is absorbed slowly. This will help with watering because of the water-retentive quality of tufa.

CREATING YOUR ROOT-IN-ROCK BONSAI

You will need
- rock
- soil
- branch cutters
- scissors
- knife
- scoop
- chopstick
- moss
- basin

1 Using your fingers, carefully press the root-ball of the plant into the hole until it is securely in place. Fill in the cavity with soil.

2 Using a sharp pair of cutters, remove all the branches, except those that are cascading down over the side of the rock.

3 Here, it is clear which branches need to be pruned so that only downward-growing branches remain in place.

4 With the piece of rock standing in its finished position, offer up the second plant to ascertain where the second hole needs to be placed.

5 Tufa is very soft and is easily carved using a spatula or other similar instrument. Make sure that the hole is large enough to receive the roots of the second plant.

6 Gently press the second plant into position, filling in any spaces around the roots of both plants with soil. Place a layer of moss over the soil of both trees in order to complete the natural effect.

7 The completed planting can then be placed in a shallow basin which has been filled with water. As tufa is very porous, it will absorb enough water to suit the needs of the plants.

8 Allow the two plants to settle in for several weeks until the roots begin to grow into the porous tufa. At a later date, the two trees can be wired into shape so that they closely follow the contour of the rock.

Right: *The two trees, having been planted in the tufa, will require several years to reach maturity.*

Root-over-rock planting – *sekijoju*

This style can be achieved by choosing a tree that has a long root system and washing away all the soil to expose the roots. If such a tree cannot be found, encourage the roots of your chosen plant to grow by placing it in a very long temporary container, such as a plastic tree guard, until the roots reach the bottom. Then, remove the tree from the tube and spread the roots over a piece of rock with an interesting shape until they fit closely to it. Tie the roots securely to the rock using wire. The preparation of a plant for root-over-rock planting can take several years, as the process of producing the long roots can be very slow, but, once you have achieved your first set of long roots, it is rewarding to know that it really can be done. This will encourage you to try something bigger and better.

Above: *This mountain pine,* Pinus mugo *'Pumilio', underwent extensive wiring and shaping several weeks prior to this exercise and has been allowed enough time to settle in before the next stage of the process.*

Plant the chosen tree – here a *Pinus mugo* 'Pumilio' – in a deep container, covering the whole root-ball (roots), including the rock, with some soil. Over the next few years, the roots will expand and develop a close fit with the rock, appearing to cascade over it. This means that when the rock is eventually exposed, a very interesting root structure should have developed that follows its contours.

This style is probably one of the most difficult of all the bonsai designs to tackle and ultimately perfect because, while the roots are maturing under the surface of the soil, it is not possible to know what, if anything, is actually happening.

However, you should rest assured that, given sufficient time, the roots of the tree will eventually thicken and become attached, as well as cross over with other roots. The roots will also become naturally grafted to each other while they are submerged beneath the soil. Time is perhaps one of the most important considerations for the successful development of this style.

Patience will also be necessary because it is a serious mistake to uncover the roots too soon. It is crucial that they stay covered with soil if they are to enlarge correctly.

The container for this style should be rugged in appearance to suit the ruggedness of the rock.

CREATING YOUR ROCK-OVER-ROOT PLANTING BONSAI

You will need
- hook
- rock
- wire cutters
- wire
- branch cutters
- scissors
- pliers
- rake
- scoop
- chopstick
- pot
- mesh
- soil
- sphagnum moss

1 Following the removal of the lower half of the root-ball (roots), rake out the rest of the roots using a suitable single hook.

2 Rake away the rest of the soil until the roots are free of soil.

3 Wash the roots thoroughly using a low-pressure water jet from a garden hose.

4 You need to wash the roots very thoroughly, so that they can be placed easily and cleanly over the rock.

5 Carefully spread out the roots by hand and then place them over the rock.

6 Press the roots into place so that they straddle as many sides of the rock as possible.

7 Using a length of 3mm (⅛in) wire, tie the tree firmly to the rock and secure by twisting the two ends of the wire together.

8 Wind a longer length of 3mm (⅛in) wire several times around the roots, securing them all in close proximity with the rock, and again twist the ends together.

9 Choose a pot that is large enough to accept the whole rock-and-root system, and place a layer of soil in the bottom.

10 Press the rock, complete with the roots, into the soil, making sure that the top of the rock does not come above the level of the pot rim, and fill in with soil.

11 Add a layer of sphagnum moss to the surface of the soil in order to keep the surface roots moist and soft.

12 Covering the surface of the soil completely with moss is absolutely essential.

13 Following the planting of the whole rock into the pot, the project is now complete, but it will take several years for the roots to grow in close contact with the rock. Eventually, the rock and the roots around it will be exposed.

Right: *The completed tree is finally placed in a temporary pot with the roots and rock below the surface of the soil.*

Literati – *bunjin*

This is an unusual style which does not conform to the general rules of bonsai styling. It often appears in nature when a number of trees have grown together over many years, and then some have died or been removed, leaving just a few individual trees. These trees will have grown tall in the stiff competition for available light, and the resulting foliage will be on or near the top of the trees. Examples of this style growing in the wild are often pines. This style of tree can also be seen growing with tall, slim, freestyle-type trunks, with just a few branches positioned quite high up on the tree. The literati style is a very useful one because it can be used to make a bonsai from almost any plant that is tall and gangly, and which does not fit into any other bonsai category.

Trees in the literati style normally have a tall, slim, free-style trunk, often with very little taper, culminating in a small number of branches in the apex of the tree. The trunk is very important: it is almost never straight and should be full of character, with slight twists and turns, although nothing too accentuated.

When you are choosing a tree that is suitable for turning into a literati bonsai, you will need to find one that may have been neglected, damaged, or both, making it unsuitable for any other style. It need not have a particularly good surface root system, as in nature this type of tree tends to grow that way; in fact, they appear to rise straight from the soil with very little visible support. If you intend to start from scratch, making the branches droop severely means that the effect of considerable age can be easily achieved.

Most conifers, but particularly pines (*Pinus*), will make good literati. In fact, it is species or varieties of this genus that seem to adopt the literati shape when growing naturally in the wild.

Above: *This Scots pine (Pinus sylvestris) was collected from the wild and grown in a temporary timber training box. It is partially wired and styled, and shown here from its best angle before final styling.*

As this style is tall and slender, suitable pots would be circular, relatively shallow and not too large, as anything too big could overpower the elegant but rugged character of the trees. A rather rough, primitive pot would be suitable for this style, as it would enhance its rugged nature.

You will need
- branch cutters
- scissors
- wire cutters
- pliers
- rake
- pot
- mesh
- wire
- soil
- scoop
- chopstick

CREATING YOUR LITERATI BONSAI

1 Close-up of the triple-wiring technique used during the application of the wire.

2 The appearance of the triple-wiring technique after the application of the wire.

3 View of the right-hand side of the partially wired and styled tree.

4 The rear of the partially wired and styled pine showing the extent of branch repositioning.

5 Following the wiring of all the branches, this is now the preferred front of the tree.

6 The left-hand side of the tree after wiring and shaping.

7 Rear view of the tree after final wiring and shaping.

8 Right-hand side of the tree after the final wiring and shaping process. The tree is now beginning to take on the shape of an old mature specimen.

Right: The finished styled bonsai has been repotted into a drum pot, which is ideally suited to the literati style.

Driftwood – *sharimiki*

The driftwood style is considered a more advanced technique. It reflects the natural look of old junipers and pines, which have areas of trunk that are totally free of bark. In the wild, this is caused by natural die-back or by lightning. Whatever the cause, the result can be dramatic and exciting. This style can be formed by taking a plant with a thick trunk and stripping part of the bark away to create the driftwood. It can also be formed by using a piece of suitable driftwood and attaching a younger plant to it. This is often called a "wraparound" as the living material is simply wrapped around a piece of dead wood.

Above: A Cedrus deodara *nursery plant and a piece of driftwood, both of which are suitable for creating a driftwood-style bonsai.*

Driftwood techniques can be used in several other styles of bonsai, including the literati, informal upright, cascade and windswept styles. If you are going to create a driftwood-style bonsai from a single plant, then you will need one that has a thick trunk so that you can strip away the bark from the main trunk to form the basis of the driftwood.

A much simpler method is to use a piece of collected driftwood or perhaps even the dead trunk of an old bonsai.

If you use the latter, then treat it with a wood preservative which will soak completely into the dead wood. This may need to be repeated several times over a period of months to make sure that the wood is properly protected against the normal decaying process that wood undergoes, particularly when wet. The piece of treated wood will then need to be left to dry thoroughly, so that all traces of any unsafe liquids in the preservative have evaporated away.

You will need various tools for attaching the plant to the driftwood, including stainless-steel screws, raffia and wire, as well as a power drill. When using power tools, follow the manufacturer's safety guidelines.

Suitable pots for this style vary, but as the form is rugged and primitive, the pot should reflect these qualities.

CREATING YOUR DRIFTWOOD BONSAI

You will need
- branch cutters
- knife
- rake
- sprayer
- screwdriver
- screws
- raffia
- wire cutters
- wire
- scissors
- pot
- mesh
- soil
- scoop
- chopstick

1 Remove the shoots and branches completely on one side of the plant and, using a sharp knife, cut away approximately half of the trunk on the side from which the branches have been removed.

2 Rake out the root-ball (roots) in order to remove excess soil, and trim the roots into a compact system. Spray the roots regularly to prevent them drying out because this style takes a long time to produce. Using a power tool or hand screwdriver, attach the lower trunk to the lower part of the driftwood. Stainless-steel screws are preferable, but brass would be a good second choice.

3 Continue to attach the trunk with screws, making sure that the cut side of the trunk sits adjacent to the driftwood.

4 The trunk can be curved around to the front of the driftwood so that it follows any curving features of the driftwood, and then secured with raffia.

5 When the trunk becomes too narrow to accept a screw, continue to attach it to the driftwood by tying it tightly with raffia.

6 While you are attaching the plant to the driftwood, keep spraying the roots regularly and cover them with a plastic bag to retain moisture. This will assist the tree during the lengthy attachment process. ▷

7 The tree is planted in a suitable pot and secured firmly with wire as described in the repotting section. The most exposed and best-looking part of the driftwood normally forms the front of the bonsai.

8 Some of the branches are removed, with the remaining branches being wired and carefully manipulated into place to create a tree-like shape.

9 With the wiring and shaping now complete, any downward-growing foliage is removed in order to leave the tree with a tidy and compact shape.

11 Close-up of the top of the tree, showing the raffia attachment and branch wiring in detail.

12 The interesting structure of the lower part of the driftwood which will eventually be the main lower trunk of the finished bonsai.

10 This is the back of the driftwood on the upper part of the tree, showing the position of the trunk and branch in relation to it.

Right: *The finished styling shows the basic shape of the tree. This will be enhanced over the following years as the foliage areas bulk out and the real bonsai emerges.*

Twisted trunk – *nejkan*

This style clearly has a very strong Chinese connection because it is followed by many Chinese bonsai artists. Indeed, ancient Chinese artefacts often contain paintings of trees such as this. Many different types of plants can be trained in this style of bonsai, but it is obviously advisable to choose a variety that has a very flexible trunk so that its shape can easily be altered with a suitable application of wire. Once the wire has been added, it is then possible to manipulate the trunk line into virtually any shape you wish, as long as the trunk is flexible enough. The structure of the branches is then styled so that they blend well with the line of the trunk.

Above: *A mountain pine* (Pinus mugo) *which has been grown in a shallow container for several years to obtain a shallow root system suitable for bonsai training.*

The twisted trunk is not a very popular style for bonsai because it does not have a particularly natural appearance. The trunk is actually spiral-shaped, and this can be achieved by using thick wire to manipulate it into place. You will need a tree with a fairly thick trunk that is flexible enough to be curved into the required shape. Use a rake to scrape away the surface soil so that you can check the healthiness of the root system and establish which is the best side to form the front. Select branches that will make a natural-looking tree.

Using branch or knob cutters, remove any unwanted branches so that the full trunk line is exposed. The complete tree is then wired with wires of an appropriate thickness, so that the structure can be formed by gently bending the branches. Always make sure that a single piece of wire is used to travel from the branch around the trunk and along another so that two branches can be anchored by each other. It is important to wire all branches, however large or small, so that every single part of the tree can be

worked into a suitable position. This will ultimately result in a design that is pleasing to the eye.

When the final shape of the bonsai has been achieved, you will need to trim back all the shoot tips lightly in order to encourage the generation of more new buds within the inner parts of the tree.

CREATING YOUR TWISTED TRUNK BONSAI

You will need
- branch cutters
- scissors
- wire
- wire cutters
- rake
- pot
- mesh
- soil
- scoop

1 Tilt the tree by resting the rear of the root-ball on the back edge of the seed tray. This will give a better appearance to the line of the trunk.

2 Use branch cutters to remove the branch that is obscuring the front trunk-line of the tree.

4 Using branch cutters, prune out any long, uninteresting branches.

5 Wire the remaining branches and carefully bend them into place.

3 Cut out all the minor inner branches with a pair of scissors, so that the full extent of the twisted-trunk line is shown at its best.

6 Bend the rest of the branches into place, and trim away excessively long shoots to refine the outline.

Right: Following the completion of the styling, the bonsai is placed in a pot that reflects the curvaceous nature of the tree.

Exposed root – *neagari*

The roots of many trees in the wild are uncovered by years of exposure to natural elements such as rain and wind. Indeed, some elderly trees have a large number of roots exposed, so that the tree looks as if it is standing on stilts. In the world of bonsai, these natural features can be artificially created by growing roots specially for the purpose, but it is easier for novices in the art and culture of bonsai to acquire a plant that already has thickened roots. When visiting plant centres or bonsai nurseries, you will need to examine the root systems of your potential purchase, but be careful not to disturb them too much, unless you are confident that you will buy the tree, because the staff may not be pleased. As with all bonsai, the appearance of this style can be improved by adding some moss to the surface of the soil.

In the exposed-root style, you are trying to copy a natural feature, as you are with all bonsai, whatever the style. Indeed, the first task you must carry out to turn a garden-centre plant into a bonsai is to rake the surface soil away from the roots to expose some of them. This gives the lower part of the tree a mature and established look. You should find a tree that has long, mature roots by probing into the soil before you buy. Virtually any species of tree may be used and a suitable pot would be simple and rugged.

The exposed part of the root system now technically becomes part of the bonsai trunk and must be treated in the same way as normal. The exposed roots will need to be kept clean and free of the moss that will slowly cover the lower part of the trunk if it is not kept in check. A stiff brush, such as an old toothbrush, is ideal for this purpose, but bonsai suppliers will also have a range of suitable brushes that will allow you to access narrow gaps between some of the exposed roots.

Above: *This trident maple (*Acer buergerianum*) has been purchased from a bonsai nursery. It is highly suited to the exposed-root style.*

Some people are tempted to fill the gap in the exposed-root system with a rock of some kind, but this will only turn your exposed-root bonsai into a root-over-rock style and would defeat the original purpose. It would be acceptable to add a rock alongside the tree, but do not fill in any gaps between the roots.

CREATING YOUR EXPOSED ROOT BONSAI

You will need
- rake
- brush
- root shears
- scissors
- pot
- mesh
- wire
- soil
- scoop
- chopstick

1 Remove the tree from the pot, taking care not to damage the branches because they can be quite brittle in a trident maple.

2 Rake the soil away to expose the thickened roots that will become the exposed part of the bonsai root system.

3 Brush the main roots clean, using a stiff brush, until the mature part of the root-ball (roots) is completely exposed.

4 Trim the fibrous root-ball with root shears so that the bottom is neat and flat. This will help you to fit the tree into a suitably sized bonsai pot.

5 Settle the tree into a prepared pot with the best roots to the front.

6 Fill the pot with soil using a scoop, and work it around the roots with a chopstick.

Above: *When the roots are securely placed in the pot, the appearance of the soil surface can be improved with the application of some moss to make the finished tree look more natural.*

Clump – *kabubuki* or *kabudachi*

There are several ways that this design can be created, but the most common involves gathering several young trees together and tying them tightly at the base for several years so that they naturally graft together. You must make sure that the trees do not become strangulated. If it looks as though this is likely to happen, then the tie should be released and another applied. This style can be seen quite often in the wild, usually in woodland areas where many seeds have germinated, grown in close proximity, and then grafted together over a number of years. It is a very simple bonsai style to create because it needs little in the way of materials, tools and spare time. Simple young plants will be ideal to use, as they will grow rapidly to produce the desired result.

Above: *Five common beech (*Fagus sylvatica*) hedging plants, which are suitable for creating a clump-style bonsai.*

There are very many plant varieties that are suitable for this fairly simple style. Deciduous trees are recommended in particular because they graft together more easily than coniferous plants. For beginners to bonsai, it would be much better to start with young plants that can be easily obtained from your local plant centre. Small self-seeded plants would also make ideal plant material, but they may be smaller than those plants that are commercially available and your bonsai would take longer to mature.

If you are a little more ambitious, the process described can be carried out on very much larger plants, which will provide a more challenging, and possibly more interesting, final design. You will need a more substantial tying mechanism, such as wire, to hold all the plants together and a larger pot to accommodate the root system.

As with any bonsai styling and arrangement process, you will need to be very patient because the growth rate of plants can vary considerably. Young plants tend to graft together quickly,

while older plants will inevitably be very much slower. Always take your time when constructing any bonsai arrangement and never allow the roots to dry out completely. Simply make sure that you have a water spray to hand, so that regular applications of water can be made to the roots. This will enhance the survival rate of the bonsai following completion.

CREATING YOUR CLUMP BONSAI

You will need
- rake
- scissors
- raffia
- pot
- mesh
- wire
- wire cutters
- soil
- scoop
- chopstick

1 Remove any roots that appear high up on the trunk, leaving radial roots for development.

2 Remove the thick tap roots completely, so that only fine fibrous roots remain. This will encourage more fibrous roots to develop.

3 Shorten the remaining fibrous roots, leaving a reasonable amount to ensure the survival of the plant.

4 All five plants have been root-pruned and are now ready for assembly into the initial clump design.

5 Using a length of raffia, tie the five tightly together immediately above the root system of each plant.

6 Prepare a shallow, oval pot and then add some soil before carefully placing the clump of trees in the soil.

7 The roots should be worked well into the soil, so that the raffia is approximately level with the rim of the pot.

9 The initial styling of the clump-style bonsai is now complete. The clump will now need to grow and become more refined over several seasons before achieving its full potential as a bonsai.

8 Top up with dry soil using a scoop and work the soil into the root system using a chopstick. Water the arrangement well, allow it to drain and then keep in a shaded place for several weeks.

Right: *The finished clump has had the raffia disguised with soil and the completed planting is displayed on a dark wood stand against a suitable background. The five plants will mature so that they all eventually graft together at the base. At this point, the trunk base can be exposed.*

Broom – *hokidachi*

This style looks similar to the traditional broom used for sweeping, which is made from a bunch of twigs tied to a wooden handle. As full-size trees, this style can be seen in parks and gardens all over the world. It was initially derived from the natural shape of several varieties of *Zelkova*. It is, therefore, best suited to these trees, but other species can also be successfully grown in this style. Deciduous trees in particular lend themselves to training into broom-style bonsai because they quickly produce a good array of branches that will form a tight, twiggy, upper structure to the tree. Frequent pinching of the leading shoots on all the branches throughout the growing season will lead to excellent branch ramification with very little physical effort.

Above: *An old elm tree (*Ulmus*) that has been prepared with air layering in readiness for developing into a new bonsai.*

The form is based around a straight section of trunk with the branches coming from the top. There may be a continuation of the initial part of the trunk, but it will taper fairly abruptly and have smaller branches emerging along its length.

As each branch is developed, it should take on a finely branched, twiggy form. Frequent pinching out of the shoot tips is one of the most important aspects of the year-by-year improvement of this style, so do not neglect this part of the process.

If the weekly shoot pinching through the growing season from mid-spring to late summer is missed, and the branches become too long, they can be reduced by pruning fairly hard and starting again. If this pinching is carried out regularly, then the emerging leaves will naturally be slightly smaller than the previous batch that have been removed by the pruning process. This means that as time goes by, a spectacular bonsai will develop, as long as the correct pruning regime has been followed.

Never forget that a bonsai will continue growing if it is not controlled. This is especially true of the broom as it depends on concentrated pruning every spring and summer to maintain a compact structure. As the bonsai matures, study it in the winter when it is free of foliage. This is the best time to remove branches that are becoming too dense or are causing confusion.

CREATING YOUR BROOM BONSAI

You will need
- saw
- wound sealer
- branch cutters
- scissors
- rake
- pot
- mesh
- wire
- wire cutters
- soil
- scoop

1 Close-up of the root system produced during the air-layering technique. This is one year on from the initial preparation.

2 Using a saw, remove the air-layered section to leave a stump that will eventually produce many new shoots.

3 Cut the top of the stump into a "V" shape to encourage shoots to appear from slightly different positions around the trunk circumference.

4 Close-up of the "V"-cut, which will need to be sealed with a suitable wound sealing paste to assist the plant in the production of shoots. The plant will take some time to produce a suitable number of shoots.

5 On another elm that has already produced a suitable number of shoots, it can be seen how the initial development takes place.

6 The top of the stump needs to be tidied up using branch or knob cutters, and trimmed back to the uppermost shoots.

7 The lower shoots are removed using a pair of scissors until a group of shoots remains at the top of the trunk. The plant is then potted up in a temporary pot so that it can grow on and develop into a proper broom-style bonsai.

Above: *The remaining shoots are all growing at approximately the same level, albeit radiating out around the trunk. These will mature into a dense branch structure that will enhance the tree's appearance.*

INDOOR BONSAI

Most people, when starting out in the bonsai world, often keep their first bonsai indoors because it is a commonly held view that all bonsai are indoor plants. This misunderstanding normally leads to disaster and an instant withdrawal from the bonsai scene. Most bonsai are actually outdoor plants if they are kept in the correct conditions. However, if kept in areas outside their normal habitat, they will need special environmental conditions to ensure their survival. Tropical and subtropical plants will be classified as indoor bonsai when grown in colder areas of the world and temperate climate plants will need special environmental conditions if they are grown in hotter areas. In temperate climates, tropical and subtropical plants will always be called indoor bonsai, but it is not so easy to provide them with the warmer and more humid conditions they require. They will need good light, but not direct sunlight through a window, and a warm, slightly humid atmosphere.

Above: *An evergreen shrub, the Chinese sweet plum* (Sageretia theezans) *is a classic specimen for bonsai.*
Left: *A weeping fig (*Ficus benjamina *'Wiandii') in the early stages of training, showing the initial wiring process that will help in the formation of the final branch structure.*

Aralia elegantissima

These plants, commonly known as finger aralia, can have one or more trunks and make a very attractive landscape. *Aralia* is a member of the ivy family which consists of trees, shrubs and palm-like plants, some of which have spines. They often have woody stems, even the smaller varieties such as the one described here. This variety is ideally suited to a group situation, as it tends to be upright with a relatively slim trunk. When grouped fairly closely together, a very pleasant indoor forest can be achieved. These plants can be sourced quite easily from plant centres or nurseries and have a compact root structure suited to shallow containers.

When growing bonsai plants in a group, always make sure that the tallest plant is somewhere in the central third of the arrangement and that the rest of the plants get progressively smaller towards the sides and rear.

Trim away all lower side shoots so that the trunks or main stems can be clearly seen. As with all group plantings or forests, the plants should always be placed very close together in order to give a mature feeling to the arrangement. The plants can be split into two groups so that an impression is given of a footpath running through the forest.

Small stones or rocks can be included in the composition to give a more rugged feel to the group and moss or very small plants can be planted under the main trees to enhance the natural look of the forest.

Containers should be shallow and can be rectangular or oval. The pot should not be too bright in colour and should complement the foliage colour of the trees. As with all bonsai

Above: *Suitable* Aralia *plants can be bought from many plant centres and will be sold simply as houseplants; these can be quickly turned into an indoor-bonsai planting.*

containers, it should never clash with the trees in any way, but just be there for growing support and minimal decorative appearance. Pots normally have a subtle glaze or a matt (flat) finish and should, of course, have good-sized drainage holes.

As with all indoor bonsai, it is a good idea to mist regularly to maintain the health and vigour of the trees.

STYLING YOUR *ARALIA ELEGANTISSIMA*

You will need
- scissors
- pot
- mesh
- wire
- wire cutters
- soil
- scoop
- chopstick
- rake
- rocks

1 Cut off the lower and inner leaves of the plants using a pair of scissors, so that the trunks can be clearly seen. This will immediately open up the stems so that they look like trunks and create a more tree-like effect. It is surprising how different a simple plant can look when the main stem, or trunk, is cleared of foliage. This applies to almost any plant that has a woody stem, and is one of the first features you should look for when choosing a plant for a bonsai.

2 Place in the prepared pot, arranging the seven trunks so that they are slightly spread out at the top.

3 Add extra soil and work well in with a chopstick until the plants are firmly arranged in the pot. Press the soil well into the roots, but do not compact it too tightly because the roots will not be able to breathe.

4 Carefully position several pieces of rock or tufa to give the effect of a miniature landscape. Make sure the pieces of rock are firmly embedded in the soil so they look as if they have always been there. This will greatly enhance the overall appearance of the finished bonsai.

Right: *Once the styling is complete and a stone and some soil decoration have been put in place, the group makes a very attractive indoor bonsai that will give great pleasure as long as the soil is kept just moist at all times. Do not forget to mist spray the foliage regularly as this will help the tree to cope with the drier indoor atmosphere.*

Crassula arborescens

Commonly known as the money tree or jade plant, this is often underestimated as bonsai material. Many species of crassula are available and *C. arborescens* is one of the best. There are many varieties available that have smaller leaves which may be even more suitable as bonsai. Most of them produce flowers at some time in the year and therefore can make very interesting indoor bonsai. Being succulents, they are prone to frosts that will almost certainly kill the plant in a very short time. Some are semi-hardy and may be suitable for cold conservatories (sun rooms) and greenhouses. Most, however, are quite happy outdoors providing they are slowly acclimatized. Crassula can be defoliated and pruned very hard if required and need very little water, so are ideal if they need to be left untended for several weeks.

Crassula arborescens has thick leaves and is strictly a succulent. The leaves and stems hold a large quantity of water, which allows the plant to go for several weeks without showing any signs of wilting. This characteristic makes the plant easy to look after as it needs watering less often than most plants. Even if it dries out, wilts and looks dehydrated, it will almost always recover once watering is resumed.

Propagation is also easy; just break off a leaf, leave until the end is dry (for about four days), and lay it on the surface of some dry soil. In about one month the leaf will have sprouted new roots. Do not water until you can see signs of new growth. Feed as with other houseplants, but only with a weak mixture of fertilizer.

When you are controlling the growth of your bonsai *Crassula*, you should wait until two or three pairs of leaves have been produced and then trim back to just one pair. Each time you do this, the growth pattern will double up. That is to say, each pruned shoot will produce two new shoots.

Above: *This is a typical garden centre or supermarket plant which can be trained into an attractive indoor bonsai.*

Never allow the plant to be exposed to frost, because its high water content will freeze and, on thawing, the tree will just collapse.

Overall, this is a very easy plant for bonsai because it has a compact root system that requires little water. The leaves will become overlarge if too much water is given, so keep watering to a minimum.

STYLING YOUR *CRASSULA ARBORESCENS*

You will need
- branch cutters
- scissors
- rake
- pot
- mesh
- wire cutters
- soil
- scoop
- chopstick

1 Cut off the left-hand trunk using branch cutters, so that the main trunk in the centre is dominant.

2 Clean up the stump, using branch or knob cutters to form a natural-looking trunk base free from excess plant growth.

3 Pull off the lower leaves to expose the line of the tree's main trunk.

4 Having removed the leaves, it is clear that the other low branch should also be removed. This allows you to see the main trunk at its best.

5 Using scissors, reduce the length of the leading shoots.

6 Place in a suitable pot and top up with soil, working it in and around the roots with a chopstick until the soil fills every space.

Above: *Once the styled plant is complete, some moss can be added to the surface of the soil to give a more natural look which will enhance the line of the trunk. New shoots will soon begin to appear from the pruned shoot ends.*

Ficus benjamina 'Wiandii'

This *Ficus* has a compact growth habit and well-proportioned leaves. Plants may have one or more trunks and generally have an interesting root system. Regular misting of the foliage with water is beneficial and the soil should be kept just moist at all times. Feed lightly, but regularly, during the main growing season from spring to autumn. As the shoots grow, prune them back to one or two leaves. This plant will enjoy warm, humid conditions, so it would be ideal for keeping in a conservatory (sun room) or similar surroundings. It is fairly tolerant of slightly dry conditions when allied to higher humidity, as the humidity will help the survival of the relatively thick leaves. A negative aspect of this *Ficus* is that the branches can be brittle and so should be handled with care.

Above: Ficus benjamina *'Wiandii'* can be bought from the indoor plant section of most plant centres or superstores. This is good material for training into an indoor bonsai because it is a tropical or semitropical plant.

A serious point to note about *Ficus* is that, when pruned, the wounds will produce a sticky white latex solution that is toxic and should be kept away from the eyes and not ingested. This latex solution also appears when the plant is root pruned, so you should be cautious whenever pruning any part of this fig. Always wash your hands thoroughly after you have been working on these plants.

Many varieties and cultivars are now available, so the choice of a plant for bonsai culture is very wide-ranging. There are extremely drooping varieties, as well as more formal upright forms, some with very small rather thin leaves and some with very large, thick leaves. Variegated varieties are also very popular as houseplants, and these, too, will make very interesting and different additions to a bonsai collection.

Ficus can be purchased as single-trunk plants or multiple-trunk specimens in a wide range of sizes, so there should be something available to suit every bonsai grower's taste.

Figs can be shaped by pruning or wiring, but take care that you do not break the branches when you are manipulating them after wiring because they can be very brittle. As figs usually have smooth bark, they can be easily damaged if the wire is left on for too long, so check them regularly.

STYLING YOUR *FICUS BENJAMINA* 'WIANDII'

You will need
- branch cutters
- wound sealer
- wire
- wire cutters
- scissors
- rake
- pot
- mesh
- soil
- scoop
- chopstick

1 Leaves growing directly from the trunk and branches must be removed to create a clean-looking plant. White latex fluid oozes from cut areas of the *Ficus* family and contact with the mouth or eyes should be avoided at all times.

2 A small amount of wiring has been carried out and excess shoots cut out in order to create a tree-like shape.

3 Use a sharp, clean pair of cutters to remove the excess shoots.

4 This is the final shape of the bonsai, before it is placed in a bonsai pot.

5 The tree has been repotted using the techniques described in the potting section and the dry soil is being worked into the root system using a chopstick. After repotting, water the soil and allow any excess water to drain away.

Right: *The tree blends well with the cream glazed pot and has been displayed on a dark, modern Chinese stand that shows the pot and tree to advantage.*

Myrtus communis

This variety is commonly known as dwarf myrtle, and only young plants are usually available, but it is relatively easy to train as bonsai. If you can buy some small plants, a miniature landscape can be constructed using a combination of plants, soil and rocks. Try to thin out the top growth to achieve a branched structure. It will be tempting to "clip" the foliage, but that would be topiary rather than bonsai. You will also need to be persistent with the thinning-out process because a dense mass of foliage can quickly regrow. Myrtle is relatively small-leaved in most of its forms and is therefore highly suited to this type of miniature landscape. The leaves will become substantially smaller with pruning and over time, and the plants will make attractive small bonsai that are suitable for grouping together.

Above: *These are typical of commercially available* Myrtus communis *plants. They are small, compact and very suitable for constructing a small landscape planting.*

This species requires regular misting to maintain the health of the foliage, particularly in the summer. As with most indoor bonsai, this variety can be placed outside in a shady spot in warmer weather. Water when the soil starts to dry out, but never allow the roots to stand in water as they will quickly rot. Good light is important, but do not place your tree in direct sunlight as this will scorch the leaves.

Because myrtles develop into compact bonsai easily, they can be planted in a variety of arrangements using different rock formations. They grow well in rocks as they have compact root systems and will fit into even the smallest of cavities. They would, however, be more suited to low-lying rockscapes as they generally grow into compact bush-like structures.

Try to be bold and use your imagination when planting any size or arrangement of landscape, as it is individual ideas that produce the great diversity of shapes and forms which make growing bonsai such an inspiring art form.

Pots or containers should be shallow and possibly slab-like in shape. If the pot is too deep, it will dominate the composition, so ensure that the pot is complementary to the bonsai and not overpowering. You will also need to add some ground-cover plants to give a natural and weathered feel to the composition.

STYLING YOUR *MYRTUS COMMUNIS*

You will need
- rake
- scissors
- pot
- mesh
- wire
- wire cutters
- soil
- scoop
- rocks

1 Having removed the plants from their pots, rake away the soil to obtain a suitable root-ball and expose the trunk base. Using scissors, remove some of the lower branches to expose the trunk line.

2 Trim each plant into a tree-like form by shortening the long shoots and branches.

3 Prepare the pot in the normal way and add a layer of soil.

4 Arrange some rocks, in this case tufa, so that there is enough space to plant the trees around them, and add extra soil.

5 Place the medium-size tree on the left and settle it into the pot, using a back-and-forth rotating motion so that the plant is bedded well into the soil.

6 Having placed the smallest tree on the right, plant the largest beside it and to the right of the rock. Ensure that this tree is slightly higher than the others. Never finish with the tops of all trees at the same level.

Right: *The final effect should be that of a miniature landscape which has been in existence for many years, so it will be necessary to add various mosses and tiny plants to the surface of the soil.*

Sageretia theezans

Commonly known as the bird plum cherry, *Sageretia theezans* is a popular species for indoor bonsai. Specimens of this plant are normally sold as fully trained trees. This particular specimen has been allowed to grow on and has lost its original shape. The bird plum cherry originates from the Far East where it is often used as a hedging plant, largely because it grows very quickly into medium-sized, shrubby shapes and even small trees. When fully developed, it produces an excellent, textured trunk that thickens very quickly and eventually forms a good, mature, flaking trunk which is especially suitable for bonsai styling.

These trees have delicate leaves which can lose their moisture quickly and dry out. Regular misting of the foliage should control this situation. The roots develop quickly, so repot every year. As the bark matures and flakes away, it will leave a very attractive patchy yellow and orange colouring that is particularly pleasing when the plant has dropped its leaves.

As with many other shrubby plants, the roots of *Sageretia* develop into very compact structures that are ideal for bonsai culture as they will flourish in shallow bonsai pots. This indoor bonsai can also be kept outdoors during frost-free periods of the year, but, because of its very thin, delicate leaves, it can be very vulnerable to many conditions. Strong wind and strong sun – either separately or, even worse, together – can quickly destroy the foliage, so great care should be taken to avoid adverse conditions such as these.

When it is necessary to prune the thick branches or even the trunk of a *Sageretia*, it will soon become very

Above: *This* Sageretia theezans *has been grown in a pot for several years until suitable for pruning and planting in a bonsai pot.*

clear how hard the wood can be. In fact, it may take several smaller cuts to carry out a pruning operation that would need just one cut if you were working with a plant that has much softer wood. For this reason, you will need to make sure that all your pruning tools are extremely sharp, so that the pruning process is made as easy as possible.

STYLING YOUR *SAGERETIA THEEZANS*

You will need
- rake
- branch cutters
- pot
- mesh
- wire
- wire cutters
- soil
- scoop
- chopstick
- scissors
- sprayer

1 Having removed the plant from its pot and raked out the roots very carefully, use branch cutters to cut out the central branch which would otherwise spoil the line of the finished tree.

2 Settle the tree into the pot just off centre and fill up with some soil using a scoop. Work the soil into the roots with a chopstick.

3 Using a pair of scissors, cut back the long shoots, leaving just one or two leaves.

4 Mist the soil and plant to create a high humidity. This species has thin leaves that can dry out quickly after repotting, so do this regularly.

Below: *After placing the finished tree in a crackle-glaze pot and shaping it by pruning, press some moss into the soil surface to add a little more realism to the design.*

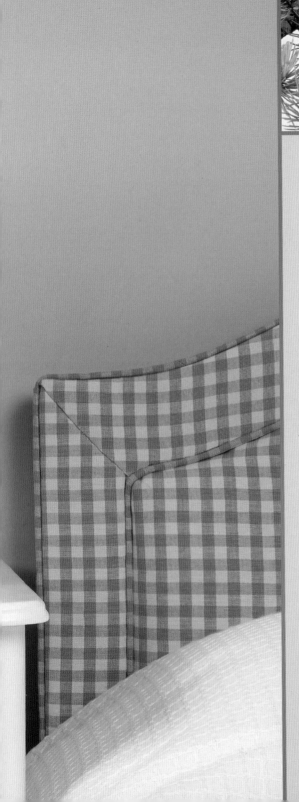

DISPLAYING BONSAI

When displaying bonsai indoors, remember that they need an airy position in good light, whereas outdoor bonsai require full light and an open situation. Indoors, bonsai are best displayed on some type of display table, perhaps on a suitable mat. Any background used indoors should also complement the tree, being as plain as possible, so that the tree form is not compromised in any way. Outdoors, bonsai can be displayed on specially built stands or benches. It is important that these are high enough for the trees to be viewed at approximately eye-level.

The choice of pot is also important. Indeed, the size, shape, colour and texture of the pot, whether it is glazed or unglazed, and whether it has bold or insignificant feet, are all features that can make or break the appearance of an individual bonsai. None of these elements must dominate the tree, but they must gently complement and frame it.

Above: *The Japanese white pine* (Pinus parviflora) *is a dense tree with a magnificent spread.*
Left: *A broom-style Chinese elm* (Ulmus parvifolia) *in an indoor situation. Remember to protect furniture from possible damage from water or pot feet.*

Pots & containers

To the untrained eye, it may seem that the bonsai pot is just the container in which to grow the tree. Nothing could be further from the truth, however, as the pot is one of the most important parts of the overall effect. The relationship between the pot and the tree is a complex one, and it is most important that the pot blends well with the tree, so that the final composition of tree and pot becomes a complementary and well-balanced single unit. A bonsai in a suitable container can be compared with a classical work of art mounted in a similarly suitable frame. In both cases, your eye should be drawn first by the painting or tree, with the frame or pot later being perceived as the complementary mount. If the reverse is true, then the framing feature will be seen to dominate the intended subject.

Above: *A common beech (*Fagus sylvatica*) in a pot that some might consider too deep, but which works quite well with this tree.*

With bonsai, the pot is the frame, and there should be no conflict over which part of the composition is viewed first. The eye should be drawn first to the lower trunk of the tree, then move up into its apex before considering the pot as framing the whole presentation.

CONSTRUCTION

Bonsai pots will need to be frost-proof if they are going to contain hardy outdoor trees in a temperate climate, and should therefore be made from high-temperature fired stoneware. (Even if trees are to be kept in tropical or subtropical areas, frost-proof pots would be recommended, as they are much tougher.) Pots and containers that are constructed of less sturdy materials, such as mica and plastic, are fine for use by beginners or as temporary training pots, but stoneware pots certainly give the trees a far superior appearance.

Choose pots that have one or more large drainage holes. Larger pots may have a series of small holes around the perimeter of their base; these are for use when you are tying the tree into the pot. The floor of the pot should be flat, so that there are no areas where water can become trapped for any prolonged period.

Make sure that any pots you purchase have good feet. These will raise the base of the pot above the display stand, so allowing free airflow around and under the base of the pot, which will increase the chances of your trees remaining healthy.

Left: *An informal upright Japanese maple,* Acer palmatum *'Nomura', planted in a suitably coloured and shaped pot.*

STYLES OF POT

Bonsai pots are produced in a huge range of different shapes, sizes and colours designed to suit all styles and species. The accompanying pictures show a small range of available pots. When choosing a pot, it is advisable to take your tree to a pot supplier, who will have a wide range of suitable pots, to make sure that you obtain the best container for your individual tree.

GLAZING

As a general rule when choosing a pot, opt for glazed or semi-glazed pots for deciduous trees and matt (flat) or unglazed pots for conifers and evergreens. Bonsai pots should always be unglazed on the inside, as this will help to keep the tree stable within the pot when the roots have grown sufficiently to come into contact with the pot sides. Any external glazing should run over the rim and a short way down the inside edge of the pot.

Above: *A small ceramic Japanese pot that is good enough to display on its own. Only a small, pretty flowering tree would suit this pot.*

Right: *An unusual cascade bonsai in a pot made by the tree's owner, and exhibited at a Bonsai Kai bonsai competition.*

A RANGE OF POTS AND CONTAINERS

There are some general rules to follow when you are deciding which container is most suitable for a particular bonsai tree. Glazed pots of various colours are much better for displaying broadleaf trees, but remember that they must never be very bright in colour. Instead, the colour should blend beautifully with the shade of the foliage or with the colour of the trunk. Unglazed pots, which are available in varying shades of matt (flat) brown or grey, are much more suitable for conifers and evergreen trees. Outdoor trees, which are more likely to be exposed to frosts, will also require a container that is totally frost-proof.

The container that you choose should also accentuate the form and colour of the bonsai specimen, while at the same time not dominating the tree. Think very carefully before choosing your container, and if you are in any doubt, consult an experienced bonsai artist who will help you to select a pot that complements your bonsai perfectly.

Right: *A tall pot such as this is ideal for cascade bonsai because it allows the form of the cascading tree to be seen to advantage.*

Japanese slip-cast
lipped rectangle

Japanese slip-cast lipped rectangle

Japanese slip-cast
lipped rectangle

Japanese slip-cast
lipped rectangle

English hand-made
crescent

English hand-made
round

English hand-made
square cascade

English primitive hand-made
shallow round

Chinese decorated
square cascade

English primitive hand-
made shallow crescent

Japanese shallow rectangle

English primitive hand-made
shallow crescent

English primitive
hand-made round

Japanese fluted round slip-cast

English hand-made
rectangle

Japanese slip-cast
lipped rectangle

Japanese slip-cast lipped oval

Japanese shallow
oval

Japanese slip-cast
lipped oval

English hand-made
round

Japanese slip-cast lipped
rectangle

Display stands

It is very important when displaying any size or style of bonsai to make sure that each element of the display complements the others, as well as the chosen bonsai. This means that the colour and design of any display tables, stands, matting and background should be subtle and blend with the bonsai pot, trunk, foliage and any accent plant involved. Display tables and stands can be purchased from bonsai suppliers or found in stores that sell oriental-style furniture. These accessories will normally be used when displaying any type of bonsai indoors in your own home or at special bonsai exhibitions and shows. All bonsai can be displayed indoors as long as you ensure that outdoor trees are only kept inside for a day or two at the most. As with the pot, the display stand must not dominate the tree.

Above: *This is a typical outdoor display using stands made from pre-treated timber and coloured to taste.*

Display tables should always be carefully selected so that they blend well with each individual tree. They are available in a very wide variety of sizes, shapes, designs and colours and are mostly constructed in various types of wood, from oak and rosewood through to ebony or teak – in fact, virtually any wood can be suitable providing it blends with the tree to be displayed. However, good-quality display tables can be difficult to obtain. If you have the ability and skill, and think you can construct your own display tables, then this may be an easier way forward, as you can then custom-build them to your own requirements.

Instead of formal-style display tables, consider using thin slices of good-quality timber as a form of display. These are probably best suited to displaying groups or forests that are contained in or on a large flat slab or pot. The slice of timber will need to be slightly larger than the slab or pot and be properly finished so that it looks like a quality piece of furniture.

Stand shapes include rectangular, square, round and multi-sided, and range from very low to extremely tall.

Left: *This elegant Chinese elm (*Ulmus parvifolia*) cascade bonsai is being displayed to great effect on a tall Chinese mahogany stand.*

Right: *A modern Chinese tall rosewood stand (left) and an antique Chinese mahogany stand (right), both of which are suitable for cascade-style bonsai.*

Low stands are suitable for most trees, be they formal upright, informal upright, leaning or multi-trunk, while tall stands would normally be used to display cascade or semi-cascade trees, which need the height so that they can cascade down over the side of the stand. The height of the stands depends largely on the overall height of the tree. Again, if you have the facilities, knowledge, skill and ability to produce your own display stands, then you can tailor-make them to suit a specific bonsai.

Above and right:
The photographs here show clearly how important the choice of stand is for your bonsai. Low and tall stands have been used to display the same bonsai, but, because the tree is a cascade, it is much better suited to the tall stand.

Below: *Clockwise from top right: English oak rectangle; Chinese mahogany round; English oak rectangle; Chinese rectangle (stained softwood).*

Below right: *Rectangular rosewood stand from Taiwan (top) and a Japanese oak rectangular stand from Nihonmatsu City (below).*

Slabs & rocks

Bonsai are traditionally grown in pots and containers of a certain depth in order to enclose the root structure of each individual tree. However, this is not always the case, because some styles of bonsai can actually benefit from being planted on a thin, flat slab made from stone or slate. If this technique is required, then the bonsai will need to be securely attached to the slab because there are no sides for support as there are with a pot. Suitable slabs can be made of slate, sandstone or, in fact, any type of real rock, because artificial slabs which are made of concrete will almost certainly never look as attractive. Slabs that are made from clay in the same way as pots can be very good and, if made by a good potter, they will look as good as any natural rock.

Above: *Although this bonsai is in the process of being repotted, it can still be displayed on the slab on which it is resting after repotting.*

Ideally, these flat slabs should be formed of a material that is strong enough to take the weight of the individual planting involved. Although the pieces of rock need to be thin for aesthetic reasons, they must not be so thin and weak that they break when they are transported.

There are many types of rock for this purpose, but the best is slate, which is structurally very strong. Sandstone can be very weak when in thin section, so this may not be very suitable, although if a thicker slab were needed, it might be satisfactory.

If you find natural stone slabs hard to find, then a good bonsai potter will make you a slab, provided he or she has a good-sized kiln. You can make an artificial slab using a metal frame covered in glass fibre with a sand-and-cement surface that has been coloured to create the appearance of natural rock.

You might find stone slabs locally, but good bonsai suppliers will be able to advise you. Look out for natural products, such as real sandstone or slate. A visit to a local quarry or stonemason could reveal suitable pieces of stone. As a last resort, you can buy reinforced concrete slabs (the type normally sold as paving), but these are heavy and do not look natural enough.

Left: *A "mame" box (Buxus sempervirens) displayed on a thin piece of slate. This image was taken at an RHS bonsai show in London.*

SLAB PLANTING A *COTONEASTER* 'CORAL BEAUTY'

1 Select a good-quality specimen of *Cotoneaster* 'Coral Beauty' from a plant nursery.

2 Remove approximately three-quarters of the upper growth and half of the root-ball (roots). Carry out a trial placement of the pruned and styled plant on a sandstone slab.

3 Drill four "tying-in" holes through the slab using a power drill and a masonry drill bit. Always wear safety glasses or goggles when you are using power tools.

4 Pass two pieces of wire through the holes from under the slab.

5 After carrying out initial pruning, place the plant on the slab between the wires.

6 Twist the ends of the two pieces of wire tightly together to secure the tree to the slab. Cut off the spare wire ends.

7 Contour the root-ball by adding a small amount of soil and cover the soil completely with moss in order to create a natural effect.

8 The final arrangement of the bonsai with its slab is pictured here on a suitable surface and against a striking purple background. The tree, soil mound and slab all complement each other beautifully.

Accessories

There are many accessories that can be used with bonsai. These range from stands to labels, and must always complement the bonsai that is on display. Other types of display material, such as bamboo matting, gravel, stone or slate, as well as many other substances, may also be used in the display of bonsai, and you can use a selection of these items to design suitable settings for your bonsai. In all instances, when using accessories such as those already mentioned, consideration must be given to the style, shape, size and colour of both the bonsai and the pot in which it is planted. None of these accessories should clash with or detract the viewer from looking at the bonsai, as it is the bonsai that is always the most important part of each display. That said, all items must be complementary to each other.

Some people like to include all sorts of accessories around their bonsai, but, if too many items are introduced, there could be confusion as to what is the most important item on view, which should always be the bonsai. Therefore, there should never be any item that is not connected with that bonsai, as it will inevitably detract from the appearance of the tree. For example, small figures or figurines incorporated alongside or on the soil of a bonsai are totally inappropriate, as they would catch the eye first and distract the viewer from the beauty of the bonsai.

Above: *This indoor bird plum cherry (*Sageretia theezans*) bonsai has been grown in a glazed pot and displayed on a cut-rush mat.*

MATS

You can use various styles and textures of matting as a base for bonsai as long as they complement, not distract from, the tree itself. You might like to try rush or bamboo matting. Again, it is important to choose matting with a colour and texture that complements the choice of container.

LANTERNS

Stone lanterns can be used in a garden situation where one or, at the most, two (depending upon the size of your garden display area) can be placed strategically alongside some bonsai display stands to give an oriental look to your garden. Any more than two would overdo the situation.

LABELS

Bonsai will benefit from having name labels next to them so that anyone viewing them can instantly identify the species and variety. Any labels should

Left: *Broom-style Japanese grey bark elm (*Zelkova serrata*) on a dark bamboo mat that was chosen to complement the style of pot.*

Left: *Mame-style, informal upright English elm (Ulmus procera), standing on a pale-coloured, thin rush mat. The thin mat complements the small tree.*

Below: *Japanese black pine (Pinus thunbergii) on a piece of mahogany furniture with two accessories that tend to distract the eye from the tree.*

be subtle and the information they display should be kept to a minimum so that the appearance of the bonsai is not compromised.

OTHER DISPLAY ELEMENTS

The time and application that goes into the creation of bonsai trees means that you will want to display them to the best effect. Top-dressings, such as moss and gravel, various fabrics as well as many other substances may well be suitable for use in the display of bonsai. A potted bonsai can be displayed on a thin layer of grit, which can be acquired in many different colours and sizes to suit your tree.

Above: Frankenia thymifolia *accent plant on a hexagonal stand that matches the pot shape. The label is typical of that used at exhibitions.*

Above: *Moss is used as an accessory for decorating the soil surface and is essential for giving a natural look to the completed arrangement.*

Accent planting

Accent or complementary plants are used to enhance the natural appearance of a bonsai. Full-size trees growing in the wild have various other plants and natural objects around them, including wild flowers, grasses, mosses, lichens and even stones or rocks, some of which may have very interesting shapes. We can draw on these natural features for inspiration when searching for items to display with a bonsai specimen, so creating a more exciting arrangement for the viewer that does not detract attention from the tree itself. Small plants are the most suitable as accents for the majority of displays because their size does not overpower the bonsai. Much larger plants can be used as accents in an outdoor display where they can be used on the ground at the base of a single bonsai display stand.

Suitable material that can be used as accent plants include the dwarf forms of *Equisetum*, *Miscanthus* and *Pennisetum*, as well as *Ophiopogon planiscarpus* 'Nigrescens', *Hakonechloa macra*, *Acorus gramineus*, *Imperata cylindrica*, *Aruncus aethusifolius* and some dwarf forms of *Astilbe*. Many other plants are also suitable for use as accent plants, including daisies, gentians and dandelions, as well as very small bamboos.

In all cases, the accent plants should be potted in complementary containers in just the same way as the bonsai pots complement the trees. When choosing plants as accents for bonsai, it is possible to collect plants from the garden or from woodland areas, as well as buying from plant centres. It is easy to develop a blinkered view when deciding on a plant variety as an accent so try to be open-minded and look at any type of small herbaceous or alpine plant. You may be surprised to find that there are many more plants available than you first imagined which would be suitable.

Right: *This Japanese black pine (*Pinus thunbergii*) is being displayed with a wild violet accent plant. The rustic accent pot blends well with the rugged trunk of the bonsai.*

Below: *Korean hornbeam (*Carpinus laxiflora*) with a cyclamen accent plant. Both are displayed on a slice of polished yew wood.*

Above: *Sisyrinchiums make good accent plants. The botanist Theophrastus used the word sisyrinchium for a plant related to the iris.*

SUITABLE ACCENT PLANTS

Above: Frankenia thymifolia *with its russet-coloured foliage is planted here in a deep, hexagonal, matt (flat) brown pot and displayed on a complementary hexagonal rosewood stand.*

Above: Aruncus aethusifolius *growing in a shallow, primitive-style pot. This is a large accent plant and for this reason is more suited to an outdoor display.*

Above: Hakonechloa macra *'Alboaurea' is quite a large plant with red stems and stripes within the leaves, so the chosen red pot shows off the plant superbly.*

Above: Astilbe × crispa *'Lilliput' has fern-like leaves and eventually upright stems with pale pink flowers. Again, this is a fairly large plant, planted in this case in a primitive-style pot.*

Above: Ophiopogon planiscarpus *'Nigrescens' is a very attractive, almost black-leaved plant. The pot is more decorative than normal because it matches well with the curly leaves.*

Above: Any small or alpine variety of cyclamen will make a very good accent plant for use with bonsai. Here, a cyclamen is planted in a pot and displayed on a rosewood stand.

Suiseki

These are decorative stones. In traditional Japanese settings, bonsai and *suiseki* are often positioned very close to each other when these two art forms are displayed together. They may, in fact, be regarded as an art form in their own right. Suitable stones can be collected from almost anywhere, such as beaches, river beds, mountain areas, quarries, garden centres and even from your own garden. The main criterion is that each stone must have an interesting shape that can tell a story of its own. Its appearance should also give the impression of a mountain or cliff or other natural features such as these. If the stone has a vein running through it, this might even represent a mountainside with a waterfall or other similar watery outlet.

Above: *English Lake District quartz formed into an interesting shape that closely resembles a craggy mountain peak.*

It is thought that the first *penjing* (the original Chinese form of tree and rock landscapes) and *gongshi* (viewing stones) were given to the Empress Regent Suiko of Japan by the Chinese imperial court around AD592–628. These stones were considered to be of great interest to the Japanese aristocracy by virtue of their amazing shapes, which included various features that resembled mountains, caves, waterfalls and many other natural-looking features. They tended to be in the form of stones that emulated the massive, almost vertical, mountains of China. This type of decorative stone became very popular with the Japanese for many hundreds of years.

The samurai warrior class came to power in Japan in the late Kamakura period (1185–1392). The teachings of Zen Buddhism became widely accepted by the samurai as a result of the highly active trading that took place between China and Japan. The disciplines of Zen Buddhism – including austerity, meditation and intuitive insight – meant that apparently simple items in keeping with this philosophy, such as stones with interesting but subtle shapes and colours, were much sought after.

This preference was further emphasized by Zen monks during the Muromachi period (1393–1568), when the stones were cleaned of all other elements, such as soil, dirt and possibly plant material, thus accentuating their simple but interesting detail.

Over a considerable period of time, stones came to be selected that suggested, by their form, representations of natural landscapes, such as mountains, valleys, caves and waterfalls etc. The Zen monks had a powerful influence over the Japanese ruling class, and these stones were considered to lead to spiritual refinement, enlightenment and inner awareness.

During the Edo period (1603–1867), the wealthy merchants who came to the fore began to challenge the

Left: *A piece of* ibigawa rock, displayed here as an accent to an Acer palmatum 'Kiyohime', which is showing the beautiful branch ramification of its winter form.

Right: *Californian black jade mountain* suiseki *used as an accent to a* Juniperus chinensis *on an English bonsai stand.*

aristocracy with their interest in *suiseki* and began collecting and competing with them for these stones. During this period, Japan became extremely isolated as a result of closing its borders to all outsiders, but this closure meant that the Japanese arts expanded and flourished without influence from other countries, religions and regimes.

The Meiji period (1868–1912) saw a lull in the interest in *suiseki* largely because of the decrease in wealth of the samurai and upper classes, but in some ways it began to develop. It was during this period that *suiseki* first came to be classified and given names for certain shapes and styles.

From the middle of the twentieth century, interest in *suiseki* began to regenerate, and it spread into the international arena, as did bonsai.

It continues to rise in interest today, so much so that there are now *suiseki* societies, clubs and associations throughout the world.

DIFFERENT *SUISEKI* STONES

Above: *Beautiful slate* suiseki *resembling a mountain with vertical rock faces and sheer drops.*

Above: *Japanese* ibigawa *stone which has many different colours, interesting textures and caves.*

Above: *Coastal rocky island with interesting, water-shaped erosion and textures in a sea of fine white gravel.*

Above: *This Californian jade mountain stone has intriguing caves, waterfalls and sheer rock faces.*

Above: *Another slate* suiseki *with a graduating slope that leads to a dramatic vertical rock face.*

Above: *Very interesting mountain range that culminates in a typically high, imposing alpine peak.*

Indoor displays

Whatever the climate of your area, and whatever types of tree you have, at some time you will want to display one, some or all of your bonsai indoors. You will need to make sure that the trees you select are in pots suitable for the surroundings in which they are to be displayed. You will also need to take into account the amount of light there is, as well as any direct source of heating, since these aspects may well affect the health of the bonsai in question. With contemporary styling in our homes comes the need to try different ideas when planting and displaying bonsai indoors. Trying different, minimalist containers and placing trees in various rooms can bring a whole new meaning to a bonsai display, but never forget the importance of good light and humidity.

Above: *Broom-style Chinese elm (Ulmus parvifolia) on a table by a north-facing window, a good source of natural light.*

Bonsai should be kept in the correct environmental conditions for the species of plant being grown. Their position also depends very much upon where you live in relation to the natural growing environment of any particular bonsai that you are growing. They will always need to be in receipt of very good natural light, but not placed on a windowsill where the sun can shine directly on to the tree because this could lead to irreparable damage to the bonsai.

It is advisable to place your trees on a table or bench that is covered with a suitable piece of fabric or any sort of natural material that will enhance rather than detract from the appearance of the tree. The tree can then be placed on a smaller table or mat of some description on top of the chosen fabric or natural material. None of these props should detract from the tree in any way: they are simply meant to contribute to the satisfactory display of the tree.

TYPE OF ROOM

A bonsai can be displayed in virtually any room in the home, as long it is checked carefully and regularly to see if it needs watering or feeding and whether the atmospheric conditions are right. You will also need to ensure that it is pruned correctly. Central heating can severely affect any plant when kept indoors, as the conditions will be far too warm and dry for successful plant growth. This can be overcome, to some extent, by mist-spraying with water.

The best room for displaying a bonsai is obviously one in which the bonsai can be seen by you and any friends or visitors, such as the sitting room. However, this is not the best room as far as the atmospheric conditions are concerned and, for this reason, a kitchen, bathroom or anywhere that may experience a certain amount of humidity is

Left: *Twisted-trunk Chinese elm (Ulmus parvifolia) planted in a clean, contemporary container and displayed in a bathroom which will provide good humidity.*

Above: *This bird plum cherry (Sageretia theezans) has been displayed to good effect in a curved dish and placed on a sideboard.*

preferable. Indeed, the best rooms in which to display bonsai are the kitchen and bathroom because they have an inbuilt humidity as a result of the water systems in place there.

Tropical and sub-tropical plants may be kept in slightly warm and humid indoor conditions for quite long periods of time, but hardy temperate trees can remain indoors for only a maximum of one or two days before they begin to show signs of stress. If you have to spray the foliage of any tree while it is being displayed indoors, you will need to take care that water droplets do not fall on to polished wood surfaces, especially if the piece of furniture is of any value.

Right: *This Chinese elm (Ulmus parvifolia) has been planted in a traditional pot and placed in a kitchen near to a window in order to obtain good natural light.*

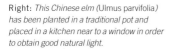

DISPLAY TABLES AND STANDS

The tables upon which bonsai are displayed will need to vary in style depending on the tree that has been chosen for display. For example, if the tree is powerful and masculine in form, then it will need a stand or table that is strong and powerful, though not so dominant that it detracts from the main appearance of the tree. Similarly, if the tree is soft and feminine in appearance, then the stand should have similar features so that it complements and does not overpower the tree. The stand should always be complementary to the tree that is being displayed and should never appear to be the main item in the display; nor should it be of a completely opposing colour or design. If the tree has a simple shape, then the stand should be simple. If the tree is more complex, then a more complicated design may be suitable.

TRADITIONAL BONSAI DISPLAYS

Traditionally, in Japan, bonsai are displayed in a specially designed area called a *tokonoma* or alcove, which can be quite a large construction. It is basically a bench with sides and background within which any object of interest can be displayed. The description given here is very basic, but the finished *tokonoma* must have simple, crisp, clean and elegant features. Most people do not have the space at home to construct this type of alcove display area, and therefore the most likely place to find this type of display will be at a horticultural show, such as the Chelsea Flower Show, or a major exhibition that deals only with bonsai and related subjects.

In Japan, there are many different shapes and sizes of *tokonoma*, depending on their intended use. Some are used in a teahouse and others for displaying such items as

bonsai. The most common version used for bonsai display is called "Kekomi-doko"; it has a wooden floor usually covered with tatami matting and basically looks like a step up from the surrounding normal floor.

Above: *Tree of a thousand stars (Serissa foetida) standing on a cabinet. Ensure that protection for the polished surface is supplied.*

Right: *The variegation of this weeping fig (Ficus benjamina 'Variegata') is picked up by the white of the table on which it is displayed.*

Right: *You can display an outdoor bonsai indoors for a maximum of a day or two as it cannot tolerate indoor conditions for longer.*

Left: *A Podocarpus* bonsai has been displayed on a mantelpiece. This is possible as long as there is not a burning fire beneath it. This would certainly be very dangerous to a bonsai. This type of display situation should only be temporary.

Right: *Several trees have been placed indoors on a long, heavy, timber shelf. This looks rather attractive, but the thickness of the shelf tends to dominate the trees.*

When you are displaying a bonsai in such an alcove or *tokonoma*, it is important that the bonsai is placed on a suitably sympathetic stand or table along with an accent plant, which must also be placed on a suitable stand. In traditional *tokonomas*, there is often a scroll of some description hanging on the back wall. All the items in the display must complement each other. If, however, you are simply displaying a tree for your own enjoyment in your home, then you can place a bonsai on a normal piece of furniture, as long as this does not overpower the appearance of the bonsai specimen.

MODERN BONSAI DISPLAYS

With the advent of more minimalist decor in our interiors, there has been a natural progression into a similarly minimalist style for bonsai planting and displays. So, why not try out some different types of pots, such as glass containers and vases, variously shaped bowls and wooden dishes for

Right: *Sacred bamboo (*Nandina domestica*) growing in a piece of rock. Good light and humidity must be maintained.*

displaying your bonsai? These containers can all be displayed on modern pieces of furniture made of any type of material such as glass or various plastics, but always remember that good light is required for healthy plant growth. Try standing your bonsai on a shelf in a bathroom,

kitchen or sitting room, by all means, but always make sure that any polished wood surfaces are meticulously maintained. An office desk is often used to display a bonsai, but, unless it is near to a window, it will not be very good for the tree because of the low light levels.

SINGLE SPECIMENS AND GROUPS

Whether you have only one tree or many, it is worth making the effort to display your bonsai to best advantage. When showing more than one bonsai in a particular place, try to arrange them so that they complement each other, with pots of varying heights and sizes that are suitably positioned. When displaying several trees in a line, it can be difficult to find a suitable tray for them all, so you may have to find individual trays or dishes on which to stand each tree, as this will be a good way to protect your furniture from damage by water.

BACKDROPS

It is important to use relatively plain backgrounds or backdrops behind bonsai or *penjing* so that you do not detract from the impact of the tree. The tree is always the most important feature at all times and a very busy background may distract the viewer.

Left: Serissa foetida, *tree of a thousand stars, with a bowl of potpourri as an accessory, standing on a polished wood table, which should be protected.*

Above: *Japanese black pine (Pinus thunbergii) placed on a windowsill. As it is an outdoor variety, it can only be kept indoors for one day.*

Outdoor displays

Display stands for bonsai kept outside can be very varied and much more rustic in appearance than stands for indoor bonsai. Whatever style of stand you choose, give the trees the dignity they deserve by placing them on good-quality display units. Do not forget the background that will be behind your collection of trees. If they are displayed in your garden in front of a hedge or other trees, you may not even be able to distinguish them. Try to set them against a fence or even a plain painted wall, so that they can be seen in all their glory. When displaying bonsai against a wall or fence, it is also important not to place the trees too close to the background because the tree will "search" for the best light and grow in one direction away from the background. You should also turn your trees regularly to avoid this problem.

Above: *A purple Japanese maple (Acer palmatum) displayed in front of garden plants will be lost in the background, unless it is backlit, as here.*

OUTDOOR BENCHING AND STANDS

Benches made from timber that has been treated with a plant-safe preservative are ideal. They can be supported on timber stands, legs or even concrete, brick or stone blocks. Reinforced concrete slabs are also suitable if they are available and can be laid across the top of concrete block stands to create a long-lasting display. Remember that most timber has a limited lifespan because it is subjected to all types of weather, so any timber benches will need to be replaced every 5–10 years, depending on how well they have been maintained.

Strong display benching is very important, and it is well worth making sure that the size and weight of any benching used is suitable for the trees to be displayed. The most suitable height at which to display your bonsai trees is approximately eye-level, so that you can look into the trees from just above the level of the pot rim. Remember that if you were viewing a full-size tree, you would be looking at it from just above ground-level, so when viewing a bonsai you must use the same criteria by imagining that you are looking at your trees with the eye of a suitably scaled-down person.

DISPLAYING A LARGE OUTDOOR COLLECTION

If you have a large collection outdoors, then it may not always be possible to provide benching that can be used to display a variety of trees at the correct

Left: *Bonsai should be displayed so that their features can be clearly seen. A split-level stand such as this can be used to display trees of different sizes perfectly.*

Above: *Part of the author's collection of bonsai at Leonardslee Gardens, West Sussex, England, where the trees are on permanent display on a variety of stands.*

height. It may, therefore, be a good idea to vary the height of the stands to suit each tree. Your main aim should be to provide a pleasing overall effect, while allowing easy access for all general maintenance purposes. If you have several large trees, using a table-top that can be rotated will prove to be a considerable advantage because you will need to turn the trees from time to time in order to maintain even growth all round.

Right: *A typical bonsai display belonging to a Japanese bonsai grower, showing heavy timber benches of varying heights. Heavy-duty benches are required if each bench has to support a large number of bonsai.*

Above: *A large, old Japanese white pine (Pinus parviflora) in a garden situation and displayed on timber decking next to a small pool. This situation will help any bonsai by providing it with additional humidity. The deck should always be raised substantially above ground-level to prevent possible damage by animals.*

Left: *Many bonsai nurseries use this type of concrete block-and-timber display bench as a good way of showing off their trees to customers. Each tree should never be too close to its neighbour.*

SUITABLE BACKDROPS

Any bonsai will look its best if it is displayed against a suitable backdrop. On earlier pages, the points that need to be considered when displaying bonsai indoors have been discussed. Most of these are the same for outdoor bonsai, although there are other points that you will also need to consider.

Backgrounds for bonsai are normally made from natural materials such as timber, stone, or other varieties of plant. In the case of timber, the most common is some sort of fence and, if you regard bamboo as a type of timber, then this too can be used to form a flat, fence-style background. If you would like to use a wall as a backdrop for bonsai, then remember that it should

always be very plain so that it is not confused with the tree displayed in front. Indeed, a brick or stone wall may be very distracting behind a bonsai, so it is best to paint it with some pale-coloured paint. Should the wall be of an uneven texture, it may also be necessary to render it to achieve a smooth, uninterrupted surface. When the rendered wall is painted, it will provide an excellent solid backdrop, allowing the bonsai trees to stand out so that their true forms can be truly appreciated.

If there needs to be any form of joint in a fence or wall, then it is preferable for these to run vertically, rather than horizontally. Horizontal lines will detract from the appearance of any

Above: *A beautiful Japanese maple (Acer palmatum) placed on a small table in a private garden. In this instance, the tree is standing in an open position, so that it does not become confused with the background.*

bonsai because they will "cut through" the form of the tree, whereas vertical lines or joints will accentuate the line of the tree.

If you have hedges in your garden, then you will need to position your bonsai specimens so that they are far enough away from the hedges to stand out and be clearly seen. If you place the trees too close to any form of hedge, however, the whole picture will become very confusing and rather uninteresting.

▷

Any background must always be high enough to allow the whole tree to be viewed in front of it and not so short that the top of the fence, wall or hedge simply cuts across the top of the tree.

Backgrounds to a bonsai display can be a very controversial talking-point because what seems acceptable to one person does not always please another. For this reason, it is actually very difficult to define what is good and what is bad as a backdrop. Be prepared to try something new, by all means, but remember that the bonsai tree must remain the most important feature at all times and you should do all you can to ensure that its appearance is never compromised.

OTHER POINTS TO CONSIDER

If you are designing a purpose-built bonsai display area in your garden, then you will need to give careful consideration to the backgrounds so that the correct environmental conditions are achieved for your bonsai specimens. For example, both sides of a wall or fence can be used to provide a background for two different displays

Left: *An 80-year-old Japanese white pine (Pinus parviflora) on an outdoor bench.*

Right: *European olive (Olea europaea) that has been grown as a garden bonsai, although it does not follow the proportional relationship between the plant and the pot, as is customary with traditional bonsai specimens.*

of bonsai, as long as you can ensure that the trees can flourish in the conditions in each area.

Many other accessories, such as lanterns and wind chimes, can be included in an outdoor display, but these should be kept to a minimum. Also ensure that they do not distract the viewer from the bonsai, which should be the main feature.

It is sometimes difficult for people to understand the concept of bonsai as an art, but the most important point to note when you are displaying bonsai of any description is that all backgrounds and accessories must complement the bonsai so that the viewer can appreciate the beauty of this living art form.

Above: *Japanese maple (Acer palmatum) growing in a temporary training pot until its final bonsai form is achieved.*

Above: *Japanese white pine (Pinus parviflora) on a timber stand in front of a painted brick wall that distracts the eye slightly from the bonsai.*

Above: *Japanese white pine (Pinus parviflora) trained as a garden bonsai in a pot that is not normally suitable for a traditional-style bonsai.*

Above: *Chinese juniper (Juniperus chinensis) in an English handmade pot that shows off the cascade styling to perfection.*

Bonsai shows

Many of the best bonsai are in private collections and are rarely seen by members of the public except when they appear at horticultural shows or special bonsai exhibitions and conventions. It is at these special events that the owners of such collections have the opportunity to display their bonsai when they are looking their very best. Such shows and conventions occur in most parts of the world and it is worth attending one of these events to see top-quality bonsai correctly displayed by very experienced bonsai growers and collectors. Most people who exhibit at bonsai shows and competitions are amateur growers who are members of their local bonsai club or society and who may have been growing bonsai for anything from a few months to many decades.

Above: *This Virginia creeper (*Parthenocissus*), with its ivy-like leaves, belongs to a member of Bonsai Kai and is an unusual subject for bonsai.*

One of the most well-known shows at which you can view bonsai is the Royal Horticultural Society's Chelsea Flower Show. This takes place in late May every year in the grounds of the Royal Hospital in London. At this show there are normally about six bonsai exhibits staged by both professional and amateur bonsai growers, as well as bonsai societies.

Below: *General view of a Bonsai Kai members' competition at one of the Royal Horticultural Society's London shows.*

The Chelsea Flower Show is the world's most prestigious horticultural show and normally draws people from most countries around the world. It is considered to be the pinnacle of any grower's life to be invited to exhibit at this show and, to date, the author and his wife have exhibited eighteen times consecutively and been awarded six Gold Medals.

Similar gardening shows, as well as shows devoted purely to the exhibition of bonsai, take place all over the world and are very well patronized by people from all nations. This is because bonsai is such a very absorbing and popular pastime.

When displaying bonsai at a show or exhibition, it is absolutely critical that every piece of equipment involved in the display, including the bonsai tree, is complementary to every other item, such as stands, backdrops, *suiseki*, accent plants and table coverings.

POINTS TO CONSIDER WHEN SHOWING BONSAI

- Your bonsai trees should be correctly trimmed so that they are presented at their very best and do justice to your efforts. Bonsai judges are very meticulous in their observations.

- The pot must be suitable for the tree in terms of design and colour and the pot and tree should be in balance.

- The pot must be thoroughly clean; its appearance can be enhanced by a light application of oil or leaf-shine to the pot's outer surface.

- Foliage on the tree must be clean and free from any type of pest or disease. Check well in advance to be certain of a healthy-looking tree for the show.

- If there is any wire or other shaping aid on a bonsai, it must be unnoticeable when viewed from any angle.

- The soil surface should always look as natural as possible, with moss or other very small ground-cover plants strategically placed. Grit is not recommended as a soil decoration.

Above: *A variety of bonsai on show at a Royal Horticultural Society spring show in London. This club competition is open to all members who are amateur bonsai growers.*

Left: *The author judging the Bonsai Kai bonsai competition at the 2005 spring show organized by the Royal Horticultural Society.*

THE BONSAI YEAR

Throughout the year, bonsai trees can change dramatically in appearance. Some trees, such as junipers and pines, may not look that different from one season to the next, but those that produce prominent flowers and fruit, as well as those that change their foliage colours every season, can be breathtaking to look at. Most trees look different as the seasons pass, but many deciduous trees, such as maples, often develop brilliantly coloured leaves in both spring and autumn. It is this spectacular transformation throughout the seasons that captures the imagination of so many bonsai enthusiasts. Even if you have just one or two flowering or fruiting bonsai, this will certainly make an interesting contribution to your collection.

Above: *The green summer leaves of the Oriental hornbeam* (Carpinus laxiflora).
Left: *This Oriental hornbeam* (Carpinus laxiflora) *group is just beginning to attain its autumn colour. From green summer foliage, it progresses through a mixture of yellow, orange and red.*

Spring

Early spring brings about the first signs of active growth in your trees following their dormant period throughout the winter months. This certainly makes it one of the busiest times in the bonsai year. In the northern hemisphere, spring encompasses the months of March, April and May whereas, in the southern hemisphere, spring covers September, October and November. In real terms, this means that the work which needs to be carried out in spring varies by six months over the two areas of the world. It is important to make sure that all necessary procedures for this period of the year are carried out so that the health of your bonsai is not compromised. General housekeeping tasks, such as watering and feeding trees, as well as maintaining the cleanliness of trees and pots, are all necessary in spring.

Above: *A relatively young Japanese crab apple (*Malus floribunda*) with delicate spring flowers. These become small fruits in autumn.*

SPRING CARE

Most deciduous trees should have been repotted in late winter, but, if there are a few still to be done at this time of year, then they must be dealt with as soon as possible. Any sign of hard frosts means that freshly repotted trees may need to be provided with some form of protection. You can easily do this by placing your bonsai in a garden shed or perhaps a cold greenhouse or cool conservatory (sun room) until the threat of frosts is over. Just before the buds break, any repotting required should be done, so make sure that you have everything prepared in order to repot your bonsai when the time is right.

Some pruning can be carried out now because this is by far the best time of the year for tidying up both deciduous and coniferous trees. In the case of deciduous trees, it is easy to see any twigs or branches that have died back or need removing just before the buds burst. So, trees should be trimmed now so that they start the year in good shape. When the shoots begin to extend, cut them back to one pair of leaves in order to maintain a compact growth pattern.

Wire for shaping can be applied now to conifers, such as pines (*Pinus*) and junipers (*Juniperus*), but preferably not to deciduous trees. These should not be wired until a little later in the year when the sap is flowing freely because they will be more flexible if branch bending is required. Monitor any wire on trees at all times of the year; it can be surprising how quickly the branches swell. Remove any wire that appears to be cutting into the bark.

Left: Acer palmatum *'Deshojo' with its late-spring leaf colouring, which fades from pink at bud-break to bronze in the summer.*

Fertilizer must never be applied to recently repotted and/or root-pruned trees because this can easily result in severe damage to the roots that were pruned during the repotting process or to very young, freshly growing roots.

Watering should be of a moderate nature and only when it is required, but it will be necessary to increase the amount of water as the weather begins to warm up with the approach of summer. Freshly potted trees must also never be over-watered because they can easily become waterlogged. This is because freshly pruned roots do not take up moisture until the new young roots begin to develop.

BONSAI FEATURES IN SPRING

Spring is a very colourful and vibrant time of the year for bonsai, and for plants in general for that matter, so you should make the most of the huge variety of fresh and beautiful colours both of foliage and of any blossom that may appear.

Foliage colours in spring can vary from brilliant pink to bright yellow or green and almost any other colour variation that you can imagine. The really brilliant colours are normally courtesy of deciduous trees because conifers and evergreen plants are generally not so colourful at this time of year. Japanese maples (*Acer palmatum*) will produce some of the most spectacular spring leaf colours with such a wide range of colours available that it would be impossible to classify them all here.

The leaf forms of the spring growth of this type of plant are also very varied. As the leaves unfurl, they present a multitude of shapes that cannot be easily matched by any other variety of tree used for bonsai culture.

Flowers are another very important and colourful aspect of spring within the bonsai world. There are many different species of plant suited to bonsai growing that will produce flowers of many different shapes and

Above: *This* Acer palmatum *'Deshojo', with its brilliant pink colouring, will draw admiring comments throughout early spring.*

Left: Prunus incisa *'Kojo-no-mai' in mid-spring showing its delicate flowers that are closely followed by the fresh new leaves.*

colours. The size of blossom on bonsai is crucial to the overall look of the tree, so it is necessary to research the eventual size of the flowers before you embark on a bonsai that will produce flowers.

Most flowers are too large in proportion to the plant when grown in a miniature form such as that encountered with bonsai. Look out for small-flowered plants, such as crab apple (*Malus*) and flowering cherry

Below: *Informal upright Japanese crab apple* (*Malus floribunda*) *in mid-spring with an abundance of white flowers.*

(*Prunus*), which will give a balanced feel when the plant actually produces its flowers. It is also important that you do not forget that many flowering plants will also go on to develop fruit later in the year. The size of any eventual fruit on the bonsai specimen must also be taken into account when you are choosing a plant from which to create and style a bonsai.

Whatever aspect of your bonsai is important in spring, it must always be considered for its balance relating to the size of the tree, as well as the size, shape and colour of any flowers that may develop.

SEASONAL FEATURE PLANT: WISTERIA

Wisteria, when it is grown naturally to its full size as a climber, is perhaps one of the most spectacular hardy plants in the world. When it is used in an open garden or decorative situation, wisteria is normally seen growing against a garden wall or fence, or even cladding the side of a house.

Wisteria is native to China and Japan and can provide some of the most spectacular spring floral displays in its native habitat or in a garden. The flowers consist of long, pendulous racemes of fragrant, pea-like flowers that hang in dense clusters, giving the plants a weeping appearance. The flowers, which appear in late spring and early summer, vary in colour from white and mauve through to blue and are often at their best when the new leaves are just beginning to break behind them. This provides a breathtaking and stunning start to the garden year and should you be lucky enough to own a bonsai version it will give your collection a much-needed boost of spectacular colour. Wisteria flowers also have the added bonus of a deliciously intoxicating scent.

Because of its pendulous appearance when it is in flower, the wisteria is usually grown as a weeping-style tree. The racemes of flowers, depending on the variety, can be from as little as 10cm (4in) to as much as 1m (40in) in length, with the longer ones being preferred for a weeping-style bonsai.

Because of their long flower formation, wisteria are best grown as informal upright, slanting, weeping, semi-cascade and cascade-style bonsai. They are also normally grown as fairly large specimens because of the size and scale of the flowers.

Bonsai wisteria need protection from frost in the winter as they have rather thick, succulent-like roots that can be very easily damaged if the temperature drops below about

Right: *Wisteria make beautiful bonsai, but only for a few weeks in late spring. The racemes of flowers can be white, pink or various shades of blue, depending upon the variety.*

-5°C (23°F). During the summer months, a wisteria bonsai will need copious amounts of water and, during the really warm parts of the summer, it is advisable to stand the pot in a shallow tray of water so that the plant has a continuous supply of water throughout this hot period. It is most important that wisteria bonsai are never allowed to dry out completely. This is, of course, a rule that applies to all bonsai, although some species can tolerate a certain amount of dryness. However, in general, allowing a bonsai to dry out can quickly result in its death.

You will need to feed your wisteria bonsai about once a week following flowering until midsummer, commencing again in early autumn through to late autumn. Repot wisteria bonsai every two to three years and prune back to two buds following flowering in the summer, as well as in the autumn.

To obtain good flowering plants, propagation should be carried out using hardwood cuttings or grafting in early spring or by air layering from late spring to early summer using the techniques described in the appropriate section of this book. Propagation from seed produces plants very quickly, but they do require anything from seven to ten years to produce flowers whereas the other propagation methods should produce flowers the following year.

KEY TASKS FOR SPRING

ROOT PRUNING AND REPOTTING

- Root-prune and repot any deciduous trees as soon as possible, although most should have been done in late winter. Make sure that all repotting is done before the buds break.

- Never apply fertilizer to recently root-pruned and repotted trees, as this could damage roots pruned during the repotting process.

- Protect freshly repotted trees by placing them in a shed or unheated greenhouse until all threat of frost has passed.

PRUNING

- Tidy up deciduous and coniferous trees. With deciduous trees, it is easy to see twigs or branches that have died back or need removing before the buds burst. Trimming them now means they start the year in good shape. When shoots begin to extend, cut back to one pair of leaves to maintain compact growth. With some conifers, such as juniper (*Juniperus*) or larch (*Larix*), pinch out any new soft shoot tips. This encourages more shoots to grow and the process can be repeated. With pines (*Pinus*), pinch back new candles by about two-thirds when they reach about 2.5cm (1in).

WIRING

- Apply the wire for shaping to conifers such as pine (*Pinus*) and juniper (*Juniperus*), but preferably not to deciduous trees. These should not be wired until a little later in the year when the sap is flowing freely. This means that the trees will be more flexible if the branches need to be bent during the shaping process.

WATERING

- Water moderately when required, increasing the amount as the weather warms up, but never over-water freshly repotted trees.

Summer

June, July and August constitute the summer months in the northern hemisphere, whereas in the southern hemisphere, summer is the period that includes December, January and February. All repotting should have been finished by the beginning of the summer. If you have trees in your collection that require a different pot for display purposes only, then it is possible to remove them carefully and plant them in a more suitably sized pot. Do not seriously disturb the roots; simply loosen them slightly and place the bonsai in its new pot, filling in the gaps with fresh soil. It is not advisable to repot any trees during the summer months, but, if this is necessary, then careful consideration of the placement and care of the trees is very important immediately following repotting.

Above: Acer palmatum *showing the colour variation that appears on the leaves as a result of stronger sunlight. The balance would improve if the lower right branch were removed.*

SUMMER CARE

Most trees should be growing at their maximum rate at this time of the year and any rapidly extending shoots will need to be pruned, trimmed or thinned on a regular basis. Deciduous trees will need their shoots cut back to one or two pairs of leaves and the buds on conifers should be carefully plucked out as they begin to swell and extend. The use of wire for training purposes can be brought into the equation now and applied to most species of tree at this time of year. However, it is vital that you always remember to keep a close watch on wire that was applied earlier in the season and remove any that appears to be cutting into the tree or if you think the branch or trunk has already become set in its required position. If, after removing any wire, you find that the branch or trunk springs back towards its original position, then you will need to rewire for a few more weeks or months.

Watering daily is required as the weather gets warmer. If it becomes very hot, then watering may be needed more than once each day and extra care should be taken of very small trees. At all times, the condition of the soil needs to be monitored and the bonsai watered if required.

When there is a sudden burst of torrential rain, your trees will not necessarily have gained sufficient water. Trees with a heavy foliage canopy can shed rain rather like an umbrella, so water beneath the canopy directly on to the soil.

Feeding is also very important at this time of the year and most trees will need to be fed throughout the summer months, making sure that you lower the amount of nitrogen applied as you progress from late summer into the autumn.

Left: *Japanese hornbeam (Carpinus laxiflora) in full foliage which will remain rich green in colour throughout the summer. Note the close proximity of the trunks in this group.*

Above: *This Japanese maple (Acer palmatum) is displaying its beautiful summer colouring. Maples undergo many colour changes through the year.*

BONSAI FEATURES IN SUMMER

This is an interesting time in the bonsai calendar, with many unusual trees making an appearance. You can, for example, create stunning bonsai from fruiting plants such as kumquats and olive trees (*Olea europaea*). Flowering bonsai include fuchsias, while the summer foliage of more traditional bonsai can also provide a burst of colour, including the fresh green Japanese hornbeam (*Carpinus laxiflora*) and the beautiful colour variations of certain varieties of Japanese maple (*Acer palmatum*).

SEASONAL FEATURE PLANT: RHODODENDRON

This genus includes some of the most spectacular varieties of flowering plant. Azaleas fall within this genus and, contrary to popular opinion, there is no botanical difference between azaleas and rhododendrons. A large number of species originate in Japan and many named varieties are now available. Their hybridization and propagation has been taking place in Japan over the last four centuries with the evergreen Satsuki azaleas being the most popular. These have a wide range of flower sizes and colours. The Kirishima or Kurume azaleas also make beautiful bonsai and have smaller blooms than the Satsuki, which makes their proportions appear much more in keeping with bonsai sizes.

Rhododendrons can be trained into most bonsai styles, except broom, and of course the larger-flowered varieties are more suitable for larger bonsai. Those with smaller flowers are generally grown as small bonsai, but when grown as large bonsai they will appear to be much more in proportion.

These plants are acid-loving, needing an ericaceous compost (acid soil mix) for the best results and watering with rainwater in areas with a hard water supply. Protect them from heavy rain

Above: *A small* Rhododendron *bonsai with pale pink, double flowers. This bonsai has a very chunky trunk and has been placed in a* similarly rugged-looking pot. This tree has been developed from the stump of a very much larger plant.

▷

when in flower as the blooms damage easily. Remove the new shoots after flowering. Give a lighter shoot prune in midsummer to encourage new flower buds for the following spring.

Rhododendrons need repotting and root pruning once the flowers have dropped. There will be few repotting problems as they have a compact, fine, fibrous root system. Keep them in partial shade, giving little water in winter, and feeding fortnightly in spring, leading up to the flowering period.

Rhododendrons can be propagated either by air layering or softwood cuttings in early summer and quickly produce vigorous new roots. A good way to obtain a *Rhododendron* bonsai is to find an old plant in the garden, prune it hard back to the main trunk, lift it from the ground and pot it into a temporary container. Once re-established, it quickly puts on new growth that can be selectively pruned to produce a good bonsai in two or three years and a very good bonsai in ten years.

SEASONAL FEATURE PLANT: FUCHSIA

As the interest in using hardy, woody, shrubby perennials for bonsai increases, plants such as fuchsias have been found to exhibit good woody growth that eventually develops into a mature, tree-like form given the correct pruning and shaping.

A very common method of growing fuchsias is with a tall straight stem, supported by a cane. Side shoots are continually pinched off until a tall,

GROWING A BONSAI FUCHSIA

1 Remove the plant from its pot and tease the potting compost (soil mix) from around the roots of the plant using a fork or rake.

2 Using a sharp pair of scissors or secateurs (pruners), carefully cut away approximately two-thirds of the roots.

3 Cut down a plastic flowerpot to leave a small, low pot that will provide a temporary training pot for the fuchsia.

4 Repot the fuchsia, holding the plant upright and trickling charcoal-rich, gritty potting compost around the roots.

5 Gently firm down the potting compost, using a stick to ensure that all the spaces are filled. Water the fuchsia.

Above: *This young bonsai fuchsia is clearly in the early stages of shaping and styling, and there is further work to be done. If you want to* encourage a "windswept" growth form, then you can lay the plant on its side or at an angle for a couple of weeks.

thick stem is produced, before finally pinching out the lead shoot to encourage a twiggy, branched canopy of blooms.

The training of fuchsia bonsai is very similar to this procedure in that some side shoots are removed leaving a few selected shoots in suitable positions so as to form a tree-like trunk and branch structure.

Fuchsias are indigenous to South and Central America and are therefore not totally hardy in a temperate climate, although a few varieties are able to withstand some degree of frost.

To avoid die-back of the trunk and branch structure, growth must be maintained throughout the winter months and this can be achieved by making sure that the plant retains its foliage throughout the colder part of the year. It is therefore recommended that fuchsia bonsai be given winter protection where the temperature remains below 6–7°C (43–45°F).

As with other flowering bonsai, varieties with small leaves and flowers are preferred because they create a

lifelike and balanced specimen. In the same way as the chrysanthemum, fuchsia bonsai can be trained in all the usual bonsai styles with informal upright and cascade being two of the most frequently grown forms. Most shaping and styling can be achieved by pruning to shape rather than using wire because fuchsias are capable of developing compact, twiggy structures by constant pruning of the shoot tips. At all times, remember that the flowers normally appear from the tip of the shoots and, therefore, as the flowering

Left: Fuchsias are becoming increasingly popular as subjects for pruning and shaping into highly decorative bonsai.

season approaches, care should be taken not to remove any forming flower buds.

When in bloom, fuchsia bonsai can be spectacular, being covered in brightly coloured, pendulous flowers that last many weeks before sometimes developing richly coloured seed pods. As with any bonsai that produces fruit or seed pods, it is not advisable to allow too many to remain on the plant as it can overpower the appearance and overtax the strength of the tree.

The normal method of propagation is by softwood or semi-ripe cuttings taken from the parent plant in mid-summer. These should be inserted into good-quality cuttings compost (soil mix) and kept in a slightly shaded place until the first signs of growth are observed. The cuttings can then be moved to larger pots to establish a good root structure and initial top growth.

KEY TASKS FOR SUMMER

ROOT PRUNING AND REPOTTING
• All root pruning and repotting should have been finished by the beginning of the summer, but if there is a tree that seems to be too large for its pot, just repot it without pruning the roots at all. Avoid seriously disturbing the roots by just loosening them slightly, then place the tree in its new pot and fill the gaps with fresh soil.

PRUNING
• Prune, trim or thin rapidly extending shoots of your bonsai regularly, as most trees should be growing at their maximum rate at this time of year.

• Cut the shoots of deciduous trees back to one or two pairs of leaves, and carefully pluck out buds on conifers as they begin to swell and extend.

WIRING
• Most species of tree can be trained by wiring at this time of year, but keep a close watch on any wire you have already applied and remove any that appears to be cutting into a tree.

• Remove any training wires if you think a branch or trunk has already become set in its required position. If, after removing any wire, you find that the branch or trunk springs back toward its original position, you will need to rewire for a few more weeks or months.

WATERING
• Water regularly as the weather gets warmer, and every day should it become hot. You may need to water more than once each day if the temperature becomes very hot.

• Take special care if your trees are small and in very small pots.

• In all cases, keep a very close watch and monitor the soil regularly, watering if it begins to dry out. Do not be fooled into thinking that a sudden burst of torrential rain will provide your trees with sufficient water.

• Some trees have a heavy foliage canopy that can shed rain just like an umbrella, so be vigilant and water beneath the canopy and on to the soil.

FEEDING
• This is an important time of year for feeding and most trees will need to be fed throughout the summer. Ensure you lower the amount of nitrogen applied as late summer passes into autumn.

Autumn

A northern hemisphere autumn covers the months of September, October and November and a southern hemisphere autumn takes place in March, April and May. The rate of growth in most plants begins to slow down in early autumn, dropping off to almost nothing by late autumn. Deciduous leaves will change colour and eventually fall, leaving the trees bare during winter. The inner leaves will be the first to fall, as these were the earliest to develop, leaving those on the ends of the branches to fall last. Some conifers change foliage colour for the winter, so do not think that some of your trees may be dying – they are just acquiring their autumn colours. Root growth will slow right down, and any buds that have already formed for the following year will harden up with the colder weather to prepare for winter.

Above: *An informal-upright Japanese holly (*Ilex crenata*) with the bright red berries that remain on the tree from autumn to winter.*

AUTUMN CARE

You can continue pruning pines (*Pinus*) and junipers (*Juniperus*), but avoid pruning deciduous trees in early autumn, as this can induce a spurt of new growth that can be damaged by early frost. When growth has stopped, the pruning or trimming of shoots is not necessary, with the exception of some conifers like junipers and cryptomerias. The shoot tips of some species can be pinched out one last time before winter sets in.

Wiring is not generally necessary in autumn, but if some conifers like pines still need to retain their wire, you must keep a close watch on them as they often produce a late burst of growth and may well suffer serious damage from wire that has been inadvertently left in place. Should this appear to be happening, the wire must be removed as soon as possible.

Do not apply wire in late autumn; in fact, it is more beneficial to remove it, allowing your trees to have a rest during the colder winter months.

With the cooling of the weather, the need to water will drop almost completely away as the trees are going into a temporary dormancy. Look at and check the condition of the soil daily and apply water sparingly if required. When deciduous trees have shed their leaves, they will need very little water as transpiration through the leaves will have ceased, but remember that very strong, cold winds can dry the soil just as quickly, if not quicker, than strong sun, so you may need to protect conifers that retain

their foliage by placing them under cover. Two applications of nitrogen-free fertilizer should be given to most trees in the autumn to harden off the current year's growth. One should be applied in mid-autumn. This is an excellent way of helping to protect your trees in winter.

Left: *A spectacular* Acer palmatum *specimen, displaying the brilliant red leaves that are such an important feature of any display during the autumn.*

Above: *Autumn colour varies tremendously with species and variety, and this Japanese grey bark elm (*Zelkova serrata*) has beautiful golden-yellow foliage at this time of year.*

BONSAI FEATURES IN AUTUMN

This is one of the most colourful periods in the bonsai year, with many trees going through stunning colour changes. The Japanese grey bark elm (*Zelkova serrata*), for example, has golden foliage in the autumn, while Japanese maples (*Acer palmatum*) can be relied upon to provide a stunning display of colour. Early berries are also a feature of autumn, with the bright red berries of the Japanese holly (*Ilex serrata*) making a welcome appearance.

SEASONAL PLANT FEATURE: CHRYSANTHEMUM

Growing chrysanthemum as bonsai is relatively recent. It has become popular in Japan over the past three centuries and is beginning to gain a foothold worldwide. This form of bonsai-growing is a little quicker than normal in that the finished product can be achieved in a reasonably short time. It can, however, take much longer than this to create a mature-looking tree.

The art of producing any bonsai relies on the plant producing a woody trunk and branch structure that looks very old. In the case of a chrysanthemum, the plant should develop the mature characteristics, such as roots, trunks and branches, within the first year of training.

Being a perennial flowering plant, it produces blooms each year and, as with any other flowering bonsai, you need to choose varieties that produce small, compact flowers. Over several hundred years of chrysanthemum cultivation, many miniature flowering forms with characteristics suitable for bonsai have been developed. These include short internodal growth, compact habit, multi-branching habit, strong root and trunk growth, and the all-important profusion of long-lasting blooms on very short stems.

Chrysanthemum varieties for this type of culture should also have very pliable young growth that allows for easy manipulation and styling into tree forms.

Above: *Japanese hornbeam* (Carpinus laxiflora) *planted in a group and displaying its initial autumn colour of yellow progressing through to brilliant red. This group holds its changing coloured foliage for many weeks.*

Left: *This is a root-over-rock* Chrysanthemum, *showing how the roots cling to the rock. The rocks are normally soft building blocks that are easily carved into any shape with grooves to accommodate the roots.* ▷

Developing a chrysanthemum for bonsai is no more difficult than using any other type of material as the techniques involved are the same as those already described. Using techniques such as wiring, pruning and pinching could well produce an acceptable result in between ten and fifteen months, depending on the skill and vision of the grower.

As the chrysanthemum tends to grow quicker than any other tree or shrub, it is possible to make changes or correct mistakes that will improve the overall appearance of your chrysanthemum bonsai. As it takes relatively little time to produce an attractively shaped bonsai, it need not be a massive disaster if the odd failure occurs as a new plant can be formed fairly easily.

Flowers can vary in colour from pure white through yellow and orange to pink and red. Continual pinching out of the shoots will produce densely flowering pads of colour, which will last for anything up to two months.

Chrysanthemum can be trained in all the usual bonsai styles and make spectacular displays throughout mid-

and late autumn each year. The chosen plants should be of the hardy varieties and kept outside for as long as possible, placed under cover for protection in the most severe winter conditions.

Propagation is normally carried out using cuttings or stolon growth. The use of cuttings is very popular for propagating chrysanthemum as many plants can be produced from a single stock plant. Cuttings should be approximately 7.5–10cm (3–4in) in

Left: Chrysanthemum *plants trained over artificial rock make for a very natural root-over-rock display.*

length with five or six leaves. The lower two leaves should be removed before the cutting is inserted into the cuttings compost (soil mix).

Stolons are shoots that emerge from the crown of the root system of a mature plant and can develop either just above or just below the soil surface. Propagation from stolon growth generally provides a more vigorous plant and is more suited to much larger styles of *Chrysanthemum* culture. Like normal cuttings, these are carefully removed from the parent plant using a sharp knife or scalpel and inserted into a good-quality rooting compost as with cuttings.

SEASONAL FEATURE PLANT: CRAB APPLE (*MALUS*)

The crab apple is a popular plant that can be styled into a most attractive flowering and fruiting bonsai. Remember that the smaller flowering and fruiting varieties are most suitable for bonsai, so that the correct balance

Right: *Large* Chrysanthemum *bonsai created from a piece of dead tree stump with flexible-stemmed* Chrysanthemum *plants being trained up the rear and into the branch structure to create an impressive exhibit.*

Above: *The apex of a crab apple bonsai with fairly well-proportioned fruits.*

Left: *Very attractive Nagasaki crab (Malus cerasifera) with individual fruits showing various colours as they mature.*

between tree size, foliage, flower and fruit is maintained through the year. One of the most common varieties used for bonsai work is *Malus cerasifera*, or the Nagasaki crab, as it produces both dense foliage and masses of compact clusters of flowers, followed by reasonably small fruits.

The crab apple is normally grown as an informal upright bonsai that often resembles a full-size apple tree, only in miniature, but other styles can be successfully created if desired.

Some varieties have relatively smooth bark, while others may develop a knobbly, gnarled bark structure. As with any tree with a smooth bark, extreme care must be taken to avoid damage as a result of any wiring used in the training process.

Most varieties of *Malus* are totally hardy, but when grown as bonsai in shallow pots, they may require some light winter protection for their slightly tender, succulent roots. With full-size trees growing naturally in the

ground, these roots would normally be below the frost level in the soil and the plants would therefore be considered hardy.

As *Malus* produce a prolific number of fibrous roots, plants should be repotted every year in spring before the flower buds begin to break. The soil, as with most bonsai, should be an open, gritty, free-draining compost (soil mix) that allows good fibrous root development, which in turn will result in a strong, healthy flowering plant.

KEY TASKS FOR AUTUMN

PRUNING

• Prune pines (*Pinus*) and junipers (*Juniperus*).

• Avoid pruning the deciduous trees in your collection in the early autumn because this could induce a sudden spurt of new growth, which could be severely damaged by an early frost.

• Once all plant growth has stopped in the autumn, no more pruning or trimming will be necessary, except perhaps of some conifers, such as junipers and cryptomeria.

• Pinch out the shoot tips of some species one last time before the winter.

WIRING

• Look out for wiring on some of your conifers such as pines which often produce a late burst of growth and may be damaged by wire left in place. Remove the wire as soon as possible. Generally speaking, it is beneficial to remove any wiring to give your trees a rest during the colder winter months.

WATERING

• Assess the condition of the soil daily and apply water sparingly if this is required. Deciduous trees will need almost no water, but conifers that retain their foliage are vulnerable to strong, cold winds, so place them under cover for protection.

FEEDING

• Give two applications of nitrogen-free fertilizer to most trees in late autumn to harden off the current year's growth. and to protect your trees through the winter months.

REMOVING DEAD LEAVES

• Pick up any leaves that fall on the soil surface, the surrounding display benches and the ground below.

• Regularly remove all dead leaves that become trapped in the branches.

• Keep the trunks and branches of all your trees clean and free of all algae and moss.

Winter

The winter months cover December, January and February in the northern hemisphere and June, July and August in the southern hemisphere. It is a quiet time for your bonsai, but there will still be some general maintenance required and, unless you live in a reasonably mild area, you will need to protect your trees from severe weather. Do not, however, over-protect hardy varieties that would normally survive well in your area. Winter is a time to study trees that have lost their leaves and assess their structure with a view to deciding what can be done to improve them. It is not advisable to carry out severe pruning, however: leave this until early spring when the wounds will heal quicker. Conifers and any other evergreens will need to have old, dead internal foliage removed to allow light and air to penetrate.

Above: *Looking at this Acer palmatum 'Deshojo' in winter allows the true form to be seen and it is now that any structural changes which may be required can be identified.*

WINTER CARE

Wiring and pruning should not be carried out in early winter. However, at a time when deciduous trees have dropped all their leaves, it is a good idea to look closely at the form of all your bonsai trees with a view to making an assessment of which branches may need to be pruned or adjusted in the early part of the following spring. Assess whether branches or trunks need to be reshaped or if any major or minor branches need to be removed altogether in order to improve the overall appearance of the tree.

Bonsai trees left out in the open will not need watering from mid-autumn through to late winter because they should receive enough water from dew, mist, rain, and even snow. However, bonsai need to be monitored at all times to check on the moisture levels around their roots. Should any appear dry, then it is advisable to give them a splash of water in order to maintain a "just-moist" situation in the soil. If they become too wet, they can be placed under cover, but you should still ensure that they are open to all atmospheric conditions except rain until they dry out a little. A good tip is to prop up one end of the pots of your bonsai with a brick or something similar so that they are tilted to one side. Any excess water will then quickly drain away, returning the root system again to that "just-moist" situation that will ensure a healthy tree throughout the winter.

Left: *The pale bark of this Japanese beech (Fagus crenata) looks striking in winter. It has been recently pruned and rewired.*

Right: *Korean hornbeam (Carpinus laxiflora) following the shedding of its foliage gives a very good view of the excellent structural form of the tree.*

Some bonsai growers always tilt all their trees throughout the winter months and place as many deciduous trees under rain protection as possible.

Hardy bonsai will come to no harm if they become covered with a blanket of snow; it will actually keep the root-ball (roots) at a more even temperature. However, if there is a heavy snowfall where large amounts of snow collect on bonsai branches, then it is always advisable to knock the snow away so that its weight cannot damage the branches in any way.

Preparations for the onset of spring will need to be made during the winter. Start by sourcing any new pots that may be required, along with new soil and all accessories such as grit, wire, tools and anything that you think may be useful for the coming new bonsai season. All of these items may

be needed when you begin repotting in early spring, so make sure you have all the materials you may require. Sift and mix the necessary soils, grit and humus so that repotting can be started in late winter, but always be careful to protect freshly potted trees from frost.

Outdoor bonsai can be very attractive in their winter form and make an excellent short-term indoor display, as long as you remember that they can be indoors for only a very short time and then only where the temperature is fairly low in a room with an airy atmosphere.

Tropical or subtropical trees are better suited for indoor use during the winter and they will need warmer and more humid conditions than their outdoor counterparts.

Left: *During the winter Japanese beech (Fagus crenata) can retain their leaves in a bronze form and these will need removing in the spring if they do not fall naturally.* ▷

Right: This is the attractive winter form of a Japanese maple (Acer palmatum). Its broom style clearly shows in its winter silhouette. Bonsai can be attractive all-year-round.

YOUR BONSAI IN WINTER

Winter is the ideal time to sit and study your trees because there will be little or no apparent activity. Trees, of course, do not stand still and there will always be something happening over the winter period in readiness for the new season. It is important to understand exactly what happens during a tree's so-called dormant period. For example, buds will be setting and the roots settling down and getting ready to leap into action when temperatures begin to rise in early spring.

The autumn application of a low- or zero-nitrogen fertilizer will have begun to do its work in the preparation of both roots and buds. It will have helped to harden up the previous year's growth and will therefore take the trees through the winter months without too much stress caused by any very cold weather.

During this time, you will be able to take stock of the individual style and structure of each tree, especially the deciduous trees that have shed their leaves. Now is the time to decide which, if any, branches will need to be adjusted or removed. However, you will probably carry out the most severe pruning in early spring as the healing rate of wounds is much greater in spring than winter. The growth rate of all your trees will have slowed down, so callousing of wounds will not take place and the risk of infections leading to decay within the tree's structure will be higher than in spring.

KEY TASKS FOR WINTER

PLANNING WIRING AND PRUNING

- Do not carry out wiring and pruning in early winter, but this is a good time to look closely at the form of all bonsai trees, now that deciduous trees have dropped all their leaves. You can then make an assessment of which branches may need to be pruned or adjusted in the early part of the following spring.

WATERING

- Bonsai trees that are kept out in the open should not need watering, as they should receive enough water from dew, mist and rain. You should, however, give them a splash of water if they become dry. If they become too wet, place them under cover, in the open, until they dry out a little.

- Prop up one end of your bonsai pots so that they are tilted; any excess water will then quickly drain away.

OUTDOOR CARE

- Hardy bonsai will come to no harm if they are covered with a blanket of snow; in fact, it will keep the root-ball (roots) at a more even temperature. Remove heavy snow from any branches, however, as the weight could damage them.

ROOT PRUNING AND REPOTTING

- Prepare for the onset of the spring now by sourcing any suitable new pots and containers that may be required, along with sufficient new soil for the root pruning and repotting processes that need to take place during the following year.

- Sift and mix the necessary soil ingredients, and make sure you have everything you need before starting work on any deciduous trees that need this treatment. Be careful to protect any freshly root-pruned and repotted trees from frost.

SEASONAL PLANT: FLOWERING HAZEL (*HAMAMELIS*)

Flowering bonsai specimens, such as hazel (*Hamamelis* x *intermedia*) are very popular, but the choice of plant needs to be considered very carefully because not every flowering or fruiting tree or shrub is suitable for bonsai.

It is important to know that when you are applying the normal techniques used for bonsai training, the foliage usually tends to decrease in size with age. It is equally important to remember that, unlike the foliage, neither the flowers nor the fruit of any plant will reduce in size due to any type of pruning or any other bonsai technique. It is therefore absolutely

essential that you select trees that have naturally small flowers and fruit and which will be in proportion to the size of bonsai that you are growing. Care should also be taken to ensure that the growth which will bear the flowers is not pruned off before it blooms.

Hamamelis is now available in many varieties which produce autumn leaf colours ranging from yellow, orange and red, and flowers in brillant yellow, orange and rusty red.

Left: *Hardy* Hamamelis *x* intermedia *showing the highly attractive flower formations covered with ice. It would be preferable to remove any snow from the branches before it freezes into an ice block.*

STYLING A FLOWERING HAZEL (*HAMAMELIS* × *INTERMEDIA*)

1 The unpruned plant has a nice even shape, making it a suitable subject. Remove any inward-growing branches with scissors.

2 Using a pair of side cutters, prune out the very long top growth from the plant.

3 Scrape away the soil with a rake to see where the roots begin to flare out. This will ensure the best blend of trunk to soil surface.

4 Place the tree in a prepared pot and secure in place with wire.

Above: *The finished tree is potted up in a cream glazed pot, which blends with, but does not detract from, the impact of the flowers. Given several years of pruning and shaping, the structure of this tree will improve dramatically.*

BONSAI
DIRECTORY

This section provides a comprehensive list of plants that can be trained and styled into bonsai. This is a guide only as there are many other plants that are suitable; in fact, almost any plant that produces a woody main stem will have characteristics that are suitable for bonsai growing. For many of the plants described, there is a photograph of the typical foliage shape and colour, as well as descriptions of the texture of the bark and the colour of the flowers and fruit where applicable. The styles of bonsai to which the plant is most suited are given where relevant, as is a recommendation of the preferred size for the bonsai, which will depend upon the characteristics of each plant. The details provided on each plant also include its country of origin and the environmental conditions in which the plant should be grown.

Above: *The evergreen Jade tree (*Crassula arborescens*)*
should be grown indoors; the soft, bulbous leaves are
attractive to behold.
Left: *The beautiful late spring appearance of an* Acer
palmatum *'Deshojo'. This shows every detail of a most*
attractively foliated plant highly suited to bonsai culture.

A to Z of bonsai plants

Acer buergerianum
Trident or Three-lobed maple

Smooth-barked deciduous tree, eventually producing flaking bark that exposes attractive red-orange patches. Leaves are dark green, paler underneath and three-lobed, turning red, orange or yellow in autumn. An excellent plant for bonsai as it responds well to hard pruning, resulting in a dense, twiggy growth pattern. Slightly tender in winter as it produces rather fleshy roots, but it should not require much winter protection if it is grown in good, open, granular soil.

Country of origin Japan and Eastern China
Suitable bonsai styles Informal upright, slanting, twin trunk, group, root-over-rock
Environmental conditions Hardy in temperate climates; slight protection required below -5°C (23°F). Z5–9

Acer palmatum
Japanese maple

Deciduous tree growing to about 8m (25ft) in the wild. This is one of the most popular and easy-to-grow plants for bonsai culture. The leaves are bright green with paler undersides, have five to seven deeply divided lobes and turn red in autumn. There are hundreds of cultivars of Japanese, European and American origin, some of which are listed separately in this plant directory. Other good cultivars

Acer palmatum

Acer buergerianum

include 'Osakazuki' (with brilliant red leaves in autumn) and 'Senkaki' (which has bright coral-pink young shoots in the winter). They are all hardy and need protection only in the most severe conditions.

Country of origin Japan and Central China
Suitable bonsai styles Informal upright, slanting, cascade, twin trunk, group, root-over-rock
Environmental conditions Hardy outdoors in temperate climates. Z5–8

Acer palmatum 'Deshojo'
Japanese maple

This is one of the most popular cultivars of *Acer palmatum* and is a deciduous tree that has bright carmine-red leaves in the very early stages of spring. The five-lobed leaves develop into rich red at the start of summer, changing to red/green in late summer and brilliant red in autumn. The red leaf colour will be retained for a longer period if the bonsai is kept in very good light conditions for as long as possible.

Country of origin Japan
Suitable bonsai styles Informal upright, slanting, cascade, twin trunk, group, root-over-rock
Environmental conditions Hardy outdoors in temperate climates. Z5–8

Acer palmatum 'Kamagata'

Acer palmatum 'Kamagata'
Dwarf Japanese maple

A dwarf deciduous cultivar with mainly five-lobed, sometimes only three-lobed, green leaves edged in rich or rusty red in spring, changing to brilliant light green in summer. Autumn colours range from yellow to orange and sometimes red, and remain on the tree into late autumn.

Country of origin Japan
Suitable bonsai styles Informal upright, group
Environmental conditions Hardy outdoors in temperate climates. Z5–8

Right: *Acer palmatum*

Acer palmatum 'Deshojo'

Acer palmatum 'Kiyohime'
Dwarf Japanese maple
A dwarf cultivar of *Acer palmatum* of low, compact, spreading habit with small, five-lobed, green leaves edged with orange-red in spring, changing to rich green in summer, and then yellow, orange and red in autumn. This is one of the earliest deciduous trees to break bud in spring and one of the last to drop its leaves in the autumn.
Country of origin Japan
Suitable bonsai styles Twin trunk, broom, clump
Environmental conditions Hardy outdoors in temperate climates. Z5–8

Acer palmatum 'Shindeshojo'
Japanese maple
The name means "new Deshojo" because this plant is a later selection of cultivar than 'Deshojo'. It has many more brilliant flaming or crimson leaves in the early stages of spring as the leaves unfold. The five-lobed leaves retain their red colour well into summer, changing to reddish-green in late summer and a mixture of orange and red in autumn. As with 'Deshojo', the leaf colour will be retained for a longer period when the tree is placed in very good light conditions for as long as possible.
Country of origin Japan
Suitable bonsai styles Informal upright, slanting, cascade, twin trunk, group, root-over-rock
Environmental conditions Hardy outdoors in temperate climates. Z5–8

Aralia elegantissima
Finger aralia
This plant has attractive straight stems when young, with deeply cut, purple-brown, more or less deeply serrate, somewhat pendulous leaves, not dissimilar to those of *Acer palmatum dissectum*. The juvenile stage can be up to 1.8m (6ft) or so in height, unbranched with many leaves. The stems and petioles are smooth, with leaves up to 23cm (9in) long and 2.5cm (1in) wide, narrowing from the middle to the tip. The juvenile stage is best for bonsai use.

Country of origin New Hebrides
Suitable bonsai styles Groups
Environmental conditions Half hardy; protection required below -5°C (23°F). Z10

Berberis thunbergii
Barberry
A round and compact shrub that can reach a height of approximately 1.2m (4ft), barberry has a strikingly different appearance in the various seasons. It has pale to mid-green leaves that turn a brilliant red in the autumn. Long clusters of pale yellow flowers, which appear in mid-spring, are followed by small, scarlet-red berries. Two other good varieties of barberry which are suitable for bonsai are 'Atropurpurea', with rich purple-red leaves throughout spring and summer, and 'Atropurpurea Nana', which has similar leaves, but a more compact habit.
Country of origin Japan
Suitable bonsai styles Informal upright, clump, semi-cascade, cascade, twin trunk
Environmental conditions Totally hardy in most areas. Z5–9

Bougainvillea spectabilis
Bougainvillea
Tender, shrubby, climbing, deciduous plant, with spiny growths and dark green elliptic leaves. Long flower panicles with magenta bracts are produced from

Bougainvillea glabra

mid-summer to early autumn and there are many varieties with various shades of colour from cerise and scarlet through to deep pink. Its very rigid twigs and branches mean that bonsai shaping is normally achieved by simple pruning techniques. *B. glabra* (often known as the paper flower) is an evergreen or semi-evergreen, rambling climber that has clusters of floral bracts in shades of cyclamen purple in the summer.
Country of origin Brazil
Suitable bonsai styles Informal upright, semi-cascade, cascade
Environmental conditions Tender in temperate areas with minimum temperature of 10°C (50°F). Z10

Berberis thunbergii 'Atropurpurea'

Buxus sempervirens

Buxus sempervirens
Common box

A hardy, evergreen, slow-growing shrub with a bushy habit. It has dark green, glossy leaves as well as inconspicuous, honey-scented, pale green flowers in mid-spring. Box is commonly used for closely clipped hedges and topiary and is therefore highly suited for bonsai use, as the clipping procedure promotes the dense twiggy structure required for bonsai.

Country of origin Europe, North Africa and Western Asia

Suitable bonsai styles Informal upright, clump, twin trunk, broom

Environmental conditions Totally hardy. Z6–9

Carpinus betulus
European hornbeam

Deciduous tree with oblong, pointed, deep green leaves, turning to various shades of yellow in autumn. Catkin-like fruits sometimes appear when it is grown as a bonsai. Commonly grown as hedging around fields, it responds well to hard pruning, producing compact growth suitable for most bonsai styles.

Country of origin Europe and Asia Minor

Suitable bonsai styles Informal upright, slanting, twin trunk, group

Environmental conditions Hardy outdoors in temperate climates. Z5–9

Carpinus laxiflora
Japanese hornbeam

Deciduous tree growing to 15m (50ft), with pointed green leaves which turn to yellow, orange and red in autumn. Excellent for bonsai training as this plant responds extremely well to shoot pruning and quickly develops a good twiggy form. Catkin-like fruits sometimes appear when it is grown as a bonsai.

Country of origin Japan and Korea

Suitable bonsai styles Most styles, but normally informal upright, slanting, group or forest

Environmental conditions Totally hardy outdoors in temperate climates, but may need some protection from extreme heat in tropical areas. Z5–9

Cedrus deodara
Himalayan cedar

Evergreen tree of pendulous habit, with rich green to grey-green, very sharp, needle-like leaves. Not as good for bonsai training as *Cedrus libani* but can produce acceptable results with persistent effort. Can be very sparse in foliage if consistent and regular shoot pruning is not carried out properly.

Country of origin Western Himalayas, Afghanistan and Eastern Nepal

Suitable bonsai styles Informal upright, cascade

Environmental conditions Hardy outdoors in temperate climates. Z7–9

Cedrus libani
Cedar of Lebanon

Large evergreen tree growing to 45m (150ft) in natural conditions, with roughly horizontal branches and mid-green, sometimes bluish, needle-like leaves. Provides very good material for bonsai, especially the dwarf variety 'Brevifolia'. Produces cones, but often when grown as bonsai they are too large and so out of proportion with any miniaturized tree.

Country of origin Syria and south-east Turkey

Suitable bonsai styles Formal upright, informal upright, literati

Environmental conditions Hardy outdoors in temperate climates. Z7–9

Carpinus laxiflora leaves

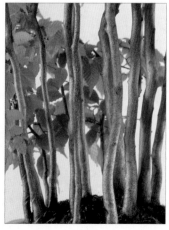

Carpinus laxiflora stems

Cedrus libani subsp. *atlantica*

Cedrus libani 'Brevifolia'

Cedrus libani subsp. *atlantica*
Atlas cedar

Evergreen subspecies of *Cedrus libani*, but with slightly ascending branches. Needle-like leaves can be dark green, blue-green or blue-grey. Another good plant for bonsai, as it develops dense, twiggy foliage when pruned using bonsai techniques.

Country of origin North Africa (Atlas Mountains)

Suitable bonsai styles Formal upright, informal upright, literati

Environmental conditions Totally hardy outdoors in temperate climates and will not need any protection from extreme heat as originates from very hot areas. Z7–9

Cedrus libani subsp. *atlantica* 'Glauca'
Blue Atlas cedar

Another very good plant that can be developed into high-quality bonsai. This is the blue form of the *Cedrus libani* subsp. *atlantica*, which has silver-blue, needle-like foliage and is generally known as the blue Atlas cedar. There are many slightly different forms of this plant, which include weeping and fastigiate versions.

Country of origin North Africa (Atlas Mountains)

Suitable bonsai styles Formal upright, informal upright, literati

Environmental conditions Hardy outdoors in temperate climates. Z7–9

Celtis bungeana
Nettle tree or Hackberry

This is a deciduous tree which reaches a height of 15m (50ft) in the wild. It has oval leaves that are glossy and dark green. The smooth, light grey bark is damaged easily if the tree is wired during bonsai training, so wiring is not recommended for this particular plant. *Celtis australis* is a very similar plant, but it has oval to lanceolate, rough, dark-green leaves that are downy on the underside.

Country of origin Central and northern Asia

Suitable bonsai styles Formal upright, informal upright, twin trunk, group

Environmental conditions Hardy in most temperate areas of the world. Z2–9

Cercis siliquastrum
Judas tree or Love tree

This is a deciduous tree or shrub that grows naturally to approximately 10m (30ft). It has maroon young shoots with rounded, matt, grey-green leaves which turn bright yellow in the autumn. Pale rose to rich magenta, pea-shaped flowers on very short racemes break from naked old wood in late spring and are then followed by flat seed pods which are similar in shape to mangetout (snow peas). These seed pods turn brown and are retained well into the following year.

Country of origin Eastern Mediterranean

Suitable bonsai styles Informal upright

Environmental conditions Hardy in temperate climates. Z8–9

Cercis siliquastrum developing seed pods

Cercis siliquastrum foliage

Chaenomeles japonica

Chrysanthemum

Chaenomeles japonica
Japanese or Maule's quince

This delightful spreading, deciduous, thorny shrub grows to approximately 1m (3ft) in height. It has mid-green, ovate to round leaves. The flowers, which resemble the flowers of apple trees, can be orange-red, scarlet or crimson and are borne on the old wood from early to late spring. The flowers are followed by apple-shaped yellow fruits, which are sometimes tinged with red.

Country of origin Japan

Suitable bonsai styles Informal upright, clump

Environmental conditions Hardy in temperate climates. Z5–9

Chamaecyparis obtusa
Hinoki cypress

This is a slow-growing evergreen tree which reaches approximately 40m (130ft) in height when growing in the wild. The hinoki cypress bears blunt, deep green, scale-like leaves, with silver-white undersides, which are sweetly aromatic when they are crushed. The bark has a brown, flaky, very attractive appearance and can be peeled to reveal deep reddish-brown colouring. There are several dwarf forms available, all of which are highly recommended for bonsai.

Country of origin Japan

Suitable bonsai styles Formal upright, informal upright, twin trunk

Environmental conditions Hardy in temperate climates. Z4–8

Chamaecyparis pisifera
Sawara cypress

Evergreen tree that has bright, mossy-green foliage in fern-like sprays, with fine silver-white undersides. The foliage is acridly aromatic when it is crushed. The bark is rusty-brown and peels into thin strips that can be removed, as with *Chamaecyparis obtusa*. Makes excellent material for bonsai training as it develops a very compact form with correct shoot pinching.

Country of origin Japan

Suitable bonsai styles Informal upright

Environmental conditions Hardy in temperate climates. Z5–8

Chrysanthemum

About 20 species of scented herbs, often woody at the base. Flowers range in size, but the best varieties for bonsai will have the smallest flowers. Flowers usually borne in autumn and remain on the plant for several weeks. Results will be achieved in less time than most hardy, woody varieties of plant. Suitable varieties include 'Hokuto' (red), 'Ohko' (yellow) and 'Sumi' (yellow).

Country of origin Europe and North Africa

Suitable bonsai styles Groups, informal upright, formal upright, root-over-rock, root-in-rock

Environmental conditions Half hardy; protection required below -5°C (23°F). Z8–9

Chamaecyparis obtusa

Chamaecyparis pisifera

Cotoneaster × suecicus 'Coral Beauty'

Crassula arborescens

Cotoneaster horizontalis
Cotoneaster

This is a deciduous shrub with a flat-growing habit and a striking, herringbone-like branch structure. The broad, glossy, dark green leaves turn brilliant red in the autumn. Depending on the atmospheric conditions, some or all of the leaves may remain throughout the winter period. The very small pink flowers, which appear during the spring, are followed by cheerful red berries in the autumn.

Country of origin Western China
Suitable bonsai styles Informal upright, semi-cascade, cascade, root-over-rock
Environmental conditions Hardy in temperate climates. Z5–9

Cotoneaster × suecicus 'Coral Beauty'

Evergreen, low-growing, spreading shrub with oval, bright green leaves and outstanding brilliant red berries in autumn. This is a very good plant for bonsai culture as it can be easily pruned into shape with very little need for wiring, and can tolerate virtually any weather conditions imaginable.

Country of origin China
Suitable bonsai styles Semi-cascade, cascade, any form of rock planting
Environmental conditions Very hardy. Z5–9

Crassula arborescens
Jade or Money tree

Named from the Latin *crassus*, which means thick or swollen, and refers to the succulent nature of the plant. There are many species and varieties, but *C. arborescens* is one of the most widely available. Leaves are oval, thick and succulent and are borne in opposite pairs. Clusters of very small white flowers appear on vertical stems in the leading ends of shoots from late autumn to early spring.

Country of origin South Africa
Suitable bonsai styles Informal upright, twin trunk

Environmental conditions Minimum temperature of 10°C (50°F). Ideal low-maintenance indoor bonsai. Z10

Crataegus monogyna
Common hawthorn or May

This is a thorny, deciduous, very hardy small tree with glossy, lobed and toothed, very dark green leaves. Bears dense clusters of white flowers in late spring followed by dense clusters of small crimson haws in autumn. Numerous very hard thorns, which can grow to 2–2.5cm (¾–1in) in length, appear on most of the shoots; these can prick your hands when

Crataegus monogyna

Cryptomeria japonica

Cryptomeria japonica 'Tens Sans'

you are training this plant as a bonsai specimen, so take great care. *C. laevigata* is similar to *C. monogyna*, but it can have white, pink or red flowers and bright crimson, double flowers as in the cultivar 'Paul's Scarlet'.

Country of origin United Kingdom and Europe

Suitable bonsai styles Informal upright, semi-cascade

Environmental conditions Hardy in temperate climates. Z5–7

Cryptomeria japonica
Japanese red cedar

This is an evergreen tree with mid- to dark green, needle-like leaves which turn bronze in the winter, but remain green on some cultivars. The thick, peeling bark is red-brown. Dwarf varieties, such as 'Jindai-sugi', are highly recommended for bonsai culture. The different varieties of the Japanese red cedar can vary considerably in their habit, but when the shoots are pinched out regularly, very dense growth patterns will result.

Country of origin Japan and China

Suitable bonsai styles Formal upright, group

Environmental conditions Extremely hardy in temperate climates, but when grown as a bonsai, it will benefit from a slightly shady position. Z6–9

Fagus crenata
Japanese beech

Large deciduous tree with long, pointed buds leading to pointed, soft green leaves in spring, changing to glossy, mid- to dark green leaves in summer, and then russet in autumn. When trained as bonsai, the leaves are retained throughout the winter, eventually falling in spring. It has a very smooth, pale grey bark. There are many species of beech, all of which would make good bonsai.

Country of origin Japan

Suitable bonsai styles Formal upright, informal upright, twin trunk, clump, group

Environmental conditions Hardy in temperate climates. Z4–7

Fagus sylvatica
Common or European beech

This is a very large, long-lived, deciduous tree with ovate, pointed, wavy-margined foliage, which is bright green in spring, turning mid-green in the summer and yellow to russet in the autumn. When grown as bonsai, the russet leaves remain in place until bud-break in spring. As with the Japanese beech, this tree has smooth grey bark, but in a slightly darker shade of grey.

Country of origin Europe

Suitable bonsai styles Informal upright, twin trunk, clump, group

Environmental conditions Hardy in temperate climate and very tolerant of most conditions. Z4–7

Fagus sylvatica

Ficus benjamina

Ficus benjamina 'Variegata'

Ficus benjamina
Weeping fig

An evergreen tree with pendulous branches and slender, pointed leaves that are soft green when young, maturing to dark glossy green. The bark is grey. Aerial roots often appear, particularly when kept in humid conditions. During pruning, the wounds will produce a sticky, white latex solution that is toxic and should not be ingested.
Country of origin India
Suitable bonsai styles Informal upright, cascade, twin trunk, clump
Environmental conditions Maintain temperature above 10°C (50°F) in winter. Z10

Ficus benjamina 'Variegata'
Variegated weeping fig

Evergreen tree similar to *Ficus benjamina* but with leaves that are green with creamy-white variable edges.
Country of origin India
Suitable bonsai styles Informal upright, cascade, twin trunk, clump
Environmental conditions Maintain temperature above 10°C (50°F) in winter. Z10

Ficus microcarpa
Indian laurel, Curtain fig, Malay banyan, Chinese banyan or Glossy-leaved fig

This plant was previously misnamed *Ficus retusa* and is often still known by this name. It is an evergreen tree with a spreading crown and ascending branches, from which many aerial roots descend to form curtains around the trunk. The glossy leaves are similar to *Ficus benjamina*, but darker green, and the bark is grey and rougher. As with *F. benjamina*, pruning produces a white, toxic latex solution.
Country of origin India
Suitable bonsai styles Informal upright, cascade, twin trunk, clump
Environmental conditions Maintain temperature above 10°C (50°F) in winter. Z10

Fuchsia
Lady's ear drops

There are over 100 species of procumbent, erect or climbing shrubs or small to medium trees in this genus. The leaves are alternate, opposite or in whorls. Flowers are solitary and axillary, or gathered into terminal paniculate groups and are often drooping, tubular, and with nectar at the base. Flowers vary in size from about 5mm to 10cm (¼ to 4in) in length and come in a large variety of colours from white to deep purple. The flowers form the most spectacular part of these plants in bonsai. Suitable varieties include 'Tom Thumb' or 'Lady Thumb'.
Country of origin Central and South America, Mexico, New Zealand, Tahiti
Suitable bonsai styles Groups, informal upright, formal upright, root-over-rock, root-in-rock, cascade
Environmental conditions Half hardy; varieties require protection below -5°C (23°F). Z8–9

Gingko biloba
Maidenhair tree

This ancient deciduous tree is thought to have been around for about 200 million years and is now often grown as a curiosity because of its historical value. It has leathery, fan-shaped leaves, partially divided in the middle and similar to the maidenhair fern. Leaves are pale green in spring, dark to mid-green in summer and brilliant gold in autumn. Once the leaves have turned gold, they drop very quickly.
Country of origin China
Suitable bonsai styles Informal upright, twin trunk, broom
Environmental conditions Hardy in temperate climates. Z5–9

Fuchsia

Hamamelis x intermedia
Witch hazel

A cross between *H. japonica* (Japanese witch hazel) and *H. mollis* (Chinese witch hazel). Medium-sized shrub with broad leaves which are 10–15cm (4–6in) long. Autumn leaf colours are yellow with tints of red and orange. Flowers are butter yellow, 2.5cm (1in) or so in diameter, with crumpled petals, borne in midwinter. Various forms have different flower colours, ranging from pale yellow through orange to deep rust red.

Country of origin China, Japan, North America and Europe

Suitable bonsai styles Formal upright, informal upright

Environmental conditions All varieties totally hardy. Z5–9

Hamamelis mollis 'Pallida'

Ilex crenata
Japanese or Box-leaved holly

Evergreen shrub or small tree with dark green leaves and numerous lustrous, small white flowers followed by small, glossy black fruits. Ideal for bonsai culture because of its small leaves, flowers and fruit and its easy persuasion, by pruning, to form tight twiggy growth.

Country of origin Japan and Korea

Suitable bonsai styles Informal upright

Environmental conditions Hardy in temperate climates. Z6–8

Ilex serrata
Japanese winterberry

This deciduous shrub has mid-green leaves and small pink flowers. The flowers are followed by small red berries in autumn. It is widely used for bonsai in Japan, but seldom seen in other countries. It responds well to pruning and produces good, branched growth patterns, making it an ideal subject for bonsai culture.

Country of origin Japan and China

Suitable bonsai styles Informal upright

Environmental conditions Hardy in temperate climates. Z6–9

Jasminum nudiflorum
Winter jasmine

A deciduous shrub with a rambling growth pattern and dark green leaves. Fragrant yellow flowers are borne on previous years' growth from winter to early spring. It develops a rough bark at a young age.

Country of origin Northern China

Suitable bonsai styles Informal upright, slanting, semi-cascade, cascade, root-over-rock, exposed root

Environmental conditions Extremely hardy and tolerates sub-tropical and tropical conditions. Z6–9

Ilex serrata

Jasminum nudiflorum

Juniperus chinensis
Chinese juniper

This is an evergreen bushy tree that has dark green, scale-like adult foliage with needle-like juvenile leaves internally or when the plant is severely pruned. The insignificant flowers develop into small, blue-black fruits. The bark is red-brown in colour, peels very easily and can be lightly brushed in order to give a beautiful reddish appearance. There are many cultivars of Chinese juniper to choose from, some of which carry the scale-like adult foliage and others that bear only the needle-like juvenile foliage.

Country of origin China
Suitable bonsai styles Informal upright, cascade, group
Environmental conditions Hardy in temperate climates. Z5–9

Juniperus communis
Common juniper

This is a densely branching evergreen tree or shrub which has needle-like foliage, deep green on the outer surface with a blue-white band on the inner surface. The fruits of the common juniper are berry-like and green in appearance, ripening to blue-black in approximately two years. It is not one of the easiest trees to form into a bonsai, but it will make a superb specimen with persistence.

Country of origin Europe, Asia and North America
Suitable bonsai styles Informal upright, semi-cascade, cascade
Environmental conditions Hardy in temperate climates. Z3–7

Juniperus chinensis

Juniperus horizontalis
Creeping or prostrate juniper

Evergreen, low-spreading, mat-forming species developing into thick cushions with grey-green leaves; it may produce dark blue cones. There are many cultivars in various shades of green that will provide very good material for bonsai production.

Country of origin North-east America
Suitable bonsai styles Semi-cascade and cascade
Environmental conditions Hardy in temperate climates. Z3–9

Juniperus procumbens
Procumbent juniper

Evergreen species with maroon-brown bark and light green foliage. This is an excellent plant for bonsai, especially the very compact variety 'Nana' or any of the less common varieties that are now available in plant centres and nurseries.

Country of origin Japan
Suitable bonsai styles Semi-cascade and cascade
Environmental conditions Hardy in temperate climates. Z5–9

Juniperus rigida
Needle or Temple juniper

This small evergreen tree reaches a height of 15m (50ft) in the wild and is highly sought-after by bonsai enthusiasts. It has yellow-brown peeling bark and very sharply pointed, needle-like, bright green leaves, which have a blue-grey line in a dorsal groove. The cones mature in about two years into spherical, dark purple, eventually black, berry-like fruit.

Country of origin Japan, Korea and northern China
Suitable bonsai styles Formal upright, informal upright, driftwood
Environmental conditions Hardy in temperate climates. Z6–9

Larix decidua
European larch

This is a deciduous conifer with bright green needle-like leaves on the young shoots and in whorls on spurs on the older growth. The young shoots are yellow-brown in colour, with grey-brown bark which matures to flaking plates. The female flowers are red-purple, developing into small, woody cones which can remain on the trees for many years. The cones are small enough to be in proportion when they are allowed to remain on larger bonsai specimens.

Country of origin Central Europe
Suitable bonsai styles Formal upright, informal upright, cascade, group or forest
Environmental conditions Hardy in temperate climates. Z3–6

Right: *Juniperus chinensis*

Juniperus horizontalis

Larix decidua

Larix kaempferi
(syn. L. leptolepis)
Japanese larch

Deciduous conifer with rusty-brown, fissured and scaly bark and red-brown shoots. These are grey at first, but eventually bear needle-like green leaves that are slightly broader than *Larix decidua*. The small squat cones that are produced in profusion are retained on the branches for several years. A very good plant for bonsai as it responds extremely well to any bonsai styling technique.

Country of origin Japan

Suitable bonsai styles Formal upright, informal upright, cascade, twin trunk, group

Environmental conditions Hardy in temperate climates. Z5–7

Lespedeza bicolor
Bush clover

Bushy, woody shrub with vivid green leaves that are paler beneath. Small flowers can be in short racemes or terminal clusters and are purple-rose or rose-violet. A very attractive plant that is relatively easy to care for and will produce a good-looking bonsai in a fairly short time.

Country of origin Japan, China, Manchuria, Korea and Taiwan

Suitable bonsai styles Informal upright, twin trunk, broom, root over rock

Environmental conditions Normally hardy but susceptible to die-back in very cold conditions.

Lonicera nitida
Hedging honeysuckle

Dense, branched, evergreen shrub growing to about 3.5m (11ft), with young purple shoots carrying ovate to rounded glossy dark green leaves. Insignificant cream to white flowers from early to mid-spring followed by shiny, semi-translucent, blue-purple, globular berries in late spring and early summer. Has the potential to make superb bonsai.

Country of origin China

Suitable bonsai styles Informal upright, semi-cascade, twin trunk, windswept

Environmental conditions Hardy in temperate climates. Z7–9

Malus floribunda

Lonicera pileata
Shrubby honeysuckle

Low-growing, often prostrate, evergreen or semi-deciduous shrub with young purple shoots. Leaves are shiny, mid- to dark green. Inconspicuous yellow-white flowers on underside of shoots in the spring are followed by semi-translucent, amethyst-coloured, globular berries in late spring. A first-class plant for bonsai training, this species develops a flaking woody trunk while still quite young.

Country of origin China

Suitable bonsai styles Informal upright, semi-cascade, twin trunk

Environmental conditions Hardy in temperate climates. Z5–9

Malus floribunda
Japanese crab

Deciduous tree or shrub growing up to 10m (30ft) with mid-green, toothed leaves. Flowers are abundant along the length of branches in spring, beginning deep pink in bud, fading to pale pink with white inside, and followed by yellow fruits in autumn. Makes a good flowering bonsai, but is not easy material from which to achieve a pleasing tree-like shape.

Country of origin Japan

Suitable bonsai styles Informal upright

Environmental conditions Hardy in temperate climates with some frost protection being required when the flowers are about to break. Z5–8

Lonicera nitida

Morus alba
White mulberry

A small, rounded tree with downy young shoots eventually bearing glossy, bright green leaves with serrated edges. Flowers are white-green, leading to green-white fruit, ripening to pink or dark red with a sweet but poor flavour. Capable of producing, with persistence, a good, rough-barked, twiggy bonsai.

Country of origin China
Suitable bonsai styles Informal upright, twin trunk, broom, root-over-rock
Environmental conditions Relatively hardy but needs protection in very serious winter conditions. Z5–9

Myrtus communis
Myrtle

A much branched, erect shrub, to 3m (10ft), with dense, dark lustrous green foliage that is strongly scented when crushed. The fragrant, slender flowers are white or pink-white, 2.5cm (1in) in diameter and up to 2.5cm (1in) long. Fruit is blue-black when ripe. Widely cultivated from ancient times with its native range therefore uncertain. Many different varieties are now available, most with fragrant flowers and small leaves, which are suitable for bonsai culture.

Country of origin North Africa, Mediterranean and south-west European countries

Olea europaea

Suitable bonsai styles Informal upright, formal upright and groups
Environmental conditions Half hardy; protection required below -5°C (23°F). Z9–10

Nandina domestica
Sacred or Heavenly bamboo

An upright evergreen or semi-deciduous, multi-stemmed shrub, with green leaves tinged with red when young and turning to red-purple in autumn. Profuse flowers are followed by red, pea-sized fruits that remain in place for long periods. Will not produce classical bonsai styles, but makes for an interesting variation in a collection.

Country of origin Japan
Suitable bonsai styles Informal upright, clump, twin trunk, group, landscape
Environmental conditions Hardy, but young shoots can be damaged by frost. Z7–10

Olea europaea
European, Common or Edible olive

Multi-branched evergreen tree that grows to 7m (23ft), with grey-green leaves that are silvery beneath. Off-white, fragrant flowers turn to red, followed by purple-black fruit. Makes a good indoor bonsai because the normal habitat is dry and arid.

Country of origin Mediterranean
Suitable bonsai styles Informal upright, broom
Environmental conditions Hardy down to freezing, but could be damaged below this temperature. Z9–10

Picea mariana
Black spruce

Medium-sized evergreen tree with red-brown bark and densely arranged blue-green needles. The dwarf variety 'Nana' is highly suited for bonsai, as it is very compact with short, blue-green needles. Excellent for small group plantings and rock landscapes, where the trees can be pruned into very mature-looking designs.

Country of origin Canada
Suitable bonsai styles Root-on-rock, landscape
Environmental conditions Very hardy in temperate climates and will need no protection at all in any area. Z3–6

Myrtus communis

Picea mariana 'Nana'

Pinus parviflora

Podocarpus macrophyllus

Pinus parviflora (syn. *Pinus pentaphylla*)
Japanese white pine
Evergreen tree with blue-green, short needles in fives on the upper side of shoots. The bark is smooth and grey-black, developing small plates when it is mature. This is one of the classical varieties from which bonsai are grown and it can be very long-lived in the bonsai form.
Country of origin Japan
Suitable bonsai styles Informal upright, slanting
Environmental conditions Hardy in temperate climates. Z6–9

Pinus sylvestris
Scots pine
Extremely hardy evergreen tree with grey-green needles borne in pairs. The bark is thin, red-brown and flaky when young, exposing rusty-brown colouring beneath, and becomes thick and plate-like with extreme age. Superb tree for bonsai

Pinus sylvestris

culture because of its hardiness and willingness to be manipulated and pruned. Particularly good for literati-style bonsai.
Country of origin Europe, Siberia and Eastern Asia
Suitable bonsai styles Formal upright, informal upright, semi-cascade, cascade, literati, driftwood
Environmental conditions Hardy in temperate climates. Z3–7

Pinus sylvestris including 'Beuvronensis', 'Jeremy' and 'Watereri' syn. 'Nana'
Dwarf Scots pine
These are compact, slow-growing varieties of the Scots pine, all having shorter needles than the species *Pinus sylvestris*. 'Beuvronensis' has blue-tinted needles, 'Jeremy' has green needles, and 'Watereri' has rich blue-grey needles. They are all grafted on to rootstocks of *P. sylvestris* and exhibit features that make them ideal for bonsai training.
Country of origin Europe
Suitable bonsai styles Formal upright, informal upright, semi-cascade, cascade, literati, driftwood
Environmental conditions Hardy in temperate climates. Z3–7

Pinus thunbergii
Japanese black pine
This is an evergreen tree with black-grey, furrowed bark and orange-yellow young shoots. The dark green needles are borne in pairs of two and are densely arranged on the shoots. This pine makes good material

for bonsai and is much prized in Japan. It is grown less abundantly as a bonsai specimen outside Japan, but it is still very popular with bonsai enthusiasts worldwide.
Country of origin Japan and Korea
Suitable bonsai styles Informal upright
Environmental conditions Hardy in temperate climates. Z5–8

Podocarpus macrophyllus
Big-leafed podocarp
Evergreen tree or shrub with densely arranged, mid- to dark green leaves that are tinged yellow beneath. Normally sold as an indoor tree in temperate areas, but is totally hardy and makes a good evergreen bonsai. The leaves are slightly long, but they do reduce in size with time.
Country of origin Japan
Suitable bonsai styles Informal upright, semi-cascade, cascade
Environmental conditions Suitable for both indoors and outdoors in most areas. Z7–10

Pinus thunbergii

Prunus cerasifera
Cherry plum

Deciduous, tree-like, sometimes spiny shrub with bright green leaves. The small, pure white, solitary flowers on twigs in late winter and early spring are followed by red to yellow, cherry-shaped fruit. This makes a good flowering bonsai, but it is not easy to maintain this particular plant in a good tree-like shape.

Country of origin Asia Minor and Caucasus
Suitable bonsai styles Informal upright
Environmental conditions Hardy in temperate climates. Z5–9

Pyracantha

Prunus spinosa
Blackthorn or sloe

Very spiny, dense, bushy shrub or tree, which has dark green leaves. Masses of small, snow-white flowers in early and mid-spring are followed by small green fruit in late spring, turning to black damson-like fruit (sloes) in late summer and early autumn. The fruit is used to make sloe gin. In the right hands, the plant will make a handsome bonsai.

Country of origin Great Britain, North Africa and north Asia
Suitable bonsai styles Informal upright
Environmental conditions Hardy in temperate climates. Z5–9

Prunus yedoensis
Tokyo cherry

A cross between *P. × subhirtella* (winter flowering cherry) and *P. speciosa* (Oshima cherry). This small tree, growing to 15m (50ft), is mainly upright with smooth bark and young ascending branches. The leaves, up to 12cm (4½in) in length, are vivid green above and paler beneath. The pure white flowers can be 4cm (1½in) across. The fruits are round, pea-sized and black when ripe. 'Shidare Yoshino' ('Pendula') has a weeping habit with snow-white flowers.

Country of origin Japan
Suitable bonsai styles Informal upright, formal upright.
Environmental conditions Mostly hardy, but protection required to prevent frost damage to opening flower buds. Z6–8

Punica granatum
Pomegranate

Deciduous shrub or small tree with glossy, pale green leaves and often spiny branches. The funnel-shaped flowers are orange-red and the fruits are spherical, up to 12cm (4½in) in diameter, with many seeds in a fleshy, sweet, edible coating. There are several cultivars, the best of which is the dwarf variety 'Nana', which makes a good small bonsai.

Country of origin Eastern Mediterranean to Himalayas
Suitable bonsai styles Informal upright, semi-cascade, twin trunk, group, raft, root-over-rock
Environmental conditions Able to endure only light short frosts; otherwise hardy. Z8–10

Pyracantha
Firethorn

Extremely hardy evergreen shrub closely related to *Cotoneaster* and *Crataegus*. Depending on variety, the leaves range from entire to crenate. Flowers are white on most varieties, but the fruits vary from yellow through to brick red and are borne in dense clusters throughout. Excellent, hardy material from which beginners can learn the art and culture of bonsai.

Country of origin South-eastern Europe to China
Suitable bonsai styles Informal upright, semi-cascade, cascade, twin trunk, broom, root-over-rock
Environmental conditions Very hardy in all climatic conditions and will endure wide-ranging temperatures. Z6–9

Prunus yedoensis

Rhododendron 'Double Pink'

Azalea

Quercus robur
English oak, Common oak or Pendunculate oak

Large, long-lived tree with grey-brown, deeply fissured bark and dark green leaves that have rounded lobes. This is not one of the easiest trees to turn into a bonsai, but is worth the effort because of its popularity as a well-known tree. There are many oaks that are not suitable because they have quite large leaves which are difficult to miniaturize for the purposes of bonsai.

Country of origin Great Britain through Europe to Russia

Suitable bonsai styles Informal upright, twin trunk, group

Environmental conditions Hardy, but roots can be slightly tender when potted as bonsai. Z5–8

Quercus robur

Rhododendron indicum
Satsuki azalea

This is an evergreen shrub with dark, glossy green leaves. There is a profuse display of wide, funnel-shaped flowers in mid-summer, ranging from white through to deep pink, sometimes variously striped, depending on the variety. There are hundreds of cultivars and varieties, available from most good garden centres, but the smaller-flowered varieties are best suited to bonsai.

Country of origin Japan

Suitable bonsai styles Informal upright

Environmental conditions Hardy in temperate climates. Z5–8

Rhododendron obtusum 'Amoenum'
Kirishima azalea

This is a semi-deciduous, small-leaved rhododendron which has dark green leaves and small, magenta flowers. The Kirishima azalea is particularly good for bonsai culture because of its small flowers and its good response to bonsai shoot-pruning techniques. It is widely planted in large ornamental gardens and is, therefore, a possible source of very old plants from which to make excellent bonsai specimens.

Country of origin Japan

Suitable bonsai styles Informal upright, slanting, group

Environmental conditions Hardy in temperate climates. Z5–8

Sageretia theezans
Bird plum cherry

Evergreen shrub with shiny, mid-green leaves and insignificant, green-white flowers followed by small blue berries. Stiff, straight branches produce compact twiggy growth when regularly shoot-pruned. Indoor bonsai of this species, which are imported from China, need to have their foliage sprayed regularly to encourage healthy growth.

Country of origin Central and southern Asia; some regions in North America

Suitable bonsai styles Formal upright, informal upright, multi-trunk, slanting, semi-cascade, cascade

Environmental conditions Need winter protection below 12°C (54°F). Z5–8

Right: *Rhododendron*

Sageretia theezans

Styrax japonicus

Serissa foetida

Serissa foetida
Tree of a thousand stars

This is an attractive evergreen shrub with dark green leaves. It also bears small, double, white, rose-like flowers.

Country of origin South-east Asia

Suitable bonsai styles Most normal bonsai styles, but best for informal upright and broom

Environmental conditions Needs winter protection below 15°C (59°F). Z9–10

Styrax japonicus
Snowbell or Silverballs

This is a deciduous shrub or small tree, which grows up to approximately 10m (30ft) in height, with elliptic to oblong, slightly toothed, glossy, dark green leaves. The bark is attractive because of its smooth, sometimes flaky, appearance and the flowers are generally white in colour. Snowbells are very popular in Japan as bonsai specimens and are rapidly gaining popularity among bonsai enthusiasts in other parts of the world.

Country of origin China and Japan

Suitable bonsai styles Formal upright, informal upright

Environmental conditions Extremely hardy in temperate climates, but, when grown as a bonsai, will benefit from a slightly shady situation. Z5–9

Taxus baccata
Yew

This is a very long-lived evergreen tree which is native to many areas of the northern hemisphere. The bark is brown-tinged purple, smooth, but also slightly flaky. The attractive leaves are glossy and dark green. This plant makes extremely good material for creating bonsai specimens and will respond reliably to all bonsai styling and training techniques.

Country of origin Europe, North Africa (Atlas Mountains) and Asia Minor

Suitable bonsai styles Formal upright, informal upright, twin trunk, clump, group, windswept

Environmental conditions Very hardy. Z6–7

Ulmus glabra
Wych elm

Large tree to 40m (130ft) with a wide spreading, open crown and smooth bark, becoming fissured when very old. Leaves 5–16cm (2–6¼in), oval and occasionally three-lobed at the apex. Leaves uneven at base, partially covering the petiole, rough, dull green above and lighter green beneath. Flowers formed in dense clusters with red stigmas and the fruit up to 2.5cm (1in), broadly elliptic with a notched apex.

Country of origin North and Central Europe to Asia Minor

Suitable bonsai styles Informal upright, formal upright

Environmental conditions Totally hardy in most areas of the world. Z5–7

Taxus baccata

Ulmus parvifolia

Wisteria floribunda

Ulmus parvifolia
Chinese elm
This is a deciduous tree when it is kept outdoors, but it is an evergreen when it is treated as an indoor bonsai. Chinese elms have rich green leaves with toothed margins and often develop interesting corky bark.

Country of origin Many temperate areas of the world

Suitable bonsai styles Informal upright, semi-cascade, cascade, twin trunk, broom

Environmental conditions Mostly hardy, but those elms that originate from southern China and Taiwan should be considered as indoor bonsai in temperate areas. Z5–9

Ulmus procera
English elm
Deciduous tree with mid- to deep green leaves that turn bright yellow in the autumn. It is popular with bonsai enthusiasts because it responds well to all bonsai techniques.

Country of origin Great Britain, western and southern Europe

Suitable bonsai styles Informal upright and group

Environmental conditions Hardy in temperate climates. Z5–8

Wisteria floribunda
Japanese wisteria
Hardy, deciduous, climbing shrub with light to mid-green, pinnate leaves, each with 12 to 19 leaflets. Fragrant, violet-blue flowers in 24–30cm (10–12in) drooping racemes. White and pink forms available.

Country of origin Japan

Suitable bonsai styles Informal upright

Environmental conditions Hardy in temperate climates. Z4–10

Wisteria sinensis
Chinese wisteria
Hardy, deciduous, climbing shrub with dark to mid-green, pinnate leaves, with up to 11 leaflets. Dense, 20–30cm (8–12in), pendulous racemes of fragrant, mauve flowers. White and double mauve-flowered forms available.

Country of origin China

Suitable bonsai styles Informal upright

Environmental conditions Hardy in temperate climates. Z5–9

Zelkova serrata
Japanese grey bark elm
A large deciduous tree that can grow to over 30m (100ft). It has mid-green leaves that turn yellow-orange and red in autumn. The bark is smooth and grey, and prone to damage if wired during bonsai training.

Country of origin Japan

Suitable bonsai styles Informal upright, broom, group

Environmental conditions Hardy in all temperate climates and will endure wide ranging temperatures. Z6–8

Ulmus glabra

Wisteria sinensis

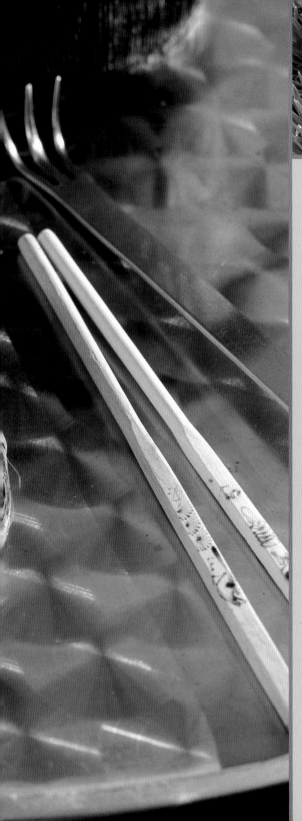

CARE &
MAINTENANCE

Having spent time establishing your Japanese garden, or having nurtured a variety of bonsai specimens, you must then develop housekeeping routines to keep them in order, and to ensure that your tools and equipment are tidy and ready to hand.

For Japanese gardening, general upkeep will normally involve weeding, pruning, trimming, shaping, brushing and raking. There will also be general maintenance demands, such as keeping water features clean and in working order, the repair of fences and gates and the provision of winter protection for less hardy plants.

Wherever you decide to display your bonsai collection, make sure that all your trees and pots are clean and tidy, so they will always look at their best. To achieve this top-quality appearance you should wash and dry the pots containing the trees that you wish to display. You should also make sure that the trees are clean and free of any pests and diseases, as well as free of damaged foliage.

Above: *Despite being widely used for bonsai, the Japanese black pine* (Pinus thunbergii) *has individual growth patterns which mean that they are more successfully managed by an experienced bonsai practitioner.*
Left: *Pliers, scissors, a brush, chopsticks and a rake form a typical range of tools that may be required when root pruning and repotting a collection of bonsai.*

Maintaining a Japanese garden

There is a curious ambiguity about the Japanese garden. As a first impression, one might think that maintaining a spread of gravel, a rock or two, a pine tree and a bamboo would require very little work. However, a dynamic Japanese garden, even on a small scale, carpeted with moss and planted with several trees and shrubs around a pond, can in fact involve a high level of maintenance. What is more, Japanese gardeners are meticulous in the way they keep their gardens, and pay extraordinary attention to small details such as training, staking and pruning.

Even the more naturalistic tea gardens are treated with the same high level of care. Traditionally, the work involved in looking after a garden has been seen as spiritually valuable in itself, but it is important to be realistic when creating your design, and think about the time you will have available. On the following pages we look at the main activities to ensure the upkeep of the garden: weeding, pruning, raking, sweeping, tidying, as well as repair and maintenance work.

Above: *Most tree work can be dangerous and should be carried out by professionals who have safety certificates and insurance.*

Below: *The twisting stem of a weeping* Sophora *has been carefully propped up and bound with jute.*

Opposite: *This pine tree was in poor health with the resin bleeding from the bark, so as a precaution it has been bound with hessian.*

Left: *Gardeners at Kenroku-en in Kanazawa, Japan, tie boughs with rope to protect the old pine trees from breaking branches in the snow.*

WEEDING

While Japanese gardens do not have flower borders, they do need regular weeding. Weed-suppressing matting and weedkillers could be used – Western recreations of Japanese gardens routinely use at least the former under gravel – but Japanese gardening is meant to be meditative and calming, and the process of weeding is therefore part of the experience.

Weeding tools

Some of the tools used in Japanese gardens are less well known in Western gardens, but they can be useful for weeding and cultivating in naturalistic garden settings. There are various small choppers and chisel-like planting tools for working between plants and rocks, and a right-angled, short-handled hoe or cultivation tool that is ideal for working in tight spaces. Hand scythes or sickles are used for controlling ground cover plants and for cutting grass in hard-to-reach places or on sloping sites that are unsuitable for lawnmowers. You can also use nylon-line trimmers.

PRUNING

In Japan, teams of professionals descend on public and private gardens once or twice a year to carry out the

Above: *The weeds that break up the smooth surface of the grass at Kenroku-en Garden in Honshu are broken loose with a hand sickle, and then carefully collected in baskets.*

specialized job of pruning. Most shrubs and trees can be tackled in early to late autumn, but some plants, such as plums, require pruning immediately after flowering in the spring. Pruning is vital because plants in the Japanese garden are used for their structural qualities as well as the beauty of their flowers and foliage, and so their growth must be kept in check. Because Japanese gardens are often quite densely planted, you need to decide how much light should fall on the ground between shrubs to encourage the growth of moss, mondo grass or other ground cover plants. Too much light and some plants will burn in the sun; too much shade might stunt or kill plants, leaving the earth exposed, dusty and brown. Aim for an attractive dappled shade and a green surface.

The term *niwaki* in Japanese means "garden trees", and also applies to a technique of pruning a tree to achieve some very striking effects. Trees may be made to look older than they really are by encouraging a broad trunk supporting gnarled branches; they

may also be made to imitate windswept or lightning-struck trees in the wild.

Other pruning techniques include *tama-mono*, the art of creating simple semi-spherical shapes of azaleas, shapes that are often combined with rocks and carefully pruned trees, such as a windswept pine. Another technique called *hako-zukuri* is designed to create box shapes that complement and echo architectural elements within a garden.

Trimming and shaping tools

Japanese gardeners use a wide range of tools which are designed to shape, prune and clip shrubs and trees.

For large hedges, or gardens with a large number of shrubs, powered trimmers (though obviously not traditional) are the easiest option, but large-leaved plants such as camellias should be pruned by hand using secateurs (pruners) to avoid shredding the foliage. Small, shaped shrubs are also best trimmed by hand for accuracy.

Many trimming tools are similar to those used in topiary, and indeed some Western topiary artists favour Japanese tools because of their diversity and suitability for carrying out intricate tasks. For example, as well as a range of standard anvil and bypass secateurs or pruners, there are also special long-

Above: *Gardeners use bamboo structures to prune the leaves of topiaries in Suizen-ji Park, Kumamoto, Japan.*

bladed, narrow-nosed cutters that are used to shorten the new growths or "candles" on pine trees and to thin the bundles of needles. This kind of tool is useful for precision shaping and trimming individual twigs in topiary.

Individual tree branches are often trained to achieve the desired shape and angle using bamboo canes and galvanized or plastic-coated training wire. You can use ladders to reach taller trees, but you may find long-handled or telescopic pruners, loppers and pruning saws useful with their longer reach.

Another essential tool for a Japanese garden containing large shrubs and small trees is a small pruning saw with a curved blade that folds or retracts into the handle for safe storage.

Shears with short blades and narrow noses, sometimes sold as "ladies' shears", are perfect for trimming over the rounded or flattened plates of cloud-pruned trees and shrubs and also for shaping azaleas and other evergreens such as box to resemble rounded boulders. For precise snipping and trimming of foliage on a smaller scale you can buy sprung one-handed cutters or "sheep shears", as well as scissor-like trimming tools. So-called sheep shears are not suitable for extended use as they are heavy, and will tire your hand.

PRUNING A DWARF PINE

This step-by-step process illustrates how to improve the general shape of a dwarf Japanese red pine (*Pinus densiflora umbraculifera*), a small rounded shrub that can be used in small compositions, especially those employing *shukkei* or "condensed landscape". The process could also be used on old junipers and boxwood, and other evergreens such as *Osmanthus* and yew. The aim is to give the impression that the tree is older than it is, and to give it a more open and attractive habit. Dwarf pines and many other conifers become very dense and twiggy with age, creating a dull, uninteresting mass. If you remove old growth, exposing the trunk of the tree and clipping excess growth, you can transform a shrub or small tree into a plant of much greater beauty.

2 Prune off the old dead and half-dead wood inside the bush, plus any crossing branches or weak, spindly twigs and branches. Stand back from time to time to get a good look at how the plant is shaping up. Prune the inside of the plant, removing larger branches so that you can see the branch structure.

4 Collect up the dust sheet around the red pine and dispose of the prunings.

You will need
- a pair of secateurs (pruners) or specialist Japanese pruners
- a small pruning saw
- a dust sheet (optional)

1 The specimen to be pruned is a dwarf Japanese red pine and has grown generally dense and lacking in character. If you have one, lay the dust sheet under the shrub. This is to catch all the prunings as they fall.

3 Prune out leading shoots to encourage the growth of side branches. This will give the plant a more balanced shape, and is important if you need to keep the plant contained within a small space. Do not make the plant too rounded but try to work with, and enhance, its innate form.

5 The plant is now more open and shapely. Continue the process each year, and the plant will develop more shape as it matures.

RAKING GRAVEL AND SAND

One of the most meditative practices in a Japanese garden is raking gravel or sand in a dry garden (*kare-sansui*). In temple gardens the rhythmic, focused motions of raking are still part of the spiritual practices of Zen monks. The softer and finer the texture of the sand, grit or gravel, the more frequently it will need raking.

Sourcing rakes

Used for making and maintaining patterns in grit, and often sand too,

rakes are not easy to get hold of, even from specialist companies. You can buy three- and four-pronged metal hand rakes, but these are not traditionally used in Zen gardens or *kare-sansui*. For such gardens as these you may need to make your own.

You can fashion a traditional Japanese rake from a rectangular piece of wood with broadly cut, saw-like teeth, which can be held with two hands and used at ground level or with a handle attached. Alternatively, you can make a rake from a row of dowel rods fitted into a block of wood.

Look critically at the area to be raked: the tool must be able to fit between rocks and between rock groupings and

pathways or boundaries. A wide rake may be unwieldy in a restricted area, but for a large, open expanse of sand, a bigger rake will cover the space more quickly. When making your own rake, adjust the size of the teeth or the thickness of the dowel rods and their spacing according to the grain diameter of sand or gravel. The larger the gravel, the wider the space required.

Making a wooden sand rake

A sand rake can be a "dowel-tooth" rake, made using wooden dowelling, which looks rather like a small hay rake. The other option is to make a slightly simpler "saw-tooth" rake. Choose whichever is best suited to the size and style of sand patterns you wish to create (see page 85 for pattern suggestions).

To make a dowel-tooth rake, follow the step-by-step method for the saw-tooth rake (see opposite), but use a block of wood that is about 6cm (2½in) wide so that you can drill holes in which to insert the dowelling. Each piece should be 2cm (¾in) in diameter and 10cm (4in) long.

Making a saw-tooth rake

Before designing your rake, consider how deep and how wide you want your ripples or waves to be. This will obviously affect how many teeth your rake will need, and how long each tooth should be. You will also need to know how fine your gravel or sand for raking will be, as a fine-toothed rake will not make much impression on coarser gravel.

1 The first stage is to prepare the wood for the saw teeth. Take the block of wood for the rake end and lay it flat. Then make a mark with a pencil on the long edge of the block, 4cm (1½in) from one end and then every 8cm (3in) along the length. The last mark should be 4cm (1½in) from the other end. Trim the timber to fit the measurements (you may prefer to have a wider or narrower rake, or teeth of a different size).

2 Using a set square, make lines at 60 degrees in both directions from each mark that you have already made. Carry on along the length until you have made the zigzag outline of your saw pattern.

3 Clamp the board in a vice and saw out the teeth. You could use an electric jigsaw, but a fine-toothed cross-cut saw would also be suitable for a small project of this type. If you prefer to saw vertically, then clamp the board in the vice at an angle.

4 Prepare to attach the handle by making a notch in the rake end. The notch needs to fit the exact width of the timber that you have bought for the handle but should be only 2cm (¾in) deep, so that when the handle is placed into the notch, 2cm (¾in) of it will be left proud.

You will need

- for the rake end: block of timber measuring 60cm (24in) long, 5cm (2in) thick (6cm or 2½in wide for a dowel-tooth rake) and 15–20cm (6–8in) wide
- for the handle: length of 4 x 4cm (1½ x 1½in) timber 150–200cm (5–6½ft) long
- for bracing the handle: 2 strips of wood, each 2cm x 3cm x 60cm (¾in x 1¼in x 2ft)
- wood screws
- an electric drill
- a cross-cut hand-saw, or electric jigsaw
- a work-bench vice
- an angle-measuring device, such as a set square
- a wood chisel
- a wood rasp and sandpaper

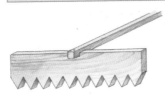

5 Fit the handle into the notch and screw it down into the board.

6 Brace the handle by resting each brace in turn against the handle 45cm (18in) from the rake end, and on the rake end, and mark off the angles. Cut these angles off the braces.

7 Fix the braces by screwing one end to the rake handle, and the other to the rake end.

8 Round off the square edges of the handle along the area where you will be holding the rake with a coarse rasp, then follow this with a good sanding.

BRUSHING, SWEEPING AND TIDYING

In the famous garden of Shisendo, in Kyoto, the surface of the dry garden is covered by light sand, which requires brushing rather than raking. Soft brushwood brooms or besoms made from bundled twigs are used to sweep the sand into patterns. These brooms are also used to sweep debris and leaves off paths and mossy areas.

At the risk of shattering the peace and tranquillity of a Japanese garden, you could also use a powered leaf blower, but in this case take great care not to disturb any raked or levelled areas of sand or fine grit.

You will also need to check paths made of stepping stones are kept clean and free of moss and slimy algae.

Top: *A gardener using a brushwood besom to maintain the gravel patterns in a Zen garden at the Silver Pavilion Ginkaku-ji in Kyoto.*

Above: *A long hand brush is useful for sweeping debris from pathways and removing leaves and blossoms from cobbles and clipped topiary.*

OTHER TASKS

Other occasional maintenance work:

• the repair and re-binding of bamboo fences and gates.

• making or repairing tree supports, elaborate constructs, with black and natural-coloured jute and sisal being used to bind branches to their supports (synthetic black "jute" is available and lasts longer).

• cutting ground cover plants. Some larger Japanese gardens have lawns, but the grass is coarse and cannot be mown too closely. Where spreading dwarf bamboos are used instead of grass, they will need shearing once or twice a year to keep them down to 10cm (4in) at most.

• maintaining water features. Unless you have a natural stream or spring, water gardens will need a certain amount of upkeep. Pump filters must be cleaned and pools dredged to prevent them from silting up and to keep the water clean and fresh.

Left: *The Japanese walk carefully on mossy ground with soft-soled shoes and brush the autumn leaves with twig brooms (besoms).*

Below: *Bamboo fences do not last for many years and will often need repairing. This gardener is tying on new bamboo stays with natural black jute.*

Above: *In cooler areas some plants, such as this cycad, are wrapped and bound with rice straw and twine to protect them from heavy frosts.*

Below: *Elaborate frames are used to extend the weeping boughs of cherries to lift the canopy so that it stretches over walkways and paths.*

Bonsai: environmental conditions

Once you have decided that you want to own a bonsai, you will have to choose between buying a ready-made tree and styling your own. In either case, you will also need to decide whether you wish to keep the bonsai indoors or outdoors because you need to select the type of tree that best suits the chosen environment. Growing, training, styling and general maintenance techniques for both indoor and outdoor bonsai are virtually identical; it is only the environmental climate that is different. All outdoor trees are happy to be grown in their natural climatic conditions, but when they are moved to a position with different conditions, such as those that occur in other parts of the world, they may need special treatment to maintain an environment more akin to that of their natural habitat.

Above: *Deciduous bonsai stored in a rain-free environment from late autumn to winter, so that moisture levels of the roots can be monitored.*

The local climatic conditions in the area of the world in which you live will inevitably determine the type of trees you can keep indoors or outdoors. Wherever you live, it is generally trees that naturally grow outdoors in your area that will be most suitable as outdoor bonsai, while those from different climatic conditions to the area in which you live, such as tropical or sub-tropical in a temperate climate, will need to be kept indoors or in controlled environmental conditions.

INDOOR BONSAI

Trees to be kept indoors normally need warm conditions with fairly high humidity, which can often be difficult to achieve in centrally heated homes. They will also need to be kept in very bright conditions, but not in front of a sunny window, as this could result in serious drying-out of the foliage.

Their situation means that indoor trees often require extra humidity in and around the foliage. You can supply this by placing the tree, in its pot, on a layer of absorbent granules within a shallow tray or dish. Keep the granules constantly moist so that as the water evaporates from the granules it drifts up and around the foliage, slowing down the transpiration rate of water from the leaves and therefore decreasing the risk of the leaves drying out and shrivelling up.

Left: Ficus benjamina *bonsai used as a table decoration. Remember that this variety needs good light and humidity.*

Above: *Japanese black pine (*Pinus thunbergii*) kept temporarily indoors. This can done only for a maximum of one or two days.*

OUTDOOR BONSAI

Trees to be kept outdoors in a temperate climate will always be those species and varieties that are hardy in those climatic conditions. They will normally be able to accept very cold conditions (from about -10°C/14°F) up to quite hot summer conditions (30–40°C/86–104°F).

If hardy trees are placed under cover during normal cold winters, they may become slightly tender and could be susceptible to damage from late spring frosts when they are removed from that winter protection. It is therefore advisable not to protect such trees too much, as it could lead to greater problems than might be caused if they were left outdoors throughout the winter.

Deciduous trees will need much less water in the winter, as they will not have any foliage to keep supplied with fluid. It may therefore be necessary to give only a light splash of water every month over the winter period. You must, however, always keep a close watch on the moisture levels, as total drying out could be a disaster and result in the death of the tree.

Above: *A very useful outdoor display area, incorporating several different heights of stand that show off a variety of different bonsai.*

Left: *A bonsai on a timber deck next to a pond will be provided with extra humidity.*

Left: *This is winter housing for bonsai, with the slightly more vulnerable trees placed beneath the bench for added protection from the elements.*

Watering bonsai

As with all plants, water is vital to the survival and healthy growth of bonsai. If bonsai are kept outside, then rainfall will supply some of their needs, but if they are kept inside, they will be totally reliant on their owner for their water supply. This may seem obvious at first, but it is a fact that cannot be overstated because so many people find it difficult to assess the watering needs of bonsai, whether they are indoor or outdoor varieties. It is therefore crucial that the correct watering regime is carried out in order to maintain the health and vigour of any type of bonsai. Bonsai must never be allowed to dry out or become waterlogged because it can prove fatal in both instances. The death of a bonsai is demoralizing when you consider the time and effort that goes into creating it.

Above: *Use a watering can with a very fine rose attachment when applying a light watering to the soil of a bonsai.*

OUTDOOR BONSAI

Although outdoor trees will benefit from rainfall, you should not think that if it rains, even heavily, watering will be unnecessary. A tree may have a very heavy foliage canopy, similar to an umbrella, which even heavy rain cannot penetrate, and so the soil may not get wet at all. You will therefore still need to supply your bonsai with water, making sure that it is applied under the foliage canopy and on to the soil itself. Even a tree with a small canopy, and therefore one more suited to being watered naturally, may still need hand-watering, since the fact that most bonsai are grown in fairly shallow containers means that they will be able to retain little of the rainwater they receive.

Keep the soil moist at all times, but never water it to such a degree that the soil and roots become waterlogged because this could quickly result in the roots getting too wet, which will encourage root rot and possibly the death of the tree.

A watering can with a fine rose is ideal, but if your collection of bonsai is very large you can use a hose with a fine rose attached.

The frequency of watering will depend on many things. Strong wind or sun, or a combination of both factors, can be lethal to bonsai, as the soil can quickly dry out. For this reason, you should monitor moisture levels in the growing medium every day in the summer, spring and early autumn.

Right: *Here, a rooted cutting is being watered in using a pressure sprayer, so that the plant receives only a very light watering. This will prevent any disturbance of the fresh soil.*

Left: *A good-quality galvanized watering can with a fine rose is ideal for watering bonsai.*

1 Fill a bowl with water and immerse the pot in the water until the bubbles cease to rise; remove from the water and leave to drain.

2 Use a watering can with a fine rose in order to water the soil and roots. If the soil is very dry, use several applications of water.

3 The same watering can may be used to water the foliage weekly, particularly if there has not been any rain for a while.

4 You can also water with a pressure sprayer or with a hose fitted with a fine rose. Never water with a high-pressure hose.

INDOOR BONSAI

So-called indoor trees require a somewhat different approach to watering. It is very easy to water any indoor bonsai: simply place the whole container in a bowl of water, completely submerging both the container and the soil. Leave the plant submerged until the air bubbles stop rising to the surface, then remove the

container from the water, place it on a suitable surface, and allow any excess water to drain away.

You can also water indoor bonsai with a small watering can, preferably one fitted with a very fine rose, but be careful that the pots are not standing on a piece of valuable furniture that will be damaged by having water splashed on its surface.

Take the tree outdoors or to a kitchen draining board or even to the bathroom where moisture in the area will not create a problem. Feeding can also cause problems with furniture, so at all times take care with these tasks. For this reason, it is advisable to apply a dry granular fertilizer to the soil surface of your indoor trees.

Feeding bonsai

Regular feeding with the correct type and dose of fertilizer, and at the correct intervals throughout the year, is just as important to bonsai as watering. In fact, feeding is absolutely essential if good, healthy growth is to be maintained. Like all plants, bonsai will take up a certain amount of the fertilizer's nutrients in the soil, but watering will leach away any fertilizer that is left in the soil. This means that a regular input of nutrients is required. Although fertilizers are absolutely necessary to the health of your bonsai, they should always be used sparingly, so that the trees do not put on a massive amount of "forced" growth that will make it difficult to maintain their compact nature. Conversely, too little feeding leads to unhealthy specimens that will struggle to survive.

Above: *A good, balanced general-purpose fertilizer will provide most bonsai with healthy foliage and roots throughout the year.*

Fertilizers can be purchased in a variety of forms, including liquids, slow-release granules and soluble powders. Some of these can be applied as foliar feeds by spraying them on to the foliage with an atomizing spray or by watering them into the soil using a watering can. Pellets can be placed on the soil surface or pushed into the soil and covered over.

Fertilizer pellets that are specially formulated for bonsai can be obtained from specialist bonsai suppliers; they normally take the form of a rapeseed cake. They are a slow-release organic fertilizer that will supply nutrients, and therefore all the necessary feeding requirements, to bonsai for several weeks or months.

When using liquid feed, apply only the recommended dose, or less. Frequent applications of half-strength fertilizer, say once a week or once every two weeks through the spring and summer, will ensure that your trees receive a gentle feeding regime. Once autumn approaches, a feed of very low- or zero-nitrogen content will be required to harden off the current year's growth, which will help your trees to survive better over the winter.

FERTILIZER CONTENT

Most widely available fertilizers contain nitrogen (N), phosphorus (P) and potassium (K), and this combination is usually quoted on the packet as an NPK ratio, such as an NPK of 6:12:10 (which means 6 parts of nitrogen to 12 parts of phosphorus to 10 parts of potassium).

Nitrogen is absolutely essential for vegetative stem and leaf growth, and it is the constituent part of a fertilizer that is responsible for the rich green colours of the leaves. Too much nitrogen will not be good for bonsai, as their growing method means that they do not need to have masses of long, lush, green shoots. Although bonsai need healthy green shoots, they should

Left: *An application of low- or zero-nitrogen fertilizer can be given in late summer and early autumn. This is necessary to harden off the current season's growth in readiness for the winter.*

FEEDING YOUR BONSAI

1 You can apply liquid fertilizers to the roots using a watering-can. Dilute recommended fertilizers as specified.

2 Make sure the fertilizer has been absorbed into the water, then apply the mixture to the soil with care.

3 Pellets made of rapeseed cake can be applied by laying them on the soil surface with tweezers or fingers, about 5cm (2in) apart.

4 After placing the pellets on the soil surface, water over them to start the feeding process which will last two to three months.

be encouraged to grow with short internodal lengths by feeding them with a fertilizer with a relatively low-nitrogen content.

The phosphorus content of a fertilizer is mostly responsible for healthy root growth, but it also helps with bud formation, protection against diseases and poor winter conditions.

Potassium, which is often known as potash, will help to encourage the formation of flowers and fruit. This is also the most essential component in fertilizers in the fight against various diseases. It will also assist with hardening off any new growth produced throughout the season before the winter.

Most commercially available fertilizers contain all three main nutrients, plus some trace elements that will maintain good, healthy growth. There is just one type of fertilizer that is normally available only through specialist bonsai nurseries, and this is a late-autumn feed with an NPK of 0:10:10.

FEEDING GUIDE FOR BONSAI

(Number of applications per month in brackets)

SEASON	COMMONLY GROWN SPECIES		FLOWERING BONSAI
	Liquid and foliar fertilizer	Slow-release fertilizer	Type of fertilizer
Midwinter			
Late Winter			
Early Spring	High Nitrogen (1)	3 months release (1)	
Mid-spring	High Nitrogen (2) Balanced (1)		Balanced (2)
Late Spring	Balanced (3)		Balanced (1) Tomato/rose fertilizer (2)
Early Summer	Balanced (4)	3 months release (1)	Tomato/rose fertilizer (4)
Midsummer	Balanced (4)		Tomato/rose fertilizer (4)
Late Summer	Balanced (2)	Low Nitrogen (2) Low Nitrogen (1)	Low Nitrogen (2) Tomato/rose fertilizer (2)
Early Autumn	Low Nitrogen (1)	Low Nitrogen (4)	Low Nitrogen (4)
Mid-autumn	Low Nitrogen (1)	Low Nitrogen (2)	Low Nitrogen (2)
Late Autumn	Low Nitrogen (1)	Pines only (1)	Low Nitrogen (1)
Early Winter			

Bonsai: general maintenance

Whether you grow your trees purely for pleasure or display them at bonsai shows and exhibitions, you will want to make sure that your bonsai look their best at all times. Poor maintenance can result in plants that look untidy, unkempt and generally of reduced quality, so make sure you keep your trees clean and tidy following the instructions below, so that the very best impression of your trees is given to anyone viewing them. If any of your trees cannot be seen at their best, then it is advisable not to include them in a display or exhibition. You will find that the cleaner your trees are, the less likely they are to be infested with insects of any kind, or to be susceptible to attacks from fungal or viral diseases that could prove to be highly problematic to your trees.

Above: *Despite having large drainage holes, the flat base of a bonsai pot tends to retain a lot of water. This Chinese juniper (Juniperus chinensis) is tilted for winter drainage.*

POT MAINTENANCE

The pots containing all the prized bonsai specimens that you intend to display or exhibit should be washed thoroughly and also dried. If you encounter a problem when cleaning your bonsai pots, then a kitchen scouring pad is an ideal aid for scrubbing dirty pots and will remove algae, calcium deposits and any stubborn dirt.

To enhance the appearance and colour of a pot, spray it with a leaf-shine product. This dries quickly and gives the pot a very natural appearance; it also tends to protect the pot against the return of any algae, deposits and dirt. Alternatively, you can wipe over the pot with some vegetable oil, using a lint-free cloth so that no small particles of lint are left behind to spoil the effect.

TREE MAINTENANCE

It is also important to make sure that the trees themselves are clean, free from any pests and diseases, and have no damaged foliage. These factors are unsightly and will compromise the appearance of your bonsai display.

Remove any damaged leaves or foliage by pinching them off with your fingers or with a pair of tweezers. You can also simply snip them with a pair of scissors. If they are difficult to reach, then you may need to use a pair of scissors with extra-long blades. If there is any die-back within the branch structure, remove it using scissors for small items and branch or knob cutters for larger pieces.

You may find that over a period of time, there is a build-up of dirt, moss, algae, lichen or even insects on some of the trunk and branch structures of your trees. Brushing with a stiff brush and water will easily remove all of these problems. Spraying with water

Left: *Various bonsai on temporary benches for winter storage under cover.*

CARING FOR YOUR POTS

1 Brush the surface of the soil in order to remove any debris, such as dead leaves, and top up with more soil if required.

2 Add some moss and press it into the surface of the soil while spraying. This helps the moss to establish quickly and results in a very natural look.

3 Brush the sides and rim of the pot to remove any loose dust, and then wash off any dirt that still remains.

4 Using a lint-free cloth that has been soaked with vegetable oil, wipe the pot to bring out its texture and colour.

MAINTAINING YOUR TREES

1 Remove any odd bits of dead bark from the trunk with a pair of tweezers in order to create a clean appearance.

2 Brush the trunk clean with a dry, stiff brush. You can use an old toothbrush if necessary.

3 Using the brush and some water, clean off any algae from the tree.

4 Spraying with water while you are brushing will help to wash away any loose debris.

while brushing will also help to wash away any unwanted debris that is spoiling the effect.

If any loose pieces of bark are unsightly, carefully remove them from the trunk with your fingers or with tweezers, making sure that you do not damage any features of the tree's trunk that could ultimately enhance the overall appearance of the tree. If there are any signs of disease or insect attack, you should take all the necessary steps to stop any recurrence of such a problem and it would be best not to exhibit the tree until the problem has been completely cleared up.

REFINING TECHNIQUES

As bonsai mature, they will always need some form of refining and pruning to keep them looking their best. When refining broad-leaf trees, minor adjustments can be made to the shape using wiring techniques. Young shoots sprout from various places on trunks and branches, and some of these will need to be removed to maintain the mature look of the tree. Tidying up old pruning cuts, removing dead branches and thinning out the branch structure are all essential to ensure continued improvement of your bonsai.

As with deciduous trees, refining techniques for conifers include pruning shoots, cutting out unwanted branches and thinning foliage, as well as the introduction of jin, shari and other artificial aging processes. The relationship of one branch to another and the space between them is important, because this enables the tree to be seen at its best. Creating spaces between branches also allows the sunlight to reach all the foliage and this will lead to healthier, more compact growth. Pinch out young growth with your fingers but use scissors for hardened growth.

SOIL MAINTENANCE

The condition of the soil surface is also very important, not only for the general health of your bonsai trees, but also for their overall appearance when you are preparing for an exhibition. Removing fallen leaves or needles from the soil surface is a high-priority task, along with removing any moss and troublesome weeds such as liverwort and pearlwort. These should be removed as soon as possible so that they do not over-run the roots of your trees. Liverwort is generally a sign that the soil is too wet, while pearlwort can quickly choke the tree's roots, since its own roots can go deep into and under the root-ball, quite often blocking the drainage holes in the pot. This makes the soil too wet, which can in turn lead to the development of large areas of liverwort.

You can deal with most of these problems by picking out any small, individual plants that are not wanted with a pair of tweezers and then brushing the surface of the soil clean with a suitable brush.

WINTER STORAGE

Whether or not your bonsai need protection for the winter depends on the climate in which you live. If your trees are going to be exposed to conditions below freezing, then you may have to take extra precautions. These may include placing the trees in a greenhouse, shade tunnel or just under the display benching.

When placing bonsai trees under benches, it is advisable to put them on some form of timber staging to keep them off the ground. You will also need to provide extra protection at the front, sides and back of the benching. Small trees can be placed in containers filled to the brim with peat so that the root-ball and pot are covered. These methods for extra-winter protection should only be carried out if it becomes necessary because over-protecting normally hardy species can lead to problems with new growth in the spring.

REFINING BROAD-LEAF TREES

1 Using a pair of concave branch cutters, remove any stubs left from previous pruning.

2 Cut out any small adventitious shoots with a pair of scissors.

3 Apply wire to those branches that cover the front of the tree.

4 Reposition the branches to give a balanced appearance, and seal all the cuts with wound sealer.

REFINING CONIFERS

1 Use a pair of scissors to remove all downward-facing growth.

2 Similarly, remove all upward-facing growth in order to produce a clean outline.

3 Using branch cutters, prune out any large or heavy growth from the inner part to show the main branch at its best.

4 Gather up the foliage in bunches and pinch the tips off using your fingers or a pair of tweezers to thin out the leaves.

CREATING A HYGIENIC ENVIRONMENT

1 Leaves and rubbish on and around your bonsai trees can harbour all sorts of unwanted insects and diseases.

2 The removal of rubbish not only makes the trees look better, but it keeps them healthier too.

3 Here, you can see that the pot is dirty and there is fallen foliage on the surface of the soil.

4 The removal of debris, and the cleaning and oiling of the pot, will keep the tree healthier, as well as improving its overall appearance.

STORING YOUR BONSAI OVER WINTER

1 Trees can be placed on timber slats beneath the normal bonsai benches for added protection through the winter months.

2 Cover the front and sides (and rear if it is open) with greenhouse shade netting. Here, it is partially covered to show the placement of the trees, but it will be completely covered when the temperature falls below freezing.

3 You can provide added protection for the roots of your bonsai by placing them in a box or basket filled with organic matter.

4 Here, the two trees have their pots and roots protected from severe winter frosts. Water sparingly during the winter months.

Bonsai: pests and diseases

Most bonsai are created from hardy shrubs and trees and are therefore not very susceptible to many pests or diseases. Instances of both of these will occur, however, and so it is important to know what to do. The actual process of identifying a pest or disease is very important and, if this is done correctly, then a suitable remedy can be applied. Cleanliness is the best form of attack that you have. In fact, good hygiene practices will normally keep most pests and diseases under control. This should avoid the unnecessary use of insecticides and pesticides. Pesticides can be dangerous and most bonsai growers would recommend the use of such chemicals only as a very last resort. If you do decide to apply pesticide, ensure that you have properly read the instructions and are wearing suitably protective clothing.

Above: *Aphids can be a real problem because they can quickly take over a plant, sucking the sap from its stems, leaves and fruit.*

PESTS

There are a few pests that can be a problem to bonsai trees, as follows:

Vine weevil

This insect is difficult to eradicate. The vine weevil larvae act by devouring the root system of a plant and can quickly kill a tree. They feed on the roots and destroy the tree's lifeline. The larvae will strip the roots bare right up to soil level. It will not be obvious that there is a problem until the tree shows signs of stress, begins to wilt and then dies. The soil should be treated at regular intervals with a suitable product to prevent infestation by these fat, creamy white, maggot-like larvae. Repot your bonsai regularly each year, if appropriate, with fresh soil in early spring just before the buds begin to break. If you discover vine weevil

Vine weevil larvae

Vine weevil adult

larvae when repotting, wash the roots clean of all soil, destroy any larvae, and repot the bonsai in the usual way.

The adult vine weevil is difficult to spot, as it hides away during the day, emerging only at night when it climbs to the top of plants to eat notches from the edges of the leaves. Treatment with a soil insecticide will deal with the larvae, or you can go out at night with a torch, collect the adults and destroy them.

Scale insect

This is another creature that can be very difficult to find until the limpet-like shell lifts to reveal a fluffy, sticky, white mass on its underside. Scale insects are one of the most difficult pests to get rid of if they get a hold in any indoor bonsai collection.

The application of a systemic insecticide should prevent this insect from becoming a problem for your bonsai, or you can physically remove the adults one at a time, although that process can be very time-consuming and laborious. A cotton bud (swab) soaked in methylated spirits (methyl alcohol) and used as a removal tool is also a very effective way to remove scale insects from the trunks of your bonsai. Alternatively, brushing with a stiff brush such as an old toothbrush

will also remove them. This technique may, however, simply transfer the insects to the soil, from where they could reappear later on, so treatment with a systemic insecticide is probably the only true solution to this rather difficult problem.

Aphids

These can be a serious problem, as they colonize plants and systematically suck the sap from stems, leaves and fruit. They are especially attracted to early spring growth on trees such as Japanese maples (*Acer palmatum*). The first indication that there is an infestation of aphids is usually when the leaves begin to curl up and become distorted. They come in a variety of colours, but the most common are greenfly, blackfly and whitefly. The latter is one of the most troublesome pests that attack indoor bonsai, but regular applications of a systemic insecticide will usually eradicate them from most plants.

The woolly aphid can be a serious problem on pine, larch and beech trees, and manifests itself as a white,

Soft scales

Brown scale insects

White soft scale insects

Young scale insects

Leaf-cutter bee damage

Caterpillar

fluffy, sticky mass. On pines and larch it appears among the needles and is very difficult to remove without applying a systemic insecticide; on beech trees it appears on the underside of the leaves. Once again, the application of a systemic insecticide should be sufficient to deal with this problem.

Leaf-cutter bee

These can be a problem to the bonsai grower, but not one that will cause any serious damage. It will definitely not result in long-term damage to any tree. The symptoms of leaf-cutter bee infestation are large, circular notches cut into the edges of leaves. This is carried out by the leaf-cutter bee and only disfigures the foliage. There is no control method other than removing the damaged leaves. This will, of course, act in the same way as leaf pruning, and will simply encourage more leaves to grow.

Caterpillars

Many varieties of caterpillar can attack the foliage of your bonsai plants. The easiest method of controlling these unwanted visitors is simply to pick them off by hand and destroy them. Alternatively, you can place them on another plant in your garden, so that they eat the foliage of something other than your prized bonsai specimens.

Snails and slugs

These cause a lot of damage in a short time, so it is important to discourage them from areas around your bonsai by making sure that there are no hiding places for them. They do most damage at night or when it is wet, so keep everything clean by removing dead and unwanted leaves from areas near your trees, especially if you do not wish to use dangerous chemicals.

Snail

Slug

DISEASES

These are less frequently encountered than bonsai pests, mostly taking the form of leaf disorders. These can normally be controlled by removing and destroying affected leaves and stems. However, regular applications of a good systemic fungicide will control the most common diseases.

Powdery mildew

This is a white dusty growth that appears on leaf surfaces and young stems, and can be treated by regular spraying with fungicide.

Damping off

This condition is where seedlings begin to rot at the base of the stem, resulting in the seedling falling over and then dying. Spray with a copper-based fungicide.

Rust

This unsightly disease appears on leaves as slightly raised orange/yellow spots. If you see this tell-tale coloration, then quickly remove any affected leaves and destroy them. You should also spray the bonsai specimen with a zinc-based fungicide.

Verticillium wilt

This is a disease that causes die-back in maples. It attacks the sapwood and is difficult to detect, and most trees should be treated with a systemic fungicide as a preventative measure.

Peach leaf curl

This can be a problem on trees belonging to the *Prunus* family and appears as reddish-brown blistery shapes on the leaves. These quickly multiply, causing the leaves to curl up into distorted shapes. Treat with a copper-based fungicide.

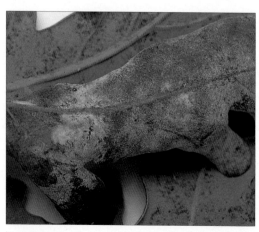

Powdery mildew

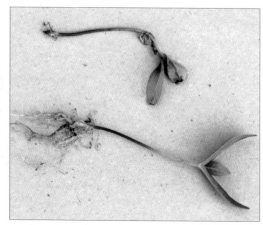

Damping off

Rust

Verticillium wilt

Peach leaf curl

Grey mould

Grey mould

This is a fungus that occurs on the leaves of plants that are kept in conditions of high humidity. It is possible to control it by increasing ventilation and spraying with a systemic fungicide. Always make sure that you adhere closely to the directions on the packaging, and if there are any safety precautions, follow them to the letter.

A NOTE ON SPRAYING

Although you may not use insecticides or fungicides, it is worth noting that regular spraying with them will keep most pests and diseases under control. If an infestation builds up in your bonsai, then some sort of remedy will be required. Systemic remedies are normally sprayed on to the plant using an atomizing sprayer, and precautions should be taken to prevent inhalation of any of these types of spray, as they can be very dangerous to humans, animals and fish.

Systemic insecticides and fungicides act by being absorbed into the tissues and sap of the plant, which then transport them around the entire plant, giving protection for up to about six weeks at a time. Systemic solutions will need to be applied about three to four times during the growing season, but care should be taken not to apply them when the leaves are very fresh, as the chemicals can damage them. Another reliable form of deterrent is to spray your trees with a winter wash, which will destroy any overwintering eggs, larvae, insects and fungi. This means that you will not be plagued with problems in the following spring.

Below: *Garden centres and supermarkets sell a wide range of garden chemicals. Always follow the manufacturer's instructions, wear protective clothing and store products safely.*

Bonsai calendar of care

Throughout the year, you will need to carry out various tasks in order to maintain the health, appearance, growth and general well-being of your bonsai, whether they are indoor or outdoor varieties. Keeping the trunks, branches, soil surfaces and pots clean is just one element of a general maintenance programme that needs to be followed at all times, regardless of season and weather. If any of the following tasks are ignored, you may run into serious problems later in the year or even later in the life of your bonsai specimens. So, make sure that you clean your tools and equipment thoroughly and keep a constant look-out at all times for any signs of distress in your plants, and you will eventually reap great rewards from your bonsai collection.

Above: *Japanese maple* (Acer palmatum*) in a pot ideal for future bonsai training. Check water content of the soil daily to prevent drying out.*

EARLY SPRING

- As the days lengthen, many trees will begin to come out of their dormant period. This will be evident in the swelling of buds, although some bonsai will not start any new growth yet. Keep a close watch on all trees from now on, and repot when each tree is ready. Most trees will not need larger pots because, once their roots have been pruned, they will fit into the same pot, as long as it is still suitable for that tree. Before repotting, allow the tree's root-ball (roots) to dry out a little, as this will help when removing old soil and adding new.

- Watering may need to increase as the weather warms up, but be careful not to overwater.
- Begin to take hardwood cuttings towards the end of early spring, as well as sow seeds in trays of good open soil to encourage root growth on both seedlings and cuttings.

MID-SPRING

- Hardy trees can be taken out from their winter quarters if they have been under any sort of cover. Remember that hardy trees require winter cover in only the most exceptional circumstances.

- Most repotting should have been completed by now, but some conifers can be left until late spring before being repotted.
- If your trees have been left out throughout the winter, their buds will be hardy and should not suffer from late frosts. However, some species, such as Japanese maples (*Acer palmatum*) or anything that has delicate new leaves, may need a little protection from any late frosts.

CARING FOR YOUR BONSAI IN SPRING

Early Spring: *Clean, spread out and prune roots of cuttings prior to potting into larger pots.*

Mid-spring: *Tidy up the shape of all bonsai as they start growing to achieve a neat outline.*

Late Spring: *Repotting a three-year-old cutting into a training pot to obtain good root growth.*

- Watering will now need to be stepped up, as trees are beginning to get into their full growing mode.
- Applications of fertilizer should be started now, as trees will be requiring their first nutrients of the year. The first application of slow-release feed can be given now, but avoid applying fertilizer to freshly root-pruned trees. Leave them for three to four weeks before feeding so as to avoid any root scorch by the fertilizer.
- Tidy up the shape of your bonsai as they begin to grow so that their appearance remains satisfactory.

LATE SPRING

- All bonsai should be in full active growth by now, and daily watering may be required from now on to avoid allowing any trees to dry out. Be careful not to overwater pines (*Pinus*), as this can make them grow too rapidly and produce needles that are too long and look out of proportion to the trees. For this reason pines must definitely be kept on the dry side.
- Feed weekly with liquid fertilizer if you have not given a slow-release application in mid-spring.
- Trees will vary enormously in the strength of their growth, and pruning will have to be carried out to suit each individual tree so that a good shape is always maintained.

Above: *Fresh growth on a* Cryptomeria japonica *a few weeks after the shoots have been pinched out in midsummer.*

Both light and heavy pruning can be carried out in late spring, as most trees are in full growth mode and any pruning cuts will heal very quickly.
- Shaping using wire is acceptable at this time of year on most trees, but take care when applying wire so that you do not damage growth that is important to the shape of your trees.
- If there are any conifers still to be repotted, get this done quickly so that they have a good period of time to re-establish themselves before winter sets in once again.

EARLY SUMMER

- This is quite often one of the hottest times of the year, and with the correct watering and feeding regime, most bonsai will be at their peak growth rate.

- Maples will require almost daily pinching out of shoot tips so that their form, compactness and tight growth are maintained throughout.
- Early summer is a good time to defoliate any deciduous trees that need this treatment, as there is enough time before autumn to ensure that the second set of leaves can reach maturity.
- All root pruning and repotting should have been carried out by now except in very rare emergency situations.
- Take softwood cuttings now. Insert them into a good-quality cuttings compost (soil mix) and provide them with some shade to avoid drying out the soil and any leaves left on the cutting.
- While your bonsai may be growing fast, so too are the weeds, so it is a good idea to remove any unwanted plants from the soil surface as soon as possible. Never allow them to mature and seed, as this just allows them to proliferate.
- Watch out for insects and diseases from now on as most flourish in the warmer weather. Apply systemic insecticides or fungicides when this is necessary, but avoid their use if at all possible because they can be dangerous to adults, children, pets and fish if correct precautions are not taken.

CARING FOR YOUR BONSAI IN SUMMER

Early Summer: *Deciduous trees can be defoliated now.*

Midsummer: *Apply wire to any bonsai that require it.*

Late Summer: *Continue to prune as needed by pinching out shoots with fingers or tweezers.*

MIDSUMMER

- Weather conditions are similar to the early summer, and most bonsai activities are the same. Pruning, pinching, wiring, watering, feeding, etc may all need to be carried out.
- Indoor trees can be placed outdoors now, as they will benefit from the fresh air and good light at this time of year. Give them slight shading when they are first placed outside, then move them into full sun once they have hardened off.
- Continue to take softwood cuttings as well as semi-ripe cuttings and place them in trays.
- Do not root prune or repot other than in extreme emergencies.

LATE SUMMER

- The growth rate of bonsai will be starting to slow down, and overnight dew and some slightly misty evenings mean that some may require less watering now.
- Continue to prune where needed.
- Slow down on feeding, and use low-nitrogen fertilizer at about two-weekly intervals. The low-nitrogen fertilizer will help to harden off the current year's growth, so aiding the trees' survival through the winter.
- Conifers can still be repotted towards the end of late summer, but make sure that enough time is left before the winter for the roots to make

Above: *Autumn is a time of year when you can enjoy the spectacular colour of deciduous bonsai foliage.*

some new growth before winter sets in. If this root growth does not happen, then the tree could sit in wet soil, with cut root ends, which will make the tree vulnerable to root rot during the winter months.

EARLY AUTUMN

- Bonsai will have mostly stopped growing by now, so you will need to water less. Monitor the situation, however, and water where necessary. Give an application of low- or zero-nitrogen fertilizer, as this will help with winter survival.
- Wiring can still be carried out, but is not advisable. Think about removing wire to give the trees a rest and to avoid any damage in winter. Watch pines closely if they still have wire on them, as they often put on a spurt of

growth from early autumn onwards; the wire will become embedded in the bark, with disastrous results. Avoid this by removing wire in good time.

MID-AUTUMN

- Very little watering needs to be done in mid-autumn, as overnight dew and autumn mists will supply a reasonable amount of water.
- Deciduous trees will begin to show some beautiful autumn colour and also to drop a few of their leaves. Some of these trees will look spectacular and should be placed where their beauty can be admired.
- Take all indoor trees back under cover and supply them with some mild heating and humidity.
- Apply the last low-nitrogen feed of the year.
- Carry out any pruning needed to tidy up the shape of your trees.
- Keep all trees clean and remove any fallen leaves from the soil surface, as well as around and under bonsai benches and stands. This will help to deter unwanted pests and diseases.

LATE AUTUMN

- There is very little to do now except for tidying up fallen leaves and giving a splash of water where needed. Make sure that any winter shelter areas are ready so that trees can be moved to them quickly.

CARING FOR YOUR BONSAI IN AUTUMN

Early Autumn: *Prop up one end of the pots to assist drainage and prevent waterlogging.*

Mid-autumn: *Autumn colour is now at its best. Place your trees where they can be seen.*

Late Autumn: *Begin to provide some winter protection, but only in the most severe conditions.*

EARLY WINTER

- This is probably an even quieter month in the bonsai world than late autumn, but bonsai should always be checked regularly, whatever the time of year, to make sure that there are no problems developing. This is a good time to study the structure of your trees, especially that of deciduous trees, as all the foliage has dropped, leaving the branch formation easy to see. An assessment can be made now of any serious pruning required that can take place in spring just before growth restarts. So, once you have recovered from the seasonal festivities you can begin to think ahead to the New Year and all that is needed to once again bring your trees to their best for the spring.

MIDWINTER

- This is normally the coldest time of the year, and there is very little need for watering outdoor trees, though they should be checked regularly and given a splash of water if required. Indoor bonsai continue to grow over the winter period despite taking a little bit of a rest, and they will need regular light watering to keep them just moist at all times.
- Feeding is not required on outdoor trees, but light, regular doses of fertilizer can be given to indoor or less hardy varieties.

Above: *Even in winter, you still need to water your bonsai plants. You cannot simply rely on rainfall at this time of year.*

- Tidy up twigs of both indoor and outdoor trees if you did not do this during late autumn.
- Conifers can be very vulnerable to the effects of strong, cold winds at this time of the year, especially if their root-ball becomes frozen. They will still need to be watered in order to keep the foliage going, and, if the soil is frozen, it will have the same effect as drying out in the summer. (If any of the root-balls of your conifers freeze for more than five days, it is advisable to thaw them out gently by placing the affected plants in a cold greenhouse or shed until they have thawed, then leave them for a few days so that the trees can take up water before returning them to their normal outdoor position.)

- Apply wire to trees such as larch (*Larix*), as it is easier to do this when there is no foliage on the tree, but do not wire deciduous trees such as maples, as they can be very brittle at this time of year.
- There will be no need to begin root pruning or repotting during midwinter, although the pots, soil and any other materials and tools relating to repotting and root pruning should be prepared at around this time.

LATE WINTER

- Conditions in late winter are very similar to those in midwinter, and it is wise to keep deciduous trees a little on the dry side while never allowing them to dry out completely. This can be achieved by placing your outdoor trees under a roof cover.
- Continue to prepare potting supplies and make sure bags of soil are open to allow the soil to dry out, as it is better to use totally dry soil for repotting. If trees show signs of buds swelling, then repot before they begin to break bud. Following repotting they may need some frost protection, as cut root ends are very vulnerable.
- Some heavier pruning can be dealt with now, as the new growth is beginning and wounds will heal fairly quickly.

CARING FOR YOUR BONSAI IN WINTER

Early Winter: *Check on the shape of your bonsai trees regularly in winter.*

Midwinter: *This is a good time of year to admire the structural framework of bonsai.*

Late Winter: *Provide some winter protection for your bonsai trees outside.*

Japanese gardening glossary

Amida Buddha The form of the Buddha whose promise of a western Paradise influenced Heian-period garden makers.

Aminoshidate A long pine-clad peninsula on the north coast of Honshu, and one of the five most famous scenic spots in Japan, often symbolically reproduced in gardens.

Aware Lamenting the passing of things, a heightened awareness of fleeting beauty. An emotional attitude to the natural world that infected the sensibility of Heian courtiers.

Bakufu The military bureaucracies that acted for the emperor.

Carp stone A stone placed at the base of waterfalls to represent a leaping fish. This indicates the strivings of humanity.

Cha-niwa tea garden. Garden immediately around the tea house.

Cha-noyu The tea ceremony.

Chonin The merchant class, especially those who enjoyed a period of wealth during the Edo period but were forced to hide it. They made elaborate gardens inside their unobtrusive houses.

Chozubachi Taller style of water basin, often placed where it can be reached from a veranda.

Confucius (d. 479 BC) Chinese sage who laid down principles and morals. These were especially popular during the Edo period when Buddhism waned.

Crane island (*tsuru-shima*) Part of the Mystic isles myth. Cranes carried the immortals on their backs, and became symbols of longevity. The crane island is portrayed by rocks indicating long necks or an upheld wing.

Daimyo A lord who owned land.

Dyana meditation. The Sanskrit word that is at the root of the word Zen.

Edo period From 1603 to 1867, when the Tokugawa shogunate ruled Japan from its new capital in Edo, now known as Tokyo.

Eisai The Buddhist monk attributed with bringing both Zen Buddhism and the first successfully transplanted tea plants to Japan in the 13th century.

Enshu, Kabori 17th-century garden designer and town planner, whose plans set new standards for garden design, influencing the Katsura palace and many temple gardens.

Fuji-san, **Mount Fuji** ("san" means mountain) sacred mountain whose form can be reproduced symbolically in gardens.

Fuzei taste.

Genji, The Tale of Highly influential novel of the Heian period, written by Murasaki Shikibu.

Geomancy Chinese system that brings together many beliefs as to how buildings, cities and gardens should be laid out relative to directions, colours and elements. This system is also

applied in systems of government. Includes such principles as yin-yang and feng-shui.

Go-shintai Shinto term for an area that is considered to be the abode of the gods.

Heian Period from 794 to 1185, marking the period from when a new capital was created in Kyoto until the shogunate moved its headquarters to Kamakura.

Hiei-san Mountain overlooking Kyoto, views of which were coveted by garden designers. See *shakkei*.

Hojo The abbot's quarters in Zen temples, where the majority of dry Zen gardens were laid out.

Horai The central island in the ancient Chinese myth of the Mystic Isles, often portrayed by a large upright rock.

Immortals Inhabitants of the Mystic Isles who possessed the secret of the elixir of eternal youth. Mystic Isles were constructed in pond gardens in the hope of luring the immortals to earth.

Ishe-tate-so The "rock-setting priests" of the 14th and 15th centuries, who designed the first *kare-sansui* or dry gardens.

Iwa-kura Literally "boulder-seat". Shintoists believed rocks possessed spirits, and certain rocks were given the status of gods, a factor that may well have influenced the way rocks were used in Japanese gardens.

Kamakura Period from 1185 to 1392, following the Heian period, when the shogunate moved its headquarters from Kyoto to Kamakura, south of modern-day Tokyo.

Kame-shima see Turtle islands.

Kami The Shinto term for gods.

Kare-sansui The dry landscape garden, where the element of water is represented by sand and gravel.

Kawara-mono The lowest caste in Japan, attributed with having helped to build *kare-sansui* dry gardens during the Muromachi period, especially Ryoan-ji.

Koan Zen riddle to aid emptiness of mind, and a trigger for enlightenment.

Kyoto The most important capital city in the history of Japanese garden design.

Machiya Smaller town houses belonging to merchants, containing small *tsubo-niwa* or courtyard gardens.

Mappo The Buddhist age of "ending law" said to have started in the 11th century. The last of three ages predicted by the Buddha, inducing a sense of pessimism.

Matsushima Pine-clad islands off the north-east coast of Japan that inspired reproduction in many gardens.

Meiji restoration The restoration of the emperor as acting head of state in 1868, and the end of the shogunate rule. The emperor moved to the new capital of Tokyo.

Mitate Recycled second-hand building materials, such as millstones, incorporated into garden paths and buildings, which show the refined taste of their owner.

Momoyama Period from 1568 to 1603. The era of the generals, especially Totomi Hideyoshi, who fought on behalf of daimyo Nobunaga, and eventually unified Japan. The last of the generals was Ieyasu Tokugawa, whose family ruled throughout the Edo period.

Mu nothingness. An aspect of Zen that reveals itself in the empty spaces of sand in some dry Zen gardens.

Muromachi Period from 1393 to 1568, when the shogunate returned from Kamakura to Kyoto. Possibly the most intensely creative period in Japanese history, which saw both the dry *kare-sansui* gardens and tea gardens come of age.

Mystic Isles See Horai, Crane island and Turtle island.

Naka-kuguri Literally a middle crawl-through gate or stooping gate, a gate that deliberately induced a sense of humility along the tea path before a guest entered the tea house.

Nara Period from 710 to 794. Nara was the last of the ancient capitals, standing 50 miles south of Kyoto, before a new capital was built in Kyoto.

Nigiriguchi A small hatch-like entrance to the tea house, whereby the guest entered on hands and knees.

No-da-te An informal tea ceremony conducted outdoors.

O-karikomi The Japanese form of topiary, where plants of many kinds are clipped into abstract shapes.

Pagoda A Japanese or Chinese building that contained relics of the Buddha or his saints. These were often symbolically carved in stone and placed in gardens.

Peng-lai The original name for Mount Horai.

Pure Land paradise Thought to be in the West, this was the Buddha's abode for the afterlife. Ponds were made to evoke this paradise, especially in the Heian and Kamakura periods.

Rikyu Japan's most famous tea-master, whose influence on the tea ceremony and tea garden is still felt today.

Roji Literally "dewy path", the tea path that leads to the tea house.

Roji-mon The entrance gate to the tea garden or roji.

Ryoan-ji The most famous of all the dry Zen gardens in Kyoto, believed to have been built in 1499.

Sakuteiki The first and most influential garden treatise, which was written in the 11th century.

Samurai A soldier in service of a lord (*daimyo*).

Sanzon Buddhist trinity stone arrangement, meaning one large, vertical stone complemented by two smaller, horizontal stones.

Sesshu The most influential of Japanese brush and ink painters during the 15th century, who was also a gardener and a Zen priest.

Shakkei Literally "borrowed landscape". The inclusion of distant views to become part of the garden scene.

Shibumi This term is derived from the word meaning "astringent". It describes the minimalist, unpretentious worldly aesthetic of the Edo period that replaced the earlier and more spiritual term *wabi-sabi*.

Shigemori, Mirei The most influential and celebrated Japanese garden designer of the 20th century.

Shiki-no-himorogi Sacred areas covered with pebbles.

Shime The binding of artefacts, rocks and trees as part of the Shinto religion. The word *shima*, meaning garden, may have derived from this source.

Shin, gyo and **so** An expression to suggest the mixture of formal (*shin*), semi-formal (*gyo*) and informal (*so*) that describes different physical patterns, such as paving, in garden design.

Shinden Literally "sleeping hall". The main residence at the centre of the pond gardens of the Heian period.

Shinto The native animistic religion of Japan, meaning "the way of the gods". It is characterized by the idea that men are fundamentally good, and evil is created by spirits.

Shishi-odoshi A deer scarer. A bamboo device that repeatedly fills with water, then tips and smacks against a rock.

Shogun Military leader. It literally means "barbarian-quelling general".

Shoin architecture The style of architecture developed in Japan during the Muromachi (1393–1568) period that included a study room.

Soan The rustic style of architecture of tea houses.

Sode-gaki Sleeve fences. Small sections of bamboo and rush fences that divide up views of the garden from the house.

Sumeru Originally a Hindu mountain (Meru) that became Mount Shumisen to the Japanese Buddhists.

Tatami The woven rush matting that was especially favoured for the floor of Japanese tea houses.

Tokonoma The alcove in a tea house used for arrangements of Japanese wall-scrolls and symbolic art objects.

Tsubo-niwa A courtyard garden.

Tsukubai A low basin found by the path to the tea house, usually accompanied by a lantern.

Tsuru-shima See Crane island.

Turtle island Derived from the myth of the Mystic Isles, which were said to float on the backs of turtles. Turtle islands (*kame-shima*) are abstract rock arrangements with flippers and heads suggested.

Wabi-sabi Can be literally interpreted as "withered loneliness". An aesthetic term that was originally used in poetry, and later came to describe aspects of the tea ceremony, including its pottery, gardens and architecture.

Yatsuhashi An eight-plank zigzag bridge that crosses over streams and ponds which are often planted with irises.

Yugen Literally meaning "too deep to see", suggesting a mystery or depth that goes beyond what can be seen. A quality sought by Japanese artists of all kinds, including garden makers.

Zen Buddhism A form of Buddhism introduced to Japan from China in the 13th century. Zen heavily influenced the arts, especially gardens such as the *kare-sansui* and tea garden.

Bonsai glossary

Accent plant Separate planting of small plants such as bulbs, grasses or herbaceous plants. Normally used alongside a bonsai.

Acid soil Soil with pH less than 7.0.

Adult foliage Mature leaves of a plant that has different juvenile and mature foliage.

Adventitious Shoots originating from parts of a plant other than the growing points. Usually found on older wood.

Air layering Technique used to produce roots from a wound on a branch or trunk by covering it with sphagnum moss.

Akadama Japanese red clay, granular, nutrient-free, general-purpose soil.

Alkaline soil Soil with a pH over 7.0 or rich in lime.

Apex The crown of a tree.

Apical Shoot at the tip of a branch or bud.

Axil The angle between leaf and shoot.

Back budding New buds within the branch structure that have been encouraged by pruning the tip growth.

Bark Protective outer layer of trunk and branches formed by the cambium and dead cells on the outside of the tree.

Bole The trunk of a tree between ground level and the lowest branch.

Branch cutters Japanese pruning tool with single, concave cutting edges used for pruning branches. Sometimes known as side cutters.

Broad-leaved Trees that have broad and flat leaves as distinct from needles.

Bud Embryonic shoot protected by scales formed by modified leaves

Bunjingi Literati-style bonsai, usually a tall, slender, freestyle and flowing tree with a few branches normally in the upper trunk.

Buttress Base of the trunk from where the surface roots emerge.

Callus Growth developed over a wound.

Cambium A thin, growing layer between the bark and the heartwood, responsible for producing new bark on the outside and new wood on the inside.

Candle New tip growth on pines.

Canopy The foliage of the outer and upper parts of the tree.

Chokkan Formal-upright style, normally with a straight vertical trunk and horizontal main branches.

Clamp Tool used to bend heavy trunks or branches.

Collected tree Tree taken from the wild or from a garden, suitable for training into a bonsai specimen.

Compost (potting mix) A mixture of humus, sand and grit used as the growing medium and sometimes described as soil.

Conifer Usually evergreen trees bearing needle like leaves and cones.

Cross Hybrid plant resulting from cross-fertilization between species or varieties.

Crown Uppermost part of tree, sometimes referred to as the apex.

Cultivar Garden variety of a plant identified by certain characteristics when propagated vegetatively or from seed.

Cut-leaved Description of a plant which has leaves with finely divided segments.

Cuttings Plant shoots used for propagation.

Deciduous Trees or shrubs that lose their leaves in the autumn.

Defoliation Complete leaf removal to encourage the growth of smaller leaves.

Dendrology The study of trees.

Die-back Deterioration of shoots or branches normally caused by drought, disease or incorrect pruning.

Dormancy Period of rest for plants during the winter months, and the condition of seeds before germination.

Drainage mesh Normally plastic, mesh used to cover drainage holes in bonsai pots.

Drawn Plants that have characteristic extended, spindly growth caused by overcrowding or poor light.

Dwarf Genetic mutation producing plants of small compact habit.

Ericaceous Plants normally requiring acidic growing conditions.

Evergreen Plants bearing foliage all year.

Eye level The ideal viewing position for bonsai, between one third and two thirds up the trunk.

Fertilizer Substance that provides essential nutrients for plant growth.

Fruit Part of a plant that carries its seeds.

Fungicide Substance for controlling fungal diseases.

Fukinagashii Windswept-style bonsai that emulates a tree in nature that has been exposed to the elements. A slanting trunk indicates a strong wind that blows in one direction.

Genus Group of plants with common structural characteristics.

Germination Earliest stage in the growth of plants from seed.

Girth Circumference of a tree trunk measured at chest height on full-size trees and just above soil-level in bonsai.

Habit Plant's characteristic growth pattern.

Half-hardy Plants requiring some winter protection.

Han-Kengai Semi-cascade bonsai style, normally with horizontal trunk or just dipping below the horizontal. The semi-cascade trunk will not grow below the bottom of the pot.

Hardening off Introducing plants grown under protection to outside conditions.

Hardwood Mature shoots used for cuttings and timber from broad-leaved trees.

Hardy Plants that can survive severe conditions outside during winter.

Heel cutting The base of a side shoot after it is pulled away from main stem.

Hoki-Zukuri Broom-style bonsai, also known as *Hokidachi*. The trunk is chopped and a deep V cut is performed on the remaining trunk.

Humidity The water content in the atmosphere, expressed as a percentage.

Humus Partially decayed organic material used in soil for potting bonsai.

Kengai Cascade-style bonsai, normally with the trunk angled down below the pot by 45 degrees or more.

Ibigawa Japanese rock formed by the amalgamation of various rocks.

Ikadabuki Raft-style bonsai, emulating a tree that has fallen with the trunk lying on the ground in a horizontal position, subsequently re-rooting and with the branches developing into the trunks.

Inarching Grafting technique used for introducing a new branch into a tree trunk.

Inorganic Chemical compound not containing carbon; horticulturally manufactured fertilizers, treatments and growing mediums.

Internode Distance between leaf nodes.

Ishizuki Generally, a bonsai with roots growing in, on or over a piece of rock.

Jin Branch or trunk apex with its bark removed exposing shaped, bleached and preserved heartwood for artistic effect.

Juvenile foliage Leaves produced during rapid stages of growth.

Kanuma Japanese granular acidic subsoil, suitable for ericaceous plants like azaleas.

Kiryu Japanese granular alkaline subsoil, suitable for pines and junipers.

Knob cutters Japanese cutting tool similar to side cutters but with double concave cutting edges, also known as wen cutters.

Jinning tool A tool similar to electrician's pliers, used for creating jin.

Lateral Side shoots from a branch or trunk.

Lava Wingless grub that is the second stage of an insect lifecycle.

Leader Upper part of main stem.

Leaf mould Partly decayed dead leaves used in compost.

Leaf scorch Damage to foliage caused by the action of strong wind or sun.

Lime Calcium as a soil component.

Lime sulphur Strong-smelling compound used to bleach and preserve jin and sharimiki (shari).

Loam A rich, fertile soil originating from pastureland and used in potting composts (soil mixes).

Mame Miniature bonsai, normally up to about 15cm (6in) high.

Microclimate Local climatic conditions within the immediate vicinity of a plant.

Misting Fine watering of plants using an atomizing spray.

Moyogi Informal upright style, usually with a slightly curved, interesting trunk.

Needle A very narrow leaf such as that on a pine or larch.

Nitrogen One of the most essential elements of plant nutrition. Responsible for the green vegetative growth in stems and leaves and identified by the letter N.

Node The position on a shoot from which leaves or new shoots appear.

NPK An abbreviation used to denote the proportions of the three main elements in fertilizer, which are are nitrogen (N), phosphorous (P) and potassium (K).

Old wood Any plant part that originated during the previous season's growth.

Organic Chemical compound which contains carbon; horticulturally a compound or growing medium that is not manufactured or synthetic.

Peat Partially decayed organic matter, such as sphagnum moss, that is found in bogs or marshy ground. Often used as a moisture-retaining ingredient in potting mixes.

Penjing Chinese version of bonsai. The meaning is the same as the Japanese "plant in a container".

Petiole The stalk of a leaf.

pH Unit of measurement describing the acid or alkaline level in soil.

Phosphorous One of the most essential elements of plant nutrition. Encourages root growth and the ripening of shoots, fruit and seeds. Identified by the letter P.

Photosynthesis The production of food substances by leaves using sunlight, water and carbon dioxide.

Pinching out Removing shoots or foliage with the fingers.

Potassium One of the most essential elements of plant nutrition. Responsible for encouraging new strong growth and development of flower buds and fruit formation, and identified by the letter K.

Pot-bound The condition of a plant that has been grown in a pot when the roots have completely filled the space inside. This will eliminate all the air space and may result in the premature death of the plant.

Prostrate A plant that has a habit of growing along the ground.

Pruning Removing leaves, shoots or branches to stimulate new growth.

Raffia Natural fibre that is wrapped around a trunk or branches prior to wiring. The raffia protects the bark from wire damage and assists regeneration of tissues following bending of trunk or branch.

Ramification The division of branches into a dense formation of shoots and twigs. Achieved by pinching of shoot tips.

Repotting The process of removing a pot-grown plant from its pot at regular intervals and replanting with fresh soil to encourage new root growth.

Root Part of plant used to absorb water and nutrients from within the growing medium.

Root-ball Mass of soil and roots seen when a plant is lifted from the ground or removed from its pot.

Rootstock The main stem and root system when used as the basis for a new plant for propagation by grafting.

Root grafting Technique for attaching new roots to a tree using a stump of the root system and a part of the trunk.

Root pruning Reduction of root mass to encourage new healthy root growth.

Root burn Damage to roots normally caused by a fertilizer overdose or by applying fertilizer too soon following repotting and root pruning.

Saikei Miniature landscape of rocks and plants grown in a shallow container.

Sapwood Living tissues forming the wood layers beneath the bark.

Scion Small section of a plant that is used to propagate a new plant by grafting. This will retain the characteristics of the parent plant.

Seedling Early stages of plant growth.

Semi hardwood Half-ripe shoots used for cuttings.

Shakan Slanting-trunk-style bonsai.

Sharimiki (or shari) Part of trunk that has had the bark removed for artistic effect.

Shohin Small bonsai measuring from 15cm (6in) up to about 30cm (12in).

Sieve Screening device for separating soil particles of different sizes.

Slow release Normally used to refer to a fertilizer that releases nutrients over an extended period.

Softwood Immature shoots used for cuttings.

Sokan Bonsai style with twin trunks in which the trunks must be visibly connected at the buttress.

Soju Twin-tree bonsai style made up of two separate trees as distinct from twin trunk or *Sokan*.

Species Subordinate classification to genus differing from genus in detail only.

Sphagnum moss Type of moss common in bogs and marshy land, used in bonsai for air layering and root formation.

Stratification The overwintering of hardy plant seeds outdoors or in a refrigerator to break seed dormancy and thereby induce germination.

Systemic A fungicide or insecticide that enters the sap of a plant to prevent infestation by disease or insects.

Tap root Main root which normally acts to anchor a tree or plant in the ground.

Tender Trees that are unable to tolerate low temperatures and will require winter protection. Tenderness is measured relative to the local climate.

Training pot Container suitable to enable the tree to form strong, vigorous growth during initial styling and training.

Transpiration Natural water loss from the leaves and stems.

Tufa Type of sedimentary limestone often used for rock plantings because of its porous, moisture-retaining nature.

Turntable Rotating platform for displaying trees and for practical purposes whilst repotting and styling.

Variety Sub-division of species displaying variations from the naturally occurring parent plant.

Viability The ability of seeds to germinate.

Wire Usually aluminium, anodized aluminium or copper; used extensively for bonsai shaping.

Wiring The practice of applying wire to the trunk or branches of bonsai during the styling and training process.

Woody A plant stem that has hardened, will not die and has taken on the appearance of an old trunk.

Wound sealer Protective paste used to cover cuts following pruning and along the edges of jins and sharis.

Yose-uye Bonsai forest or group planting style combining separate trees of one variety to form a natural looking group.

Useful addresses

JAPANESE GARDENING SUPPLIERS

AUSTRALIA

Cyclone Industries Pty Ltd
Victoria, Tasmania
Tel (613) 8791 9300
Wide range of cutting tools

Garden Grove
1150 Golden Grove Road, Golden
Grove, Adelaide SA 5125
Tel (618) 8251 1111
www.gardengrove.com
Nursery and garden supplies centre

Universal Rocks
20 Hearne Street, Mortdale, NSW 2223
www.universalrocks.com.au

CANADA

The Angelgrove Tree Seed Co.
P.O. Box 74, 141 Hart Path Road,
Riverhead
Harbour Grace NL A0A 3P0
www.angelgroveseeds.com

Burns Water Gardens
Baltimore
Ontario KOK 1C0
Tel (905) 372-2737
Waterlilies, aquatic plants, ponds

UNITED KINGDOM

UK Bamboo Supplies Limited
Unit 18, Donkin Road
Armstrong Industrial Estate,
Washington
Tyne and Wear NE37 1PF
Tel 0191 417 2915;
www.ukbamboosupplies.com

Glendoick Gardens Ltd
Glendoick, Glencarse
Perth PH2 7NS, Scotland
Tel 01738 860205
Rhododendrons and azaleas

Japan Garden Company
15 Bank Crescent, Ledbury,
Herefordshire HR8 1AA
Tel 01531 630091
Japangarden.co.uk
Lanterns, screens, fences

Japanese Garden Supplies
Millstone, Mill Lane, Worthing
West Sussex BN13 3DF
Tel 01903 691167

Japanese Garden Supplies
Addlestone Road, East Peckham,
Tonbridge TN12 5DP
Tel 01622 872403

Jungle Giants
Ferney Hall, Onibury, Craven Arms,
Shropshire SY7 9BJ
Tel 01584 856200
Bamboo plants and materials

Junker's Nursery Ltd
PMA Plant Specialists, Lower Mead,
West Hatch, Taunton
Somerset TA3 5RN
Tel 01823 480774
www.junker.net

Kenchester Water Gardens
Church Road, Lyde
Hereford HR1 3AB
Tel 01432 270981
Water products, waterlilies and irises

Rockfeatures
Wilton Farm, Marlow Road
Little Marlow
Buckinghamshire SL7 3RR
Tel 01628 533335
www.rockfeatures.co.uk
Fibreglass and cement, imitation rocks

Silverland Stone
Holloway Hill, Chertsey
Surrey KT16 0AE
Tel 01932 570094
www.silverlandstone.co.uk

www.mudmom.com
full size and table-top Zen rakes

UNITED STATES

Bamboo Gardens of Washington
5035 – 196th Ave NE
Redmond WA 98074
Tel (425) 868-5166
Bamboos, fences, lanterns and basins

Bamboo and Koi Garden
2115 SW Borland Road
West Linn OR 97068
Tel (503) 638-0888
bambookoigarden@aol.com

Cherry Blossom Gardens
Tel (952) 758-1923
www.cherryblossomgardens.com
Japanese garden ornaments

Japanese Garden
PO Box 3847, Portland, OR 97208
Tel (503) 223-1321
www.japanesegarden.com
Bells, lanterns, bonsai and ikebana

Japanese Garden Fences Inc.
P.O. Box 2212, Pawcatuck CT 06379
Tel (860) 599-2348
Handcrafted *sode-gaki* fences

Riverside Enterprises
Tel toll-free on 1-888-773-8769
or call (518) 272-3800
www.wirestore.com

Tatami Room
466 20th Street, Oakland, CA 94612
Tatamiroom@yahoo.com
Blinds, tatami, lanterns and water basins

BONSAI SUPPLIERS

AUSTRALIA

Bonsai Emporium
4433 West Swan Road, West Swan
Western Australia
Tel: (618) 9374 0555

Bonsai Kingdom
10 Haywards Road, Gosnells
Western Australia
www.bonsaikingdom.com

Bonsai-n-Bamboo
848 Forest Road, Jandakot
Western Australia
Tel: (618) 9414 9966

Bonsai Palace
Stock Road Markets, Bibra Lake
Western Australia
Tel: (614) 19047244

Lee's Bonsai World
180 Grand Promenade
Bedford, Western Australia
Tel: (618) 9370 5915

EUROPE

Bonsai Vaerkstedet
Bonsai & Satsuki Centre
V/Hans Jurgen Nielsen
Strynovej 36
6710 Esberg V
Denmark
Tel: (45) 7515 6734

Bryan Albright Bonsai Pots
Tel: 01263 587587
www.bonsai.free-online.co.uk

Bushukan Bonsai
Ricbra, Lower Road
Hockley, Essex SS5 5HL
Tel: 01702 201029
www.bushukan-bonsai.com

Dai-Ichi Bonsai
Hillier Garden Centre
Priors Court Road, Hermitage
Newbury
Berkshire RG18 9TG
Tel: 01635 200667
www.dai-ichibonsai.com

Erin Pottery and Bonsai
41 Savoy Road, Brislington
Bristol BS4 3SZ
www.erinpottery.com

Ginkgo Bonsai Centre
Heireg 190
9270 Laarne
Belgium
Tel: (32) 9 355 1485
www.ginkgobonsai.be

Glenbrook Bonsai Nursery
Tickenham
Clevedon
North Somerset BS21 6SE
Tel: 01275 858596
www.glenbrookbonsai.co.uk

Green Lawns Bonsai
Hadleigh Road, Boxford
Nr Sudbury
Suffolk CO10 5JH
Tel: 01787 210501
www.greenlawns.co.uk

Greenwood Bonsai Studio
Ollerton Road, Arnold
Nottingham NG5 8PR
Tel: 0115 920 5757
www.bonsai.co.uk

John Hanby Bonsai School
Newstead Lane, Havercroft
Wakefield
West Yorkshire WF4 2HW
Tel: 01977 610040
www.johnhanbybonsai.co.uk

A. Harriman – Bonsai Pottery
58 Station Road, Misterton
Nr Doncaster
South Yorkshire DN10 4DE
Tel: 01437 890434
www.chinamist.co.uk

Herons Bonsai Ltd
Wire Mill Lane, Newchapel
Nr Lingfield
Surrey RH7 6HJ
Tel: 01342 832657
www.herons.co.uk

Kaizen Bonsai
Tel: 0800 4580672
www.kaizenbonsai.com

Observatory Bonsai
Cardiff
Tel: 02920 484892 or 07980 897264
www.observatorybonsai.co.uk

John Pitt Bonsai Ceramics
Etwall, Derbyshire
Tel: 01283 733479
john@johnpittbonsaiceramics.co.uk
http://johnpittbonsaiceramics.co.uk/
Visitors by appointment only.

Pius Notter Bonsai Arboretum
Boswil, Lucerne, Switzerland
mail@swiss-bonsai.ch

Salvatori Liporace
Studio Botanico, Via Rubens 9-20148
Milan, Italy
Tel: (39) 02 404 5565
www.liporace.it

Tokonoma Bonsai Nursery
London Road, Shenley
Radlett
Hertfordshire WD7 9EN
Tel: 01923 858587
or 01923 855670
www.tokonomabonsai.co.uk

Walsall Studio Ceramics
Tantara Street, Walsall
West Midlands WS1 2HU
Tel: 01922 645707
www.walsall-studio-ceramics.com

Kevin Willson Yamadori Bonsai
15 Oxley Hill
Tolleshunt, Darcy
Maldon, Essex CN9 8ES
Tel: 01621 815285
www.kevinwillsonbonsai.com

Windybank Bonsai
60 Woodmansterne Lane
Carshalton, Surrey SM5 4BJ
Tel: 020 8669 8847
www.windybankbonsai.co.uk

NEW ZEALAND

Bonsai Boutique
PO Box 9113, Tauranga
Tel: (64) 7578 4854
www.home.clear.net.nz/pages/
bonsai-boutique

Bonsai New Zealand Ltd
147 Seabrook Avenue, New Lyn
Auckland
Tel: (64) 9 827 3439
www.bonsai.co.nz

Catlins Natural
Balclutha
Tel: (64) 3 418 1798
www.catlinesnatural.co.nz

Cedar Lodge Nurseries Ltd
63 Egmont Road, R.D.2
New Plymouth
Tel: (64) 6 755 0369
www.conifers.co.nz

EfilDoog
Akatarawa Valley Road, Upper Hutt
Tel: (64) 4 526 7924
www.efildoog-nz.com/index.htm

Joy's Bonsai Studio
6 Torquay Street
Abbotsford, Dunedin
Tel: (64) 3 488 4592
joys-bonsai@clear.net.nz
www.home.clear.net.nz/pages/joys-
bonsai

Vanz Bonsai & Pottery
27 Raxworthy Street
Ilam, Christchurch
Tel: (64) 3 358 2591
vanzsa@xtra.co.nz

SOUTH AFRICA

Dunmau Bonsai
130 Major Road, Clayville
East Olifantsfontein, Gauteng
Tel: (27) 11 316 2910
wiles@icon.co.za

Imithi Bonsai
85B Longwy Road
Lorraine, Port Elizabeth
Eastern Cape
Tel: (27) 41 379 4789

Misty Moon Bonsai
204 Kay Ridge Road
Assegay, Kwa-Zulu Natal
Tel: (27) 031 768 1198
mistymoon@mweb.co.za

CANADA AND UNITED STATES

PFM Bonsai Studio
7 Western Avenue
West Charlton
New York
Tel: (518) 882-1039
www.pfmbonsai.com

Rosade Bonsai Studio
6912 Ely Road
Solebury, New Hope
PA 18938-9634
Tel: (215) 862-5925
www.rosadebonsai.com

Shikoku Bonsai
Vancouver
British Columbia
Canada
Tel: (604) 886-3915

JAPANESE GARDENS

INTERNATIONAL

The Japanese Garden Database
www.jgarden.org
Worldwide listing of gardens

AUSTRALIA

Cowra Japanese Garden
Binni Creek Road, Cowra, NSW 2794
Tel (612) 6341 2233

Edogawa Commemorative Garden
36 Webb Street, East Gosford
NSW 2250
Tel (612) 4325 0056

The Melbourne Zoo Japanese Garden
Elliott Avenue, P.O. Box 74
Parkville, Victoria 3052
Tel (613) 9285 9300

BELGIUM

Hasselt Japanese Garden
Gouverneur Verwilghensingel,
3500 Hasselt
Tel (32) 11 23 95 40
www.trabel.com/hasselt-japanesegarden

CANADA

Kurimoto Japanese Garden
Devonian Botanic Gardens
Edmonton
Alberta
Tel (780) 987-3054

Nitobe Memorial Garden
895 Lower Mall
Vancouver
British Columbia
Tel (604) 822-6038
www.nitobe.org

FRANCE

Citroën Garden
Parc André-Citroën
Quai André-Citroën
75015 Paris
Tel: (01) 40 71 76 07

Jardins Albert Kahn
Musée Albert-Kahn
14 rue du Port
92100 Boulogne-Billancourt
Paris
Tel (01) 55 19 28 00

UNESCO Japanese Gardens
7, place de Fontenoy
Paris 75007
Tel (01) 45 68 10 00
www.unesco.org

GERMANY

Bonn Japanese Garden
Rheinaue Park
Nordrhein-Westfalen

Freiburg Japanese Garden
Ökostation Freiburg
Seeparkgelände
Falkenbergstrasse 21b
Freiburg 79100

Karlsruhe Japanese Garden
Stadt Karlsruhe
Gartenbauamt
76124 Karlsruhe

Augsburg Japanese Garden
Botanischer Garten, Dr.-Ziegenspeck-
Weg 10, D-86161 Augsburg

JAPAN

Daisen-in (Kyoto)
Kita-ku, Murasakino, Daitokuji-cho,
Kyoto-shi, Kyoto-hu

Ginkaku-ji (Kyoto)
Sakyo-ku, Ginkakuji-cho, Kyoto-shi

Joei-ji in (Yamaguchi)
Miyano-mura, Yoshiki-gun

Katsura Palace (Kyoto)
Ukyo-ku, Katsura, Shimizu-cho
Get permission from the Imperial Park
Agency, Kyoto Gosho, 3 Kyoto-Gyoen,
Kamigyo-ku, Kyoto
Tel (075) 211-6348

Jiko-in (Nara)
Nara-shi, Nara-ken

Joju-en (Kumamoto)
Kumamoto, Kyushi

Kenroku-en (Kanazawa)
1-4 Kenroku-machi Kanazawa-city,
Ishikawa I

Koishikawa-Koraku-en (Tokyo)
1-6-6 Kouraku, Bunkyo-ku
Tokyo 112-0004
Tel (03) 3811-3015

Koraku-en (Okayama)
1-5 Korakuen, Okayama-shi, Okayama

Motsu-ji (Iwate)
58 Osawa, Hiraizumi-cho
Nishi-Iwai-gun, Iwate

Raikyu-ji (Takahashi)
18 Raikyuji-cho, Takahashi, Okayama

Ryogen-in Zen Garden (Kyoto)
Daitoku-ji-cho, Murasakina
Kyoto-shi

Ryoan-ji (Kyoto), Ukyo-ku
Ryoanji, Goryoshita-cho, Kyoto-shi

Saiho-ji (Kyoto)
Write for permission: Saiho-ji
Nishigyo-ku, Kamigatani-cho
Matsuo, Kyoto

Sanzen-in (Kyoto)
Sakyo-ku, Ohara, Raigoin-cho, Kyoto-shi

Shisen-do (Kyoto)
27 Monguchi-cho, Ichijoji, Sakyo-ku,
Kyoto-shi

Shugakuin Palace (Kyoto)
Sakyo-ku, Shugakuin, Kyoto-shi

Tōfuku-ji Hojo (Kyoto)
15-778 Honmachi, Higashiyama-ku,
Kyoto-shi www.tofukuji.jp/english.html

NEW ZEALAND

Waitakere Japanese Garden
Waitakere City Council
6 Waipareira Avenue
Waitakere
Tel (09) 836 8000

UNITED KINGDOM

Brunei Gallery Roof Garden
SOAS, Thornhaugh Street
Russell Square
Bloomsbury
London WC1H 0XG
Tel 020 7898 4915

Compton Acres
Canford Cliffs Road
Poole
Dorset BH13 7ES
Tel 01202 700778

Heale Garden and Plant Centre
Middle Woodford
Salisbury
Wiltshire SP4 6NT
Tel 01722 782207

Holland Park Gardens
London W8 6LU
Tel 020 7471 9813

Japanese Garden and Bonsai Nursery
St Mawgan, nr Newquay
Cornwall TR8 4ET
Tel 01637 860116

Newstead Abbey
Newstead Abbey Park
Nottinghamshire NG15 8NA
Tel 01623 455900

Pine Lodge Gardens
Holmbush, St Austell
Cornwall PL25 3RQ
Tel 01726 735000
www.pine-lodge.co.uk

Pureland Zen Garden
North Clifton
Nottinghamshire NG23 7AP
Tel 01777 228567

Royal Botanic Gardens
Kew, Richmond
Surrey TW9 3AB
Tel 020 8332 5655
www.rbgkew.org.uk

Tatton Park
Knutsford
Cheshire WA16 6QN
Tel 01625 534400
www.tattonpark.org.uk

Tully Japanese Garden
Irish National Stud, Tully
Co. Kildare, Ireland
Tel +353-45-522963
www.irish-national-stud.ie

UNITED STATES

Brooklyn Botanical Gardens
1000 Washington Ave.
Brooklyn, NY 11225
Tel (718) 623-7200
www.bbg.org

Earl Burns Miller Japanese Garden
California State University
Long Beach
Tel (562) 985-5930

Hakone Gardens
21000 Big Basin Way
Saratoga CA 95070
Tel (408) 741-4994
www.hakone.com

Hammond Japanese Stroll Garden
North Salem NY 10560
Tel (914) 669-5033
www.hammondmuseum.org

The Japanese Friendship Garden
1125 N. 3rd Ave Phoenix, AZ
Tel (602) 265 -3204

Huntington Botanical Gardens
1151 Oxford Road, San Marino CA 91108
Tel (626) 405 -398

Japanese Garden
11 Southwest Kingston Avenue
Portland, Oregon 97205
Tel (503) 223-1321
www.japanesegarden.com

The Japanese Tea Garden
Golden Gate Park, San Francisco
CA 94117

Morikami Japanese Gardens
4000 Morikami Park Road
Delray Beach, Florida 33446
Tel (561) 495-0233
www.morikami.org

BONSAI COLLECTIONS

AUSTRALIA

Auburn Japanese Gardens
Chiswick and Chisholm Roads
Auburn, New South Wales
Tel: (612) 9871 5630
shellan@bigpond.com.au

The Bonsai House
The Brisbane Botanic Gardens
Mount Coot-tha Road, Toowang,
Brisbane, Queensland 4066
www.bonsaihouse.com

EUROPE

Belgium Bonsai Museum
Ginkgo Bonsai Centre
Antwerpsesteenweg 148-9080
Lochristi, Nr Ghent, Belgium
Tel: 32 (0) 9 355 14 85

Bonsai Centrum
Mannheimerstr. 401
9123 Heidelberg-Wieblingen, Germany
Tel: 06221 84910
www.bonsai-centrum.de

NEW ZEALAND

Bonsaiville
Mount Albert, Auckland
Tel: (9) 629 3662
www.bonsaiville.co.nz

North Canterbury Bonsai
Christchurch
Tel: (3) 355 5411

UNITED KINGDOM

**Ken and Ann Norman Bonsai
Collection (Norman Bonsai)**
Leonardslee Gardens
West Sussex RH13 6PP
Tel: 01273 506476 or 01403 891457
www.hortic.com/normanbonsai

National Bonsai Collection
Birmingham Botanical Gardens and
Glasshouse (BBGG)
Westbourne Road, Edgbaston
Birmingham B15 3TR
Tel: 0121 454 1860
www.nationalbonsaicollection.org

**Royal Horticultural Society Garden
at Wisley Bonsai Collection**
Woking, Surrey GU23 6QB
Tel: 01483 224234
www.rhs.org.uk

UNITED STATES AND CANADA

Brooklyn Botanic Garden
Bonsai Collection, 1000 Washington
Avenue, Brooklyn, NY 11225-1099
Tel: (718) 623-7200; www.bbg.org

International Bonsai Arboretum
William N Valavanis
1070 Martin Road, West Henrietta
Rochester
NY 14692-3894
Tel: (585) 334-2595
wnv@internationalbonsai.com

**Montreal Botanical Garden Bonsai
Collection**
4101 Sherbrooke East, Montreal
Quebec
Tel: (514) 872-1400
www.ville.montreal.qc.ca/jardin/
vedettes/bonsai.htm

National Bonsai Foundation
National Bonsai and Penjing Museum
US National Arboretum
3501 New York Avenue
North East Washington DC
www.bonsai-nbf.org

North Carolina Arboretum
100 Frederick Law Olmstead Way
Asheville, North Carolina 28806
Tel: (828) 665-2492
www.ncarboretum.org

Pacific Rim Bonsai Collection
33633 Weyerhaeuser Way South
Federal Way
Washington 98003
Tel: (253) 924-5206

Southern California Bonsai Collection
Huntingdon Library
1151 Oxford Road
San Marino CA 91108
Tel: (625) 405-2100
www.huntingdon.org

SOCIETIES & ORGANIZATIONS

INTERNATIONAL

Bonsai Clubs International
www.bonsai-bci.com

International Bonsai Magazine
www.international bonsai.com

World Bonsai Friendship Federation (WBFF)
www.bonsai-wbff.org

AUSTRALIA

Australian Associated Bonsai Clubs
http://godzilla.zeta.org.au
Bonsai Northwest Inc.
135 Stephen Yarraville, Victoria
www.bonsainorthwest.com.au

Bonsai Society of Australia Inc.
West Pennant Hills Community Centre
42 Hill Road, West Pennant Hills
New South Wales
www.bonsai.asn.au

Suiseki Australia
Don Moore Centre
North Rocks Road
North Rocks
New South Wales
shellan@bigpond.com.au

Waverley Garden Club Bonsai Group
St Johns Uniting Church Hall
Virginia Street
Mount Waverley
Victoria 3149
Tel: 9544 5039

EUROPE

European Bonsai Association (EBA)
Contact: Reg Bolton
Tel: 01793 822470
reg.bolton@ic24.net
www.ebabonsai.com

NEW ZEALAND

New Zealand Bonsai Association
16 Elder Street, Dunedin
Tel: 3 7323 7560
www.bonsaiTALK.com

SOUTH AFRICA

South African Bonsai Association
www.saba.org.za

UNITED KINGDOM

Association of British Bonsai Artists
Tel: 01803 872856
enquiries@bonsaiartists.co.uk
www.bonsaiartists.co.uk

Federation of British Bonsai Societies
Tel: 01793 822470
reg.bolton@ic24.net; www.fobbs.info

Japanese Garden Society
www.jgs.org.uk
Arranges events and meetings
throughout the UK.

Journal of Japanese Gardening
www.rotheien.com

UNITED STATES AND CANADA

American Bonsai Society
PO Box 351604, Toledo
OH 43635-1604
www.absbonsai.org

North American Bonsai Federation
www.bonsai-wbff.org

Toronto Bonsai Society
PO Box 155, Toronto
Ontario M3C 2E8
www.torontobonsai.org

Index

Plant hardiness zones

Plant entries in the directory have been given hardiness descriptions and zone numbers. The former are as follows:

FROST TENDER

A plant which needs heated greenhouse protection through the winter in the local area. May be damaged by temperatures below 5°C (41°F).

HALF HARDY

A plant which cannot be grown outside during the colder months in the local area and needs greenhouse protection through the winter. Can withstand temperatures down to 0°C (32°F).

FROST HARDY

A plant which, when outside, survives through milder winters in the local area, with additional protection. Can withstand temperatures down to -5°C (23°F).

FULLY HARDY

A plant which, when planted outside, will survive reliably through the winter in the local area. Can withstand temperatures down to -15°C (5°F).

There is widespread use of the zone number system to express the hardiness of many plant species and cultivars. The zonal system used, shown below, was developed by the Agricultural Research Service of the United States Department of Agriculture. According to this system, there are 11 zones in total, based on the average annual minimum temperature in a particular geographical zone.

The zone rating for each plant indicates the coldest zone in which a correctly planted subject can survive the winter. Where hardiness is borderline, the first number indicates the marginal zone and the second the safer zone.

This is not a hard and fast system, simply an indicator, as many factors other than temperature play an important part where hardiness is concerned. These include altitude, wind exposure, proximity to water, soil type, the presence of snow or shade, night temperature, and the amount of water received by a plant. These factors can easily alter a plant's hardiness by as much as two zones. The presence of long-term snow cover in the winter especially can allow plants to survive in colder zones.

Zone 1   Below -45°C (-50°F)
Zone 2   -45 to -40°C (-50 to -40°F)
Zone 3   -40 to -34°C (-40 to -30°F)
Zone 4   -34 to -29°C (-30 to -20°F)
Zone 5   -29 to -23°C (-20 to -10°F)
Zone 6   -23 to -18°C (-10 to 0°F)
Zone 7   -18 to -12°C (0 to 10°F)
Zone 8   -12 to -7°C (10 to 20°F)
Zone 9   -7 to -1°C (20 to 30°F)
Zone 10   -1 to 4°C (30 to 40°F)
Zone 11   Above 4°C (40°F)